Date Due

DEC 1 1 1995		
APR 1 5 1996		
MAY 2 8 1996		

The Life of Joseph Conrad

B

BLACKWELL CRITICAL BIOGRAPHIES

General Editor: Claude Rawson

The Life of
JOSEPH CONRAD

A Critical Biography

172 174425

John Batchelor

BLACKWELL
Oxford UK & Cambridge USA

Copyright © John Batchelor 1994

The right of John Batchelor to be identified
as author of this work has been asserted in accordance with the
Copyright, Designs and Patents Act 1988.

First published 1994

Blackwell Publishers
108 Cowley Road
Oxford   OX4 1JF
UK

238 Main Street, Suite 501
Cambridge, Massachusetts 02142
USA

British Library Cataloguing in Publication Data

A CIP catalogue record for this book is available from the British Library.

Library of Congress Cataloging-in-Publication Data

Batchelor, John, 1942–
The life of Joseph Conrad : a critical biography / John Batchelor.
    p.   cm. — (Blackwell critical biographies : 4)
Includes bibliographical references (p.) and index.
ISBN 0–631–16416–2 (alk. paper)
1. Conrad, Joseph, 1857–1924.   2. Novelists, English—20th
century—Biography.   I. Title.   II. Series.
PR6005.04Z557   1994
823'.912—dc20
            [B]   93–3674
                                                     CIP

Typeset in 10 on 11 pt Baskerville
by Graphicraft Typesetters Ltd., Hong Kong
Printed in Great Britain by T.J. Press Ltd, Padstow, Cornwall

This book is printed on acid-free paper

For my son Leo

Contents

Illustrations

14 Conrad and H. G. Wells together. Their friendship resulted from Wells's review of *An Outcast of the Islands* in 1896. Conrad wrote at the time, 'He descended from his "time machine" to be kind as he knew how.'

15 Pent Farm, near Hythe in South West Kent. Conrad lived here from 1898 to 1907, a period in which he wrote some of his best works.

16 R. B. Cunninghame Graham dressed as a gaucho, probably soon after his return from South America in the late 1870s. Conrad's friendship with him lasted from 1897 until Conrad's death in 1924. In a letter to Graham in 1920, Conrad wrote: 'May you ride firm as ever in the saddle, to the very last moment, et la lance toujours en arrêt, against The Enemy whom you have defied all your life!'

17 Stephen Crane.

18 Conrad's wife, Jessie, with their eldest son, Borys, at Pent Farm, in 1900.

19 Ford Madox Ford.

20 J. B. Pinker and Conrad at Pinker's home in 1922. Pinker approached Conrad in 1899 and later acted as his literary agent until Pinker's death in the year this photograph was taken. Pinker was agent for many leading writers of the day. When he recognized talent he was generous with his financial aid, as Conrad and Arnold Bennett knew from experience.

21 Joseph Conrad with his son Borys and Edmund Oliver on the occasion of Borys's joining *HMS Worcester* in 1911. Edmund Oliver was owner of Capel House.

22 Capel House, Conrad's residence from June 1910 to March 1919.

23 Mr and Mrs Joseph Conrad and their son John.

24 Joseph Conrad, c.1911.

25 Oswalds, Bishopbourne, near Canterbury. This was Conrad's last home, where he lived from 1919.

26 Conrad in the garden at Oswalds, June 1924, shortly before his death.

Acknowledgements

I would like to express my gratitude to the British Academy for a research grant which enabled me to visit the Conrad archives in the USA, to the Trustees of the Joseph Conrad Estate for permission to quote copyright material, to the Warden and Fellows of New College, Oxford, for two periods of sabbatical leave and to the University of Newcastle-upon-Tyne for research equipment, and to the following institutions and individuals: the Beinecke Museum and Library, Yale University; the Berg Collection, New York Public Library; the Harry Ransome Humanities Research Centre, University of Texas; the Rosenbach Museum and Library, Philadelphia; Birmingham University Library, the Bodleian Library, the British Library, Cambridge University Library, Durham University Library, the Oxford English Faculty Library, Rhodes House Library and the Robinson Library, University of Newcastle-upon-Tyne; Claude Rawson who commissioned this biography and Andrew McNeillie my editor at Blackwell, my agent, Felicity Bryan, who has nurtured this project from its inception, Hermann Moisl who taught me how to use the computer on which it was written, David Saunders who alerted me to some of Conrad's source material, my wife, Henrietta, who has lived with my preoccupation with Conrad for many years, and Andrzej Busza, Zdzisław Najder, Tony Nuttall, Ken Robinson and Cedric Watts who read my drafts and made a large number of detailed and valuable comments. The book's limitations are, of course, all my own.

JBB
April 1993

1

Conrad and Poland

'My first object is to bring up Konradek not as a democrat, aristocrat, demagogue, republican monarchist, or as a servant and flunkey of those parties – but only as a Pole.'

Apollo Korzeniowski to Stefan Buszczyński, 5/17 March 1868[1]

'What ish my nation? Ish a villain and a bastard and a knave and a rascal? What ish my nation? Who talks of my nation?'

Henry V, III, ii.

When Joseph Conrad was born, in 1857, the 'Congress Kingdom' of Poland (established in 1815) was all that remained of a great medieval empire.[2] 'Poland' existed as a culture, a history, a language and a geographical region, but not as an independent nation. In 1795 it became an administrative area split up between three different states, Russia, Prussia and Austria. At the Congress of Vienna in 1815 the map was redrawn and a nucleus of the old Poland, 'the Congress Kingdom of Poland', centred on Warsaw, was created. Recognition of this restored 'Poland' as a separate entity did not mean independence for the Poles: the King of this 'Kingdom' was the Tsar of Russia. The Kingdom's constitution, designed by Prince Czartoryski, conferred some degree of autonomy on its inhabitants but that independence was drastically curtailed in 1831 and finally lost in 1864. An armed patriotic rising in 1830, the 'November Rising', organized by young army officers, led to a punitive expedition sent out by Tsar Nicholas I who declared that 'Russia or Poland must now perish'. After the military defeat of Poland in 1831 severe punishment was handed out: 254 of the military and political leaders of the 1830 rising were sentenced to death and some 80,000 other Poles were condemned to deportation to Siberia. Among those punished was Prince Roman Sanguszko, a courageous young man who refused, at his trial, to accept the prosecution's suggestion that he had joined the rising because he was depressed by his wife's death and without seeing the consequences of his actions. He declared that he joined the rising out of conviction: he was sentenced to deportation. Nicholas I personally insisted that Prince Roman should make the whole journey to Siberia – five thousand miles – on foot. Conrad's only Polish narrative, his story 'Prince Roman', is based on his uncle Bobrowski's account of Roman Sanguszko's heroism.[3] The relatively liberal constitution set up for the Polish Kingdom in 1815 was replaced by a 'constitution' whereby Poland was in practice governed by military decree.[4] A further patriotic rising in 1863 directly involved Joseph Conrad's family: his father, Apollo Korzeniowski and one of his maternal uncles, Stefan Bobrowski were members of the committee of 'Reds' which had planned the rising. Stefan Bobrowski died in a duel in April 1863 and another maternal uncle, Kazimierz Bobrowski, was imprisoned after resigning his commission in the (Russian controlled) army. Two other uncles, Apollo Korzeniowski's brothers, were also involved: Robert Korzeniowski was killed in May 1863 and Hilary Korzeniowski was imprisoned and later (1865) deported to Tomsk: he died in exile.[5]

The rising of 1863 was ruthlessly suppressed by the Russians by 1864 and in 1865 the Congress Kingdom was dissolved. Russian punishment for the 1863 rising inflicted unprecedented damage on Poland. There was mass slaughter in Lithuania, and in Poland itself a whole generation of political and cultural leaders was lost. The most able and courageous (including Conrad's parents) were sent into exile and for most of them there was to be no reprieve. Some partisans of 1864–5 were still living out their punishment in Siberia forty years after the event.[6]

Józef Teodor Konrad Korzeniowski, 'coat of arms Nałecz', was born 3 December 1857 at Berdyczów, in Podolia, one of the provinces of what was then known as Ruthenia and is now known as the Ukraine.[7] His parents were figures of extraordinary and exemplary qualities. His father, Apollo Korzeniowski, was a member of the *szlachta*. This term, commonly translated as 'nobility', has no exact equivalent in English.[8] The 'coat of arms Nałecz' in Conrad's name refers to the way – unique in Europe – in which the *szlachta* organized themselves into clans. These clans were based not only on kinship but also to some extent on community of interest (so that the Polish coat of arms is not an exact equivalent of the coat of arms of an English aristocratic family).[9] In medieval Poland the *szlachta* were an hereditary class of landowning gentry. In 1573 Poland became an elective monarchy and this enhanced the political role of the *szlachta* who now had the right to elect the King. In theory at least any member of this class might himself be elected King. The *szlachta* were about ten per cent of the population – a much larger group than the aristocracies of Britain or France – and although many of them were wealthy, land and serf-owning figures who became effectively local princes, others were reduced to an economic level no better than that of the peasants (but they retained their political privileges).

The Korzeniowskis at the time of Conrad's birth were no longer land-owning. Their estates had been confiscated because of their participation in the uprisings of 1794 and 1830. Apollo Korzeniowski was a brilliant, passionate, courageous patriot, totally committed to the liberation of Poland from Russia. From 1840 he had studied Law and languages at St Petersburg university but seems to have left without taking a degree. From 1846 onwards he helped his father to manage various leasehold properties in the Ukraine, and probably in 1847 he met and fell in love with Ewa Bobrowska, who was twelve years his junior. The Bobrowskis, Ewa's family, were much more prudent (and much richer) than the Korzeniowskis, and resisted the match between Ewa and Apollo until, under the pressure of Ewa's illness (depression) in 1855, they gave in, and Apollo and Ewa Korzeniowski were married at Oratów, the family estate of the Bobrowskis, on 4 May 1856.[10] Apollo was already marked out as a patriot and a radical: his poems, 'Purgatorial Cantos' (1849–55), could not be published because of their patriotic and subversive content, and were circulated among the Polish-Ukrainian gentry in handwritten copies. His play, *Komedia* (1854), regarded as dangerously radical when it was performed in the 1850s, advocates an alliance between the patriotic gentry and the peasants against newly enriched landowners (landowners who prospered under the Russians – like the Bobrowskis – could, of course, be seen by fervent Polish patriots such as the Korzeniowskis as collaborators).[11] From 1852 onwards Korzeniowski worked in effect as a tenant farmer; his wife's dowry enabled him in 1857 to take on a farm at Derebczynka, in Podolia, but through a combination of financial mismanagement and a policy of generosity to-wards the peasants on the estate he seems to have lost most of their money by 1859, and moved with his wife and small son to Żytomierz, where he became a shareholder in a publishing company. He wrote and translated, and became increasingly involved in politics. In 1861 he committed himself entirely to politics, moving to Warsaw in order to take part in the resistance movement against the Russians, as a member of the 'Reds'. Polish patriots had split into two camps, the Reds, who advocated direct action and the Whites, who advocated negotiation. He had introduced his brother-in-law, Stefan Bobrowski, to the Reds. Stefan soon became one of their leaders but was killed, as we have seen, in a duel with a White in 1863.[12] Stefan Bobrowski is of particular interest to us as I shall show[13] because his life and death may have contributed to Conrad's dramatizations of Haldin in *Under Western Eyes* and Jim in *Lord Jim*.[14]

In October 1861 Apollo Korzeniowski was arrested by the Russians and imprisoned in the Warsaw citadel.[15] Both Apollo and Ewa Korzeniowski were convicted of 'political activism', but their real, and serious, political activities remained undiscovered by the Russians and they were convicted on trumped-up charges.[16] They were exiled to Vologda, a town in the Northern part of European Russia which had a penal settlement. In June 1862, about two weeks after their arrival at Vologda, Apollo Korzeniowski wrote to his cousins Gabriela and Jan Zagórski:

Vologda is a huge quagmire stretching over three versts, cut up with parallel and intersecting lines of wooden foot-bridges, all rotten and shaky under one's feet.... A year here has two seasons: white winter and green winter. The white winter lasts nine and a half months, the green winter two and a half. Now is the beginning of the green winter: it has been raining continually for twenty-one days and it will do so till the end.... We do not regard exile as a punishment but as a new way of serving our country. There can be no punishment for us, since we are innocent. Whatever the form of service may be, it always means living for others – so let our Lord Jesus Christ be praised for having rewarded us more than we deserve! Our serene faces, proud bearing and defiant eyes cause great wonder here: because after what we have seen and what God saw a luminous glow has remained in our eyes, a glow which will not be dimmed by anything and which will stay with us like a testimony when one day we appear before God's tribunal. So do not pity us and do not think of us as martyrs.[17]

This letter demonstrates Korzeniowski's best qualities, his courage, high self-esteem, stoicism and fidelity (qualities which Conrad would, of course, dramatize as exemplary in his novels). It brings out, too, the strength of the Korzeniowskis' Christian conviction and the extent to which their Catholic faith sustained the couple in exile. To be Catholic was itself part of the composite which made up the identity of a Pole in the absence of a Polish nation. In 1863 Conrad, aged five, wrote an inscription on the back of a photograph which he addressed to his grandmother: 'To my beloved Grandma who helped me send cakes to my poor Daddy in prison – grandson, Pole, Catholic, nobleman – 6 July 1863 – Konrad'.[18] Although Korzeniowski says in the above letter 'Do not think of us as martyrs' his and his wife's plight is, in a way, analogous with that of the early Christian martyrs in that the physical privation, which led directly to their deaths, was endured for the sake of convictions which they held passionately and unwaveringly.

Ewa Korzeniowska's health deteriorated, with some remissions, from the date of her exile until her death on 18 April 1865. Najder says of her that she was 'the only person in Konrad Korzeniowski's whole family about whom there are no conflicting reports. All the evidence points to her exceptional qualities. ... For many years she kept her faith in the man she loved, even when his hope was waning, and her unshakable decision to participate in all his activities testifies to her strong character'.[19] At the time of her death Conrad was seven. After his wife's death Apollo Korzeniowski, himself suffering from tuberculosis, broke down. He became the figure whom Conrad recalled from his own childhood: the popular, brilliant and romantic patriot who had always been at the centre of highly charged political activity was transformed into something of a recluse, though not a despairing recluse. He engaged in a series of literary projects and tried to educate his little son, his 'Konradek', himself. The patriotism was undimmed. His central preoccupation, Polish national freedom, remained with him until his death in 1869.

Conrad was, then, the son of a man who was both a hero and a man of letters. *Under Western Eyes* is a major political novel expressing, in a refracted way, Conrad's feelings about Russia's relationship with Poland,[20] and it is an interesting fact that Conrad's father might himself have written a somewhat similar novel, had he lived. In October 1868, when he was already mortally ill, Apollo Korzeniowski wrote to his closest friend, Stefan Buszczyński: 'A long Polish novel is in my head – about the depravity flowing to us from Moscow through the Asiatic splendour, the bureacratic honours, the disbelief inculcated into public education, the baubles of civilized fashionable Muscovy, and finally by penetration through inter-marriage. It would begin in '54 and end in 1861.' He adds in the same letter a phrase which anticipates one of Conrad's titles: 'Usually those at the end of their tether keep making plans: I suppose I am not unlike them'.[21] Korzeniowski did not write his patriotic novel but he was productive, and respected, as a poet, playwright, critic, political essayist and translator. The *Purgatorial Cantos*, written between 1849 and 1854, express his disappointment at the failure of the Poles to join the majority of other nations of Europe in revolution in 1848. The poetry is full, as Andrzej Busza says, of despair and patriotic grief:

> So many days and so many years
> have we groaned with the voice of orphans
> on this our mother's grave,
> accompanied by the music of thunder;
> on our own soil – yet dispossessed,
> in our own homes – yet homeless!
> This once proud domain of our fathers
> is now but a cemetery and a ruin.
> Our fame and greatness have melted away
> in a stream of blood and tears;
> and our sole patrimony
> is the dust and bones of our ancestors.[22]

His best known work, his play *Komedia*, deals, with a poet, Henryk, an idealist and revolutionary, who is at odds with the materialist society surrounding him (*Komedia* was revived in Wroclaw in 1952 and was very successful).[23] It is important for a reader of Conrad to note that Apollo Korzeniowski worshipped Shakespeare, and published in 1868 a long essay, 'Studies on the Dramatic Element in the Works of Shakespeare'. This essay displays exalted admiration for the poet's universality and, interestingly, for the England that he may be said to embody:

Shakespeare! It is enough to pronounce this name and at once a whole world of alluring visions deludes the mind. Before one's eyes, the man and the poet, his people and its civilization, and his age stand out – enigmatical and alluring ... The new pattern of dramatic art was born in his [Shakespeare's] soul through an insight into *the essence of man*. The bard's genius was moved and inspired by a universal spectacle; a spectacle of almost daily recurrence and yet one which goes unperceived by mankind, in spite of the fact that man is in it both the author and the spectator. This spectacle is the deadly struggle of the might of *Man* with the powers of Fate.[24]

Andrzej Busza suggests that the ideas here can be compared with parts of the *Preface* to *The Nigger of the 'Narcissus'*.[25] I agree with that and I would make more of it: it seems to me that the Preface's post-romantic view of the relationship between the artist, the art and the audience is more likely to be indebted to Apollo Korzeniowski's mid-nineteenth-century post-Romantic view of Shakespeare than it is, as some critics maintain, to the English romantic tradition as expressed in Wordsworth's and Coleridge's Preface to the *Lyrical Ballads*.[26] We will see that in much of his work, especially *Lord Jim*, *Chance* and *Victory*, Conrad displays a desire to do homage to Shakespeare.

In *A Personal Record* Conrad tells us that Shakespeare was the first English writer whom he read, and he read him in his father's translations: 'My first introduction to English literature [was] the "Two Gentlemen of Verona", and in the very MS. of my father's translation. It was during our exile in Russia, and it must have been less than a year after my mother's death, because I remember myself in the black blouse with a white border of my heavy mourning' (p. 71). This memory, which must date from 1866 (when Conrad was in his ninth year), reminds us that much of Korzeniowski's literary work consisted of translations: his other Shakespeare translations were *The Comedy of Errors* and *Much Ado About Nothing*, and he translated all Victor Hugo's plays (except *Cromwell*) and two of his novels (*Les Misérables* and *Les Travailleurs de la mer*). Conrad says that his father's translation of *Les Travailleurs de la mer* was his, Conrad's, 'first introduction to the sea in literature'. He gives Hugo's title as 'Toilers of the Sea' (*A Personal Record* p. 72): it is peculiarly relevant to Conrad's own preoccupations with the duties of sailors that *work* at sea should have been his introduction to sea literature. Among other French works Korzeniowski translated de Vigny's tragedy *Chatterton* and Dickens's *Hard Times* (this latter translation was reissued in Poland as recently as 1955). Bobrowski said that Korzeniowski also translated some of Heine's poetry into Polish. Andrzej Busza remarks that 'It is worthwhile noticing that Korzeniowski's choice of the materials which he translated was not haphazard. Three of the writers, Hugo, Heine and Dickens, whom he wished to introduce to the Polish reader were radicals who shared, in some measure, his own social and political creed'.[27] His translations would presumably have passed into Stefan Buszczyński's hands after Korzeniowski's death and some of those that were unpublished were subsequently lost (Buszczyńsky published a memoir on Korzeniowski, *Mało znany poeta* ['The Little-Known Poet'], in Cracow in 1870[28]). His political essay, 'Poland and Muscovy,' was published in 1864, anonymously and allegedly 'posthumously'. The editors undoubtedly knew that the author was alive and under police supervision in Russia. This essay foreshadows Conrad's own political essays, 'Autocracy and War' (1905) and 'The Crime of Partition' (1919). Apollo Korzeniowski writes [Najder's translation]:

> The aim of Muscovy's development is to bring to a standstill all progress of humankind. So there is nothing surprising that Muscovy should keep this aim secret, and if it were not for her history I could be accused of exaggeration. Muscovy's history, however, shows that ever since she wriggled her way into European affairs, she has launched passionate attacks against every holy principle which happened to bloom in the civilized world, devouring or maiming it dangerously.[29]

Compare Conrad's treatment of Russia as a mindless and carnivorous force:

> Holy Russia, arrogating to itself the supreme power to torment and slaughter the bodies of its subjects like a God-sent scourge, has been most cruel to those whom it allowed to live under the shadow of its dispensations. The worst crime against humanity of that system we behold now crouching at bay behind vast heaps of mangled corpses is the ruthless destruction of innumerable minds. The greatest horror of the world – madness – walked faithfully in its train ('Autocracy and War', *Notes on Life and Letters*, p. 9).

It is within this context that we need to see Apollo Korzeniowski's letters about his son. Conrad is to live under an abominable tyranny within which one needs to be strong, intelligent and highly motivated in order to survive. And, as he writes on Christmas Eve, 1868, the little boy is worryingly undirected:

> My Konradek is in good health. And this pleases me more than anything else, for his nerves were shaky. He is receiving formal education in accordance with the local school syllabus, although this year he will not attend classes. He is quite capable but has as yet no taste for learning and lacks stability. Admittedly he is only eleven. But before I close my eyes I would like to foresee the course he will follow. He likes to criticize everything from a sympathetic standpoint. He is also tender and good beyond words (to Stefan Buszczyński, 24 December 1868[30]).

This is the loving and concerned language of a father who knows that he is dying and seeks to make provision for his only child.

It will be obvious from my account that I regard Korzeniowski as a heroic figure. His behaviour, which Tadeusz Bobrowski liked to represent as Quixotic and absurd, makes perfectly good moral sense given the historical situation within which he found himself.[31] At the end of 1867, because of his extreme ill-health, Apollo Korzeniowski was given permission to leave Russia. The year and a half of life that were left to him were apportioned equally between his two greatest loves, his little son and his unhappy country: he tried to make plans for 'Konradek's' education, but he also involved himself in the setting up of a new patriotic newspaper to be published in Cracow. In February 1869 he and Conrad moved to 6 Poselska Street, Cracow. On 23 May Apollo Korzeniowski died. The funeral, on 26 May 1869, was made the occasion of a major Polish patriotic demonstration. Conrad, aged eleven, led a funeral procession of several thousand people to the graveyard a few miles away from the medieval centre of Cracow.

Apollo Korzeniowski was an idealist, a radical, a man of action and a devout Catholic. His son was to grow up a sceptic, a conservative, a thinker and a declared unbeliever, though his resistance to Christianity softened in his last years.[32] Yet the two men have much in common: they share an exalted notion of literature and of the writer and his moral duty. And, as Andrzej Busza remarks, they were both pessimists who were wholly sceptical about the prevailing nineteenth century myth of human progress.[33] In addition, they were both ironists who were, paradoxically, fascinated by heroism and convinced of the validity of a few fundamental truths, and they were both individualists who insisted on their identity as gentlemen.

The works of the Polish romantic and patriotic poet Adam Mickiewicz were of huge importance to Poles, and Conrad recalled that his father read to him *Pan Tadeusz* (1834: Mickiewicz's greatest work, a twelve-book poem which became in effect the Polish national epic) and two other works (which, he said, made more impression on him as a child) *Grażyna* (1823) and *Konrad Wallenrod* (1827).[34] 'Konrad' was habitually used as the first name when Conrad was a child and then anglicized by him as his last name when he settled in England. Apollo Korzeniowski had chosen the name 'Konrad' for his son partly because of its associations with two works by Mickiewicz, *Konrad Wallenrod* and *Dziady* ['The Forefathers' Eve'] (1832), in each of which the protagonist's name is Konrad (in *Dziady* the poet 'Gustaw' is renamed 'Konrad' and becomes a patriotic hero[35]). The Konrad of *Konrad Wallenrod* is hero of a medieval struggle between Lithuanians and Germans which was understood, by all Poles, to stand for their contemporary struggle with the Russians. Konrad was obliged, for the ultimate good of his country, to engage in actions for which he was likely in the short-term to be judged a traitor. Julian Krzyżanowski sees this kind of moral conflict, whereby the hero is perceived as a traitor by those he seeks to help, as peculiar to occupied countries like Poland, and 'entirely foreign to the happy nations that have never known servitude and alien oppression'. In his view *Under Western Eyes* dramatizes a similar moral conflict, 'the influence of the wrong and rotten social conditions that affect, poison and destroy the human soul'.[36] In Polish romantic literature the romantic hero embodies ideals of national and social responsibility and is an exceptional individual burdened with special duties to his nation. In Juliusz Słowacki's *Kordian* (1834), a work Conrad knew well, the hero wanders Europe, a 'lost soul', until he finds moral identity by fighting for his country's freedom.[37] (*Kordian* is in part a polemic with Mickiewicz's *Konrad Wallenrod*, 'Kordian' being almost an anagram of 'Konrad'.[38])

Apollo's behaviour is thus part of a distinctly Polish romantic tradition, and the naming of his son shows a clear intention to pass that tradition on.

After his father's death care of Conrad passed in the first instance to Stefan Buszczyński, his father's friend and executor. Like Apollo Korzeniowski, Buszczyński was a literary man and had been a fellow member of the 'Reds' of 1861. Buszczyński was a dramatist, a poet, a literary critic and a journalist but he was also, and preeminently, an historian. In his historical works, published between 1860 and 1890 in Polish, French and German, he showed himself a radical and patriotic opponent of foreign domination (especially Russian and Austrian) and an advocate of education and political freedom as the only truly liberalizing forces in Europe.[39] Buszczyński's guardianship was a temporary arrangement, and in 1870 the Bobrowskis and the surviving Korzeniowskis placed Conrad, now aged twelve, under the joint guardianship of his maternal grandmother, Teofila Bobrowska, and Count Władysław Mniszek (who had been a friend of Conrad's mother). Teofila Bobrowska shared her daughter's – Conrad's mother's – patriotic spirit and romanticism. Between 1870 and 1873 Conrad lived in Cracow with his grandmother. In 1873 Bobrowski sent him from Cracow to a boarding school in Lwów, the capital of Galicia, where he stayed with Bobrowski's cousin, Antoni Syroczyński, who ran a boarding-house for boys orphaned by the 1863 insurrection.

In practice Conrad's real guardian during this period was his uncle Tadeusz Bobrowski, his mother's brother. Tadeusz felt that as the son of well-known political activists Conrad would be unsafe living in Russia: hence the decision to settle him in Cracow, which was under Austrian rule, with his grandmother. We have seen that Apollo Korzeniowski had tried to educate Conrad himself, with the result that Conrad was very backward in some subjects and lacked the German and Latin that he would need to be admitted to the Gymnasium. He was placed at a boarding house run by Ludwik Georgeon in Floriańska Street in Cracow and a medical student from the Jagiellonian university, Adam Marek Pulman, was appointed as his private tutor. In 1870 Conrad passed an examination for St Anne's Gymnasium, reputedly the best school in Cracow, but it is not certain that he actually attended the school.[40] (Zdzisław Najder believes that Conrad did not go to St Anne's but Andrzej Busza puts forward good arguments for thinking that he did.[41]) If Conrad was indeed educated at that school then he went there at a fortunate time. As a result of a reform of 1867 Polish had replaced German as the official school language of 'Galicia' (Austrian Poland) and the principal text books had been translated into Polish.[42]

Conrad recalled his Cracow years very emotionally. The city centre was, and still is, small and exceptionally beautiful: the walking distances between his lodgings in Floriańska Street, St Anne's Gymnasium, and the apartment on Poselska Street where his father spent the last months of his life, were not great. He speaks of Cracow as 'that town of classical learning and historical relics' ('Poland Revisited', *Notes on Life and Letters*, p. 165) of 'glorious tombs and tragic memories' (p. 169). Even for an eleven year old it was intimate and atmospheric. The middle-aged Conrad recalls his young self walking up Floriańska Street, just off the great central square where the 'unequal massive towers of St Mary's Church soared aloft into the ethereal radiance of the air' (p. 166). To walk up Floriańska Street and into the square today is to have exactly the visual experience that Conrad describes. Sadly, though, the air is no longer 'ethereal' but dangerously polluted. The Communist regime built a huge steel-works close to Cracow. It is believed that this was done with the deliberate intention of preventing its inhabitants from retaining elitist notions of the city's royal and academic status. This measure has seriously damaged the citizens' health but has done nothing to undermine their veneration of Cracow's traditions.

Tadeusz Bobrowski had a reputation for being ambitious and self-seeking and had few friends. He wanted to control Conrad's view of his parents. Throughout Conrad's childhood Uncle Tadeusz seems to have encouraged Conrad to see his mother as a helpless victim of his father's recklessness. He concealed from Conrad the fact that his mother had been *convicted*, with his father, of fostering rebellion against the Russians. The young Conrad was given a simple scenario: that he was the child of an adored and martyred mother and of a reckless father from the consequences of whose wild actions he, Conrad, had been rescued by his prudent uncle.[43] Yet this obstinate, prickly man has been misunderstood, both at the time and by posterity: he was capable of being warm and generous and he was genuinely affectionate. He loved Conrad, who to some degree replaced in Bobrowski's affections his daughter, his only child, Józefa, who died in 1871 aged twelve. She was a year younger than Conrad and had been his playmate 'in the clean country air' of Nowochwastów (the family estate of the Lubowidzkis, Tadeusz Bobrowski's parents-in-law) in 1866 (letter from Apollo Korzeniowski, November 1866[44]). Conrad and Józefa were both lonely children and like Conrad, Józefa had had a childhood which could be seen as tragic in that her mother had died giving birth to her (27 April 1858). This woman, Józefa Lubowidzka, was from a wealthy family – Bobrowski had 'married well', as became so circumspect a man – and it is relevant to the Apollo Korzeniowski and Tadeusz Bobrowski relationship to note that Apollo had facilitated Tadeusz's courtship of Józefa Lubowidzka.[45] Apollo was nine years older than Tadeusz and had been a friend to him when they were students together at St Petersburg. Tadeusz studied Law but never practiced; on his father's death in 1850 he took on the responsibility of managing the Bobrowski estates. On 11 May 1849 Apollo, then twenty-nine, wrote to Tadeusz, who was then twenty:

> I entertain a strong affection and great respect for you;.... I wish to be worthy of your friendship, which I find most rewarding;.... I cherish blissful hopes that having read this letter you will place me among dreamers and

unrecognized geniuses and that you will laugh; but if sincere feeling may evoke a reciprocity, then in spite of our different characters you will remember that we share the same feelings on human dignity, and you will not deny me your friendship.[46]

This is affectionate but also nervous: Apollo seems very anxious to propitiate the younger man and is also seeking reassurance from him. In a curious way its tone anticipates the tone of the letters that Apollo's son in the 1890s was to write to Edward Garnett, whom – though he was much younger – Joseph Conrad treated as a senior and almost patriarchal friend. Tadeusz was to propagate the myth of Apollo as the insecure prodigal, himself as the confident anchor-man. Apollo's letter colludes with that myth: its writer clearly has little confidence – about the relationship with the recipient, at least – and is seeking reassurance. Tadeusz was then twenty.

We know far more about Tadeusz's view of Apollo than we do about Apollo's view of Tadeusz. It seems likely that Tadeusz was jealous of Apollo. While expressing affection for the older man, in his *Memoirs* (published after his death in 1900) and his letters Tadeusz fleshes out his myth of Apollo as an impulsive prodigal:

> In our part of the country he had the reputation of being very ugly and sarcastic. In fact he was not beautiful, nor even handsome, but his eyes had a very kind expression and his sarcasm was only verbal, of the drawing-room type; for I have never detected any in his feeling or in his actions. Openhearted and passionate, he had a sincere love of people. In his deeds he was impractical, often even helpless. Uncompromising in speech and writing, he was frequently over-tolerant in everyday life. . . . Although he regarded himself as an avowed democrat, and others took him for an 'ultra' or a 'Red', he had in him – as I kept telling him – a hundred times as many *szlachta* traits as I. . . . Actually it was his tender heart and his sympathetic feeling towards the poor and oppressed which made some people, including himself, believe that he was a democrat. In reality this was nothing more than the case of a well-born Nałecz being transported by his emotions and ideas, and not by any democratic principles.[47]

Najder points out that this last assertion – that Apollo had no firm political beliefs – is contradicted by Apollo's writings, where 'he expresses his democratic views quite unequivocally.'[48] In all his writings about Apollo, Tadeusz displays a natural, if uningratiating, impulse to denigrate his dead brother-in-law's impulsiveness and thus vindicate his own caution. Tadeusz outlived Apollo by many years and we know a great deal about him from his writings, including his letters to Conrad, the 'Document' that he prepared for his nephew, and his *Memoirs*. The most attractive side of Tadeusz's personality is revealed in his relationship with his nephew.[49]

Joseph Conrad's childhood can be said to have lasted until he was twenty-nine. From his father's death when he was eleven he was loved, cajoled, nagged, worried over and subsidized by Uncle Tadeusz, who saw his nephew as a gifted young man who was wasting his talent and who needed to settle to something. Most of the knowledge of this period of Conrad's life comes from Bobrowski's letters to him. Sadly Conrad's letters to Bobrowski were all destroyed by fire at Kazimierówka manor, Bobrowski's house, which was burnt down in the 1917 revolution. Bobrowski viewed the stages towards Conrad's final qualification in the British merchant marine as the father of a student might view the stages in the young man's protracted higher education, and when Conrad passed his Master's certificate in 1886 Bobrowski wrote to him in undisguised relief as a person who has at last become an independent adult: 'As the humble provider of the means for this enterprise I can only rejoice that my groats have not been wasted but have led you to the peak of your chosen profession.... You are, my dear Sir, now 29 years old and have mastered a profession'.[50] The years at the start of this process, between 1869 and 1874, are very poorly documented. And they were the crucial years of Conrad's life. As Conrad says in 'Poland Revisited', his early adolescence in Cracow was decisive: 'It was in that old royal and academical city that I ceased to be a child, became a boy, had known the friendships, the admirations, the thoughts and the indignations of that age. It was within those historical walls that I began to understand things, form affections, lay up a store of memories and a fund of sensations with which I was to break violently by throwing myself into an unrelated existence' (p. 145). He is referring obliquely to his decision to leave Poland and join the French merchant marine.[51]

The bare bones of Conrad's last years in Poland are as follows: from 1869 to 1870 Buszczyński was his guardian. Between 1870 and 1873 Conrad lived in Cracow with his grandmother. In 1873 he went to Syroczyński's school in Lwów. On 19 September 1874 Conrad left for Marseille and joined the French merchant marine.

Conrad was a difficult adolescent for Tadeusz to look after. Since childhood he had been subject to illnesses: a letter from his father in 1868 speaks of gravel in the bladder which causes gripes, and some of Tadeusz's letters seem to refer to the risk of epilepsy (there was epilepsy in the family: another of Bobrowski's nephews suffered from it).[52] Bobrowski had his hands full. As the son of a political criminal Conrad could not safely live within the Russian state and in any case Bobrowski was preoccupied with many other responsibilities including the health of his little Józefa. Also he had other wards: in his *Memoirs* he records that he was guardian to eighteen young people. Conrad presented a number of problems. The fear that he might have epilepsy was fuelled by a series of nervous illnesses and was not put to rest until he was fourteen or so: in 1873 he was sent away travelling round Europe for twelve weeks with Adam Pulman for the sake of his health.[53] He displayed challenging behaviour, resisting all forms of authority and indulging himself in illicit pleasures: a 'talent for cigars' is mentioned by his irritated uncle.[54] He was disobedient and troublesome at school both in Cracow and in Lwów.[55] And the stirrings of adolescence were giving trouble of a more normal kind: it is likely that during a holi-day in Krynica (with Adam Pulman) in 1871 or 1872 he was attracted to the girl who became the source for the early love affair reflected in *The Arrow of Gold*.[56] Syroczyński's daughter remembered Conrad in Lwów (1873–74):

> He stayed with us ten months while in the seventh class at the Gymnasium. Intellectually he was extremely advanced but disliked school routine, which he found tiring and dull; he used to say that he was very talented and planned to become a great writer. Such declarations coupled with a sarcastic expression on his face and with frequent critical remarks, shocked his teach-ers and provoked laughter among his classmates. He disliked all restrictions. At home, at school, or in the living room he would sprawl unceremoniously. He used to suffer from severe headaches and nervous attacks; the doctors thought that a stay at the seaside might cure him.[57]

Conrad was a constant source of trouble. Bobrowski was at his wit's end to know what to do with him. The plan to become a merchant seaman appears to have been conceived by Conrad in 1872 and resisted at first by the family, but Bobrowski was eventually brought round to the conclusion that for someone so undirected and seemingly unteachable a career in the French merchant marine was better than nothing. There was little more future for Conrad in Galicia than there was in the Ukraine, since attempts to obtain Austrian citizenship for him had failed. Bobrowski could thus have seen two strong reasons for consenting to Conrad's wish to seek his fortune abroad: the chance of becoming a French citizen, and the (rather more remote) possibility that the sea-life would cure Conrad's nervous illnesses. If Conrad's illnesses were all part of the mix of anger, frustration and intense anxiety that are constituents of depression then a complete change of environment could, indeed, have been an appropriate way of dealing with the problem.[58]

Absence makes the heart grow fonder. Bobrowski and Conrad seem to have become warmer, more intimate and more friendly after Conrad had left home. Both took letter-writing seriously. Conrad's side of the correspondence has been lost, as we have seen. Bobrowski's letters dis-play affection, concern, a desire to guide and to warn together with an acknowledgement of the young man's ambition and nobility of spirit. The Korzeniowski and Nałecz inheritance was blamed for Conrad's impulsiveness:

> You always, my dear boy, made me impatient – and still make me impatient by your disorder and the easy way you take things – in which you remind me of the Korzeniowski family – spoiling and wasting everything – and not my dear Sister, your Mother, who was careful about everything (27 September, old st., 1876)

> I recognize your Nałecz blood – in this tendency to fly into a passion (28 July/8 August 1877)

But Bobrowski was also able to say, with justice and foresight, that Conrad combined the best of both families, the Korzeniowskis and the Bobrowskis:

> I see with pleasure that the Nałecz in you has been modified under the influence of the Bobroszczaki, as your incomparable mother used to call her own family after she flew away to the Nałecz nest. This time I rejoice over the influence of my family, although I don't in the least deny that the Nałeczes have a spirit of initiative and enterprise greater than that which is in my blood. From the blending of these two excellent families in your worthy person there should spring a race which by its endurance and wise enterprise will astound the whole world! (28 June, old st., 1880)[59]

Apollo Korzeniowski had provided the romanticism, the ardour and the exalted self-image, Bobrowski provided the vigilance, the wit and the irony. Bobrowski kept up his correspondence with his beloved young ward for twenty years, from 1874 when Conrad left Poland until Bobrowski's death in 1894, by which time Conrad had almost completed the first novel, *Almayer's Folly*, which was to be dedicated to Bobrowski. In a sense it was Bobrowski who made Conrad a writer. Both uncle and nephew seem to have regarded letter-writing as an art form. Conrad seems to have written detailed accounts of his travels in the merchant marine for his uncle, and one of Bobrowski's letters indicates that he was encouraging the young man to write for publication:

> As thank God you do not forget your Polish (may God bless you for it, as I bless you) and your writing is not bad, I repeat what I have already written and said before – you would do well to write contributions for the *Wedrowiec*[60] in Warsaw. We have few travellers, and even fewer genuine correspondents: the words of an eyewitness would be of great interest and in time would bring you in money. It would be an exercise in your native tongue – that thread which binds you to your country and countrymen, and finally a tribute to the memory of your father who always wanted to and did serve his country by his pen. Think about this, young man, collect some reminiscences from the voyage to Australia and sent them as a sample (16/28 June 1881)[61]

But for the fact that they are written in English rather than Polish, Conrad's early novels could be said to fulfil Bobrowski's requirement here in that they are traveller's tales, bringing exotic subjects – the far East, the Malay archipelago, unknown peoples – to a European metropolitan audience.

Although not consciously literary in the way that Conrad's father had been, Bobrowski was widely read and peppers his letters to Conrad with literary references: Polish writers like Zaleski and Słowacki, and great European figures like Shakespeare, Molière, Pushkin and Cervantes. It is assumed that easy familiarity with great literature is part of the equipment of a cultivated person. Bobrowski writes in September 1886 warning Conrad that he may not be able to respond to future requests for money. He sends £30 and adds:

I do not know how much longer I shall be able to manifest my remembrance in such a tangible form. For if Hamlet said 'Something is rotten in the State of Denmark', so it has been the case for some time in our agricultural affairs. The fall in the prices of grain (in spite of the bad harvest this year our local needs can always be met) and sugar affects the rent one can get for one's land (18/30 September 1886)[62]

The fact that a very large number of Tadeusz Bobrowski's letters to his sailor nephew have survived[63] is a silent tribute to the great affection that Conrad felt for his uncle. Conrad was prodigal and careless with some of his possessions. In 1875 he lost a trunk and in September 1876 he is rebuked by Bobrowski for losing a family photograph and some Polish books: 'And you ask me to replace them! Why? So that you should take the first opportunity of losing them again!?'[64] But he obviously treasured his uncle's letters. Many of the letters show that Bobrowski and Conrad were both lonely and that they were the two people in the world best placed to understand each other. The old squire on his estate at Kazimierówka fills his life with day-to-day rural activity but is essentially lonely. As he gets older the loneliness becomes more pronounced: 'I shall . . . stay at home writing my memoirs. My health is good, and I am used to being alone. Write to me, Panie Bracie ['Sir Brother', the form of address between equal members of the *szlachta*], what your plans are for the future' (18/30 September 1886).[65] He is distressed when an old servant dies: 'My last link with the past has been broken. An ever-growing emptiness surrounds a man, till at last he falls himself' (5/17 April 1887).[66] He preoccupies himself with anxieties about his own health and worries about his vagrant nephew. He fusses persistently and touchingly over Conrad's health, especially inquiring after his 'precious little liver'.[67] On 1/13 May 1881 he writes to say that he is feeling old, missing Conrad and hopes to see him. As the expatriate son of a convict Conrad could not visit Kazimierowka while he is still a Russian subject for fear of arrest, so Bobrowski plans that they might meet at Marienbad or Wiesbaden, 'where I intend to undergo a grape cure [for haemorrhoids] – and I have chosen to take it there solely to make it nearer for you to drop in on me.' It is ten years since the death of his beloved daughter Józefa ('my Józieczka') and he intends to keep her anniversary. The letter goes on and on in the same way: Bobrowski longs to see his nephew but is assailed by scruples about making demands on his time and the scruples are set out in obsessional detail ('I know that staying on shore does not agree with you, and above all that it seems a waste of money to spend an unproductive 3 months on land while waiting for a fortnight's meeting'[68]). And he ends with fussy honesty: his health will improve ('I shall try to fight it with Marienbad and grapes'), he is not likely to die yet. Conrad wrote back to say that he ought not to take time off to visit his uncle.[69]

Bobrowski's health remains a dominant theme of his letters to Conrad throughout the 1880s: he suffers from haemorrhoids, diarrhoea, neuralgia, rheumatism, anxiety, sleeplessness and 'nerves'. He visits Marienbad regularly to drink the spa-water and he has 'electrical' treatment, grape treatment, whey treatment, rain-water baths, mud-baths and friction. Some of these cures are good, others less good: Cieplice water aggravates the haemorrhoids while Marienbad water produces gentle stools.[70] A subordinate, but important, topic in these letters is the troubles of his brother Kazimierz. Kazimierz, who had resigned his commission and been imprisoned in the uprising of 1863, now had a poorly paid job as a station-master on the railway. He had six children whom he couldn't afford to feed and educate, and Bobrowski found himself providing for Kazimierz's family as well as for Conrad. Kazimierz's fecundity prompts an earthy joke (14/26 May 1882): 'You will admit that your Uncle worked successfully in this field [begetting children]. I don't even know when he had time to achieve all that as at nights he always had to be on the look-out for trains. Probably between one train and another he devoted himself to "social work" to keep himself from falling asleep!'[71] Kazimierz died of pneumonia in 1886 and Bobrowski stoically, and characteristically, took responsibility for the children.

With regard to Conrad himself, Bobrowski's letters have two leading themes, both eminently sensible: Conrad must gain his qualifications in the British merchant marine and he must become a naturalized Englishman and thus cease to be a Russian subject. Conrad achieved both these things: he qualified as second mate in 1880, first mate in 1884 and gained his master's certificate in 1886, and on 31 March 1889 the Russian Ministry of Home Affairs released him from the status of a Russian subject. This made it possible for Conrad to visit his uncle in the Ukraine without being arrested. The letters containing these items of advice contain references to many other schemes. Conrad seems to have represented service in the British merchant marine to his uncle as a stop-gap career, and was constantly coming up with schemes for setting up partnerships to engage in trade in London. Adolf Krieger was a fellow lodger at Dynevor Road, Stoke Newington, in 1880. He was an American of German origin who had a series of jobs: as agent for Barr, Moering and Company in the later 1880s he found work for Conrad in the company's warehouse. It seems clear that Conrad and Krieger proposed to set up a trading partnership and that early in 1886 they proposed to Bobrowski that he should invest in them. At about this time Conrad borrowed an unknown, but substantial, amount of money from Krieger and did not repay it. (Later, in 1897, this was to cause estrangement between the friends. In 1898 Conrad dedicated *Tales of Unrest* to Krieger 'for the sake of old days' possibly in an attempt to placate him.) The relationship with Krieger is the background to Bobrowski's letter of 24 March/5 April 1886: 'I deduce from your and Krieger's letters [that] you intend to devote yourself to trade and stay in London. . . . I would strongly recommend a thorough investigation in London of two possibilities: *trading in wheat-flour* . . . and *trading in granulated sugar.*'[72]

His connection with uncle Tadeusz and his knowledge of merchant shipping meant that Conrad was well placed to import Polish agricultural products of the kind that Bobrowski grew on his estate – sugar and flour – into England and this could have been quite a good scheme. The letters indicate that Bobrowski sent some capital to be invested in the scheme (some £350) but later letters anxiously asking what has happened to the money suggest that it had gone on Conrad's extravagant habits. Nothing came of the proposed trading company.

Some of Bobrowski's letters to Conrad contained Shandean requests for the sailor. One of these was on behalf of Dr Kopernicki, an old friend of the family who had helped with Conrad's education between 1870 and 1873 and who treated Tadeusz at Marienbad in the late summer of 1881. He was a craniologist, and Conrad is asked to 'collect during your voyages skulls of natives, writing on each one whose skull it is and the place of origin' (3/15 August 1881).[73] The idea was that Conrad should collect these skulls and send them off in batches of a dozen to the Museum of Craniology in Cracow. Not surprisingly, Conrad refused. There is an ugly context to this letter (and the following letters of 1881): on 10 August Conrad had written to Bobrowski asking for immediate funds because a ship on which he was serving, the *Annie Frost*, had foundered and he had lost his luggage and spent several days in hospital. Bobrowski sent the money. The reality was that Conrad had been squandering money on speculations, the details of which are obscure, and had invented the *Annie Frost* calamity to lever a further subsidy out of Bobrowski (a ship called the *Annie Frost* existed but Conrad didn't serve on it).[74] Bobrowski was no fool and perhaps sensed, after a bit, that his generosity was being abused. He wrote that anxiety about the *Annie Frost* misfortune is making him ill ('your last calamity has upset me', 'the worry gave me diarrhoea'[75]), and in successive letters he pressed Conrad to explain why he had failed to obtain compensation from the owners of the *Annie Frost*. Conrad must have squirmed. It is a pity that we don't have the letters in which he tried to come up with a convincing reply.

Despite this and other deceptions, Conrad's love for Bobrowski was real. It was genuinely difficult to visit Poland, but Conrad and Bobrowski had a pleasant summer reunion at Marienbad and at Teplice in Bohemia in the summer of 1883. The reunion stirred up Conrad's sense of himself as a Pole, and on 14 August 1883 he wrote from Teplice to Stefan Buszczyński, his first guardian:

> During the last few years – that is, since my first examination,[76] I have not been too happy in my journeyings. I was nearly drowned, nearly got burned,[77] but generally my health is good, I am not short of courage or of the will to work or of love for my profession; and I always remember what you said when I was leaving Cracow: 'Remember' – you said – 'wherever you may sail you are sailing towards Poland!'[78]

Early in 1890 Conrad returned to Poland – for the first time for sixteen years – and stayed in Warsaw and then for two months with Tadeusz at

Kazimierówka. The visit was made possible by the fact that the Russians had finally (31 March 1889) released Conrad from Russian citizenship. The account of the visit in *A Personal Record* is curiously oblique: there is a mention of the stay in Warsaw and a good deal about the sleighride from Kalinówka to Kazimierówka, but very little about Kazimierówka itself. The testimony of Polish friends and neighbours who saw him at his uncle's house during this visit suggests that he was awkward and out of place, that he resented suggestions that he ought not to have gone abroad and that there were problems of adjustment for this mature man returning to a place where people were accustomed to thinking of him as a wayward child.[79] There was one more visit to Kazimierówka, in the late summer of 1893: Conrad seems to have been ill on this visit and spent a week in bed. He writes to his cousin (by marriage) Marguerite Poradowska: 'As for me, I have been very unwell and in bed for five days. This is a good place to be ill (if one must be ill). My uncle has cared for me as if I were a little child.'[80] One of the functions of this visit, seen in retrospect, was to enable Conrad to say goodbye to his childhood.

In February 1894 Bobrowski died. He had left his estate to the widow and six children of his brother Kazimierz, but to Conrad he left fifteen thousand roubles and silver and other valuables.[81] The love and loyalty for Tadeusz Bobrowski had remained unchanged by the disappointing 1890 visit, and Conrad was distressed at his loss. Several years later he wrote to Kazimierz Waliszewski (5 December 1903):

> I cannot write about Tadeusz Bobrowski, my Uncle, guardian and bene-
> factor, without emotion. Even now, after ten years, I still feel his loss. He was
> a man of great character and unusual qualities of mind. Although he did
> not understand my desire to join the mercantile marine, on principle, he
> never objected to it. I saw him four times during the thirty [sic] years of my
> wanderings (from 1874–1893) but even so I attribute to his devotion, care,
> and influence, whatever good qualities I may possess.[82]

Bobrowski had been both a second father to him and, in a sense, a literary godfather, since Bobrowski was himself a writer. In 1900 his book *The Bobrowski Memoirs*, some nine-hundred pages long, was published in Poland. There are three major strands to the memoirs: a thorough and unspar-ing criticism of contemporary Polish society, an account of the attempts of forward-looking Poles – among whom Bobrowski included himself – to reform that society (especially by pressing for the emancipation of the peasants), and the absurdity of the 1863 rising and its consquences.[83] The last of these gave offence to patriotic Poles who charged Bobrowski – quite unfairly – with collusion with the Russians. Conrad would have read the Bobrowski memoirs soon after receiving them in 1900. I have referred above to the death in a duel in 1863 of Bobrowski's brother, Stefan Bobrowski (p. 3) and to the possibility that Bobrowski's account of Stefan in the *Memoirs* has influenced the ending of *Lord Jim* and part of the Haldin

plot of *Under Western Eyes*. Stefan played a key role as a member of the
'Reds' and was challenged to a duel by Adam Grabowski, who was a member
of the 'Whites'. Stefan Bobrowski had poor eyesight and Grabowski was
well-known to be an expert marksman: a duel with Grabowski meant certain death, and Stefan Bobrowski must have known that. At first he refused
to accept the challenge but then bowed to the pressure of a 'court of
honour' which ruled that the duel must be fought. Tadeusz Bobrowski
believed that Stefan had chosen to die in a duel as an honourable alternative
to suicide: 'Having lost faith in the cause he had embraced – his mind was
too alert and realistic to harbour illusions – he no longer wished to live
and preferred to die by another's hand than by his own.' If Bobrowski's
reading of the event was correct then Stefan's death would have resembled Jim's death in *Lord Jim*: after his defeat by Brown Jim chooses to be
executed by Doramin, father of his friend whom Brown has murdered.
Bobrowski's account of the betrayal of Stefan by an informer may have
contributed to Razumov's betrayal of Haldin in *Under Western Eyes*: 'The
informer was a Warsaw Jew named Bernstein.... He was sent to Kiev
to discover the secret lithographic press [Stefan's press] which had been
causing trouble to the police for some time. In Warsaw he had been a
student, and so in Kiev he also mixed with students, pretending to be one
himself.'[84]

Conrad made use of Bobrowski's memoirs again in 1908 when he was
writing *A Personal Record*. He wrote to his literary agent, J. B. Pinker, on
7 October:

> To make Polish life enter English literature is no small ambition – to begin
> with. But I think it can be done. To reveal a very particular state of society,
> bring forward individuals with very special traditions and touch in a personal
> way upon such events for instance as the liberation of the serfs [this doesn't
> appear in *A Personal Record*] ... is a big enterprise. And yet it presents itself
> easily just because of the intimate nature of the task, and of the 2 vols of my
> uncle's Memoirs which I have by me, to refresh my recollections and settle
> my ideas.[85]

Bobrowski was Conrad's epistolary companion throughout Conrad's sea
years. The prudence and the maturity that Bobrowski displayed were
valued by Conrad and became part of the fabric of his works. He wrote
to Conrad late in 1891 as follows:

> I have gone through a lot, I have suffered over my own fate and the fate of
> my family and my Nation, and perhaps just because of these sufferings and
> disappointments I have developed in myself this calm outlook on the prob-
> lem of life, whose motto, I venture to say, was, is, and will be 'usque ad
> finem'. The devotion to duty interpreted more widely or narrowly, accord-
> ing to circumstances and time – this constitutes my practical creed (28
> October/9 November 1891)[86]

The faith in good order and the motto, *usque ad finem*, are associated with the figure of Stein in *Lord Jim*:

> He [Stein] sat down and, with both elbows on the desk, rubbed his fore-head. 'And yet it is true – it is true. In the destructive element immerse. . . .'
> He spoke in a subdued tone, without looking at me, one hand on each side of his face. 'That was the way. To follow the dream, and again to follow the dream – and so – *ewig – usque ad finem*. . . .' (chapter 20, pp. 214–15)

Seeing things through to their conclusion, tenacity, loyalty, persistence, good workmanship, judgement – these were all Uncle Tadeusz qualities. Conrad dramatizes the contrast between these virtues and the flamboyant virtues of his father – idealism, risk-taking and self-sacrifice – in all his works. And although he left Poland so young there is a sense in which Poland – the Poland of Tadeusz Bobrowski as much as the Poland of Apollo Korzeniowski – remained with him all his life. His thick Polish accent, his mannerisms and his appearance marked him off until his death from the English people among whom he lived; this included, of course, his own wife and children. After his marriage he chose to live in rural places in the south-east of England in a succession of rented farmhouses and country properties. It was often remarked that in the various country houses of his long English exile he was reproducing for himself, as far as he could, the life-style of a Polish landowner. He was a *szlachcic* to the end.

2

Officer of the Merchant Marine

Long live the 'Ordin. Master in the British Merchant Service'!! May he live long! May he be healthy and may every success attend him in every enterprise both on sea and on land!

Bobrowski to Conrad, 14/26 November, 1886, on the news of
Conrad gaining his Master's certificate.[1]

Conrad was, as has often been said, 'set' to loneliness, and yet he had two powerfully contrasting males on whom to model himself, his father and his uncle. R. R. Hodges writes of Conrad as 'the man with two fathers' . . . torn between his father's impractical idealism and his uncle's practical morality'.[2] The question of what it means to be a fully mature male as well as a complete moral being is considered in many of Conrad's novels and tales. Further, it has often been said – by, for example, Thomas Moser, Bernard Meyer and Graham Hough – that Conrad's many years in the merchant marine give a particular bias to his dramatization: that he finds it easier to dramatize relationships between men than relationships between the sexes because throughout his early adult life his experience of human interaction had been largely restricted to the society of men on a ship. In *Image and Experience* Graham Hough writes 'There is only one kind of society that Conrad had ever known intimately, had fully participated in as an adult human being – the society of a ship at sea'.[3] But it is easy for literary critics to engage in wishful thinking. Just as Polish political sympathy seems to determine the nature of some of the work that has been done on Conrad's Polish background and identity, so homosexual political conviction seems to have determined some of the work that has been done on Conrad's interaction with other men. On guilt in Conrad's writings Professor Hodges writes: 'I would suggest that in addition to patriotic guilt, which played a large and fairly conscious part in Conrad's inner life, a suppressed attraction to members of his own sex contributed to his unhappiness'.[4] There is no evidence for this, as far as I can discover. Conrad had close friendships with other men and male bonding, with its odd mix of tenderness, sentimentality and reticence – the kind of relationship that grows between Jim and Marlow – is clearly a feature both of Conrad's experience and of his fiction, but with regard to sexual preference all the evidence suggests that his orientation was heterosexual. To compare the characteristics of Conrad's heroes with those of 'closet' homosexuals and to find parallels (secrecy, private torment and a desire to transcend loneliness) is fair enough as an aid to understanding the work but tells us nothing about Conrad the man. To answer the question 'what did Conrad have to feel guilty about?' we need look no further than his guilt over having left Poland.

We have very little information about Conrad's feelings on his departure for Marseille in 1874, but from later evidence it is clear that Conrad was very sensitive to the charge that he had deserted Poland. He was very hurt by an attack made on him in April 1899 by Eliza Orzeszkowa, a Polish novelist and patriot, who had been led to believe that he was making a great commercial success with his novels in England. Orzeszkowa's article, published in Polish, was called 'The emigration of talent'. Conrad certainly read this, either at the time of publication or later.[5] He became angry when Orzeszkowa's name was mentioned during his visit to Poland in 1914 (he referred to Orzeszkowa as a 'hag'). Aniela Zagórska surmised that Orzeszkowa's words must have 'touched on his deepest and most painful emotions and thoughts [. . . because his] dual loyalty to Poland and England – with the evident supremacy of the latter – constituted a constant source of distress for him'.[6] Orzeszkowa wrote of Conrad, 'This gentleman, who writes popular and very lucrative novels in English, has almost caused me a nervous breakdown. My gorge rises when I read about him. Why, are creative artists to join the exodus? . . . Creative talent forms the very crown of the tree, the pinnacle of the tower, the life-blood of the nation. And to take away that flower, to remove that pinnacle, to drain away that life-blood in order to pass it on to the Anglo-Saxons . . . just because they pay better. . . . It is even hard to think about it without shame'.[7]

In 1874 Conrad left Poland for Marseille. An outline of the years 1874–96 could read as follows: he left Poland for Marseille to become a trainee seaman with the French merchant navy. In 1876 he served as a 'steward' on the *Saint-Antoine* and in 1877 he was possibly involved in smuggling arms from Marseille to the 'Carlists' (the Spanish royalists). In 1878 in Marseille he shot himself in the chest but was not seriously injured. As a direct result of this apparent suicide attempt his Uncle Tadeusz cleared his (very substantial) debts. In April 1878 he joined his first British ship, the *Mavis*, and later in the year joined the *Skimmer of the Sea*. In August 1886 he became a British citizen. In November he passed the examination for the Master's certificate. In 1887 he was hospitalized in Singapore with an injury sustained on the *Highland Forest*. In 1887–8 he got to know the Malay Archipelago as an officer of the *Vidar*. In 1888 he was appointed master of the *Otago*, his only command. In 1889 he resigned from the *Otago*, settled briefly in London, began to write *Almayer's Folly* and began a lasting friendship with his 'Aunt' Marguerite Poradowska. In 1890 he worked in the Belgian Congo for the Société Anonyme Belge pour le Commerce du Haut-Congo. In 1891–3 he served as an officer of the *Torrens*, his last ship.

To return to the young man who arrived in Marseille in 1874: he was in France for about three and a half years, from the age of sixteen until he was twenty, during which time he made three voyages to the West Indies. The period is badly documented: no letters from Conrad have survived for these years and his written accounts, in *The Mirror of the Sea*, *A Personal Record*, *The Sisters* and *The Arrow of Gold*, are enriched by a good deal of fabulation. From *A Personal Record* it seems that his desire to go abroad was hard for Bobrowski to understand and gave rise to arguments: 'I catch myself in hours of solitude and retrospect meeting arguments and charges made thirty-five years ago by voices now for ever still; finding things to say that an assailed boy could not have found, simply because of the mysteriousness of his impulses to himself.' The young Conrad took pleasure in the stir that he caused. Perhaps that pleasure – the simple gratification of attracting a great deal of attention to himself – contributed to his course of action: 'There was no precedent. I verily believe mine was the only case of a boy of my nationality and antecedents taking a, so to speak, standing jump out of his racial surroundings and associations.' Conrad's diction here describing his 'standing jump' from Poland resembles that of Jim in *Lord Jim* describing his jump from the *Patna*. Like Jim, Conrad claims not to have understood his own volition: 'I understood no more than the people who called upon me to explain myself' (chapter 6, p. 121). Uncle Bobrowski gave him an allowance of 2,000 francs a year and had asked two acquaintances, a Pole called Wiktor Chodźko (who was in the French merchant navy) and a Frenchman called Baptistin Solary to keep an eye on Conrad. Solary wrote to Bobrowski promising to get young Conrad experience on a French ship 'if he really wanted a taste of *ce métier de chien*' ('this dog's occupation'; chapter 6, p. 122). Slightly daunted by this last phrase, Conrad put his 'trust in the good-natured Solary's very civil letter', and when he met Solary in Marseille found him 'a quite young man, very good-looking, with a fine black, short beard, a fresh complexion, and soft, merry black eyes'. Conrad's first experiences at sea were as a tourist rather than as a sailor. The French dubbed him *le petit ami de Baptistin* (we must remember that he was only sixteen): 'Many a day and night . . . did I spend cruising with these rough, kindly men, under whose auspices my intimacy with the sea began. Many a time "the little friend of Baptistin" had the hooded cloak of the Mediterranean sailor thrown over him by their honest hands.' This reinforces our sense of Conrad as a tourist: the recollection is affectionate but at the same time somewhat patronizing. He does recall, though, and is grateful for, the fatherly tenderness that he brought out in these sailors: 'Their sea-tanned faces, whiskered or shaved, lean or full, with the intent wrinkled sea-eyes of the pilot-breed, and there and there a thin gold loop at the lobe of a hairy ear, bent over my sea-infancy.' But the tone of social distance returns when he gets on to their wives and daughters: 'I have been invited to sit in more than one tall, dark house of the old town at their hospitable board, had the *bouillabaisse* ladled out into a thick plate by their high-voiced, broad-browed wives, talked to their daughters – thick-set girls, with pure profiles, glorious masses of black hair arranged with complicated art, dark eyes, and dazzlingly white teeth' (chapter 6, pp. 123–4).

Baptistin Solary recommended Conrad to Jean-Baptiste Délestang, owner of a shipping firm. Conrad's first ship was the *Mont-Blanc*, owned by the Délestangs. Conrad embarked as a passenger on 15 December 1874 for St Pierre, Martinique. After a five month passage the *Mont-Blanc* returned to Marseille on 23 May 1875. Conrad repeated the same voyage in the *Mont-Blanc*, this time as an apprentice, between 25 June and 23 December. In 1876 he had six months of freedom in Marseille where he clearly enjoyed himself a great deal, spent far too much of Bobrowski's money, and went frequently to the theatre and the opera. He enjoyed Sardou, Scribe, Meyerbeer, Offenbach and, particularly, Bizet's *Carmen*. He neglected the educational study that Bobrowski had expected him to undertake. The tone of Bobrowski's letters shows clearly enough that he felt that Conrad needed to be reined in:

> Please write to me about your health and further plans. Please give me also full details of *your studies*. What have you been working on during the voyage? You praise the present captain. So you have presumably profited from him? Did he give you lessons? If so, in what? What did you work on yourself? and what did you teach yourself? Are you also working on English or other languages? and so on. In short, write about everything regarding your moral and physical being.[8]

On 10 July he sailed as 'steward' on the *Saint-Antoine* for Martinique. Tradition has it that on this voyage Conrad made his only landfall in South America (Colombia and Venezuela) and that this was the sole source in his experience (as opposed to his reading) for *Nostromo*; but entries in the ship's Agreement and Account of Crew show that the ship stayed at Martinique.[9] It is not known whether Conrad made an independent visit to the South American coast. The *Saint-Antoine* returned via the Virgin Islands and Haiti, and arrived back in Marseille on 15 February of the following year, 1877. On the *Saint-Antoine* he encountered Dominique Cervoni, the first mate, a Corsican sailor who became the model for Nostromo in *Nostromo* and for Peyrol in *The Rover* as well as appearing in his own person in *The Mirror of the Sea* and *The Arrow of Gold*. Cervoni was forty-two, Conrad was a late adolescent. The outcome was hero-worship of the most ardent and simple kind:

There was nothing in the world sudden enough to take Dominic [sic] unawares. His thick black moustaches, curled every morning with hot tongs by
the barber at the corner of the quay, seemed to hide a perpetual smile. But
nobody, I believe, had ever seen the true shape of his lips. From the slow,
imperturbable gravity of that broad-chested man you would think he had
never smiled in his life. In his eyes lurked a look of perfectly remorseless
irony, as though he had been provided with an extremely experienced soul,
and the slightest distension of his nostrils would give to his bronzed face a
look of extraordinary boldness. This was the only play of feature of which
he seemed capable, being a Southerner of a concentrated, deliberate type
(*The Mirror of the Sea*, chapter 42, p. 163).

Throughout his life Conrad interacts with males on whom he can build
his own sense of himself as an adult male. Korzeniowski and Bobrowski
were, of course, the first role-models. The impact of Cervoni was so great
that we can confidently call him their successor. No later role model was
to be as formative as these three.

In the 1870s the young Conrad was kicking over the traces, enjoying
himself, spending money and rebelling against all authority. One of the
authorities against whom he rebelled was Déléstang – very much a benefactor, but one whose hand Conrad now chose to bite. It seems likely that
Conrad found that Déléstang's treatment of him did not coincide with his
view of himself as a young gentleman at large: in the absence of Conrad's
letters to Bobrowski we cannot know in any detail what happened.
Bobrowski was indignant with Conrad, noting scathingly that Déléstang
must have been 'unmindful of having before him a descendant of the
excellent family of Nałecz', and pointing out that Déléstang had been
well-disposed and prepared to offer steady employment and that Conrad's
behaviour was rash and arrogant. Having broken with Déléstang, Conrad
needed a job: in the same letter (28 July/8 August 1877) there is talk, for
the first time, of Conrad joining the British merchant marine (Bobrowski
wants to know whether he has learnt any English yet), and of his naturalization abroad, which would release him from Russian citizenship. He
cannot be naturalized in France, 'mainly' Bobrowski writes 'because of the
compulsory military service which you would have to undergo, God knows
for what and for whom.' Under a Franco-Russian agreement the child of
a Russian political prisoner would be liable for military service as he would
have been if he had stayed in Russia. Bobrowski urges him to find out how
to become naturalized in Switzerland[10] and forwards a substantial sum of
money (some 3,000 francs) in the belief that he is embarking on a world
voyage.[11]

Conrad was doubtless abashed by Bobrowski's rebuke, but Bobrowski
was a long way away and unable to check up on him. One way to redeem
his honour and force his uncle to be impressed by him rather than ashamed
of him was to engage in dashing exploits, and for the rest of 1877 and the
first part of 1878 Conrad reported some startling and courageous adventures. How much truth there is in the stories Conrad told about this year

of his life is hard to fathom. He claimed that he had been involved in smuggling arms to Spain for the supporters of Don Carlos de Bourbon y de Austria-Este, Pretender to the Spanish throne. This is described in both *The Mirror of the Sea* (the 'Tremolino' episode) and *The Arrow of Gold*. On these texts Zdzisław Najder remarks that: 'A careful reading of 'The "Tremolino"' and *The Arrow of Gold* reveals that the whole Carlist plot is a sideline, a decoration that does not affect the course of action; its only function seems to be to glamorize and idealize smuggling.'[12]

Not only Conrad's participation in the Carlist movement, but also the very existence of the 'Tremolino' have been put in doubt by the work of Najder and Hans van Marle and Norman Sherry. It seems very likely indeed that the *Tremolino* itself and the account of support for the Carlists were fiction. An important anecdote in the narrative, the 'execution' of César Cervoni, was certainly fiction. In *The Mirror of the Sea* Conrad wrote that Dominique Cervoni knocked Cesar into the sea on the discovery that César had betrayed the smuggling mission to the coastguards. In fact César was alive well after 1878.[13] Conrad is displaying the young self that he would have liked to have been: adventurous, headstrong, masculine, given to derring-do.

So what was he actually doing during 1877–8 in Marseille? He was certainly spending a great deal of Bobrowski's money, presumably on such pleasures as were available in a French port to a sensual young man with upper class attitudes, cash in his pockets and no one in authority to restrain him. He was immature, emotional and prodigal and had an insecure hold on reality. One defence for his behaviour, though, is that the fictional self-portrait that he was building for himself embodied an alternative reality which contained a truth. Depression is often associated with ambition: a young man with very high hopes for himself who finds his desires thwarted and his exalted self-image brutally qualified by encounters with the real world will often react precisely by becoming profoundly depressed, though I am aware that this might be too simple. While the ambition and the depression can be associated with each other it is not at all clear which comes first, because high hopes can be part of a depressive configuration which becomes a self-reinforcing pattern: depression – high hopes – depression.[14] This pattern can be linked in Conrad's case to the losses of his childhood and specifically to his mourning the early deaths of his parents.[15] It seems likely that Conrad was profoundly depressed in Marseille in 1878, in the episode which was later represented by him as a duel over an affair of the heart (he refers to this several times and uses it as part of the dramatic action in *The Arrow of Gold*). In reality he shot himself through the chest. It seems very likely indeed that this suicide attempt was a 'cry for help'; he had left out a list of addresses of friends, and he had invited a friend, Richard Fecht (from whom he had borrowed eight hundred francs) to tea, timing the suicide attempt so that Fecht would arrive shortly after the wound was inflicted. Further, his uncle Bobrowski, who came as quickly as he could to Conrad's aid, found that Conrad was up and about ten days after the shooting, so that the wound cannot have been as life-threatening as Bobrowski himself had been led (by Conrad, presumably) to believe. (One of the effects of the shooting was to enforce the return of one of Conrad's lost parents, or at least of a parent-figure. Although not dead, Uncle Tadeusz, remote in his country house in the Ukraine, might well have been experienced by Conrad as 'lost'.[16]) Bobrowski wrote about the matter to Stefan Buszczyński:

> Suddenly, amidst all the business at the Kiev Fair in 1878, I received a telegram: 'Conrad blessé envoyez argent – arrivez.' [. . . Conrad] wishing to improve his finances, tries his luck in Monte Carlo and loses the 800 fr. he had borrowed [from Fecht]. Having managed his affairs so excellently he returns to Marseilles [sic] and one fine evening invites his friend the creditor to tea, and before his arrival attempts to take his life with a revolver. (Let this detail remain between us, as I have been telling everyone that he was wounded in a duel. From you I neither wish to nor should keep it a secret.) The bullet goes durch und durch [through and through] near his heart without damaging any vital organ. Luckily, all his addresses were left on top of his things so that this worthy Mr Fecht could instantly let me know.[17]

Najder remarks that this cover-up – disguising the suicide attempt as a wound sustained in a duel – is wholly consistent with the moral outlook of a young *szlachcic*: 'and Korzeniowski [Conrad] flaunted his family origin, perhaps not so much out of pride but from a youthful lack of self-confidence, particularly on foreign ground'.[18] The *Tremolino*, the gun-running, the Carlist cause and the duel involved a large cast of characters, most of whom have some basis in Conrad's experience at the time: how much basis is hard to determine. Jean-Aubry, Conrad's friend and first biographer, drawing on Conrad's own account of those years and reading *The Arrow of Gold* as autobiography has it as follows: a beautiful young woman who was thought to have been the mistress of the Pretender to the Spanish throne and later to have inherited money from a painter with whom she had lived, contributed to the purchase of the *Tremolino*. She has to be known as 'Rita' (the character in *The Arrow of Gold*) because her real name was not disclosed by Conrad. An American adventurer, J. K. Blunt, who had also fought for the Carlist cause, hoped to marry 'Rita' for her money and the outcome was the duel: 'Conrad . . . sent his seconds to Captain J. K. Blunt, "American, Catholic and gentleman," as he used to describe himself, and fought a duel with him. Both adversaries were wounded. "Je lui ai fracassé la patte," Conrad declared to one of his relatives a long time after the event'.[19]

Blunt existed, but did not play this kind of role in Conrad's life. 'Rita' may have existed to the extent that it would be very surprising if Conrad's enjoyable Marseille period had not included some relationship(s) with one or more women. César Cervoni is represented in Conrad's narrative as Dominique's nephew but was in fact not related to him.

In March 1878, as we have seen, Conrad shot himself in the chest and

Uncle Tadeusz paid off his debts. In April 1878 the Russian consul refused to extend Conrad's passport; as we have seen, he was liable for Russian military service (and as the son of a political prisoner he was likely to get long and arduous training). So Conrad had to leave France. On 24 April 1878 Conrad boarded the *Mavis* in Marseille, probably as an apprentice; he had to deposit five hundred francs with the captain as a fee. The ship then sailed to the Crimea (it is not known whether Conrad remained on board for the Russian part of the voyage – it would have been extremely dangerous for him to do so, as an illegal emigrant) and finally to England. Conrad set foot in England for the first time at Lowestoft in June 1878. He did not get on well with the skipper of the *Mavis*, Captain William Pine. It seems likely that 'de Korzeniowski' (as he signed himself) was somewhat arrogant in his attitude to the officers, and that on his side Conrad felt than his treatment on this ship was rough compared with the treatment he had had on Déléstang's ships. After the ship had docked he left the *Mavis* – forfeiting his deposit – and went to London, where he again spent money rapidly and had to appeal once more to Uncle Tadeusz for funds.[20] Tadeusz's reply to this further request is a sustained and vigorous performance, replete with wholly understandable indignation:

> You were idling for nearly a whole year – you fell into debt, you deliberately shot yourself – and as a result of it all, at the worst time of the year, tired out and in spite of the most terrible rate of exchange – I hasten to you, pay, spend about 2,000 roubles, I increase your allowance to meet your needs! All this is apparently not enough for you. . . . Really, you have exceeded the limits of stupidity permitted to your age! and you pass beyond the limits of my patience! What possible advice can I – so far away – give, not knowing the conditions of your profession in general and the local conditions in particular? When you decided on this unfortunate profession, I told you: I don't want and am not going to chase after you to the ends of the world – for I do not intend nor do I wish to spoil all my life because of the fantasies of a hobbledehoy. . . . I will not allow you to be idle at my expense – you will find help in me, but not for a lazy-bones and a spendthrift. I told you this when you set out to be a sailor. . . . You must think for yourself and fend for yourself, for you have chosen a career which keeps you far from your natural advisers. You wanted it – you did it – you voluntarily chose it. Submit to the results of your decision. . . . It is all the same to me in which navy you work – the choice is your affair. If you decide to join the French Navy I have nothing against it, but until you are 21 do something; don't idle, learn, and don't pretend to be a rich young gentleman and wait for someone to pull your chestnuts out of the fire – for this will not happen. If you cannot get a ship, then be a commission agent for a time, but do something, earn something, for one cannot be a parasite. . . . If you cannot pay your premium to go on a ship, go as a simple sailor; if you learn what poverty is, it will teach you the value of money. If you wish to wait before signing on for the Navy, find yourself some occupation and earn some money, for you won't get a penny from me before it is due even if you write to me that you are certain of becoming an Admiral of the Fleet in the British Navy – I have had enough of these additional payments!

The letter ends with a calculation to the effect that Conrad has cost his uncle to date the equivalent of thirty thousand French francs – between eighty and a hundred thousand pounds in English money in 1992 – and a trumpet blast of exhortation under the impact of which even the late adolescent Conrad, one feels, must have felt some degree of compunction for his behaviour: 'I now call on you to reflect! Think of your parents, of your grandmother, who sacrificed so much for you – remember my sacrifices, my fatherly indulgence and leniency – reform yourself – work – calculate – be prudent and doggedly pursue your aim and with deeds, not with words – prove that you deserve my blessing'.[21]

In July he became an Ordinary Seaman with the *Skimmer of the Sea*, a ship which carried coal between Newcastle-upon-Tyne and Lowestoft. In a letter written twenty years later (to Cunninghame Graham, 4 February 1989) he lovingly recalled this rough and dirty English coaling coaster: ' "Skimmer of the Seas" [sic] what a pretty name! But she is gone and took a whole lot of good fellows away with her into the other world [the *Skimmer* was lost with all hands in 1881]. Comme c'est vieux tout ca! In that craft I began to learn English from East Coast chaps each built as though to last for ever, and coloured like a Christmas card. Tan and pink – gold hair and blue eyes with that Northern straight-away-there look!'.[22]

Conrad's title aboard the *Skimmer of the Sea* was Ordinary Seaman, but his life-style was more that of a visitor than of an employee: a young gentleman working alongside the crew to obtain experience. His earnings were a shilling a month, but the allowance from Uncle Tadeusz put his income well above those of the other sailors (and indeed of the Captain). It was easy for him to make himself agreeable by standing drinks and entertainment to his companions. The exotic Pole was a popular figure on this humble ship.[23]

A pattern had been set: a gentlemanly style accompanied by a Timon-like prodigality with money. Uncle Tadeusz had cleared his debts after his suicide attempt but found that Conrad thereafter made repeated, and repeatedly infuriating, requests for money over and above the allowance that Tadeusz was able to make. Tadeusz's letter of 2/14 September 1878, sounds the familiar notes of mingled affection and rebuke:

> As I have told you in my last letter, I desire the reformation of the sinner and not the getting him out of my mind, thoughts, heart, and pocket; that would have been the easiest way and my concern is to be able to cherish him, love and, what is most important of all, respect him – which is all now up to you.[24]

In response to this letter, possibly, Conrad, now aged nineteen, took serious steps to find himself real employment. He went up by train to London from Lowestoft and walked into the city from the station 'with something of the feeling of a traveller penetrating into a vast and unexplored wilderness. No explorer could have been more lonely. I did not know a single

soul of all these millions that all around me peopled the mysterious distances of the streets' ('Poland Revisited', *Notes on Life and Letters*, p. 150).
Having seen an advertisement in a newspaper he was in search of James
Sutherland's sailing agency in Fenchurch Street.[25] To Conrad's literary
perception the whole scene was richly Dickensian:

> And the office I entered was Dickensian too. The dust of the Waterloo year
> lay on the panes and frames of its windows; early Georgian grime clung to
> its sombre wainscoting. It was one o'clock in the afternoon, but the day was
> gloomy. By the light of a single gas-jet depending from the smoked ceiling
> I saw an elderly man, in a long coat of black broadcloth. He had a grey
> beard, a big nose, thick lips, and heavy shoulders. His curly white hair and
> the general character of his head recalled vaguely a burly apostle in the
> *barocco* style of Italian art (p. 152).

When Conrad stated his mission the burly Sutherland declared (as 'Old
Powell' was to declare in Conrad's *Chance*, many years later) that it was
illegal for him to procure a berth for Conrad as an Ordinary Seaman, his
business being only to place young gentlemen who wanted to go to sea as
premium apprentices. Nevertheless, he found Conrad a berth – his first
real job – aboard the *Duke of Sutherland*. Conrad told Bobrowski that he
had to pay a fee of £20 and was taken on as an apprentice for a three year
contract, but in fact, signing as 'Conrad de Korzeniowski', he joined the
Duke of Sutherland as an Ordinary Seaman, paid one shilling a month.[26]
The ship sailed from London, 15 October 1878, for Australia. The voyage
itself was arduous and depressing, but Conrad seems to have liked Australia (*The Mirror of the Sea* indicates that he stayed on board as watchman
during the five-month stay in Sydney). It as at this time that he was first
attracted to the notion of working the Malay archipelago. He seems to
have sent an 'up-beat' letter to Uncle Tadeusz, who wrote to Buszczyński
(30 May 1879) that 'Konrad's letters are satisfactory – a liking for his profession and hope of a better future shines through them.' Conrad had
reported that in Sydney he had met an English trader who was famous for
his knowledge of the Malay archipelago, and who offered Conrad a job:
this would bring with it the prospect of naturalization as an Englishman
and useful experience in a region which was currently opening up to
European trades. Hans van Marle suggests that this trader was William
Henry Eldred, a founding member of the Geographical Society of Aus-
tralasia. He left England in 1839 and was sailing his own ship in Indone-
sian waters between 1848 and 1850. It is possible that the memory of
Eldred would later play an important part in the creative process leading
to Conrad's first novels, contributing to the personality of Tom Lingard in
Almayer's Folly, *An Outcast of the Islands*, and *The Rescue* (Conrad never actually
met the original Lingard).[27] But the Malay adventures were in the future;
in October 1879, after a full year with the uncomfortable *Duke of Sutherland*, Conrad returned to England and discharged himself from the ship.

He seems to have written to Bobrowski with plans to find work in the Mediterranean. Bobrowski replies (26 October/7 November 1879) that Conrad must follow his own judgement, but that he, Bobrowski, thinks of the Mediterranean as 'only "a great lake" ', and 'would like to see in you a sailor combined with a salesman' and thinks that 'distant and less known' regions (he must be thinking of the offer of work in the Malay Archipelago) would be more propitious. Whatever happens, he wants Conrad to pass his examination for second mate and to be naturalized as an English subject (both in order to avoid Russian military service and because as a Russian subject and illegal emigrant he could not take the risk of visiting Bobrowski at Kazimierówka).[28] Meanwhile Conrad's view of himself must have been undergoing profound changes. Internally he remained a Polish gentleman and a man of letters. He had been reading Flaubert and Shakespeare during the five months in Sydney[29] and given the profound immersion in English, French and Russian literature that he displayed when he began to work as a novelist it must be the case that he was reading continuously throughout these years. But externally he was a British merchant sailor seeking to advance himself in his new career and this meant that he had to sit, in due order, the examinations for Second Mate, First Mate and Master's certificate. There was bound to be tension between his perception of himself as a gentleman and a man of letters and his employers' perception of him as a foreigner finding work for himself on British ships. This tension developed into friction on several occasions, the first of which is reflected in an open conflict with the captain of his next ship, the *Europa*. Conrad enlisted on this ship as an Ordinary Seaman on 11 December 1879. He left the ship on 29 January 1880. (On the certificate of discharge Munro assessed Conrad's professional skill only as 'good' rather than the usual 'very good'.) One can easily guess that Conrad's anxieties about his own status and his resentment of the hardships of his chosen profession contributed to the trouble. Uncle Tadeusz writes (18/30 May 1880) to urge Conrad to knuckle under and accept the inevitable frustrations and restrictions of his work instead of chasing 'ever after new projects': 'You must not, Panie Bracie, believe in either good or bad luck. Worth and perseverance are the only values that never fail. . . . To expect that success should appear while one is on the threshold of life, and at any time it's needed, without any work or merit, is childish dreaming'.[30] The characteristics that Uncle Tadeusz finds here in Conrad are to be found later in Conrad's dramatized figures. Childish dreaming, and the assumption that success and high reward will come without having to work for it, are characteristic of many of Conrad's anti-heroes: Almayer, Willems and Jim all have 'follies' of this kind. These figures deal in false pretences: so did the young Conrad. When he applied for his examination for Second Mate in the merchant service he signed a declaration to the effect that he had had four years' experience with the British merchant marine, whereas in reality his experience had been about two and a half years (Najder points out that this was fraud and that he risked legal penalties if found out).[31] In May 1880 he passed the examination for Second Mate, to the great delight of Uncle Tadeusz who saw Conrad at last on the way to becoming a self-supporting adult. In May 1880 he moved into lodgings at 6 Dynevor Road, Stoke Newington, which was to be his London address until 1886; it was here that he made friends with the American A. P. Krieger, who was a fellow-lodger. At about this time Conrad also met one of his earliest and most loyal English friends, G. F. W. Hope. Hope was an ex-seaman who had sailed in the *Duke of Sutherland* a few years before Conrad joined her. He was a director of several companies and owner of a yacht, the *Nellie*, which was to be the setting for the frame-story of *Heart of Darkness*. In 1896–8 Conrad was to be a neighbour of Hope's and would often go sailing with him, and thereafter he and Hope never lost contact.[32]

Conrad's voyage on the *Loch Etive*, 1880, is recalled in *The Mirror of the Sea*. The *Loch Etive*, which he joined as third mate on 21 August 1880, was an iron-hulled sailing-ship bound for Australia (a wool clipper, like the *Duke of Sutherland*).[33] The master, Captain William Stuart, had a reputation for making quick passages in sailing ships and was frustrated by the relatively slow progress of the *Loch Etive*. Conrad's judgement was that the best qualities of the iron-hulled sailing ships on which he served as a young man were 'build, gear, seaworthy qualities, and ease of handling' but not speed: 'No iron ship of yesterday ever attained the marvels of speed which the seamanship of men famous in their time had obtained from their wooden, copper-sheeted predecessors' ('The Weight of the Burden', *The Mirror of the Sea*, p. 47). He recalls bad-tempered exchanges on the *Loch Etive* between Stuart, whose instinct was to make headway by carrying an excessive amount of sail, and the first officer, William Purdu, who was deaf:

> Captain S- [Stuart] seemed constitutionally incapable of giving his officers a definite order to shorten sail: and so [. . . an] extraordinarily vague row would go on till at last it dawned upon them both, in some particlarly alarming gust, that it was time to do something. There is nothing like the fearful inclination of your tall spars over-loaded with canvas to bring a deaf man and an angry one to their senses ('Cobwebs and Gossamer', *The Mirror of the Sea*, p. 41).

Conrad tells us that on the return journey he was promoted to officer of the watch because the second officer fell ill (p. 43; there is some doubt about this in that the promotion was not recorded in Conrad's papers[34]). Often in his autobiographical writings memory and invention are woven together and it is hard to disentangle them. He tells us of two encounters, in the course of the homeward voyage of the *Loch Etive*, of which it now seems that one was real and the other an invention. On Christmas day 1879 the ship sighted a whaler, the *Alaska*:

We passed, sailing slowly, within a hundred yards of her; and just as our steward started ringing the breakfast bell the captain and I held aloft, in good view of the figures watching us over her stern, the keg, properly headed up and containing, besides an enormous bundle of old newspapers, two boxes of figs in honour of the day. We flung it far out over the rail. Instantly our ship, sliding down the slope of a high swell, left it far behind in our wake. . . . I never saw anything so ready and so smart as the way that whaler, rolling desperately all the time, lowered one of her boats. . . . That Yankee whaler lost not a moment in picking up her Christmas present from the English wool clipper ('Christmas Day at Sea', *Last Essays*, p. 31).

In 'Initiation' (*The Mirror of the Sea*) he tells the story of the rescue of a crew from a Danish sailing ship which had been wrecked and was on the point of sinking. It is a beautifully written, fully realized narrative. As yet no source has been found for this incident and it seems almost certain that this, one of the best bits of *The Mirror of the Sea*, is a fiction. The crew see 'a black speck to the westward, apparently suspended high up in the void behind a stirring, shimmering veil.'

We did not raise our voices. 'A water-logged derelict, I think, sir,' said the second officer, quietly, coming down from aloft with the binoculars in their case slung across his shoulders; and our captain, without a word, signed to the helmsman to steer for the black speck. Presently we made out a low, jagged stump sticking up forward – all that remained of her departed masts (p. 138).

The imagery of *The Ancient Mariner* makes itself felt, as it is often to do in Conrad's works of fiction (especially in 'The Secret Sharer', *The Shadow-Line* and parts of *Lord Jim*). The *Loch Etive* 'seemed to us to have lost the power of motion, as if the sea, becoming viscous, had clung to her sides' (p. 138). Like the living dead of Coleridge's poem the Danish crew, skeletally thin and dressed in rags, are pumping to keep their wreck afloat and the *Loch Etive*'s life-boats setting out to rescue them are engaged in 'a race of two ship's boats matched against Death for a prize of nine men's lives, and Death had a long start' (p. 40).

Conrad's fabulations were at times simply creative, as in this instance of the rescue of the sinking Danes. At other times, especially when dealing with figures in authority or persons who might disburse money, they were manipulative: for example, as we have seen, having lost half his years' allowance from Bobrowski in a speculation he wrote to Bobrowski (10 August 1881) inventing an 'accident' (involving the loss of his possessions and a stay in hospital) aboard a ship called the *Annie Frost* which ensured that Bobrowski disgorged yet more money.[35]

The newly qualified second mate had difficulty finding the right berth for himself. The one that he secured, from 19 September 1881, as second mate on the *Palestine*, was to occupy him for nearly two years and has great literary importance because it provided the material for the first of his Marlow narrations, 'Youth'. The *Palestine*, commanded by Captain Elijah Beard, sailed from London on 21 September 1881, stopping at Gravesend and then proceeding slowly to Newcastle-upon-Tyne, where it remained for five weeks to load its cargo of coal. It sailed from Newcastle for Bangkok on 29 November 1881. Crossing the channel it encountered bad weather, began to leak and lost a mast: the crew refused to continue and Captain Beard was forced to return to Falmouth for repairs (24 December). The repairs took eight months: Conrad chose to stay with the ship in order to make up the time in service required for his first mate's examintion. He had leisure to visit London and to do a good deal of reading (including Carlyle's *Sartor Resartus* and Captain Fred. Burnaby's *A Ride to Khiva*).[36] The *Palestine* finally set sail from Falmouth to Bangkok on 17 September, and in March of the following year, 1883, the cargo of coal exploded and caught fire; the crew took to the ship's three lifeboats and landed at Muntok on Bangka island. In 'Youth' the outline of the story is the same – like the *Palestine*, the *Judea* is an old coaling vessel in bad condition, commanded by a Captain Beard (in life Elijah Beard, aged fifty-seven; in the story 'John Beard', who is 'sixty if a day') but it is enriched and extended in a variety of ways. In 'Youth' the disaster takes place far out at sea, whereas the *Palestine* caught fire close to the shore; in 'Youth' the lifeboats take several days to reach Java, whereas in reality the *Palestine*'s boats would have taken about twelve hours to reach Muntok. The crew in 'Youth' is described as 'Liverpool hard cases' recruited when the original crew left the ship at Falmouth, but none of the ten crewmen of the *Palestine* actually came from Liverpool. Four of them – including a 'Nigger' – were non-British.[37]

The 'Author's Note' to 'Youth' has to be read with care. It asserts that 'Youth' is based on fact in two different ways. Youth 'marks the first appearance in the world of the man Marlow' who is represented as a real person: 'The man Marlow and I came together in the casual manner of those health-resort acquaintances which sometimes ripen into friendships. . . . He haunts my hours of solitude, when, in silence, we lay our heads together in great comfort and harmony' ('Youth', pp. xxxiii–xxxiv). Marlow then, from this account, is someone whom Conrad knew and became close to, a 'secret sharer'. Yet there is no one who can be identified with Marlow in the way in which (for example) Dominique Cervoni can be identified with Nostromo and Robert Cunninghame Graham can be identified with Charles Gould. As far as one can judge, Marlow seems to be *the kind of Englishman whom Conrad would have liked to have been.*[38] Of the events of 'Youth' Conrad wrote that it is 'a feat of memory' and an 'experience' which 'in its facts, in its inwardness and in its outward colouring, begins and ends in myself' ('Youth', p. xxxv). 'Memory' in this usage refers to material laid down in the mind to be reworked by the present consciousness as Wordsworth's 'spots of time' are recreated into his poetry. The 'facts,' the 'inwardness' and the 'outward colouring' support our sense of the mind's creative relationship with that which is recalled. It is possible to pick phrases out of the 'Author's Note' which, out of context, invite us flatly to contradict them: 'Youth' is a 'record of experience', 'Heart of Darkness' is 'experience pushed a little (and only very little) beyond the actual facts of the case' ('Youth' p. xxxv). But the context of the whole 'Note' forces us to recognize that Conrad's words, 'experience' and 'memory', are being used in special senses and for his own artistic purposes.[39]

Conrad was not happy about his post on the *Palestine* because to be second mate to the semi-literate skipper of such a scruffy ship seemed to be a loss of status. In a letter of 11/23 September 1881, Bobrowski writes to him with his characteristic and inimitable mix of affection and crustiness: 'It seems to me that you are not very satisfied with your post: is it because being on a "barque" touches on your honour? Then, of course, £4 a month is disrespectful to your pocket, and, finally, the captain seems to you to be merely a "creature", which gives me a sad picture of his intellect.'

Part of Bobrowski's difficulty with his troublesome nephew was that he seldom had anything other than Conrad's own testimony on which to form a judgement of Conrad's behaviour: thus, here, he places Conrad's exacting patrician sniffiness over his new job in an ironic light without attempting directly to challenge Conrad's unflattering account of the *Palestine* and Captain Beard. He does point out, though, that Beard's limitations may give Conrad an opportunity to shine professionally: 'perhaps the last point [Beard's lack of intellect] will enable you to distinguish yourself as a "man conscious of his craft, and useful"'.[40] This is exactly what happened: when the Palestine exploded and caught fire, 14 March 1883, the young Conrad, like the young Marlow, displayed a great deal of courage. The first officer of the *Palestine* is quoted as saying of Conrad that he was an 'excellent fellow, good officer, the best second mate I ever sailed with'.[41] But the mantle of prescience and wisdom that Bobrowski dons here looks a bit tattered in the light of his next letter, written early in 1882 when the *Palestine* had to be docked for its extensive repairs. Bobrowski here gave vent to emotional reproach: 'Cool judgement seems to have deserted you when you accepted such a wretched ship as the *Palestine*.' He then makes the – in context – startling observation that 'I have never considered that I had the right to order you about' but on this occasion he has to say 'I sincerely advise you not to go to sea in such a lamentable ship as yours. Danger is certainly part of a sailor's life, but the profession itself should not prevent you from having a sensible attachment to life nor from taking sensible steps to preserve it. Both your Captain Beard and you appear to me like desperate men who look for knocks and wounds' (8/20 January 1882).[42] The indignation here is a further mark of Tadeusz's great affection for Conrad. He is really shaken by the thought that Conrad might have been killed. But the effect of such a letter on Conrad was likely to provoke disobedience and it may well be that, if Conrad was wavering about the *Palestine*, Uncle Tadeusz's well-meant advice tipped him over into sticking with the ship, thus ensuring that the world would have one of Conrad's best short stories.

In the spring of 1883 he saw the last of the ill-fated *Palestine*, and in July he hoped to take his First Mate's examination but was found not to have met the requirements for length of service.[43] In the summer of that year, as we have seen (chapter 1, p. 17), he visited Uncle Tadeusz (in Marienbad, whence they travelled together to Teplice, in Bohemia) and on 10 September, signed on with the clipper *Riversdale*, again as second mate. The *Riversdale* sailed to Port Elizabeth, South Africa, and thence to Madras (6 April 1884). Conrad had got across the skipper (L. B. McDonald) who seems to have been a despotic and conceited personality, and he made matters worse by telling a doctor in Madras that McDonald was a drunkard. This was repeated to McDonald who then determined to rid himself of Conrad. Conrad tried to extricate himself by writing a letter of apology but McDonald was implacable. On the certificate of discharge for Conrad (17 April) McDonald wrote 'very good' next to 'professional ability' but 'no comment' next to 'conduct'. (The effect of this certificate of discharge was the the Marine Board refused to permit Conrad to take his examination for first mate in the summer of 1884, but he was permitted to try later in the year.[44])

In Bombay Conrad found another berth as second mate aboard the *Narcissus*, which sailed on her homebound passage on 5 June 1884 and arrived at Dunkirk on 16 October, after 134 days at sea. Conrad brought a pet monkey back from India which gives us a rare glimpse of him making a concession to the peg-leg, eye-patch, parrot-on-shoulder stereotype of the nineteenth century sailor; usually he was very much the gentleman, 'Monsieur Georges' or 'The Russian Count', distinguished from British seamen as much by his dandified exotic appearance as by his heavy Polish accent. Najder carefully traces the relationship between Conrad's voyage on the *Narcissus* and the famous novella, *The Nigger of the 'Narcissus'* (1897). The effect of Conrad's changes was to make the crew of the fictional *Narcissus* much more English than it was in reality: 'In the real Narcissus there were seven Scandinavians; in the book Conrad gives the impression that four foreigners were on board. In fact there were ten – half the entire crew.' Najder goes on to point out that it was difficult for long distance sailing ships to recruit English crews, because the work was hard and exhausting, and as a result many of the crew members on Conrad's ships were foreign: up to sixty per cent. The 'Nigger' on board was probably one Joseph Barron who died three weeks before the ship reached England. The prototype for Belfast was a young Ulsterman called James Craig, and the source for Archie was a Scot, Archibald McLean. The name 'Sullivan' is probably recalled from Daniel Sullivan with whom Conrad was later to serve on the *Tilkhurst*, and Donkin may be based on one Charles Dutton who had been with the *Narcissus* on a previous voyage and had ended up in prison.[45]

Late in 1884 Conrad was permitted to sit the First Mate's examination:

he failed it on 17 November but passed at the second attempt, 3 December (his twenty-seventh birthday). He was qualified at the worst possible time: shipbuilding was on the decline, the demand for officers in the British merchant navy was steadily decreasing and in hard times the profession was likely to close ranks against a foreigner. It seems probable that this last was the decisive factor in Conrad's failure to find himself a job as a first mate during this year. On 27 April 1885 he accepted a post as (yet again) second mate aboard the *Tilkhurst*, a coaling clipper, sailing to Singapore. The ship first stopped for a month at the Welsh port of Penarth and during this time Conrad befriended Joseph Spiridion Kliszczewski, an emigré Pole who lived with his family in Cardiff; the Kliszczewskis were to be the recipients, later in the year, of Conrad's first letters written in English.

In sharp contrast with some of his earlier ships conrad found on the *Tilkhurst* a happy working environment. He was lucky in his skipper, Edwin John Blake, who seems to have been exceptionally successful in his dealings with his officers and crew.[46] The happiness with the *Tilkhurst* extended itself to happiness with England. On 13 October he wrote to the Kliszczewskis: 'When speaking, writing or thinking in English the word Home always means for me the hospitable shores of Great Britain'.[47]

In 1886 Conrad left the *Tilkhurst* and had several restless weeks in London, trying the possibility of a new career ashore in partnership with Krieger. *Tit-Bits* offered twenty guineas for the best article by a seaman on 'My Experiences as a Sailor', for which Conrad may have written 'The Black Mate' which would thus be his first attempt at fiction and therefore a significant mile-stone in his biography. But the priority of 'The Black Mate' was (much later) the subject of a minor matrimonial dispute: Conrad wrote to his agent, Pinker, on 19 January 1922, 'I wrote that thing in '86 for a prize competition' started, I think, by *Tit-Bits*'.[48] Jessie Conrad vigorously contradicted this, saying that she had suggested the subject of 'The Black Mate' to Conrad in 1904.[49] Conrad's memory may have played tricks with him over the question of quite what it was that he had submitted for the *Tit-Bits* competition in 1886. The overwhelming probability is that he wrote something, now lost, for the competition and that this was in itself an expression of part of the restlessness of that summer in which he was seeking a new direction for himself. His ambitions already included becoming a ship's captain or a self-employed merchant. From 1886 we can add 'writer' to the list of Conrad's possible future careers.

On 28 July, 1886, Conrad attempted the Master's examination but failed it; this set-back was followed by a success when he became a naturalized British subject on 18 August. On 10 November he resat the Master's examination and passed, prompting jubilation and affectionate pride in Uncle Bobrowski (see the epigraph to this chapter, p. 21). Bobrowski was right to be jubilant. He had cajoled, guided and supported his feckless and wayward nephew to a point where a life seemingly destined for failure had secured for itself tangible success. Conrad saw it rather differently.

Displaying a wholly human tendency to gather all the credit for his achievement to himself and to ignore other people's care and sacrifice, he sees the certificate as demonstrating that he was right to leave Poland and silencing the criticisms that he had had to endure from that same long-suffering uncle:

> It was a fact, I said to myself, that I was now a British master mariner beyond a doubt. It was not that I had an exaggerated sense of that very modest achievement, with which, however, luck, opportunity, or any extraneous influence could have had nothing to do. That fact, satisfactory and obscure in itself, had for me a certain ideal significance. It was an answer to certain outspoken scepticism, and even to some not very kind aspersions. I had vindicated myself from what had been cried upon as a stupid obstinacy or a fantastic caprice. I don't mean to say that a whole country had been convulsed by my desire to go to sea. But for a boy between fifteen and sixteen, sensitive enough, in all conscience, the commotion of his little world had seemed a very considerable thing indeed (*A Personal Record*, chapter 6, pp. 120–1.)

The certificate was not in itself any guarantee of promotion: on 28 December 1886 he signed on as second mate of the *Falconhurst* and on 18 February 1878 he signed on as first mate of the *Highland Forest*, sailing for Java. As first mate Conrad was responsible for the loading of the vessel, which lay in the port of Amsterdam. In *The Mirror of the Sea* he gives account of the period of waiting in the ice-bound Dutch city. Conrad, aged twenty-four, was left for several weeks in sole charge of the ship:

> I call to mind a winter landscape in Amsterdam – a flat foreground of waste land, with here and there stacks of timber, like the huts of a camp of some very miserable tribe . . . cold, stone-faced quays, with the snow-sprinkled ground and the hard, frozen water of the canal, in which were set ships one behind another with their frosty mooring-ropes hanging slack and their decks idle and deserted ('The Weight of the Burden', p. 48).

Conrad went into the city in search of entertainment and found it in a warm, hospitable and 'gorgeous' café, 'an immense place, lofty and gilt, upholstered in red plush, full of electric lights, and so thoroughly warmed that even the marble tables felt tepid to the touch' (p. 49). The cargo was delayed and Conrad visited the offices of the charterers to press for action and there encountered Mr Hudig (Conrad was to make use of this name for the Dutch trader from Macassar in *Almayer's Folly* and *An Outcast of the Islands*). Hudig was a similar physical type to Cervoni, thick-set and impassive. As well as being enraged by his deviousness Conrad obviously admired him: 'a big, swarthy Netherlander, with black moustaches and a bold glance. He always began by shoving me into a chair before I had time to open my mouth, gave me cordially a large cigar, and in excellent English would start to talk everlastingly about the phenomenal severity of the weather. It was impossible to threaten a man who, though he possessed the language perfectly, seemed incapable of understanding any phrase pronounced in a tone of remonstrance or discontent' (p. 51). When the cargo came Conrad loaded *The Highland Forest* according to his training but without taking advice about the ship's peculiarities (the skipper, formerly the ship's first mate, was not blameless, since he could have warned Conrad). This man, John McWhirr, was to be the source for Conrad's famously stoical and obtuse skipper in *Typhoon*. The McWhirr of life was much livelier than his fictional counterpart:

> The sudden, spontaneous agility with which he bounded aboard right off the rail afforded me the first glimpse of his real character. Without further preliminaries than a friendly nod, he addressed me: 'You have got her pretty well in her fore and aft trim. Now, what about your weights?' I told him I had managed to keep the weight sufficiently well up, as I thought, one third of the whole being in the upper part 'above the beams,' as the technical expression has it. He whistled 'Phew!' scrutinizing me from head to foot. A sort of smiling vexation was visible on his ruddy face. 'Well, we shall have a lively time of it this passage, I bet,' he said' (pp. 52–53).

As Conrad adds, 'He was right in his prophecy.' The outcome of Conrad's loading was an extremely uncomfortable voyage to Singapore in which the ship rolled excessively and Conrad himself was injured.[50] As he puts it in *The Mirror of the Sea*: 'It was only poetic justice that the chief mate who had made a mistake – perhaps a half-excusable one – about the distribution of his ship's cargo should pay the penalty. A piece of one of the minor spars that did carry away flew against the chief mate's back, and sent him sliding on his face for quite a considerable distance along the main deck' (p. 54). *The Highland Forest* berthed at Samarang and Conrad was sent from there to Singapore, where he entered the European hospital for treatment (Jim's stay in hospital in an 'Eastern Port', *Lord Jim*, chapter 2, is based on this experience). While at Singapore he joined (as first mate) the *Vidar*, an Arab owned ship which was captained by an Englishman and sailed under the British flag. Conrad made four voyages, visiting islands of the Malay archipelago between 1887 and 1888. This year was extraordinarily fruitful for his writing. Taking the novels and stories together more of Conrad's fictions (sixteen of them) are set in the Malay archipelago than anywhere else.[51] He spent a few days on the river Berau in Dutch East Borneo, a brief experience which was to be put to lasting artistic use in his novels.

William Lingard was an English adventurer in the archipelago, a figure of whom Conrad would have heard a great deal (without personal contact) who is the model for Tom Lingard in Conrad's early novels. Conrad had personal contact with William Lingard's nephew Jim Lingard and with Charles Olmeijer who was a protégé of William Lingard much as Almayer is a protégé of Tom Lingard in *Almayer's Folly*. Willems in *An Outcast of the Islands* is based partly on Jim Lingard and partly on a drunken Dutchman, Carel de Veer, whom he would also have met at Berau, and the name of

Nina, the heroine of *Almayer's Folly*, is drawn from a Ninette, known as 'Nina', who was (probably) an illegitimate half-caste and was married to a William Olmeijer who was (again, probably) Charles Olmeijer's brother.[52] The Malay material is used only in his early work, up to and including *Lord Jim* (and not counting *The Rescue*, which was planned in the 1890s although not finished until twenty years later). Conrad may well have resorted to it (as Najder suggests) to solve the problem of his foreignness: of the fact that he lacked 'common cultural background' with his English readers. He almost certainly felt that he could not write confidently and with authority about English life in English settings, nor about life in Australia or Singapore. The Malay settings had the huge advantage of being unknown to his English audience while sufficiently concrete in his own experience for him to write about them with confidence. And the first reviewers recognized precisely that, remarking of *Almayer's Folly* that 'No novelist has yet annexed the island of Borneo' and that Borneo was 'a tract hitherto untouched by the novelist'.[53]

On 4 January 1888 Conrad resigned from the *Vidar*, probably because he felt that he should be trying to make some kind of career for himself in England instead of continuing with the pleasant and easy, but directionless, life of the ship's officer in the East, the life characterized in *Lord Jim* as one of 'short passages, good deck-chairs, large native crews, and the distinction of being white' (*Lord Jim*, chapter 2, p. 13). In fact, though, the decision to leave the *Vidar* led to promotion in the East. He stayed for two weeks at the Sailors' Home in Singapore and was there offered, out of the blue, the command of an iron barque, the *Otago*, moored at Bangkok, whose master had died at sea. In this way he secured his first and only command, and the source of four of his works: 'Falk', 'The End of the Tether', 'The Secret Sharer' and *The Shadow-Line*.[54] The sequence of events leading to the command in *The Shadow-Line* – the command is offered to the narrator but the steward of the Sailors' Home tries to secure it for a defaulting creditor called Hamilton in order to get Hamilton out of the Home – is the reverse of what happened in life: the command was probably offered first to an Englishman (there was an Englishman called Hamilton in Singapore at the appropriate date) who declined it, and was then offered to Conrad. With his very foreign appearance and thick Polish accent Conrad was not an obvious first choice for a skipper of a British ship.[55]

> From my statement that I thought of this story for a long time under the title of 'First Command' the reader may guess that it is concerned with my personal experience. And as a matter of fact it *is* personal experience seen in perspective with the eye of the mind and coloured by that affection one can't help feeling for such events of one's life as one has no reason to be ashamed of (*The Shadow-Line*, 'Author's Note,' p. xxxix).

Much emphasis needs to be placed on the 'eye of the mind' and on the 'colour' given to the retrospective narrative by affection. *Some* of the tale is more or less transcription of facts. As Jeremy Hawthorn remarks: 'Clearly its basic plot corresponds quite closely to Conrad's own experiences. Moreover the names of many of the characters in the tale are close to, or identical with, many real people with whom Conrad came into contact during 1887–8. Captain Ellis *was* Master Attendant at Singapore (Conrad had used the name Elliot in *Lord Jim* and *The End of the Tether*, and in his manuscript of *The Shadow-Line* he starts to use the same name, changing it on second thoughts – perhaps because the real Ellis was now dead – back to Ellis). There *was* a John Niven who was engineer on the *Vidar*, and Conrad's first mate on the Otago was a Mr Born, who appears as Mr Burns in a number of Conrad's books apart from *The Shadow-Line*'.[56] Conrad enriches, in retrospect, the experiences both of the *Vidar* and of the *Otago*. The *Vidar* is referred to in *The Shadow-Line* as an 'excellent sea-boat, easy to keep clean, most handy in every way, and if it had not been for her internal propulsion, worthy of any man's love. I cherish to this day a profound respect for her memory' (p. 5). His account gives the impression that he left the *Vidar* for no good reason, in the 'inconsequential manner in which a bird flies away from a comfortable branch' (p. 5). In fact, though, it seems clear that he was bored by the *Vidar's* narrow circle of voyages. To be offered the command of the *Otago* was a source of excitement: 'Command is a strong magic' (p. 29). And the pleasure of taking over his command is lyrically evoked:

> A ship! My ship! She was mine, more absolutely mine for possession and care than anything in the world; an object of responsibility and devotion. She was there waiting for me, spellbound, unable to move, to live, to get out into the world (till I came), like an enchanted princess. Her call had come to me as if from the clouds. I had never suspected her existence.... I discovered how much of a seaman I was, in heart, in mind, and, as it were, physically – a man exclusively of sea and ships; the sea the only world that counted, and the ships the test of manliness, of temperament, of courage and fidelity – and of love (p. 40).

But he stayed with the *Otago* for only a year, resigning in 1889, the year in which he began to write *Almayer's Folly*. He was still very much the European gentleman at large, thinking of the sea as a staging-post to some as yet unfocused, but more glorious, destiny. He was never the typical seaman that his reading public was in due course to see in him.[57]

After the *Otago* Conrad was unable to find another command, and in the autumn of 1889, in London, he began to write *Almayer's Folly*:

> My first novel was begun in idleness – a holiday task.... It was not the outcome of a need – the famous need of self-expression which artists find in their search for motives. The necessity which impelled me was a hidden, obscure necessity, a completely masked and unaccountable phenomenon.... The conception of a planned book was entirely outside my mental range when I sat down to write; the ambition of being an author had never

turned up amongst these gracious imaginary existences one creates fondly for oneself at times in the stillness and immobility of a day-dream: yet it stands clear as the sun at noonday that from the moment I had done blacking over the first manuscript page of 'Almayer's Folly' . . . the die was cast (*A Personal Record*, chapter 4, pp. 68–9).

Conrad likes in his own accounts of his commencement as author to stress the accidental, unplanned nature of the enterprise. We have seen that this is somewhat misleading, because both as the son of Korzeniowski and as the nephew of Bobrowski – that is, both as the son of a Polish literary figure and as a declassé nobleman who was constantly praised by his uncle for the quality of his letter-writing – Conrad was, in a sense, born to the vocation of writer. But the account in *A Personal Record* is true to Conrad's sense of the matter at the time of writing. He is disclaiming responsibility for his activity as a writer (and denying ambition). Whatever made him write is 'obscure' and 'unaccountable' and the writer's state of mind was characterized by irresponsibility: 'idleness', 'a holiday task'.

If one stands back from Conrad's career as a writer one can see that the whole of it is characterized by what I would term creative irresponsibility, a state of mind related to his depressive illness. I have referred above to the 'depression – high hopes – depression' pattern,[58] setting oneself an unattainable goal and then hating oneself for failing to attain it, thus reinforcing the depression. The self-ideal set up in the *Preface* to *The Nigger of the 'Narcissus'* is one such goal: an impossibly elevated, dedicated, priest-like notion of the nature of the artist. Novels that he undertook to write and which became major stumbling blocks are further such goals: 'The Rescuer', later *The Rescue*, which dogged him for nearly twenty years, and the Tolstoyan, massively researched Napoleonic novel, *Suspense*. It seems to me that the early and abandoned autobiographical novel, published as *The Sisters*, would probably have been over-ambitious in the same way. Typically, Conrad's greatest novels were themselves 'holiday tasks', departures or acts of truancy from his declared plan: acts of disobedience inviting punishment from father figures (Blackwood or Pinker). Conrad would tell himself he was writing a short story, and the short story then grew into a full-length work. The pattern is established with his second novel, *An Outcast of the Islands*, which was originally to have been a short story, 'some twenty to twenty-five pages', called 'Two Vagabonds'.[59] *Lord Jim* was initially to have been no longer than 'Heart of Darkness' (the first three Marlow narrations, 'Youth', 'Heart of Darkness' and *Lord Jim* were to have formed a single volume). *Nostromo*, when first mentioned in Conrad's letters, was to have been a short story, *The Secret Agent* began as a short story called 'Verloc', *Under Western Eyes* as 'Razumov', *Chance* as 'Explosives', *Victory* as 'Dollars'. Conrad's great creative phase, 1899–1917, conforms to this strange pattern whereby flight from the responsibility of the artist to produce masterpieces itself, paradoxically, produces masterpieces.

And why did he write in English? In the Author's Note to *A Personal Record* (written in 1919) Conrad writes of English as the inevitable language for his work. He refers to an article written by his friend Hugh Clifford for the *North American Review* (June 1904) which represents him as having 'exercised a deliberate choice between French and English' (p. iv) and he remarks that in that article Clifford had misconstrued a conversation in which Conrad had said that if he had been making such a choice he would have decided against French because that language is too perfectly 'crystallized' for his use (p. v). This gives us a pointer. English is an anarchically full and fertile language: Najder tells us that 'For a Pole, English seems a language of immensely rich vocabulary, and one demanding an almost stark concreteness of expression'.[60] And I think that Conrad is simply to be believed when he says that English was so obviously the language for him as a writer that he had, in effect, no choice:

> The truth of the matter is that my faculty to write in English is as natural as any other aptitude with which I might have been born. I have a strange and overpowering feeling that it had always been an inherent part of myself. English was for me neither a matter of choice nor adoption. The merest idea of choice had never entered my head. And as to adoption – well, yes, there was adoption; but it was I who was adopted by the genius of the language, which directly I came out of the stammering stage made me its own so completely that its very idioms I truly believe had a direct action on my temperament and fashioned my still plastic character ('Author's Note', *A Personal Record*, p. v).

He was now English by nationality and had been immersed in English-speaking environments for – in effect – the whole of his working life. English was the medium for human interaction as he had observed it since the age of twenty. It was also the language of much of his reading in the course of his literary self-education. 'It was I who was adopted by the genius of the language'; he was also 'adopted' by the fact of his own adoption of an English identity. Conrad's closing words on this are, I think, fully to be believed: 'All I can claim after all those years of devoted practice, with the accumulated anguish of its doubts, imperfections and falterings in my heart, is the right to be believed when I say that if I had not written in English I would not have written at all' (p. vi). But this is to anticipate. The manuscript of *Almayer's Folly* accompanied Conrad for the next five years of his working life. The transition from sailor to writer was already taking place.

Early in 1890 he visited his Uncle Tadeusz in the Ukraine: he planned to go in 1889 but was delayed by the tardiness (which he interpreted, perhaps rightly, as gratuitously vindictive reluctance) of the Russian authorities in London to grant him a visa. En route for the Ukraine he visited Brussels and witnessed the deathbed of his relative Aleksander Poradowski, who died on 7 February. His wife Marguerite, who was forty-two at the time of her husband's death – 'Aunt' Poradowska, as Conrad would always refer to her – became one of Conrad's closest friends.

Marguerite Poradowska, née Gachet, was born of French parents in Brussels (and by her marriage to Poradowski was formally an Austrian subject). She was a cultivated woman, a writer who could give Conrad an entrée to the literary world of Paris and whom he could regard as an intellectual equal. Conrad was to write voluminously to her (in French); he was certainly at ease with her, indeed it seems possible – to anticipate a later part the story – that Conrad was attracted to Poradowska and that he may, despite the fact that she was about ten years' his senior, have proposed marriage to her and been rejected (and that he married Jessie George, in part, on the 'rebound'[61]).

We have seen that his visit to Uncle Bobrowski's circle in Kazimierówka seems to have been somewhat uncomfortable. He visited for ten weeks (taking with him the manuscript of *Almayer's Folly*, of which he began writing chapter 5 in Poland[62]). A contemporary witness reports that Conrad's manner was distant and arrogant: for Conrad himself the visit must have stirred conflicting feelings of guilt – over having deserted his native land for the richest and most powerful country in the world – and irritation with his former countrymen for their helplessness and self-pity.[63] On 29 April he returned to Brussels to find that earlier negotiations over a possible job in Africa had resulted in a firm offer of employment from the Société Anonyme Belge pour le Commerce du Haut-Congo. Freiesleben, the Danish master of one of the company's river-steamers, had been murdered by tribesman: Conrad was appointed to take his place.

The Congo Free State had become effectively the personal property of Leopold II of Belgium in 1885, as a result of Leopold's political wiliness. The brief of the Société was to open up the country by establishing communications and an administrative structure and (of course) a monopoly of the Congo's trade. The economic potential was vast. Conrad's contract was for three years but he served in the Congo for only about six months. His diary – one of his earliest known English texts – is largely factual, but disillusionment with the Société's declared aims as compared with the reality – the Belgians' brutal ill-treatment of the Africans – must have set in within the first two months or so and this was accompanied by a venomous personality clash with the company's manager, Camille Delcommune, which is powerfully reflected in *Heart of Darkness*. Conrad was subjected to pinpricks and petty humiliations, and was given a 'command' only when the captain of one of the river steamers, a captain Koch, became ill. He commanded the SS *Roi des Belges* from Stanley Falls downriver towards Kinshasa for about ten days, in September 1890, until Koch recovered. During this period the steamer took aboard one George Antoine Klein, the company's agent at Stanley Falls: Klein was French, aged twenty-seven, and suffering from dysentery. He died during the journey. His name and his death – but as far as we know, nothing else about him – were drawn on for 'Kurtz' in *Heart of Darkness*.[64] Towards the end of 1890 Conrad became ill and he returned to Europe: by February 1891 he was back in London. The experiences in the Congo were so shattering, physically and emotionally, that Conrad's health never fully recovered. At the end of February he was hospitalized suffering from gout, neuralgic pains in his right arm and recurrent attacks of malaria, and from psychological prostration. Najder remarks that 'all the symptoms mentioned in his letters show that he suffered from pathological depression, and depression, on reaching its crisis, quite often finds an outlet in the form of somatic illness. . . . The evidence indicating that Korzeniowski-Conrad suffered from depression in the strict psychiatric sense of the term is so strong that it is nearly impossible to doubt it'.[65] The astonishing feature of Conrad's case is of course that this chronically sick man was able to write major works of art, and I have suggested above one way in which the mechanism worked: Conrad's achievements were arrived at partly by evasion, pretending to himself that he was engaged in one activity (taking time off to write a short story) whereas in reality he was engaged in another (embarking on a major novel). They were also arrived at partly by a division of the self: much of the depressive's agony is channelled into his letters, which are characterized by self-pity, self-reproach, manipulation, lamentation and (less often) aggression. The hysterical, attention-seeking and dependent part of Conrad's personality displayed in the letters was split off, I believe, from the artist. A distinct part (the core, one has to add) of the self was thus permitted to retain the independence and self-esteem needed to permit the making of works of art.

Conrad was unable to find work after he left the hospital in London, and his health did not improve. His uncle sent money, and he went in May to Champel-les-Bains (near Geneva) for a water cure, but this lasted only for a month (perhaps because his funds ran low). He had a few friends: the most important were Adolf Krieger (who saw him into hospital in February) and G. F. W. Hope, with whom he had yachting trips in June and July. In August he took a job as a warehouse manager, which he found boring and depressing. By November he had despaired of finding a command, and was (once again) a first mate: this time of a passenger ship, the *Torrens*, bound for Australia. Between 1891 and 1893 Conrad took four long voyages with the *Torrens*. It was an agreeable ship with a civilized and companionable commander, Captain Cope, with whom Conrad had an easy relationship. In 1893 he made significant friendships with two young passengers who were returning from Australia and New Zealand to England: John Galsworthy, then twenty-five and a newly qualified lawyer (his literary ambitions were not yet developed) and Edward Sanderson, who was to help his father run a boys' preparatory school. Galsworthy later recalled Conrad as 'thin, not tall, his arms very long, his shoulders broad, his head set rather forward. He spoke to me with a strong foreign accent. He seemed to me strange on an English ship'; and he recalls Conrad's paternal kindness to the ship's apprentices.[66] In July 1893 Conrad resigned from the *Torrens*, almost certainly because he had given up hope of succeeding Captain Cope as its commander; he went back to the Ukraine to visit Uncle Tadeusz at Kazimierówka and continued to write to 'Aunt' Poradowska – but, probably significantly, did not attempt to visit her. Late in 1893 – in desperation, presumably – he signed on as second mate of the steamer *Adowa*, which was supposed to carry emigrants from France to Canada. The *Adowa* wintered at Rouen, then made a transit to London in January 1894. At that point Conrad left the ship. It is an intriguing fact that on the discharge paper he signed his name 'J. Conrad', as though his future identity was already dimly visible to him. He had taken leave of the sea for the last time. The immediate prospect for Conrad was bleak, but the benefit of hindsight enables us to see that the salient fact about this lonely, depressed and penurious figure in the latter part of 1894, living in lodgings behind Victoria station, is that he has with him the substantial part of the manuscript of a novel.

3

Man of Letters 1894–1898

'You have the style, you have the temperament; why not write another?' I believe that as far as one man may wish to influence another man's life Edward Garnett had a great desire that I should go on writing. At that time, and I may say, ever afterwards, he was always very patient and gentle with me. . . . Had he said, 'Why not go on writing,' it is very probable he would have scared me away from pen and ink for ever; but there was nothing either to frighten one or arouse one's antagonism in the mere suggestion to 'write another'

An Outcast of the Islands, 'Author's Note', p. xliv.

In February 1894 Tadeusz Bobrowski died. As we have seen[1] his legacy to Conrad was fifteen thousand roubles in cash, to be paid one year after his death: the money had been lent out at eight per cent, and the interest was payable immediately, so Conrad received twelve hundred roubles at once.[2] It has been suggested that Bobrowski was an inhibiting figure whose death freed Conrad to finish *Almayer's Folly*. As Guerard has it, 'Bobrowski's approval and disapproval were matters of the greatest concern to Conrad. Was he to such an extent an inhibiting substitute father that Conrad could do no good creative work, no successful externalizing of experience and fantasy, until his critical presence was out of the way?'[3] But it seems certain that Conrad would have finished *Almayer's Folly* anyway: he was only three chapters from the end of the first draft of the novel at the time of his uncle's death. The dedication of this first novel to the memory of his uncle tells its own story, indicating that Conrad had now learnt to give credit where credit was due, as he had not when he secured his Master's certificate. He acknowledged that Tadeusz's patient support over the years had helped him to become a writer.

For the immediate future Tadeusz's legacy was very important. Conrad was short of money and searching for work in the early months of 1894. On about May 1 he received part of his inheritance (about a hundred and twenty pounds) which gave him something to live on and permitted him to give more time to his writing.[4] On 4 July 1894 he submitted the type-script of *Almayer's Folly* to Fisher Unwin. The typescript carried the pen-name 'Kamudi' (meaning 'rudder' in Malay) because Conrad had in mind the Unwin Pseudonym Library. The typescript was read first by W. H. Chesson, who responded enthusiastically and passed it to Edward Garnett. Garnett was to become one of Conrad's closest friends and was regarded in Conrad's lifetime as the discoverer of Conrad's talent. Conrad himself was to reinforce this notion. Chesson, who of course had prior claim, modestly remarked that to have 'discovered' Conrad was not a major feat: 'the purely stylistic and academic merits of Mr Conrad's work were even in 1894 too obvious to make the "discovery" of him by a literary critic much more than evidence of reasonable attention to his business'.[5] On 4 October Conrad received the news that the book had been accepted for publication, with an advance of twenty pounds.

The manuscript of the first state of *Almayer's Folly* differs substantially from the typescript, and is the manuscript which Conrad carried around with him, adding slowly to it over a period of five years at sea. It is now in the Rosenbach Museum and Library, Philadelphia. A note in Conrad's handwriting on the front wrapper of the manuscript reads: 'Commenced in September 1889 in London then laid aside during voyages to Congo and Australia. Taken up again in 1893 and finished on the 22nd May 1894.' This manuscript has some striking features. Conrad was clearly thinking in chapters as he wrote this first novel. Each part of the manu-script is headed 'Chapter I', 'Chapter II' etc., and the page numbers of each manuscript chapter resume from page 'one' in each case; in the later works it was to become characteristic of Conrad to produce in the first draft a flow of narrative which is more or less a seamless web on which the chapter divisions were to be imposed retrospectively. Also Conrad uses the verso of some of his sheets for scribblings which may or may not be related to the novel. Some of these are financial calculations: for example on the verso of ms. Chapter V, sheet 25, there are calculations (in pounds) com-ing to a total of £264, and the phrase 'Can it be done, Can it be done?' This looks like a private memorandum rather than a note for the eyes of another person and it indicates that Conrad was habitually thinking in English at this date. The year is probably 1891: £264 was quite a large sum of money [the equivalent of three to four thousand pounds at 1992 val-ues] and the calculation is either a record of past expenses or (more probably) a note about a speculation which came to nothing. Other cal-culations seem to be word-counts, as though the novelist is carefully check-ing (for the typist?) exactly how much has been written. Elsewhere there are drawings or doodles: on the verso of page two of the manuscript of the *Preface* (Conrad's first critical statement, written in 1895, after the novel was finished) there is what I take to be a sketch map showing Almayer's house, his 'folly' built to impress the Englishmen who never came, in relation to the river on which it stands (there are similar sketches in the manuscript of *Victory*). Other doodles seem to be Conrad's reflections on his own identity. On the verso of ms. chapter 3, p. 4, there are spirited drawings of three fully rigged sailing ships and what seems to be a London cab, as though Captain Korzeniowski were setting in contrast with each other the vehicles characteristic of his two careers, naval officer and city-dwelling writer. There are also an elaborately ornamented 'K' and lower on the sheet, again in ornamental script, the word 'KONRAD'. The writer seems here to be sketching out for himself the identity that he will have as novelist: 'Konrad', the name identified with Polish national aspirations, due to be modified soon to the 'Conrad' of his title pages. On the manuscript of 'Razumov', which later became *Under Western Eyes* (now in the Beinecke Rare Book Library at Yale) a letter K, sometimes ornamented, frequently appears on the margins of the manuscript as though Konrad/ Conrad were now experiencing doubt about his own identity.[6] It seems that the need to reinforce his sense of himself, natural enough in the unpublished writer of *Almayer's Folly*, reappeared as Conrad-Korzeniowski dealt with the painful personal material in 'Razumov' and that the frequent appearance of these 'Ks' marks his attempt to pin down, or stabilize, his self-image as he worked towards the end of that personal and painful novel.

The question of his own identity was always to be a problem for Conrad. Throughout his life he spent money prodigally, and it seems likely that he did so for reasons that he didn't fully understand: that the insecurity bred in him by the fact of being so obviously a foreigner living in England drove him to live in the style which signalled 'gentleman' to the native English. Uncle Bobrowski had been a father figure who had provided the means. Now that he was dead his legacy gave Conrad a momentary sense of affluence, which was doomed to be short-term: it was not in Conrad's nature to live within his means. He behaved over money as though the loving and reproachful uncle were still there, ready to rescue him when he came to grief, with the result that the years 1894 to 1896 – between the death of Tadeusz and the marriage to Jessie George – were among the most insecure of Conrad's life.

The control displayed in his art compensates for, and imposes structure on, the disorder and lack of control in his personal affairs. In *Almayer's Folly* Conrad dramatizes, with unsparing and painful clarity, a failed life the characteristics of which are recognizably features of the way in which he saw his own career to date: pretension, depression, displacement, professional defeat and social and financial insecurity. Almayer, the Borneo merchant who has never been to Europe (though he is Dutch by birth), lives on expectation from an older man who disappoints him – Lingard – and drags out a frustrated existence in exile, fondly imagining that prosperity and secure social status await him in the future. He weakly agrees to marry Lingard's adopted daughter in the belief that he will inherit Lingard's wealth and be set up in a luxurious life-style:

He was gifted with a strong and active imagination, and . . . saw, as in a flash
of dazzling light, great piles of shining guilders, and realized all the possibilities of an opulent existence. The consideration, the indolent ease of life
– for which he felt himself so well fitted – his ships, his warehouses, his
merchandise (old Lingard would not live for ever), and, crowning all, in the
far future gleamed like a fairy palace the big mansion in Amsterdam, that
earthly paradise of his dreams, where made king amongst men by old
Lingard's money, he would pass the evening of his days in inexpressible
splendour (*Almayer's Folly*, p. 10).

Almayer's Folly, *An Outcast of the Islands* and *The Rescue* are linked narratives, telling in reverse sequence the story of Lingard and the relationships that he forms.[7] In the first two novels Lingard is a father-figure, and
the relationship is in each case a power-relationship with a weaker and
younger man, Almayer or Willems. In the third novel the relationship
is an erotic one (Lingard and Mrs Travers). The received wisdom[8] on
Conrad's difficulties with *The Rescue* (it took him twenty-four years to finish
it) is that he found it difficult to dramatize heterosexual relationships and
when blocked with *The Rescue* turned to narratives in which the significant
interaction is between men. By 1900 three of these narratives were complete – *The Nigger of the 'Narcissus'*, *Heart of Darkness* and *Lord Jim* – while
The Rescue continued to hang round Conrad's neck. The received wisdom
seems to me to offer part of the explanation for Conrad's agony with *The
Rescue* but I also think that Conrad's behaviour over his contract with
McClure to write *The Rescue* was the behaviour of the truant part of Conrad's
personality, responding to depression by refusing to engage with the task
to which he was ostensibly committed while an inner (and deeper) level
of the self – the artist – responded to the depression in a more constructive
way by getting on with the great masterpieces under cover of this surface
conflict. No-one would claim that *Almayer's Folly* and *An Outcast of the
Islands* are among the most distinguished of Conrad's novels, but the
dramatization of weakness in each case is full, rich, moving and obviously
informed by Conrad's personal difficulties. Almayer is a man from whom
everything is taken: his expectations, his friendships with the patron,
Lingard, and with his young Malay comrade Dain Maroola, and the only
human being whom he loves, his daughter Nina. His behaviour when he
knows that Nina has left him is beautifully observed:

He fell on his hands and knees, and, creeping along the sand, erased carefully with his hand all traces of Nina's footsteps. He piled up small heaps of
sand, leaving behind him a line of miniature graves right down to the water.
After burying the last slight imprint of Nina's slipper he stood up, and,
turning his face towards the headland where he had last seen the prau
[Malay canoe], he made an effort to shout out loud . . . his firm resolve to
never forgive (pp. 195–6).

After which he goes to pieces completely, takes to opium smoking and
dies. The death is, in a way, a wish–fulfilment: a merciful release from

depression. *An Outcast of the Islands* has at its centre another weak anti-hero, Willems, who behaves towards the father figure, Lingard, in a Conradian way by betraying him. Willems betrays the secret of Lingard's river; as punishment he is left in a kind of living death from which he is (in a sense) released by his Malay mistress, Aissa, when she shoots him out of sexual jealousy. The account of Willems's interior consciousness at the moment of his own death is a highly sophisticated piece of writing – an anticipation of the technique of 'delayed decoding' employed in the later masterpieces:

> He saw a burst of red flame before his eyes, and was deafened by a report that seemed to him louder than a clap of thunder. Something stopped him short, and he stood aspiring in his nostrils the acrid smell of the blue smoke that drifted from before his eyes like an immense cloud.... Missed, by Heaven! ... Thought so! ... And he saw her very far off, throwing her arms up, while the revolver, very small, lay on the ground between them.... Missed! ... He would go and pick it up now. Never before did he understand, as in that second, the joy, the triumphant delight of sunshine and of life. His mouth was full of something salt and warm. He tried to cough; spat out.... Who shrieks: In the name of God, he dies! – he dies! – Who dies? – Must pick up – Night! – What? ... Night already.... (*An Outcast of the Islands*, p. 360).

This, too, may express the author's partially acknowledged wish. From his attempt to shoot himself in 1878 and from the many letters in which he communicates the suicidal state to which depression could reduce him we know that death was, quite often, regarded by Conrad in the 1890s as a welcome possibility, a release from the intolerable burden of responsibilities with which he felt himself to be encumbered.

Depression is accompanied by dependence. At the centre of each of these narratives is a weak anti-hero trying to bolster himself by attachment to someone strong. The bond between Willems and Lingard is a far richer and more elaborate working of the theme than that between Almayer and Lingard. Lingard knows, throughout his association with Willems, that Willems is worthless. He rescues Willems for his own sake, not for Willems's: 'We are responsible for one another – worse luck' is his rule-of-thumb assessment of his own moral predicament as he takes up the burden of Willems' shipwrecked and disgraced life (p. 40). And Willems, even while he betrays Lingard and is punished by him, knows that his relationship with Lingard is deeply ambivalent: his resentment of, and dependence on, Lingard traps him in a bond so strong that its final rupture is unbearably painful to him. The complex nature of the interaction stings the two participants into articulacy and self-knowledge. When Lingard has learnt of Willems' treachery and sentences him to perpetual exile his parting speech stresses two things: his sense of his own identification with Willems, and his perception that Willems is no longer a moral being:

'You are my mistake. I shall hide you here. If I let you out you would go amongst unsuspecting men, and lie, and steal, and cheat for a little money or for some woman. I don't care about shooting you. It would be the safest way though. But I won't. Do not expect me to forgive you. To forgive one must have been angry and become contemptuous, and there is nothing in me now – no anger, no contempt, no disappointment. To me you are not Willems, the man I befriended and helped through thick and thin, and thought much of ... You are not a human being that may be destroyed or forgiven. You are a bitter thought, a something without a body and that must be hidden ... You are my shame' (p. 275).

And for Willems the loss of Lingard is the loss of a parent figure. The outrage that he experiences must draw on Conrad's childhood reaction to his father's death, revived and reinforced as it had recently been (in 1894) by the death of Uncle Tadeusz. Lingard withdraws downriver in his canoe (anticipates, in reverse, the effect of the final scene between Marlow and Jim, where Marlow sees Jim as a tiny white speck gathering all the light to himself; I am referring to the closing paragraphs of chapter 35 of *Lord Jim*): 'He could see plainly the figure of the man sitting in the middle. All his life he had felt that man behind his back, a reassuring presence ready with help, with commendation, with advice; friendly in reproof, enthusiastic in approbation; a man inspiring confidence by his strength, by his fearlessness, by the very weakness of his simple heart. And now that man was going away' (p. 281).

The first two novels draw closely, as we have seen, on observations that Conrad made during the voyages of the *Vidar*.[9] In 1887 Conrad made four trips in the *Vidar* to Berau, a trading-post on a river in Eastern Borneo, where a half-caste called William Charles Olmeijer had been employed for many years as representative for a famous trader in the region, Captain William Lingard. William Lingard had set himself up as a trader in the Archipelago in the 1860s and had, like 'Tom Lingard', discovered for himself a river where he had a monopoly of trade. On this river, the Berau in Eastern Borneo, he had appointed Olmeijer – who was related to him by marriage – as his agent. Ten years later he appointed his young nephew, Jim Lingard, as Olmeijer's assistant. It is possible that Olmeijer saw this young man as a dangerous rival. In *A Personal Record* Conrad says that the stories of Lingard and Olmeijer were present to him, quiescent but waiting, on the day on which he began writing: 'I was in no haste to take the plunge ... My whole being was steeped deep in the indolence of a sailor away from the sea' (chapter 4, p. 73). But it was 'possible and even likely that I was thinking of the man Almayer' (p. 74). Notwithstanding several pages of anecdote about 'Almayer' in *A Personal Record* Conrad's personal contact with Olmeijer was very slight ('Almayer' is simply a phonetic rendering of his name; it is likely that Conrad never saw it written down). It is important that Conrad draws attention in *A Personal Record* to the derisive local gossip about 'Almayer': he comes to Conrad as much through oral tradition, modern folk-tale, as through direct contact. Conrad apostrophizes 'Almayer' thus: 'You come to me stripped of all prestige by men's queer smiles and the disrespectful chatter of every vagrant trader in the Islands. Your name was the common property of the winds: it, as it were, floated naked over the waters about the Equator' (p. 88). So that when Conrad says 'if I had not got to know Almayer pretty well it is almost certain there would never have been a line of mine in print' (p. 87) he is not really misleading us. I disagree here with Norman Sherry, who is generally inclined, throughout his indispensable studies of Conrad's sources, to take a rather inflexible view of the nature of evidence. Conrad 'knew' Olmeijer in the way that one gets to 'know' a person who has been the subject of animated and widespread hearsay.

Lingard, the figure who links *Almayer's Folly, An Outcast of the Islands* and *The Rescue,* cannot be based on direct observation. Conrad never met William Lingard: the 'Tom Lingard' of his novels is similarly based on legend and hearsay.[10] This is the right kind of knowledge for a novelist: compare Conrad's practice with that of Henry James, whose notebooks are full of subjects which have come to him from gossip and conversation rather than first hand observation. In the case of *Almayer's Folly* Conrad's imagination could play with the material the more readily because it had come to him in the form of a living oral tradition, envious and admiring gossip among the traders of Borneo. It was a kind of far-Eastern version of the Polish oral tale known as the *gaweda,* a 'told tale' of the kind familiar to Conrad from his childhood.[11]

Both William Lingard's employees, Charles Olmeijer and Jim Lingard, were working at the trading station at the time of Conrad's visit. If it is true that Olmeijer was jealous of young Lingard, then it is possible that two dramatic patterns, Almayer's hatred of Willems and Cornelius' hatred of Jim, are based on this situation. There is also a recurrent pattern of patronage in the source: William Lingard when young was set up in trade by a man called Secretan; William Lingard took over Secretan's trading concerns; William Lingard then became the patron and benefactor of Charles Olmeijer and of Jim Lingard. A similar pattern of patronage occurs in the novels: in *An Outcast of the Islands* Lingard adopts, in sequence, first Almayer and then Willems, and in *Lord Jim* the old Scotsman Alexander McNeil (clearly based on Secretan) initially took on the young Stein as his protégé, and Stein in his later years takes on two protégés, first Cornelius and then Jim (whose presence stirs Cornelius' murderous jealousy).[12]

In *Almayer's Folly* Kaspar Almayer marries a native girl at the insistence of Tom Lingard and spends twenty years as Lingard's agent on a small river settlement, 'Sambir', trapped by the failure of Lingard's prospects: all this is close to the reality that Conrad knew about.[13] It is common for Conrad to use real names in his fictions, but *Almayer's Folly* differs from his other novels in that there he uses the name of someone who was still alive. Olmeijer died in 1900, in Java (it is not known whether he had read the novel). William Lingard had died quite recently, and in 1896 friends of his in Singapore were indignant at the publication of a novel which made no attempt to disguise him.[14] *An Outcast of the Islands* takes the same group of characters and the same setting, adds the figure of Willems and takes place at a dramatic date some twenty years earlier than the first novel. The plot of *An Outcast of the Islands* turns on the cause of the collapse of Lingard's fortune (his secret river is betrayed by Willems) while the plot of *Almayer's Folly* turns on (one) effect of that collapse (the destruction of Almayer's hopes). In the reality from which Conrad was working William Lingard's fortunes did indeed decline, not because he was betrayed but because the replacement of sail navigation by steam opened up an area which had formerly been exclusively his and made it available to all comers. There is thus a kind of parallelism between the fate of William Lingard and the fate of Conrad himself in the latter part of his career as a sailor: both were unable to prosper in the age of steam.

With the publication of *Almayer's Folly* Conrad entered the literary market place. He was to some extent writing according to a formula understood by the current market: *Almayer's Folly* could after all be regarded as a romance in the most popular sense, since it contained a love story with a happy ending; and it also fitted in with contemporary interest in exotic adventure. Following the fashion set earlier by Chateaubriand and Byron, the exotic became a major mode of later nineteenth-century literature. In the eighties, the novel about foreign lands had become an established and popular genre in France with the immensely successful Pierre Loti, and in England with Stevenson, Kipling and R. M. Ballantyne; at a lower literary level the genre had attracted many best–selling novelists, notably Rider Haggard and such prolific but now almost forgotten writers as the Australians Louis Becke and Carlton Dawes. Conrad was early compared with the first four of these, and he certainly knew their work.[15] For a first novel *Almayer's Folly* made a splash and was widely and on the whole favourably reviewed. Reviewers drew attention to the fact that Conrad was opening up a part of the world hitherto unknown to the literary public. Conrad was said to have 'annexed the island of Borneo' and to show promise of becoming 'the Kipling of the Malay Archipelago'.[16] The first novel prompted comparisons with Louis Becke and with Zola, the second stimulated favourable comparisons with Melville and Stevenson. Conrad must have been delighted by the review in the *Daily Chronicle* which was the first to make these comparisons. The reviewer begins: 'Mr Conrad has justified the expectations roused by *Almayer's Folly*. That was altogether as remarkable a first venture in fiction as we can remember. *An Outcast of the Islands* is a work of extraordinary force and charm'.[17] H. G. Wells, who had written a brief review of the first novel, wrote a long unsigned piece on *An Outcast of the Islands* for the *Saturday Review*. He recognizes Conrad as a great novelist and at the same time deplores, with justice, the length of the novel: 'his story is not so much told as seen intermittently through a haze of sentences. His style is like river-mist; for a space things are seen clearly, and then comes a great grey bank of printed matter, page on page, creeping round the reader, swallowing him up'.[18] Conrad recognized that this was a serious review which could do him nothing but good. He was delighted to discover that Wells – already a famous name – was its author. As Conrad wrote excitedly to Edward Garnett: 'I wrote to the reviewer. I did!! And he wrote to me. He did!! And who do you think it is? – He lives in Woking. Guess. Can't tell? – I will tell you. It is H. G. Wells. May I be cremated alive like a miserable moth if I suspected it! Anyway he descended from his 'Time-Machine' to be kind as he knew how.'[19]

This correspondence with Wells was the beginning of a friendship which was to be kept up, with varying degrees of closeness, for the next ten years. Though the relationship had cooled somewhat by 1907 Conrad still regarded Wells as sufficiently an equal, in literary terms, to dedicate *The Secret Agent* to him.[20] It seems that he took Wells's sound professional advice about the style of *An Outcast of the Islands* to heart and consciously pruned his prose for the next novel, *The Nigger of the 'Narcissus'*, which displays far tighter narrative control than *Almayer's Folly* and *An Outcast of the Islands.*

In 1896 he added to his responsibilities by marrying Jessie George. All commentators have legitimately asked how it was that this middle-aged Polish literary intellectual came to marry a simple upper-working-class London girl in her early twenties. Very little is known about how or when it was that he and Jessie met: Jessie herself gives conflicting dates: she says that they met 'at the end of 1893', introduced by Conrad's friend G. F. W. Hope and then elsewhere she says that the date was November 1894.[21] Conrad says in a letter of 10 March 1896 to Karol Zagórski that he met her 'a year and a half ago', when she was 'earning her living in the City as a "Typewriter" in an American business office'.[22] She was indeed working as a typist in London and lived in Peckham with her widowed mother when Conrad met her. He proposed to her in February 1896 on the steps of the National Gallery. The proposal, 'surely one of the strangest ever made', is recreated with considerable comic skill in Jessie's narrative: 'He glanced round to see that we were alone and without any preamble began: "Look here, my dear, we had better get married and out of this. Look at the weather. We will get married at once and get over to France. How soon can you be ready? In a week – a fortnight?"' He told Jessie's appalled mother that his reason for haste was 'that he hadn't very long to live' and further 'that there would be no family'.[23] Although both Conrad and Jessie were baptized Catholics they chose to be married in the registry office in Hanover Square, London, on 24 March 1896, with Hope, Krieger and Jessie's mother as witnesses.[24]

In 1911 Ford Madox Ford published a satire (under the pseudonym of 'Daniel Chaucer')[25] containing a spiteful caricature of Conrad and suggesting that Conrad married Jessie because he was unable to afford to pay her for her typing and because she had become his mistress. There is no record of Conrad reacting to this attack, and there seems no reason to suppose that Conrad knew of the book's existence since it made no general impact on the literary world and by the time it was published he and

Ford had quarrelled and parted company. Ford was a paranoid personality covertly expressing under the cloak of a pseudonym his outraged sense of having been slighted by Conrad. His mode of combat was governed by vanity and deviousness, and after the quarrel of 1909 his communications with Conrad are couched in terms of 'gentlemanly' bluffness or cringing propitiation rather than direct aggression: it is very unlikely that he would have drawn Conrad's attention to the satire himself.

But the fact remains that Ford knew Conrad well, and his view of Conrad's reasons for marrying Jessie cannot be wholly discredited: Conrad needed a typist, he was accustomed both from childhood and from his years in the navy to being waited on, and Jessie's demeanour was reassuringly servile. Lady Ottoline Morrell in her memoirs was expressing a widely perceived view of the marriage when she said that Jessie was 'a nice and good-looking fat creature, an excellent cook . . . [and] a good and reposeful mattress for this hypersensitive, nerve-wrecked man, who did not ask from his wife high intelligence, only an assuagement of life's vibrations'.[26] We may note here that the evident resentment of Conrad that Jessie expressed in her memoirs after his death[27] was not allowed into the open – and she may never have consciously acknowledged it – during his life. It is also possible, as we have seen,[28] that Marguerite Poradowska had refused him and that he married Jessie to some extent on the rebound. It could also be that Conrad felt that he simply could not afford to marry a woman whom he could regard as equivalent in social standing to the position that he had abandoned when he left Poland. And if he could not marry into his own class then it scarcely mattered how far down the social scale he went in his choice of a woman in this alien country. Jessie, from Conrad's viewpoint, belonged to that very broad inchoate band of the English social system known as the middle class. Conrad's letter to Karol Zagórski of 10 March 1896 makes it pretty clear that Conrad was aware that his future wife was likely to be regarded as in some sense his social as well as his intellectual inferior: 'She is a small, not at all striking-looking person (to tell the truth alas – rather plain!) who nevertheless is very dear to me. . . . Her father died three years ago. There are nine children in the family. The mother is a very decent woman (and I do not doubt very virtuous as well). However, I must confess that it is all the same to me, as – vous comprenez? – I am not marrying the whole family'.[29] From this letter Jessie emerges as someone who is acceptable to him as a wife precisely because she does not represent any kind of threat. She is mild, not particularly attractive (though photographs of Jessie as a young woman indicate that she was, in fact, very attractive) and comes of a family for which Conrad feels what sounds like the kind of patronizing contempt that Willems in *An Outcast of the Islands* feels for his half-caste in-laws, the Da Souzas, whose 'admiration was the great luxury of his life' (pp. 3–4).

As it turned out, she was in many respects – as Ottoline Morrell says – an excellent wife to Conrad, providing comfort and support to the great writer as he suffered his depressions and displayed his tantrums. But she was not, as most observers thought, merely placid and bovine. She suffered, both physically and psychologically, and notwithstanding Conrad's pose of chronic invalidism her health was in fact more frail than his for much of their married life. The mismatch became more equal with time: after the birth of their second child – born in August 1906, named John after their devoted friend John Galsworthy – Conrad came, I think, to love and respect Jessie and to value her loyalty, and it may well be that that loyalty was more valuable to him than intellectual equality would have been.

Writing is a lonely business, especially lonely in Conrad's case because he lived in the country with a woman who was not an intellectual companion. During the whole of his writing life he formed important friendships with other men, usually men who were his intellectual equals. Edward Garnett who, as we have seen,[30] was one of the readers who had recommended *Almayer's Folly* to Fisher Unwin, became a close friend of Conrad and his closest literary confidant and – in effect – his unpaid literary agent during the years 1895–8. It was largely as a result of Garnett's encouragement that Conrad pursued his career as a novelist, though he had in fact begun the narrative called 'Two Vagabonds' – which became *An Outcast of the Islands* – before the meeting to which he refers in the Author's Note to *An Outcast of the Islands*.[31] Garnett's version of this meeting is slightly different from Conrad's: 'in answer to Mr Unwin's casual but significant reference to "your next book", Conrad threw himself back on the broad leather lounge and in a tone that put a clear cold space between himself and his hearers, said: "I don't expect to write again. It is likely that I shall soon be going to sea"'.[32] Conrad says that he told Garnett and Unwin that he was not thinking of writing another novel, and that he would probably go back to sea. Garnett became his chosen intimate, and the midwife whose task it was to get Conrad's works through their birth-pangs. When he had finished *An Outcast of the Islands* Conrad wrote Garnett a jocular letter which gives a clear sense of the role that Garnett was playing in his life: Willems and Almayer are treated as though they have been real people. The manuscript will be delivered for Garnett to read, with the inbuilt and unquestioning assumption that it is Garnett's duty to perform this service for his friend.[33] When Garnett had read it, and marked some paragraphs which he thought Conrad should change, Conrad replied in a manner which suggests that he wants to deny responsibility for his own work: 'All my work is produced unconsciously (so to speak) and I cannot meddle to any purpose with what is within myself – I am sure you understand what I mean. – It isn't in me to improve what has got itself written'.[34]

One might have expected that after his marriage Conrad would display greater self-possession and emotional independence. But this did not happen. He took Jessie to Brittany, where she was, as he wrote to Garnett on 9 April 1896, a 'very good comrade and no bother at all',[35] and was required (on her honeymoon) to continue typing her husband's work. On 13 April 1896 he wrote a letter accompanying part of the manuscript of 'The Rescuer'[36] in which he abased himself before Garnett:

> I am so afraid of myself, of my likes and dislikes, of my thought and of my expression, that I must fly to You[37] for relief. . . . Do tell the truth. I do not mind telling you that I have become such a scoundrel that all Your remarks shall be accepted by me without a kick, without a moan, without the most abject of timid whispers! I am ready to cut, slash, erase, destroy; spit, trample, jump, wipe my feet on that MS at a word from You. Only say where, how, when. I have become one of the damned and the lost.[38]

And in response to Garnett's comments Conrad replies (2 June 1896) 'I surrender without the slightest demur to *all* your remarks.' Conrad's tone here is of a man who has become so dependent on the opinion of others that he has virtually no self-reliance or self-esteem left. He refers with anxious self-deprecation to 'The Idiots'. 'The Idiots'[39] is a sensational tale (based on observation of a local family) about a tragic peasant couple who are unable to bear normal children. It is an odd work to be written by a man on his honeymoon, not least in that its theme suggests that Conrad's mind was running on disastrous possible outcomes of his own marriage. Conrad wants to know Garnett's opinion of that tale, and reports that the agony of writing 'The Rescuer' makes him feel that he is going mad:

> Every day The Rescuer crawls a page forward – sometimes with cold despair – at times with hot hope. I have long fits of depression, that in a lunatic asylum would be called madness. I do not know what it is. It springs from nothing. It is ghastly. It lasts an hour or a day; and when it departs it leaves a fear (2 June 1896).[40]

And in the next letter he reports that 'The Rescuer' is making him suicidal: 'If you knew how idiotic the whole thing seems to me you would pity me. You would weep over me. Oh the unutterable, the inevitable Bosh! I feel as if I could go and drown myself – in a cesspool at that – for twopence'.[41]

There is a strategy in operation in these letters which was to be characteristic of Conrad's behaviour for most of his writing life. He picks on a friend with whom the relationship becomes intimate, a relationship in which Conrad can act out the tantrums and frustrations of an enraged child. He was extraordinarily skilled at finding partners in this exercise, friends who were willing to collude with this passionately self-centred and vertiginously retrogressive process, to attend to the child in him and listen to his lamentations and self-mistrust. Meanwhile, at another level, self-interest continued to propel that separate entity in Joseph Conrad, the artist. When the artist felt blocked the depressive expressed himself in epistolary screams of rage. In mid-June, 1896, he wrote that he had been sitting 'before the blank page' unable to write a single sentence. Writing is an involuntary process: if the writing won't 'emerge' then the artist – in this scenario of the self – has no control over it:

> To be able to think and unable to express is a fine torture. I am undergoing it – without patience. I don't see the end of it. It's very ridiculous and very awful. Now I've got all my people together I don't know what to do with them. The progressive episodes of the story *will* not emerge from the chaos of my sensations. I feel nothing clearly. And I am frightened when I remember that I have to drag it all out of myself. Other writers have some starting point. Something to catch hold of. They start from an anecdote – from a newspaper paragraph (a book may be suggested by a casual sentence in an old almanack). They lean on dialect – or on tradition – or on history – or on the prejudice or fad of the hour; they trade upon some tie or some conviction of their time – or upon the absence of these things – which they can abuse or praise. But at any rate they know something to begin with – while I don't. I have had some impressions, some sensations – in my time: – impressions and sensations of common things. And it's all faded (19 June 1896).[42]

The depressive displays self-knowledge. And this letter is proleptic. *Lord Jim* and *The Secret Agent* were to take as their starting-points events which had featured in the newspapers, while in the major work with which Conrad unblocked himself – *The Nigger of the 'Narcissus'* – he was to use personal experience and sensation, and his knowledge of a human community which had its own tradition and dialect. But this was in the future. As long as he struggled with 'The Rescuer' Conrad was, as he says in a letter to Garnett in August 1896, in a self-created hell, 'a place of torment so subtle and so cruel and so unavoidable that the prospect of theological damnation in the hereafter has no more terrors for me.'[43] And yet throughout this miserable period he *knew*, with part of his mind, the solution to his own problems. This knowledge emerges with remarkable clarity in letters written *before* he became locked into his hideous struggle with 'The Rescuer': the letters were written in 1895 to Edward Noble, a young sailor who was an aspiring writer. On 28 October 1895 Conrad wrote to Noble in terms which seem to anticipate Conrad's own success with the writing of *Heart of Darkness*: 'Only my dear Noble do not throw yourself away in fables. Talk about the river – the people – the events, as seen through your temperament'.[44] He urges Noble to do two things which we, Conrad's readers, with the benefit of hindsight, can see to be central virtues of Conrad's best art: firstly, to make the most of his own experiences, and secondly, to be loyal to his own uniqueness, however isolating such loyalty may become:

> Imagination ... should be used to create human souls; to disclose human hearts – and not to create events that are properly speaking *accidents* only ... You must squeeze out of yourself every sensation, every thought, every image – mercilessly, without reserve and without remorse; you must

> search the darkest corners of your heart. . . . You must search them for the
> image, for the glamour, for the right expression. And you must do it sin-
> cerely, at any cost (28 October 1895).
>
> Everyone must walk in the light of his own heart's gospel. No man's light is
> good to any of his fellows. That's my creed – from beginning to end. Thats
> my view of life – a view that rejects all formulas dogmas and principles of
> other people's making. These are only a web of illusions. We are too varied.
> Another man's truth is only a dismal lie to me (2 November 1895).[45]

The *Preface* to *The Nigger of the 'Narcissus'* (written some six months after
Conrad had finished the novel to which it is prefatory) is often taken as
Conrad's artistic credo, and it uses phrases comparable with those in the
letters to Noble (stressing, for example, the word 'temperament'), and
tells us that the artist is alone, and that his task – to break out of his
isolation and communicate the truths that he has discovered for himself
to his readers – is one of intense difficulty. Post-Conradian novelists such
as Graham Greene and Timothy Mo admire Conrad for his adventurous-
ness, his willingness to write about places that he scarcely knew, such as
South America, and to invent on a huge scale. But they need to remember
that to each of his remote settings, whether based on observation or (as
in the case of *Nostromo*) on research, he brings his depressive's knowledge
of his own temperament. To take an extreme example in a work to be
discussed later: Chinua Achebe is partly right to complain that *Heart of
Darkness* uses Africa as a backdrop for a European problem.[46]

It took Conrad time to apply the precepts set out in the letters to Noble
to his own practice. *Almayer's Folly* and *An Outcast of the Islands*, good though
they are, seek to exploit the advantage that the exotic settings give the
tyro novelist over his English readers, and are based on observation rather
than knowledge. The latter feature is also true of 'The Idiots', the story
dealing with a Breton peasant who fathers four idiot children and is killed
by his wife when he seeks to father a fifth child. The source for this was
a family who lived near the Conrads' temporary home in Brittany in 1896:
Jessie Conrad recalls that in reality the peasant family had seven idiot
children but that Conrad said that for his story 'five were enough in all
conscience'; Conrad's point was that life was more horrible than art could
dare to be.[47] Two more stories followed: 'An Outpost of Progress', based
on Conrad's experience in the Congo[48] and 'The Lagoon', which again
squeezes the Malay archipelago for its exotic content. Both these were
written as a form of holiday from the agonizing task of writing 'The Rescuer'
(as its title still was, in 1896). Conrad's letters to Garnett show that he had
no illusions about the artistic merit of 'The Lagoon': 'It's a tricky thing
with the usual forests river – stars – wind sunrise, and so on – and lots of
secondhand Conradese in it' (14 August 1896[49]).

After their rather arduous stay in Brittany the Conrads returned to
England and moved in September 1896 into a rented house in Stanford-le-
Hope, Essex: the attraction, presumably, was that Conrad's friend G. F. W.

Achebe

Hope lived nearby. Hope, whom Conrad had met in the early 1880s, was as we have seen one of Conrad's earliest English friends. He was also one of the most enduring, in both senses: he could put up with all Conrad's moods and he was around for a long time. He and Conrad often went sailing together between 1896 and 1898, and although Conrad moved away from Stanford-le-Hope in 1898 the friendship continued. It is a mark of its importance for Conrad that *Lord Jim*, that great poem of friendship in the Conrad canon, is dedicated to Hope and his wife.[50]

In Stanford-le-Hope Conrad took up a story which he had in fact started in Brittany, his 'Beloved Nigger'. This was to develop into *The Nigger of the 'Narcissus'*. In *The Nigger of the 'Narcissus'* he may be said to have learnt to take the advice he had given to Noble. He here draws on experience and communicates his own individuality. As we have seen, he had served in 1884 on a ship called the *Narcissus*. The ship sailed from Bombay to Dunkirk.[51] There were Scandinavians aboard and figures who provided sources for James Wait, Belfast and Archie,[52] while the source for Old Singleton was probably the fifty-four year old Irishman, Daniel Sullivan, who was a member of the crew of Conrad's next ship, the *Tilkhurst*. The death of a negro (Joseph Barron, who died at sea on 24 September) was part of the reality of Conrad's experience, while the storm in which the ship nearly capsizes and the outbreak of mutinous behaviour among the crew are heightenings of reality. Ian Watt points out that there had been trouble on the *Narcissus* on its outward voyage – Conrad was not then aboard, but he undoubtedly heard about it later – and that Conrad recollected (for Jean-Aubry) that the ship ran into rough weather.[53]

The Nigger of the 'Narcissus' is at one level a novel about the politics of the workplace, distilling twenty years of Conrad's experience of work. The way the members of the ship's crew interact is constantly seen in the light of the over-riding reason for which they have been employed, to get the ship to its destination. It is also a study – or rather a dramatization – of one of the power-structures that human beings are forced to devise in order to achieve their economic objectives. But only the most rigorously historical reader would think exclusively in these terms.

From the opening lines of the novella we are engaged by the voice of a narrator who is deployed with great freedom and flexibility: at times he is ubiquitous and omniscient, at other times identifiable as a crewman or (especially in the novel's closing paragraphs) an officer. Conrad is, of course, being less consistent over 'point of view' than his admired contemporary Henry James, but no reader is in a position to rebuke Conrad for violating 'rules' of narrative consistency. As Virginia Woolf was to say: 'Any method is right, every method is right, that expresses what we wish to express, if we are writers; that brings us closer to the novelist's intention if we are readers'.[54] If the narrative method works – and it obviously does – then we have no reason to quarrel with it. To my mind the narrative flexibility enacts for the reader an important feature of the novel's dramatic organization: there is a constant tension between the claims of the formal power-system, the chain of command of the ship at sea, and the human emotions (individual or collective) which work against that system. By weaving and veering in and out of the minds of the participants the narrative method constantly reminds us of the counterpoint, as one may call it, of which the novel is composed.

Liberal humanism as practised in the twentieth century by figures such as E. M. Forster and Angus Wilson tells us to put relationships above duty. Forster puts this position clearly when he says 'If I had to choose between betraying my country and betraying my friend, I hope I should have the guts to betray my country'.[55] Conrad knows that relationships and duty pull against each other and builds that knowledge into his major novels: I am thinking especially of the predicaments of Marlow in *Lord Jim* and of Razumov in *Under Western Eyes*. If one compares these predicaments with the situation in *The Nigger of the 'Narcissus'* one can see immediately that there is far less moral relativity in *The Nigger of the 'Narcissus'* than in the later works. When we finish reading *The Nigger of the 'Narcissus'* we cannot be in any serious doubt about the moral pattern that has been displayed: Allistoun has been vindicated, Donkin and Wait have been condemned. But in the course of reading we have been encouraged, by the flexibility of the narration, to share with the crew members their experience of the charm of the soft option. These 'Children of the Sea' (the title under which the novel was published in America) are put in the position of Hercules choosing between the allure of Vice and the stony highway of Virtue. When the 'Narcissus' is on her beam ends and James Wait is in danger of drowning on the far side of the bulkhead we participate in Belfast's emotional friendship for him, and we overlook – for the moment – the fact that an already over-stretched crew is being exposed to unjustifiable risk in the course of rescuing him. The reader is wholly engrossed in the physical challenge which the rescue of Jimmy represents: to get at the bulkhead his rescuers throw overboard a large number of tools – 'saws, chisels, wire rods, axes, crowbars' (p. 66) – regardless of the fact that these things may be needed later (as indeed they are; Archie has the presence of mind to keep a crowbar and an axe). The narrator, himself for the moment identifiable as one of the three crewmen (the other two are Archie and Belfast) engaged in the rescue operation, joins in the foolhardy business of gathering up the layer of nails, 'several inches thick' (p. 67), with his bare hands. The narrator is less foolishly emotional than Belfast, though less in control than Archie. At the moment of Wait's release these distinctions break down. The three men are united with one another, and with the reader, by the pressure of their common excitement:

Suddenly Jimmy's head and shoulders appeared. He stuck half-way, and with rolling eyes foamed at our feet. We flew at him with brutal impatience, we tore the shirt off his back, we tugged at his ears, we panted over him; and all at once he came away in our hands as though somebody had let go his legs. With the same movement, without a pause, we swung him up. His breath whistled, he kicked our upturned faces, he grasped two pairs of arms above his head, and he squirmed up with such precipitation that he seemed positively to escape from our hands like a bladder full of gas (p. 70).

The American title, 'The Children of the Sea', points to the moral and social immaturity of the crew. The sub-title for the serial publication in the *New Review* (and for the first American edition) was 'A Tale of the Forecastle', while the first English edition has as its subtitle 'A Tale of the Sea'. 'A Tale of the Forecastle' puts the focus on the crewmen rather than the officers, and is in many ways appropriate since much of the novella is a dramatization of the crew's collective life.[56] The dark, warm, unthinking solidarity of that life[57] is tenderly, even sentimentally, displayed in the vigorous writing of the novel's opening pages: the 'scrimmage', the 'haze of tobacco smoke' and the 'tempest of good-humoured and meaningless curses' (pp. 5, 6) give the tone, and the cohesiveness of the group is reinforced by the separateness of Singleton (his name obviously stresses his isolation), the oldest crewman who sits 'tattooed like a cannibal chief' reading Bulwer Lytton's *Pelham* (it is an intriguing and inexplicable fact that Lytton's novels were indeed popular, as the novella says, with Victorian seamen[58]). Collectively, the crew have greater wisdom than does any individual member. The narrator – momentarily omniscient – clearly displays the crew's collective judgement of Donkin on his first appearance. They recognize him as a type who is work-shy, lazy, greedy, manipulative, finding in the forecastle the arena for his particular self-interested and disruptive 'talents': 'They all knew him. Is there a spot on earth where such a man is unknown, an ominous survival testifying to the eternal fitness of lies and impudence?' (p. 10). The novella accurately observes one of the contradictions in human nature when it shows that their professional collective judgement of Donkin, as someone unfit for work, co-exists with the 'naive' and 'sentimental' pity with which they respond to his appeal for clothes and bedding (p. 12). James Wait's impact on them is of course more subtle – they do not know, until his physical deterioration makes it obvious, whether he is dying or malingering. In either case he engages their emotions: they are brought to near-mutiny when he is confined to his cabin, the ship's routine is relaxed when his death is inevitable. In its omniscient mode the narrative voice delivers clear judgement of Wait's and of the crew's behaviour: 'Jimmy's steadfastness to his untruthful attitude in the face of the inevitable truth had the proportions of a colossal enigma. . . . The latent egoism of tenderness to suffering appeared in the developing anxiety not to see him die. . . . He was demoralising. Through him we were becoming highly humanised, tender, complex, excessively decadent' (pp. 138–9).

This judgement is pronounced in the fifth and final chapter of the novella, but its content – duty is to override personal considerations – has to be recognized as pervasive when we look back through the text. Mr Baker reading the muster in the first chapter calls the names of the crew, as the omniscient narrator tells us, 'in a serious tone befitting this roll-call to unquiet loneliness, to inglorious and obscure struggle, or to the more trying endurance of small privations and wearisome duties' (p. 15). Work, duty and discipline are to prevail, and this is driven home by the climactic scene at the end of chapter 4 in which Captain Allistoun compels Donkin to return the belaying-pin – which he had used as missile – to its position in the fore-rigging.

Singleton, hero of the great storm scene in chapter 3, seems to be the only crewman who matches up to Allistoun's experience and professionalism. But the cannibal-like tattoos covering his powerful torso signal another paradox. Donkin is destructive and useless partly because he is intelligent: Singleton is effective partly because he is ignorant and belongs to a culture of amazingly primitive superstition. He believes, for example, that head-winds will prevail as long as there is a dying man aboard, and that Wait will not die until the ship is in sight of land (the fact that the sequence of events in the narrative seems to vindicate these beliefs is, of course, coincidental and ironic). Cunninghame Graham wrote to Conrad to say that he would have liked (on socialist grounds) to have seen this emblematic figure educated. Conrad repudiated the notion with spirit:

> You say: 'Singleton with an education'. Well – yes. Everything is possible, and most things come to pass (when you don't want them). However I think Singleton with an education is impossible. But first of all – what education? If it is the knowledge how to live my man essentially possessed it. He was in perfect accord with his life. . . . Would you seriously, of malice prepense cultivate in that unconscious man the power to think[?] Then he would become conscious – and much smaller – and very unhappy. Now he is simple and great like an elemental force. Nothing can touch him but the curse of decay – the eternal decree that will extinguish the sun, the stars one by one, and in another instant shall spread a frozen darkness over the whole universe. Nothing else can touch him – he does not think.[59]

H. G. Wells's presence in the culture of the time is very marked in this letter. The images associated with entropy – mankind brought to an end by the cooling of the sun and the death of the earth – had been given currency by Wells's *The Time Machine* (1895), especially by the scene in which the Time Traveller visits the remote future and there sees a stationary and cooling sun, a dying planet, and the last descendants of man reduced to small tentacled creatures which are food for huge crabs on a desolate beach. The main point of the letter is that to be effective a man does not need to be reflective. The letter focuses on the individual rather than the group, but Conrad's reluctance to educate Singleton carries with it the clear, if unspoken, notion that to keep one's crew inarticulate is likely to ensure that the chain of command will be unchallenged. *The Nigger of the 'Narcissus'* thus displays a firmly conservative, even autocratic, view of human organizations. In the final paragraph the narrator, now an officer, asks 'Haven't we, together and upon the immortal sea, wrung out a meaning from our sinful lives?' (p. 173). To which one can reasonably answer: 'Yes, and the meaning has been more or less apparent throughout the narrative.'

This may sound as though I think that *The Nigger of the 'Narcissus'* is over-long and over-explicit; but the flexibility of the narration and the force of the dramatization ensure that it is neither of those things. The reviewers who said that it had no 'plot' seem to have neglected its elaborate five part structure, of which the great storm passage is, so to speak, the apex of the arch. But they were right to observe the absence of women in the main part of the action (there are some cameo roles for women at the end: the master's wife and Archie's mother) and the prominence of the sea and the ship as 'characters' ('the only female in the book is the ship herself', as the *Daily Mail* reviewer put it, 7 December 1897[60]).

Conrad's is a godless universe, of course, but the sea is endowed with godlike characteristics in relation to the *Narcissus's* crew. This role is displayed in the first sentence of chapter 4, 'On men reprieved by its disdainful mercy, the immortal sea confers in its justice the full privilege of desired unrest' (p. 90), and in the judgement of Donkin after he has robbed James Wait's box: 'The ship slept. And the immortal sea stretched away, immense and hazy, like the image of life, with a glittering surface and lightless depths. Donkin gave it a defiant glance and slunk off noiselessly as if judged and cast out by the august silence of its might' (p. 155).

Ian Watt dislikes this use of the pathetic fallacy, remarking that 'Donkin seems rather small game for the sea' and that the authorial commentary here is 'intrusive' and 'difficult to justify'.[61] But for me the passage is wholly consistent with the way in which the sea imagery is used throughout, and is a triumphant 'closure' of the sea's role. The sea is in itself neutral but in relation to the sailors it has the attributes of a godlike, detached observer, both penetrating and impartial. Here it is 'like the image of life' and Donkin behaves '*as if* cast out by the august silence of its might'; in other words he, Donkin, knows what it is to be a moral being and is himself attributing to the sea the judgement of his own despicable action that he knows would be appropriate.

At this point I want to stand back from *The Nigger of the 'Narcissus'* and seek to 'place' it in relation to Conrad's later works. In its rich particularity and the use of an omniscient narrator who seems to have access to all the consciousness on board the ship – the crew, the officers, Donkin as he scheme to steal James Wait's savings, James Wait himself as he dies – it presents a confidently known microcosm of the human condition. We have not yet reached the Conrad who deals with the unknowable nature of human communities (in *Nostromo, The Secret Agent* and *Under Western Eyes*) and with the tragic engagement of the modern anti-hero with his own inability to live up to an unattainable self-image (Jim, Razumov and Heyst). Instead we have something which feels refreshingly like the novel as practiced by Dickens, Thackeray and Fenimore Cooper: the fiction presents a whole knowable world. That world is underpinned by a relationship

between man and the sea that goes back to the romantic movement, to
man's sense of his own identity paradoxically both diminished and enlarged
by an oceanic setting.[62] We are in the presence of a strong and simple
formula in which man tests his strength against the sea: a formula which
recurs in 'Youth' where the middle-aged Marlow tells the story of his
younger self undergoing a liminal and maturing experience, and in
'Typhoon' where Jukes discovers that the qualities required to pass the
test of the sea are not his own intelligence and imaginativeness, but (as
embodied in MacWhirr) their opposites: stolidity and unreflectiveness.

In terms both of biography and of literary history *The Nigger of the
'Narcissus'* is retrospective. It is Conrad's personal farewell to sail and it
displays literary continuity both with the romantic movement and (to set
it in a much larger historical perspective) with the *Odyssey*. The *Preface* to
The Nigger of the 'Narcissus' written probably in August 1897, some six months
after Conrad had finished writing the novel, should be read as prefatory
not primarily to *The Nigger of the 'Narcissus'* itself but to the whole of Conrad's
major work, especially those novels of the last years of the nineteenth
century – *Heart of Darkness* and *Lord Jim* – which establish his claim to be
seen, with Henry James, as one of the fathers of modernism in the English
novel. But in saying that I do not want to overstate the gap between the
Preface and *The Nigger of the 'Narcissus'* itself. It is significant that in the
foreward that he wrote in 1914 'To my readers in America' Conrad elides
the six months that separated *The Nigger of the 'Narcissus'* from its *Preface*
and describes the two works as though they were poured from the mind
in a single continuous movement:

> [*The Nigger of the 'Narcissus'*] is the book by which, not as a novelist perhaps,
> but as an artist striving for the utmost sincerity of expression, I am willing
> to stand or fall. Its pages are the tribute of my unalterable and profound
> affection for the ship, the seamen, the winds and the great sea – the mould-
> ers of my youth, the companions of the best years of my life. After writing
> the last words of that book. . . . I understood that I had done with the sea,
> and thenceforth I had to be a writer. And almost without laying down the
> pen I wrote a preface, trying to express the spirit in which I was entering on
> the task of my new life.[63]

The phrase 'an artist striving for the utmost sincerity of expression' tightens
the bond between the two texts. What they have in common is fierce pride
and ambition, and the elevation of the figure of the artist to a height
unattainable by ordinary mortals. The status of 'artist' is both hard to
reach and honourably arduous to sustain. It has been noted that the
Preface does not use the conventional language of literary criticism.[64] It does
not talk about plot, character, dramatic organization, novel or novelist. It
speaks of art and the artist.[65] In the first paragraph of the *Preface* to *The
Nigger of the 'Narcissus'* art is described as a single-minded attempt 'to render
the highest kind of justice to the visible universe, by bringing to light the
truth, manifold and one, underlying its every aspect.' A paradox which

had been steadily forcing itself on the attention of Victorian novelists (I am thinking especially of George Eliot and Henry James, with their insistence that the novelist is an historian) is central to the *Preface*: fiction is a kind of truth-telling. The philosopher and the scientist can, in their respective disciplines, arrive at exact truths, while the artist seeks a truth deeper, more universal and harder to reach than theirs. The first paragraph tells us that the scientist and the philosopher arrive at their truths by plunging into facts and ideas respectively, while the artist (in paragraph three) must seek his peculiar truth by descending within the self, that 'lonely region of stress and strife' (p. xl). The scientist and the philosopher speak to our common-sense, the artist speaks to something more primal than that. He is said to speak to 'that part of our being which is not dependent on wisdom,' to our 'capacity for delight and wonder' and to the 'subtle but invincible conviction of solidarity that knits together the loneliness of innumerable hearts' (p. xl). Conrad seems to be establishing a contrast between kinds of intelligence: we may call them active and contemplative, or, as Jacques Berthoud puts it, 'driving' and 'objective'.[66] Conrad's obscurely phrased distinction between these two kinds of mind may owe something to William James's *Principles of Psychology* (1890). James distinguishes between 'analytic' minds (scientists and philosophers) and 'splendid' (in the sense of 'shining') minds, 'men of intuition' (poets and critics).[67] By descending into the self the artist finds out what he really feels about the world. He thus remains loyal to the notion of rendering the highest kind of justice to the visible universe; he is not becoming a self-absorbed solipsist. And the sense of 'solidarity' which he has with others is *in itself* the 'test' of truth. Paragraph four moves from this general observation to the proposal – expressed defensively, though with dignity – that the 'dark corner of the earth' that he has chosen for this particular novel (the *Narcissus* and its crew) was worthy of the artist's attention. And in paragraph five we are told that: 'Fiction – if it at all aspires to be art – appeals to temperament. And in truth it must be, like painting, like music, like all art, the appeal of one temperament to all the other innumerable temperaments whose subtle and resistless power endows passing events with their true meaning' (p. xli). By 'temperament' Conrad means the mind and all that constitutes it. Ian Watt argues that Conrad's *Preface* displays continuity with (or from) Wordsworth's *Preface* to the *Lyrical Ballads*.[68] While it is true that Conrad envisages the artist and his audience united by their common humanity, it seems to me that Watt's observation doesn't take us very far because the historical contexts of the two *Prefaces* are quite different from each other. The crisis in which England found itself in the 1890s was that of a shrinking civilization, a country that had lost the large horizons and confident imperatives of the mid-Victorian world; the crisis of the 1790s was one of, in a sense, expanding horizons, in which the young radicals and Jacobins saw themselves as engaged in a political conflict that would liberate mankind. The *Preface* to the *Lyrical Ballads* is partly a political work: poetry, it says, must be democratized and made available to the people. Conrad's *Preface* contains an artistic credo which is notoriously difficult to paraphrase, but is certainly private rather than political in its bearing.[69]

In Conrad's use of the word 'temperament', as in much of Wordsworth and Coleridge, the mind itself is the determinant of the nature of reality. The appeal of one temperament to other temperaments 'endows passing events with their true meaning'. Paragraphs five to seven of the *Preface* to *The Nigger of* the '*Narcissus*' provide what may have seemed to be missing from paragraph three. Descending into the self and there finding fundamental truth, of which the sense of solidarity is the test, is only part of the novelist's task. Another part is devotion to the practice of his craft.[70] Here Conrad seems almost to quote Pater's '*All art constantly aspires towards the condition of music*' from 'The School of Giorgione' in *The Renaissance* (1873).[71] But whereas Pater is working for the autonomy of art, a condition in which art is responsible only to itself, Conrad constantly has in mind art's double responsibility: responsibility both to itself and to the 'truth' of which the sense of solidarity is the test. Representation and perception cannot be cleanly distinguished from each other, and therefore the artist's activity is never (in Conrad's term from paragraph eight) definable by a 'formula', be it 'Realism', 'Romanticism', 'Naturalism' or 'unofficial sentimentalism'. The formula 'Art for Art's sake' – the formula associated with Pater and aestheticism – won't do either, but it is seen as more 'encouraging' than the others: encouraging, I take it, to the extent that it gives the activity of the artist the kind of elevation of which Conrad's essay approves.

The most quoted bit of the *Preface* is this: 'My task which I am trying to achieve is, by the power of the written word to make you hear, to make you feel – it is, before all, to make you *see!*' (paragraph six, p. xlii). The verbs here move in a precise sequence. Auditory perception (to make you hear) merges into emotional response (to make you feel) which contributes to and enriches visual perception (to make you see).[72] Far from being vaguely majestic and hortatory, Conrad's 'to make you see' refers to something specific achieved by the writer at the end of a process which has been clearly understood (if cloudily expressed). Paragraph seven marks another change of direction. Here time is seen as a solvent or destroyer, and the duty of the artist is to 'snatch in a moment of courage, from the remorseless rush of time, a passing phase of life' and thereafter 'to hold up unquestioningly, without choice and without fear, the rescued fragment before all eyes' (p. xlii). This again has a strong echo of Walter Pater, who says that to attain a state of attentive delight in the presence of a work of art is the highest achievement available to a civilized man, enabling him to resist the rush of time and to withstand the chaotic forces of history:

> Not the fruit of experience, but experience itself, is the end. A counted number of pulses only is given to us of a variegated, dramatic life. How may we see in them all that is to be seen in them by the finest senses? How shall

we pass most swiftly from point to point, and be present always at the focus
where the greatest number of vital forces unite in their purest energy? To
burn always with this hard, gemlike flame, to maintain this ecstasy, is success
in life.[73]

But the difference between Conrad and Pater is, of course, crucial: Pater's
contemplative man is alone, while Conrad's rescued fragment awakens in
the beholder his capacity to bond with other human beings, a feeling of
unavoidable solidarity. The artist, then, as we perceive him from the vantage
point of paragraph seven, seeks to arrive at truth in three different ways:
firstly by sinking within himself, secondly by devoting himself faithfully to
the task of renewing and refreshing the medium within which he works
and, thirdly, by resisting the onrush of time and establishing a stasis in the
midst of flux. His audience's concurrence – the audience's acknowledgement, expressed by the word 'solidarity', that the artist's truth is also its
truth – is the test of his success.

Conrad was advised by Garnett to cancel a paragraph between paragraphs
eight and nine of the present text.[74] This cancelled paragraph and the last
three paragraphs of the *Preface* in its final state (nine to eleven) introduce a new idea. The artist is seen as a man at work: the spectacle of him
engaged in this activity is itself part of the audience's experience (and
furnishes an alternative route whereby the sensation of 'solidarity' can
flow between audience and artist). The artist is doing his work well if he
secures the reader's attention before the reader sinks back into the state
of unconsciousness in which most of us spend our lives: the audience
will have had 'a moment of vision, a sigh, a smile' before its 'return to an
eternal rest' (paragraph eleven, p. xliv). One may note here the extraordinary elevation, and concomitant freedom from external constraints,
conferred on the artist by the use of metaphorical diction which invites us
to think of the artist as a priest elevating the host at the sacrament: his
task is 'to hold up unquestioningly . . . the rescued fragment before all
eyes in the light of a sincere mood' and 'reveal the substance of its truth'
(paragraph seven, p. xlii). To say that art immortalizes life is a commonplace. Yet that is what Conrad is saying, and he is saying it with an indirection and obliquity suited to the conditions of the modern age. The
indirection and obliquity are forced on us by our epistemological isolation:
no one mind or 'temperament' is like any other, yet it remains the artist's
duty to seek to communicate his 'truth' to the 'innumerable temperaments'
outside the self (paragraph five, p. xli). The *Preface* expresses itself obscurely but the painful urgency of its tone unmistakably signals that it has
something central to communicate to us. It is both and obscure and painful because it is struggling with the predicament which informs Conrad's
major works: man is alone and unable to communicate with others, yet as
artist he is bound to make the attempt. Human isolation is irreducible and
communication is impossible, but the attempt to communicate remains
an absolute necessity for the artist.

Gossip, like myth or fairy-tale, makes for short-hand narratives which already have a rough shape: Almayer's delusions of grandeur lead to despair, Willems's dishonesty leads to punishment, Jim's cowardice leads to redemption in exile, Heyst's asceticism makes him easy prey to violent aggressors. Some of the plots can be expressed even more simply than those examples: Kurtz goes native, Falk eats men but gets his girl, MacWhirr imposes order. In some cases the simplicity of the underlying structure is felt in climactic moments in the narrative: the central theme of *The Nigger of the 'Narcissus'* is encapsulated in the observation that Singleton 'steered with care'. In the later novels Conrad's simple shapes are fleshed out by his narrative innovations; in *Almayer's Folly* and *An Outcast of the Islands* the shapes are fleshed out by fairly convention narrative and dramatic procedures. The charge of 'over-writing' is often brought against these early books: it is fair, and it refers to Conrad's desire for gorgeousness at the expense of pace.

In 1897, the year of publication of *The Nigger of the 'Narcissus'*, began two important friendships, with Cunninghame Graham and with Stephen Crane. Robert Bontine Cunninghame Graham was a socialist, Scottish nationalist and adventurer. Cunninghame Graham wrote to Conrad to praise 'An Outpost of Progress' and Conrad wrote back, 5 August 1897, a long letter which greets Cunninghame Graham as a fellow-spirit, one who recognizes the need for a fundamental pessimism and scepticism in human affairs. I quote part of his penultimate paragraph:

> Life is long – and art is so short that no one sees the miserable thing. Most of my life has been spent between sky and water and now I live so alone that often I fancy myself clinging stupidly to a derelict planet abandoned by its precious crew. Your voice is not a voice in the wilderness – it seems to come through the clean emptiness of space. If – under the circumstances – I hail back lustily I know You won't count it to me for a crime.[75]

Cunninghame Graham's belief that human affairs could be put right by socialism and political action provoked Conrad to harsh expressions of scepticism. One of the best of these is dated 20 December 1897, where he caricatures Cunninghame Graham's position ('You are a most hopeless idealist – your aspirations are irrealizable. You want from men faith, honour, fidelity to truth in themselves and others'). He says that while he himself may entertain somewhat similar aspirations for mankind ('*if* I desire the very same things [my stress] no one cares') he does not think they will be achieved because the universe is godless, mindless and hostile:

> There is a – let us say – a machine. It evolved itself (I am severely scientific) out of a chaos of scraps of iron and behold! – it knits. I am horrified at the horrible work and stand appalled. I feel it ought to embroider – but it goes on knitting. You come and say: 'this is all right; it's only a question of the right kind of oil. Let us use this – for instance – celestial oil and the machine shall embroider a most beautiful design in purple and gold.' Will it? Alas no.

You cannot by any special lubrication make embroidery with a knitting machine. And the most withering thought is that the infamous thing has made itself; made itself without thought, without conscience, without foresight, without eyes, without heart. It is a tragic accident – and it has happened. You can't interfere with it. The last drop of bitterness is in the suspicion that you can't even smash it. In virtue of that truth one and immortal which lurks in the force that made it spring into existence it is what it is – and it is indestructible!

It knits us in and it knits us out. It has knitted time space, pain, death, corruption, despair and all the illusions – and nothing matters. I'll admit however that to look at the remorseless process is sometimes amusing.[76]

A letter of 14 January 1898 reflects late Victorian physicists' understanding of entropy – the notion that energy was expending itself, the sun was dying, and the universe was winding down – in the 1890s. This letter has been compared[77] with the dying planet of the remote future seen by Wells's time-traveller in *The Time Machine*.

The mysteries of a universe made of drops of fire and clods of mud do not concern us in the least. The fate of a humanity condemned ultimately to perish from cold is not worth troubling about. If you take it to heart it becomes an undendurable tragedy. If you believe in improvement you must weep, for the attained perfection must end in cold, darkness and silence.[78]

A letter written partly in French, 8 February 1899, displays a much more extreme political and philosophical scepticism than does the 'knitting machine' letter of 20 December 1897. The earlier letter hints that Conrad may sympathize with Cunninghame Graham's hopes but thinks that the hostile universe will block them; here he thinks that mankind is inherently evil and that it necessarily follows that the anarchists of the period should be applauded:

L'homme est un animal méchant. Sa méchanceté doit être organisée. Le crime est une condition nécéssaire de l'existence organisée. La société est essentielment criminelle – ou elle n'existerait pas. C'est l'égoisme qui sauve tout – absolument tout – tout ce que nous abhorrons, tout ce que nous aimons. Et tout se tient. Voilà pourquoi je respecte les êxtremes anarchistes. – 'Je souhaite l'extermination générale' – Très bien. C'est juste et ce qui est plus c'est clair. On fait des compromis avec des paroles. Ça n'en finit plus. C'est comme une forêt ou personne ne connait la route. On est perdu pendant que l'on crie – 'Je suis sauvé!'

[Man is a vicious animal. His viciousness must be organized. Crime is a necessary condition of organized existence. Society is fundamentally criminal – or it would not exist. Selfishness preserves everything – absolutely everything – everything we hate and everything we love. And everything holds together. That is why I respect the extreme anarchists. – 'I hope for general extermination.' Very well. It's justifiable and, moreover, it is plain. One compromises with words. There's no end to it. It's like a forest where no one knows the way. One is lost even as one is calling out 'I am saved!'][79]

I think Conrad believes this with the French part of his mind. That is to say, he believes it as a theoretical position and as an intellectual attitude struck to impress a friend. His knowledge of anarchists was limited to indirect knowledge of people like the Garnett's Russian refugees and William Michael Rossetti's precocious children. In the published work he seems to equivocate over this matter: the story called 'An Anarchist' and the dramatization of Haldin in *Under Western Eyes* indicate some sympathy for anarchists while Kurtz's 'Exterminate all the brutes!' (*Heart of Darkness*) and the Professor's 'To the destruction of what is' (*The Secret Agent*) are advocacies of violence from figures who are – to put it mildly – 'placed'.

The friendship with Cunninghame Graham was to be one of the most enduring of Conrad's life. It has been termed by Cedric Watts an 'expanding paradox' in that Conrad's political instincts were conservative and Cunninghame Graham's were radical.[80] Cunninghame Graham's life was extraordinary. His biographers have observed with relish that 'to summarise his career is to strain syntax, imagination and credulity'.[81] The summary that they give is helpful (and a minor masterpiece of compression):

> R. B. Cunninghame Graham, 1852–1936. Alias Don Roberto because of his Spanish blood. Alias the Uncrowned King of Scotland – for he was a Scottish aristocrat descended from King Robert II and the Earls of Menteith. Educated at Harrow and Brussels, he became a traveller and fortune-seeker in South and Central America, working as a cattle-rancher and horse-dealer among gauchos and llaneros. After returning to Britain he became one of the most mercurial, eloquent and radical political figures of the late nineteenth century. Elected to Parliament as a Liberal in 1886, during his stormy parliamentary career he became, in practice, the first socialist M. P., advocating free secular education, the eight-hour working day, and the nationalization of industry and commerce; and he was jailed for six weeks at Pentonville for his part in the Bloody Sunday demonstration of 1887. He made his name as a courageous and uncompromising defender of the workers, of the poor and of the under-privileged; became a crucial figure in the emergence of the British Labour Party, after tireless campaining with William Morris, Keir Hardie and others, yet became one of the most severe critics of the Labour Party as it grew in strength, numbers and respectability. In later years he was President of the National Party of Scotland, and of its successor, the Scottish National Party.

Cunninghame Graham's courage, energy and glamour were to contribute a good deal of colouring to the personality of Charles Gould in *Nostromo*, and his writings and conversation were to contribute much to the South American topography and social observation of that novel.[82]

In October 1897 began Conrad's tragically brief friendship with the American writer Stephen Crane. Still in his twenties (he was some fourteen years younger than Conrad) Crane was famous as author of *The Red Badge of Courage* (1895) which Conrad had read and greatly admired. Quite *when* he had read it is not clear; probably shortly after he had finished *The*

Nigger of the 'Narcissus'. Crane was a brilliant and striking looking heroic young man of action and Conrad was instantly attracted to him: they met for lunch and spent the rest of the day and much of the evening walking and exchanging literary intimacies, as Conrad recalls in a preface to a book on Crane published in 1924: 'We did not feel the need to tell each other formally the story of our lives. That did not prevent us from being very intimate and also very open with each other from the first. Our affection would have been "everlasting" as he himself qualified it, had not the jealous death intervened with her cruel capriciousness by striking down the younger man.' In the same preface Conrad says that he sees *The Nigger of the 'Narcissus'* and *The Red Badge of Courage* as parallel contemporary workings of similar themes: 'Apart from the imaginative analysis of his own temperament tried by the emotions of a battlefield, Stephen Crane dealt in his book with the psychology of the mass – the army; while I – in mine – had been dealing with the same subject on a much smaller scale and in more specialized conditions – the crew of a merchant ship, brought to the test of what I may venture to call the moral problem of conduct'.[83] Yet Conrad had his reservations about Crane's work: to Garnett he wrote (about Crane's stories), 5 December 1897: 'His eye is very individual and his expression satisfies me artistically. He certainly is *the* impressionist and his temperament is curiously unique. His thought is concise, connected, never very deep – yet often startling. He is *the only* impressionist and *only* an impressionist'.[84] Clearly, Conrad is here using the word impressionist in a limiting sense, associating it with surface as against depth. Yet Conrad himself can appropriately be called an 'impressionist'. Ford Madox Ford was able to say that in writing his memoir of Conrad he was engaged on an impressionist work about a writer 'who avowed himself impressionist': Conrad's personality is progressively revealed to Ford much as Jim's personality is progressively revealed to Marlow in *Lord Jim*.[85] The difference is that for Conrad impressionism was not restricted to the eye: the *Preface* to *The Nigger of the 'Narcissus'* tells us that the artist has to bring the whole of the sensory apparatus and the moral and philosophical being into play in order to achieve the drastically difficult business of communicating private and inward perception of 'truth'. Conrad's impressionism is, as Ian Watt has said, part of 'the long process whereby in every domain of human concerns the priority passed from public systems of belief – what all men know – to private views of reality – what the individual sees. ... The concentration of philosophical thought upon epistemological problems gradually focussed attention on individual sensation as the only reliable source of ascertainable truth'.[86]

The friendship with Crane, brief as it was, was interrupted by Crane's travelling and adventures. The two men became very close early in 1898. Crane and his companion, Cora, had rented a house at Oxted in Surrey, not far from the Sussex-Kent borders and thus not far from Conrad, who went with Jessie to stay for two weeks in February 1898. Edward Garnett recalls Conrad and Crane together:

Conrad's moods of gay tenderness could be quite seductive. On the few occasions I saw him with Stephen Crane he was delightfully sunny, and bantered 'poor Steve' in the gentlest, most affectionate style, while the latter sat silent, Indian-like, turning enquiring eyes under his chiselled brow, now and then jumping up suddenly and confiding some new project with intensely electric feeling. At one of these sittings Crane passionately appealed to me to support his idea that Conrad should collaborate with him in a play on the theme of a ship wrecked on an island. I knew it was hopelessly unworkable this plan, but Crane's brilliant visualization of the scenes was so strong and infectious that I had not the heart to declare my own opinion. And Conrad's sceptical answers were couched in the tenderest, most reluctant tone. I can still hear the shades of Crane's poignant friendliness in his cry 'Joseph!' And Conrad's delight in Crane's personality glowed in the shining warmth of his brown eyes.[87]

Conrad introduced Crane to Blackwood, who advanced money to him enabling him to take nearly a year in Cuba (April 1898–January 1899) covering the Spanish-American War as a correspondent. When he returned Conrad rented a decaying medieval manor house in Sussex, Brede Place, near Winchelsea: the Conrads made many visits (they stayed with the Cranes for two weeks in June 1899, and Conrad and Crane went sailing together). When depressed with the progress of *Lord Jim* Conrad would ask Crane to come to cheer him up. At the end of 1899 the Cranes gave a famous party at Brede Place involving the performance of an entertainment called *The Ghost* (to which Conrad, James, Wells and Gissing had contributed). This party marked the end of the century and, almost, the end of Crane's life: by May 1900 Crane was fatally ill and went to Germany in search of a cure. Conrad went to Dover to say goodbye to him and he died early in June.[88]

The friendship with Crane was very intense, and it seems to me likely that Crane's famous novel and his short life affected Conrad's own writing: after the superfluities of *Almayer's Folly* and *An Outcast of the Islands* his work becomes (relatively) taut and economical, and after *The Nigger of the 'Narcissus'* he obliquely describes (in the *Preface*) a method which we can refer to as impressionist. This becomes the dominant method of the next two major works, *Heart of Darkness* and *Lord Jim*. The protagonist of *The Red Badge of Courage*, Henry Fleming, is a young soldier fighting for the Northern States in the American Civil War who deserts from the front line, becomes disoriented, and is restored to self-possession by a blow on the head from one of his own side (the consequent wound is his 'red badge'). He is restored to the solidarity of his regiment. He resembles Jim in that he redeems his cowardice by a heroic action, he sees himself as apart from his companions and he rationalizes his moment of cowardice by telling himself that his comrades had no chance of survival. His reaction when he learns that he was wrong is just like Jim's reaction to learning that the *Patna* does not sink: not remorse but anger at being betrayed by events. He and Jim are both immature and unreflective solipsists for whom reality should – but mysteriously doesn't – conform to their individual need. It is also possible that the portrait of Jim is partly based on Crane's personality: Crane was the blue eyed son of a Methodist pastor (Jim is the blue eyed son of an Anglican clergyman) and one of a large family (seven boys, in Crane's case). The age difference between Crane and Conrad resembles that between Jim and Marlow (Crane was twenty-six and Conrad forty when they met). Crane died shortly before the completion of *Lord Jim*: Marlow's elegy for Jim thus becomes Conrad's displaced elegy for Crane.[89] Certainly Crane in Conrad's life was like Jim in Marlow's life: the heroic friend who dies young is recalled tenderly, and transformed into a figure of myth or hagiography, by an older man.

4

The First Marlow Narrations, 1898–1900: 'Youth' *Heart of Darkness* and *Lord Jim*

'Youth'. . . *marks the first appearance in the world of the man Marlow, with whom my relations have grown very intimate in the course of years.*

'Youth', p. xxxiii

The end of L. J. *has been pulled off[1] with a steady drag of 21 hours. I sent wife and child out of the house (to London) and sat down at 9 am, with a desperate resolve to be done with it. Now and then I took a walk round the house out at one door in at the other. Ten-minute meals. A great hush. Cigarette ends growing into a mound similar to a cairn over a dead hero. Moon rose over the barn looked in at the window and climbed out of sight. Dawn broke, brightened. I put the lamp out and went on, with the morning breeze blowing the sheets of MS all over the room. Sun rose. I wrote the last word and went into the dining room. Six o'clock. I shared a piece of cold chicken with Escamillo [Borys's dog, named after the Toreador in* Carmen; *a gift from Stephen Crane] (who was very miserable and in want of sympathy having missed the child dreadfully all day). Felt very well only sleepy; had a bath at seven and at 8.30 was on my way to London.*

Conrad to John Galsworthy, 20 July 1900[2]

In May 1898 Conrad was writing two short stories, 'Youth' and 'Jim: A Sketch'. It was with 'Youth' that Conrad found for the first time his mature voice, with the use of Marlow as narrator. The Marlow who sailed on the *Judea* in 'Youth' was four years younger than the Conrad who had sailed on the *Palestine* in 1881–2 – 'just twenty' – and over-joyed by his promotion: 'It was one of the happiest days of my life. Fancy! Second mate for the first time – a really responsible officer' ('Youth,' pp. 4–5).

There is much comedy and misadventure in 'Youth'. Old Beard has none of the dignity or self-command that one expects of a skipper; when the *Judea* is damaged by a collision in the dock Beard's immediate – and highly unprofessional – concern is for his wife's safety. He gets her into the ship's boat which has no oars and a loose painter (further signs, I take it, of Beard's slack seamanship) and the old couple drift helplessly about the dock. The comic characterization of both the Beards strikes an elegant balance between irony and affection. Mrs Beard's solicitude for her old husband's health is sweet and engaging, but it further undermines the old man's authority, as she anxiously asks the young Marlow to look after her husband and 'keep his throat well wrapped up' ('Youth', p. 9). The adult Marlow who narrates the story is telling the tale of a leaky old crate which is in the precarious hands of an incompetent grandfather; only someone as young and innocent as his earlier self could see the *Judea* in any other way. Edward Said has written that in his use of autobiographical material Conrad 'was hiding himself within rhetoric' and that in the early works he 'failed, in the putting down of words, to rescue meaning from his un-disciplined experience'.[3] For Marlow's next narrative, *Heart of Darkness*, these observations have some force, but for 'Youth' they feel precisely wrong: Conrad is not hiding anything or anybody (or himself), he is dramatizing a clearly, affectionately perceived young Marlow: and he is not dealing in obscurities. The 'meaning' of 'Youth' does not have to be worked for. The young Marlow undergoes a rite of passage from which he emerges a more self-possessed and fully-formed person than he was at the narrative's beginning.

At the climax of the narrative – the moment at which the *Judea* blows up – the 'delayed decoding' which Ian Watt has characterized as a central feature of the narration in 'Heart of Darkness' seems to come into play for a moment. But the decoding is not delayed for very long. The whole process (registration of a sense impression, bewilderment, classification and interpretation of the initial impression) is contained within a single fine paragraph which is also (as is so much of 'Youth') comic:

The carpenter's bench stood abaft the mainmast: I leaned against it sucking at my pipe, and the carpenter, a young chap, came to talk to me. He re-marked, 'I think we have done very well, haven't we?' [he is referring to the crews' efforts to put out the fire in the cargo of coal] and then I perceived with annoyance the fool was trying to tilt the bench. I said curtly, 'Don't, Chips,' and immediately became aware of a queer sensation, of an absurd delusion, – I seemed somehow to be in the air. I heard all round me like a pent-up breath released – as if a thousand giants simultaneously had said Phoo! – and felt a dull concussion which made my ribs ache suddenly. No doubt about it – I was in the air, and my body was describing a short parabola. But short as it was, I had the time to think several thoughts in, as far as I can remember, the following order: 'This can't be the carpenter – What is it? – Some accident – Submarine volcano? – Coals, gas! – By Jove! we are being blown up – Everybody's dead – I am falling into the after-hatch – I see fire in it' ('Youth', pp. 22–3).

Conrad is one of the first to use what would in Modernist literature become a sophisticated technique, the deceleration of time to characterize physical crisis. Notice the way in which Marlow comments on the activity of his mind as he describes his parabola: internal, Bergsonian time is disengaged from external, clock-time for the duration of this disastrous moment in the ship's life. It is followed by a further comic piece of delayed decoding: the young Marlow finds that Mahon stares at him 'with a queer kind of shocked curiosity', and the curiosity is stimulated by Marlow's own appearance. 'I did not know that I had no hair, no eye-brows, no eyelashes, that my young moustache was burnt off, that my face was black, one cheek laid open, my nose cut, and my chin bleeding' ('Youth', p. 23).

Elsewhere the title of 'Youth' becomes a metaphor for the energies that assail the *Judea* (the *Judea* as an old woman, the sea as a vigorous young man):

> It lasted all down the North Sea, all down Channel; and it lasted till we were three hundred miles or so to the westward of the Lizards: then the wind went round to the sou'west and began to pipe up. In two days it blew a gale. The *Judea*, hove to, wallowed on the Atlantic like an old candle-box. It blew day after day: it blew with spite, without interval, without mercy, without rest. The world was nothing but an immensity of great foaming waves rushing at us, under a sky low enough to touch with the hand and dirty like a smoked ceiling. In the stormy space surrounding us there was as much flying spray as air. Day after day and night after night there was nothing round the ship but the howl of the wind, the tumult of the sea, the noise of water pouring over her deck. There was no rest for her and no rest for us. She tossed, she pitched, she stood on her head, she sat on her tail, she rolled, she groaned, and we had to hold on while on deck and cling to our bunks when below, in a constant effort of body and worry of mind ('Youth', p. 10).

I have quoted a complete paragraph to display a feature which is characteristic of all Conrad's major work: the shaping of the paragraph as a literary unit, functioning in the way that a stanza functions in a lyric poem. The accumulation of verbs propels the reader towards the firm closure, or coda, of the final phrase: 'constant effort of body and worry of mind'. Another paragraph – too long to quote in full here – gives a painter's account of the changing appearance of the burning ship as night gives way to day: 'Between the darkness of earth and heaven she was burning fiercely upon a disc of purple sea shot by the blood-red play of gleams. . . . At daylight she was only a charred shell, floating still under a cloud of smoke and bearing a glowing mass of coal within' ('Youth', pp. 34–5). Elsewhere in this story the shaping of the paragraphs is less successful, punctuated by obtrusive reminders that Marlow is telling his story to a group of friends: an example of that is the paragraph which begins 'We fought the fire and sailed the ship too as carefully as though nothing had been the matter' and ends 'And we had to be careful with the water. Strict allowance. The ship smoked, the sun blazed. . . . Pass the bottle' ('Youth', p. 21). 'Pass the bottle' is too abrupt, a mark of Conrad's inexperience with this narrative device of which in the later Marlow narrations he was to make himself so consummate a master. Here the machinery of the told tale creaks, the reader's attention is violently directed back from Marlow to the frame. But the conclusion of 'Youth' is both artistically perfect and autobiographically moving. The *Judea* catches fire, the situation becomes irretrievable, and the crew take to the ship's three boats. Marlow is in charge of the smallest boat: a fourteen-foot 'cockle-shell' with two men aboard and some provisions. This is his 'first command'. It fills him with pride and a sense of competitiveness, and he determines to make landfall before the other two boats. He and his crew of two spend nights and days 'knocking about in an open boat. . . . We pulled, we pulled, and the boat seemed to stand still, as if bewitched within the circle of the sea horizon' ('Youth', p. 36). As we have seen, the few hours that it took the crew of the *Palestine* to reach Muntok have been extended into a passage of several days to Java.

In September 1898 took place a decisive meeting which established a relationship central to Conrad's writing life for the next ten years. He met Ford Madox Ford, at that time known as Ford Madox Hueffer, at Edward Garnett's house, the Cearne, near Limpsfield, in Surrey (Ford Madox Hueffer changed his name to Ford Madox Ford in 1919: for simplicity I shall refer to him henceforth as Ford). Ford's father was Francis Hueffer, a cultivated German immigrant who had become music critic of *The Times*; his mother was the daughter of Ford Madox Brown, the Pre-Raphaelite painter, who was a dominant figure in Ford's childhood. Ford was brought up in the latter end of the Pre-Raphaelite movement to believe that the arts were paramount and the vocation of the artist supreme. He was re-lated to the Rossettis and his childhood companions included, as we have seen (p. 72), his cousins, the self-styled 'anarchist' children of William Michael Rossetti (a staid civil servant, much embarrassed by his offsprings' fledgeling radicalism), and the Garnett family, who also had radical polit-ical sympathies: Constance Garnett, Edward's wife, was a distinguished translator of Russian writers, and a sympathizer with anti-Tsarist Russian political activists, several of whom became personal friends of the Garnett family. Ford himself was precocious: by the age of twenty he had pub-lished four books and had eloped with and married (unwisely, as it turned out) a strong-willed doctor's daughter, Elsie Martindale. When he and Conrad met, then, Ford was a gifted young man of letters from a back-ground of brilliant and distinguished late Victorian artists and intellectu-als. Beside this young man Conrad looked a sober, even dull, figure: a respected middle-aged writer enjoying an established reputation among the discerning, but jaded by unrelentingly disappointing sales of his books. The disparity between them contributed to the mutual attraction. Although Ford was later to be spiteful about Conrad (especially, as we have seen, in *The Simple Life Limited*), at this time his attitude to the older man was all enthusiasm and generosity. (There are many things to be said against Ford but lack of generosity is not one of them.) He had recently inherited some money and felt, no doubt, that he had the world very much at his feet for one so young: he liked to adopt a patrician style and conduct himself *de haut en bas*, especially with new acquaintances with whom he might feel uneasy (this was to make him many enemies). The notion that Conrad was a difficult foreign genius who needed his help appealed to his incurable desire to patronize. Ford liked to quote against himself a remark of Stephen Crane's: 'You must not mind Hueffer, that is his way. He patronizes me; he patronizes Mr Conrad; he patronizes Mr James. When he goes to Heaven he will patronize God Almighty, but God Almighty will get used to it for Hueffer is all right!'[4]

In his account of his first meeting (in Garnett's garden) with Conrad, Ford stresses the latter's foreignness:

> Conrad came round the corner of the house. I was doing something at the open fireplace in the house-end. He was in advance of Mr Garnett who had gone inside, I suppose, to find me. Conrad stood looking at the view. His hands were in the pockets of his reefer-coat, the thumbs sticking out. His black, torpedo beard pointed at the horizon. He placed a monocle in his eye. Then he caught sight of me. I was very untidy, in my working clothes. He started back a little. I said: 'I'm Hueffer.' He had taken me for the gardener.
>
> His whole being melted together in enormous politeness. His spine inclined forward; he extended both hands to take mine. He said: 'My dear faller . . . Delighted . . . *Ench* . . . *anté*!' He added: '*What* conditions to work in. . . . Your admirable cottage. . . . Your adorable view. . . .'
>
> It was symbolic that the first remark he should make to me should be about conditions in which to work. Poor fellow: work was at once his passion and his agony and no one, till the very end of his life, had much worse conditions.[5]

Ford here, with a touch of malice, plays up Conrad's conspicuous foreignness for comic effect. But the comedy is somewhat two-edged in that Ford was also 'foreign' (and one may note here that it was courageous of him to retain his Geman surname, 'Hueffer,' while fighting for the British army in the Great War). It was perhaps in compensation for his foreignness that he cultivated what Alan Judd calls his Grand Manner, speaking languidly with an elaborate upper-class drawl. He liked the idea that Henry James had drawn on his own personality for the typical Englishman, Merton Densher.[6] He says that James 'did indeed confess to having drawn my externals in Morton [sic] Densher of *The Wings of the Dove* – the longish, leanish, loosish, rather vague Englishman who, never seeming to have anything to do with his days, occupied in journalism his night hours'.[7] So part of the attraction of Conrad, for Ford, was the flattering foil that Conrad's obvious foreignness offered to Ford's elaborately cultivated gentlemanly English demeanour.

The immediate result of the meeting was that Conrad moved into a house which was sublet to him by Ford; the house was a medium-sized cottage in the country, called Pent Farm, near Hythe in Kent. Conrad was unhappy in Stanford-le-Hope. Ford knew that the Pent was a good house for a writer to live in and it is a characteristic instance of his generosity that he offered it to Conrad, and moved himself and his wife out into a less satisfactory house. Ford was mendacious, power-hungry and sentimental but throughout his life he was loyal to his self-imposed duty to promote the cause of art, and – further – he very soon came to love Conrad. Conrad did not, and perhaps could not, respond in kind. Alan Judd remarks that he accepted Ford's willingly offered services without much thought of reciprocating: he borrowed Ford's money and didn't repay it, accepted Ford's efforts on behalf of his work without seeing any necessity to help Ford with his own work, and never thought to dedicate a book to Ford.[8] This last, perhaps minor, point was the kind of thing Ford cared about, and Conrad's behaviour in this matter looks a bit callous: Ford could reasonably have supposed that he was more important in Conrad's writing life than such dedicatees as Krieger and Hope. When he caricatured Conrad in *The Simple Life, Limited* Ford was suffering the hurt of a rejected lover. That doesn't make the book defensible but it helps to make it understandable.

The move to Pent Farm was beneficial to Conrad in a number of ways. The rent was cheap (twenty pounds a quarter, payable to Ford; it was not always paid), and the location brought him fairly close geographically to a number of other writers who live in the South–East corner of England in the Kent and Sussex countryside: Ford himself, of course, Stephen Crane, H. G. Wells, W. H. Hudson, Kipling and Henry James. The move seems to have jolted Conrad out of the depressive trap in which he found himself confined by *The Rescue* (or 'The Rescuer').[9] Conrad's temperament was such that to be (precisely) worshipped, to enjoy a relationship with a talented younger man whose posture in relationship to himself was one of slavish discipleship, helped to lift him out of his depression and to stem the seeping-away of his constantly leaking self-esteem. The relationship throughout his ten years' association with Ford was a power-relationship in which Conrad was usually the stronger partner. This state of things suited him. Jocelyn Baines regarded Conrad's friendship with Ford as 'the most important event in Conrad's literary career'[10] but Najder thinks that this is an exaggeration and that the relationship with Garnett was more important for Conrad as a writer.[11] My own view is that Baines (and Bernard Meyer[12]) are right to stress the degree which the friendship and collaboration with Ford boosted Conrad's confidence. To emphasize, as Najder does, the importance of the friendship for Ford[13] is not necessarily to diminish its importance for Conrad.

The relationship with Garnett was slightly edgy in that Garnett offered criticisms of Conrad's work which were not always welcome. It is significant that the manuscript of *The Nigger of the 'Narcissus'* is annotated in pencil by Garnett who proposes a number of changes and criticizes Conrad's sailors' diction as unidiomatic in several places. Conrad resisted most of

Garnett's proposed changes. I think we can see here Conrad's ego sustaining some damage from Garnett, a very early indication of the divisions which much later, at the time of *Under Western Eyes*, caused Conrad to distance himself from the younger man. The relationship with Ford seldom represented a threat to Conrad's ego. Conrad received from Ford relief from the depressing isolation of a writer's life (made worse by his choice of a remote house in the country), convivial male company, daily contact with another literary mind, direct practical help with his writing, financial help, and not least a model of facility: Ford wrote fast and he would sit down and write every morning, come what may, and this helped Conrad to overcome his recurrent virulent writing block and pace his own writing. Ford always rose to a crisis: on 23 June 1902 Conrad was writing the second instalment of 'The End of the Tether' at the Pent and an oil-lamp exploded and destroyed much of the work. It also damaged the table on which Conrad was working, which happened to be one of Ford's precious heirlooms; it was designed for his grandfather Ford Madox Brown by William Morris.[14] Najder thinks Conrad may have lied about the amount of work destroyed in this accident in order to keep himself out of trouble with *Blackwood's Magazine* for being behind schedule.[15] 'The End of the Tether' was being serialized in *Blackwood's Magazine* and Conrad was close to the deadline for the instalment; Ford (by his own account) set up a rescue operation whereby he and Conrad wrote the story together day and night in adjacent cottages. This story may have been heightened (as Ford's testimony often is) but it reads as though it is essentially true.[16]

For the first few months of 1904 Ford Madox Ford can be found metaphorically carrying Conrad on his back: because Conrad was prostrated with depression Ford provided fifteen manuscript pages of *Nostromo*, again to catch a dead-line for serialisation (part of part II, chapter 5, published in *T. P.'s Weekly* on 9 April, 1904). Ford says that he actually composed this section of the novel, and there is no reason to disbelieve that. The manuscript, in the Beinecke Rare Book and Manuscript Library at Yale, does not look as though it is taken from dictation, and the editing required to tie it in with Conrad's text is consistent with the notion that it is Ford's original work.[17] Ford was also taking autobiographical pieces (later *The Mirror of the Sea*) from Conrad's dictation in the evenings and collaborating with him on a one act play.[18] Ford recalls that these months were 'the most terrible period of Conrad's life and of the writer's' and that the worst burden was 'the absolute necessity of carrying Conrad every afternoon through a certain quantum of work without which he must miss his weekly instalments in the popular journal [*T. P.'s Weekly*]'.[19]

Conrad and Ford collaborated on three books, *The Inheritors* (1901), *Romance: A Tale* (1903) and *The Nature of a Crime* (1924; most of this last novel is Ford's work. He was unable to find a publisher for it and published it himself in serial form in the *English Review*, 1909, under the pseudonym Ignatz von Aschendrof). The plan to collaborate came from Conrad, as a letter to W. E. Henley (18 October 1898) makes clear. Conrad says that 'When talking with Hueffer my first thought was that the man there who couldn't find a publisher had some good stuff to use and that if we worked it up together my name, probably, would get a publisher for it. On the other hand I thought that working with him would keep under the particular devil that spoils my work for me as quick as I turn it out (that's why I work so slow and break my word to publishers)'.[20] The 'good stuff' was the story about pirates which Ford had written as the first draft of 'Seraphina' (later *Romance*). Conrad invited Ford to read this aloud to him at Pent Farm in November 1898. In October 1899 collaboration began in earnest when Ford visited Pent Farm to read out the first chapters of *The Inheritors* (*Romance* had been set aside).[21] Ford's version of the way in which they came to collaborate is characteristically self-serving:

Conrad confessed to the writer that previous to suggesting a collaboration he had consulted a number of men of letters as to its advisability. He said that he had put before them his difficulties with the language, the slowness with which he wrote and the increased fluency that he might acquire in the process of going minutely into words with an acknowledged master of English . . . He had said to Henley – Henley had published the *Nigger of the Narcissus* [sic] in his Review – 'Look here. I write with such difficulty: my intimate, automatic less expressed thoughts are in Polish; when I express myself with care I do it in French. When I write I think in French and then translate the words of my thoughts into English. This is an impossible process for one desiring to make a living by writing in the English language . . .' And Henley, according to Conrad on that evening, had said: 'Why don't you ask H. [i.e. Hueffer/Ford] to collaborate with you. He is the finest stylist in the English language of today. . . .' The writer, it should be remembered, though by ten or fifteen years the junior of Conrad was by some years his senior at any rate as a published author, and was rather the more successful of the two as far as sales went. Henley obviously had said nothing of the sort [but Ford has taken care to 'quote' it, nonetheless].[22]

Henley had greeted news of of the Conrad/Ford collaboration with dismay (hence Conrad's letter) and others expressed doubt: Edward Garnett, who had known Ford from childhood and got on with him well enough but had never really liked or trusted him, was certain that it was a mistake. H. G. Wells cycled over to Aldington, where Ford was living in 1899, to tell him that he would destroy Conrad's 'delicate oriental style', and Henry James (after the publication of *The Inheritors*) said to Olive Garnett: 'To me this is like a bad dream which one relates at breakfast. Their traditions and their gifts are so dissimilar. Collaboration between them is to me inconceivable'.[23] The collaboration wasted a great deal of time and would often cause vexation: see Conrad's letter to Pinker, 6 January 1902, where he complains that he is having to do all the work on 'Seraphina' because Ford has choked on a chicken bone and that consequently his, Ford's, 'nerves [are] all to pieces' and he is 'totally unable to work'. Conrad himself is 'nearly going mad with worry' (Ford and Conrad were competitive about their illnesses).[24] But much of the time they found each other good fun and good company. One of Ford's best anecdotes gives the atmosphere:

> I remember once we had been struggling with *Romance* for hours and hours, and he had been in complete despair, and everything that I had suggested had called forth his bitterest gibes, and he was sick, and over ears in debt and penniless. And we had come to a blank full-stop – one of those intervals when the soul *must* pause to breathe and love itself have rest. And Mrs Conrad came in and said that the mare had trotted from Postling Vents to Sandling in five minutes – say, twelve miles an hour! At once, there in the room was Conrad-Jack-ashore! The world was splendid; hope nodded from every rosebud that looked over the window-sill of the low room. We were going to get a car and go to Canterbury; the mare should have a brand-new breeching strap. And in an incredibly short space of time – say, three hours – at least half a page of *Romance* got itself written.[25]

When he was not depressed Conrad could acknowledge the value of this friendship: on 15 April 1902, when the exhausting and exhilarating task of completing *Romance* was about a month in the past, Conrad found that he greatly missed the daily contact with Ford and sent an affectionate letter saying: 'These interrupted relations must be taken up again. The cause of my silence is as usual the worry about stuff that won't get itself written. Vous connaisez cela. I miss collaboration in a most ridiculous manner. I hope you don't intend dropping me altogether'.[26] And on the 20 October 1905, he is found writing to H. G. Wells to say that he has seen no-one recently except his agent, Pinker, and Ford: 'As to Ford he is a sort of life-long habit of which I am not ashamed because he is a much better fellow than the world gives him credit for'.[27] In 1898–9 the immediate benefit of the collaboration with Ford was personal and artistic security, and this contributed to the state of mind in which Conrad was able to dig deep into himself and write, in the last year of the century, his deeply troubling modernist masterpiece, *Heart of Darkness*.

Much commentary has related *Heart of Darkness* to Conrad's biography. A recent example proposes the following view: Marlow's relationship with Kurtz is like Conrad's relationship with his romantic and eloquent father while his relationship with the Chief Accountant, who keeps his books in apple-pie order while anarchy rages about him, is compared with Conrad's relationship with prudent and time-serving Uncle Bobrowski.[28] I think that the novella does indeed draw on deep conflict within Conrad, but that the connection with the pattern of his own relationships in life cannot be as simple as this reading suggests. The relationship between Conrad the man and Conrad the artist is in a sense adversarial or oppositional, as we have seen: the man forms relationships which are in almost every case power-relationships, in which he is either dependent (as with Garnett and Galsworthy) or dominant (as with Ford and Jessie), and in these inter-actions he displays the hysteria and self-pity which are among the charac-teristics of his depression, while at the same time a core of integrated self which is secure behind (and protected by) this acting-out of despair, counteracts the depression by getting on with the central business of writing. In his letters Conrad compares *Heart of Darkness* with his first story based on his Congo experiences, 'An Outpost of Progress', first published in *Cosmopolis* in 1896 (and collected in *Tales of Unrest*). In that story Western imperialism is subjected to very direct ironic scrutiny: two middle-class Belgians in charge of a trading station on the Congo, Kayerts and Carlier, go to pieces in their isolation and quarrel over their diminishing sugar supply. Kayerts shoots Carlier and then hangs himself. The closing paragraph of the story reveals clearly its moral thrust: it displays the system which puts these inadequate men 'in charge' of a wholly alien world as politically inept and morally bankrupt. The company steamer arrives and the hanged corpse of Kayerts is discovered: 'irreverently, he was putting out a swollen tongue at his Managing Director' (p. 34). Fisher Unwin, who published Conrad's first two novels, was also publisher of *Cosmopolis*. On 22 July 1896 Conrad wrote to him about 'An Outpost of Progress', saying: 'It is a story of the Congo. . . . All the bitterness of those days, all my puzzled wonder as to the meaning of all I saw – all my indignation at masquerading philanthropy – have been with me again, while I wrote'.[29] On 31 December 1898 Conrad wrote to Blackwood to say that he had a story almost ready for *Blackwood's Magazine,* 'a narrative after the manner of youth told by the same man' and similar to 'An Outpost of Progress' but – as Conrad puts it in what has to be one of the literary understatements of all time – 'a little wider':

> The title I am thinking of is '*The Heart of Darkness*' but the narrative is not gloomy. The criminality of inefficiency and pure selfishness when tackling the civilizing work in Africa is a justifiable idea. The subject is of our time distinc[t]ly – though not topically treated. It is a story as much as my *Outpost of Progress* was but, so to speak 'takes in' more – is a little wider – is less concentrated upon individuals.[30]

What Conrad says in these letters is true to the extent that the moral observations embedded in 'An Outpost' – the Belgians working in the Congo are inadequate and greedy people, the organization that has brought them there is cruel and corrupt – are present in *Heart of Darkness*. Also, there is the intriguing detail that in 1896 (therefore between the dates of Conrad's employment on the Congo and the writing of *Heart of Darkness*) a Captain Rom, station commander of Stanley Falls – the equivalent of Kurtz's inner station – did in reality use the heads of twenty-one 'rebels' as a decorative border for the flower-bed in front of his house.[31] But however garish and horrible the source material, the experience of reading the novella is, of course, not primarily 'documentary' in its focus.

As we have seen, the Conrad who writes the novels is to be distinguished from the Conrad who agonizes in the letters. To give an example of this I want to move forward a little in time to 31 March 1899, when Conrad was writing *Lord Jim* and '*The Heart of Darkness*' (as the serial form of the novella was titled) was appearing in *Blackwood's*. Conrad writes to Garnett partly for reassurance (he wants to know whether Garnett has seen part III of the serialization), partly to apologize for seeming to discontinue his practice of consulting Garnett about every detail of his writing; he was not sending Garnett his current manuscripts. The self portrait in this letter is a self who both is depressive and equally knows that he is depressive and is using that knowledge to characterize himself and thus to manipulate his friend into a relationship which is essentially ambivalent; he seeks both intimacy and distance, he feels the relationship with Garnett both as a loving relationship in which Garnett is the nurturing parent and Conrad is the gifted child, and as a power-struggle in which Garnett is a punitive parent and Conrad is a rebellious child. A diminished sense of one's own reality can be a characteristic of depression and is often associated with, perhaps caused by, a relationship with a powerful parent (whether nurturing or punitive). Further, the imagery of this letter echoes the imagery in which Marlow expresses his relationship with Kurtz in *Heart of Darkness*:

> in Sorrow and tribulation
> Dearest Garnett. What do you think of me? Think I love you though I am a dumb dog or no better than a whining dog. There's not a bark left in me. . . . Have you seen p. III [Part Three] of *H of D* [*Heart of Darkness*]? My dear fellow I daren't sent you my *MS.* I feel it would worry you. I feel my existence alone worries you enough. . . . Fact is I am not worthy to take up your thought. The more I write the less substance do I see in my work. The scales are falling off my eyes. It is tolerably awful. And I face it, I face it but the fright is growing on me. My fortitude is shaken by the view of the monster. It does not move; its eyes are baleful; it is as still as death itself – and it will devour me. Its stare has eaten into my soul already deep, deep. I am alone with it in a chasm wih perpendicular sides of black basalt. Never were sides so perpendicular and smooth, and high. Above, your anxious head against a bit of sky peers down – in vain – in vain. There's not rope long enough for that rescue.[32]

The manuscript of *Heart of Darkness*, now in the Beinecke Library, Yale, is written in pencil, clearly at great speed, and with a confidence and flow which argue that the inner core of Conrad the writer had 'found himself' and was stabilized by the network of marriage and friendships within which he was now established, and which argue also that the use of Marlow as narrator has cleared an obstacle which has hitherto inhibited Conrad's narratives.[33] The difference between the serial title, 'The Heart of Darkness', and the book title, *Heart of Darkness*, may seem unimportant, but Cedric Watts points out that the latter state has an ambiguity which the former lacks: in its revised state the title means both 'the centre of a dark (sinister, evil, corrupt, malevolent, mysterious or obscure) region' and 'the heart which has the quality of darkness'; if he had retained the 'The' Conrad would have tilted us towards the former reading.[34] My discussion here will be of the novella in its final state, the state in which it appears in *Youth: A Narrative; and Two Other Stories* (1902), but I would like to make some preliminary remarks about the manuscript and the *Blackwood*'s serial publication ('*ms*' and '*maga*').[35] One of the paragraphs cut from both the manuscript and *Balckwood's Magazine* contains a passage in which Marlow recalls the exact words in which Kurtz expressed his desires:

> The memory of what I had heard him say afar there, with the horned shapes stirring at by my back in the glow of fires within the patient woods, those broken phrases came back to me, were heard again in their ominous and terrifying simplicity. [*ms* and *maga*:] 'I have lived – supremely! [*maga* only:] What do you want here? [*ms* and *maga*:] I have been dead – and damned.' 'Let me go – I want more of it.' More of what? More blood, more heads on stakes, more adoration, rapine, and murder.[36]

Marlow says that the heads on stakes surrounding Kurtz's house show that 'Mr Kurtz lacked restraint in the gratification of his various lusts' (*Youth*, p. 131). This wonderfully laconic understatement is deprived of its effect if Marlow is later to recall Kurtz ranting about blood, heads on stakes, adoration, rapine and murder, and Conrad's artistic instinct clearly served him well when he cut the passage. Another clear artistic gain is made by the removal of a long passage in the manuscript about a hotel. Marlow's steamer anchors off the 'seat of government' and he has dinner in the hotel, 'a grey high cube of iron with two tiers of galleries outside.' There is a tram service which runs 'only twice a day, at mealtimes' and this tram brings to the hotel 'I believe the whole government with the exception of the governor general down from the hill to be fed by contract':

> They filled the dining room, uniforms and civil clothes[,] sallow faces, pur- poseless expressions. I was astonished at their number. An air of weary bewilderment at finding themselves where they were sat upon all the faces, and in their demeanour they pretended to take themselves seriously just as [did] the greasy and dingy place that was like one of those infamous eating shops you find near the slums of cities, where every thing is suspicious, the linen, the crockery, the food[,] the owner[,] the patrons.[37]

Conrad was obviously right not to let this passage stand (I have quoted a small but representative part of it). The passage does not 'fit'. It is at odds with the prevailing sparseness of the novella's settings: the appearance of a hotel, a tram service, and a large number of sallow officials in the middle of the jungle feels unaccountable. In the final text the places Marlow visits are much more primitive than this and any development that is taking place is at a much earlier stage (the building of the railway, for example). Also, it is firmly established in the reader's imagination that the direction of the colonizing and trading activities on the great African river (the Congo, never thus named in the text) emanates from the 'Company's offices' in a European city, the 'whited sepulchre' (Brussels, not named in the text; p. 55). Further, the consistency of Marlow as a personality comes under pressure in this passage: it seems very odd indeed that the tough, amiable, laconic man of action should be found reacting to a scruffy hotel like a peevish tourist. Biographically, though, this bit of the manuscript tells us a good deal. Norman Sherry points out that the Congo was much more heavily populated and developed than it appears to be in Conrad's novella.[38] Najder remarks that Sherry's sources have led him to overstate the case somewhat, and that in the course of his journey up the Congo Conrad could well have thought that the villages were as primitive and sparsely populated as they are in the novella.[39] But the cutting of the passage about the hotel in the seat of government supports Sherry. The Congo did in reality have a seat of government (Boma) and it is to this (again unnamed) place that Conrad refers in his text. By cutting out all the detail he plays down evidence of 'civilization', and I think we can take it that a similar editing of his recollection has taken place throughout the novella. The impact of the Europeans is to be seen exclusively as mindless cruelty. Evidence of the *successful* construction of, say, a railway, or of well-organized settlements, would present imperialism in a light too ambivalent for the fiction to bear.[40] We must remember that by the very fact of accepting employment by the Belgians in the Congo in 1890 Conrad was in effect aligning himself with the Western exploiters. Marlow does the same. It is clearly necessary that Marlow's collusion with the oppressors should be played down, and that he should see all Belgian commercial and colonial activity negatively. Conrad gives himself legitimate artistic assistance by simplifying the complex historical reality that he had himself encountered.

The author of *Heart of Darkness* is, as I have suggested, a man who has won a new confidence in himself as an artist, and this confidence enables him to examine what I take to be one of the central preoccupations of the novella. A person who suffers from depression characteristically becomes disengaged from reality. *Heart of Darkness* explores this state of disengagement, and displays one well-known way of dealing with it: as Freud writes in *Civilization and its Discontents*, 'No other technique for the conduct of life attaches the individual so firmly to reality as laying emphasis on work; for his work at least gives him a secure place in a portion of reality, in the human community'.[41] This seems to be anticipated by Marlow's perception of work as therapy: 'I don't like work – no man does – but I like what is in the work, – the chance to find yourself. Your own reality – for yourself, not for others – what no other man can ever know' (p. 85). For much of the text of *Heart of Darkness* 'reality' (or an equivalent) is that which contrasts with the experiences encountered by Marlow. The 'aunt' in the European city who has got Marlow his job with the Company, as Marguerite Poradowska had helped Conrad in 1890, uses the idiom of the Company:

I was . . . one of the Workers, with a capital – you know. Something like an emissary of light, something like a lower sort of apostle. There had been

a lot of such rot let loose in print and talk just about that time, and the
excellent woman, living right in the rush of all that humbug, got carried off
her feet. She talked about 'weaning those ignorant millions from their horrid
ways' (p. 59).

And Marlow reflects that the aunt's immersion in the Company's rhetoric
has distanced her from 'fact', and that this distancing is characteristic of
the female mind:

> It's queer how out of touch with truth women are. They live in a world of
> their own, and there had never been anything like it, and never can be. It
> is too beautiful altogether, and if they were to set it up it would go to pieces
> before the first sunset. Some confounded fact we men have been living
> contentedly with ever since the day of creation would start up and knock
> the whole thing over (p. 59).

There is a mismatch between language and reality. Marlow is very confident about the nature of the mismatch, and it is a mark of his confidence
that we feel no need to attend here to the difficulty that within a literary
text reality, however understood, is itself inevitably embodied in language.[42]
'Some confounded fact', 'knock the whole thing over': these phrases belong
to a pragmatic man-of-action idiom which is – if we stop to think about it
– almost as ritualized as the rhetoric of the Company's publicity. Similar
mismatches are confidently observed by Marlow as he makes his journey:
a code rooted in European law attaches to the descriptive terms – 'enemies',
'criminals' – which are to the Africans' perception meaningless and to
Marlow's perception absurd. Kurtz's young Russian disciple adds to this
list the word 'rebels' to describe Kurtz's victims, and here the mismatch
for Marlow between language and reality becomes so intense that it
detonates in mirth: 'I shocked him excessively by laughing. Rebels! What
would be the next definition I was to hear? There had been enemies,
criminals, workers – and these were rebels. Those rebellious heads looked
very subdued to me' (p. 132). It is because his sense of himself is grounded
in 'reality', thus (in the examples hitherto given) confidently known, that
Marlow equates lying with death: 'You know I hate, detest, and can't bear
a lie, not because I am straighter than the rest of us, but simply because
it appals me. There is a taint of death, a flavour of mortality in lies' (p.
82). To disengage language from reality – to tell lies – is to undo the self
and court disintegration.

But Marlow does lie, of course, both by letting the Mephistophelean
brick-maker believe that he, Marlow, has influence at the Company's head
office in Brussels and by assuring Kurtz's 'Intended' that her name com-
prised Kurtz's dying utterance. And his description of the first of these lies
causes a kind of disturbance in the text as though that memory of having
lied immediately causes Marlow to lose both his control of his narrative
and his sense of self: 'Do you see him [Kurtz]? Do you see the story? Do
you see anything? It seems to me I am trying to tell you a dream. . . . It
is impossible to convey the life-sensation of any given epoch of one's

existence – that which makes its truth, its meaning – its subtle and penetrating essence. . . . We live, as we dream – alone . . .'(p. 82).

This knowledge – that the apparently secure and confident self can be
experienced as isolated and unstable – presses upon the reader as he or
she moves through the text of *Heart of Darkness* until it becomes the novella's alternative 'reality', the reality experienced by Marlow when, in the
course of his great dialogue with Kurtz, he finds himself plunged into a
condition of moral relativity. This is, of course, an enriching and intellec-
tually enhancing as well as a disturbing and frightening experience.

I have said that in terms of Conrad's biography I see *Heart of Darkness*
as the work in which Conrad became strong enough to confront his own
psychological illness. He confronts it most courageously, I believe, at the
point at which Marlow recognizes both that Kurtz is mad and that he,
Marlow, resembles Kurtz more closely than he resembles anyone else.
Marlow's word for this moral and epistemological ordeal is 'terror':

> The terror of the position was not in being knocked on the head. . . . but in
> this, that I had to deal with a being to whom I could not appeal in the name
> of anything high or low. I had, even like the niggers, to invoke him – himself
> – his own exalted and incredible degradation. There was nothing either
> above or below him, and I knew it. He had kicked himself loose of the earth.
> Confound the man! he had kicked the very earth to pieces. He was alone,
> and I before him did not know whether I stood on the ground or floated
> in the air (p. 144).

As earlier, the act of narrating this past crisis immediately precipitates in
Marlow anxiety about his present authority as narrator: 'I've been telling
you what we said . . . but what's the good? They were common everyday
words. . . . But what of that?' (p. 144). In his isolation Kurtz's soul (as distinct from his intelligence) has gone mad, and in his identification with
Kurtz Marlow is forced to come close to sharing that experience, too. The
full force of the 'flavour of death' that accompanies lying is felt here if
one recalls the central argument of the *Preface* to *The Nigger of the 'Narcissus'*: the duty of the artist is to communicate 'truth'. The test of truth
is 'solidarity' (as experienced by the audience with the artist) and the
passing of this test is clearly a matter of moral as well as of intellectual
endorsement. Thus here, to know that Kurtz's soul has gone mad is to
know that he has lost all moral bearings, and the terror for Marlow consists in having to share that loss: 'His intelligence was perfectly clear. . . .
But his soul was mad. Being alone in the wilderness, it had looked within
itself, and, by heavens! I tell you, it had gone mad. I had – for my sins, I
suppose – to go through the ordeal of looking into it myself' (pp. 144–5).

Note the distance that we have come from the Marlow who is con-
soled by the therapy of work and the tangibility of facts. Earlier, when he
encountered *An Inquiry into some Points of Seamanship* 'by a man Towser,
Towson' (the dog-eared book belonging to Kurtz's Russian disciple) Marlow
had felt that the simple old sailor's diction stood in opposition to the

jungle: it gave him 'a delicious sensation of having come upon something unmistakably real' (p. 99). The dialogue with Kurtz has altered Marlow's sense of the status of the 'real'. The plain practical language of Towson's *Seamanship* is replaced for Marlow by an uncomfortable (and sophisticated) awareness of the relativity and slipperiness of language. Kurtz for Marlow is a 'voice' discoursing self-importantly ('My Intended, my ivory, my station, my river' (p. 116)), and Marlow moves seamlessly (as though prompted to do so by his recollection of Kurtz's voice) from description of Kurtz's spoken eloquence to an account of the split in 'reality' that opens up in an extant document: Kurtz's report for 'the International Society for the Suppression of Savage Customs' which, after seventeen pages of enlightened eloquence undermines itself with its 'valuable postscriptum' which, coming as it does 'at the end of that moving appeal to every altruistic sentiment' reads, in Marlow's view 'like a flash of lightning in a serene sky: "Exterminate all the brutes!"' (p. 118). This exposure to a glaring contradiction within a single body of discourse has been part of the education, we may say, of the 'present' Marlow telling his story in 'real' time to the novella's anonymous frame narrator. The Marlow who speaks is different from the young man who was sent to Brussels by his 'aunt' because he has undergone the maturing and educative process displayed in the narrative. He comes to admire and identify with Kurtz and is plunged in to a condition of moral relativity by the encounter with him. But this does not last: Marlow the solid and upright Englishman comes back into place at the account of Kurtz's death, and that it is precisely those qualities in Marlow that cause him, as I see it, to *misread* Kurtz's last words.

Kurtz dies with a phrase which is usually taken to be a judgement on his own misdeeds:

I was fascinated. It was as though a veil had been rent. I saw on that ivory face the expression of sombre pride, of ruthless power, of craven terror – of an intense and hopeless despair. Did he live his life again in every detail of desire, temptation, and surrender during that supreme moment of complete knowledge? He cried in a whisper at some image, at some vision – he cried out twice, a cry that was no more than a breath – 'The horror! The horror!' (p. 149).

The question that I want to ask here is this: how can we know what is going on in Kurtz's mind? The answer is that we can't: we are dependent on Marlow's interpretation. And Marlow asks a question ('Did he live his life again in every detail,' etc.) to which the answer is, conceivably, 'no'. Later Marlow asserts that Kurtz 'had summed up – he had judged', and that his final cry was 'an affirmation, a moral victory paid for by innumerable defeats, by abominable terrors, by abominable satisfactions' (p. 151). But how can Marlow, or the reader, know what Kurtz means by his final cry? He is, after all, a devil, who has been raised like Milton's Satan to a

bad eminence: he has 'taken a high seat amongst the devils of the land
– I mean literally' (p. 116) and he may well here be inverting the moral
significance of vocabulary (as Milton's Satan says 'Evil be thou my good'[43])
and using the word 'horror' to describe that which he admires, enjoys,
and hopes to have more of in the after life. Marlow is a good-natured but
limited person whose moral and epistemological horizons have been extended by his experiences but whose moral balance and good-nature prevail.
Kurtz's hollowness ('the wilderness . . . had whispered to him things about
himself which he did not know . . . and the whisper had proved irresistibly
fascinating. It echoed loudly within him because he was hollow at the
core', p. 131) is compensated for by, so to speak, Marlow's moral fullness.
All we as readers, looking over Marlow's shoulder at the dying Kurtz, can
say confidently about 'The horror! The horror!' is that we don't know
what is going on in Kurtz's mind and therefore we cannot say what his
dying words mean. The moral reading of Kurtz's final words is Marlow's
invention, authorized by nothing but Marlow's innate moral balance.

Marlow then is a limited narrator telling the story of Kurtz from a
perspective which, though enriched by the experience embodied in the
narrative, remains restricted. The upright Englishman who tells Kurtz's
'Intended' that Kurtz's last words were her name believes that he is telling
her a lie, but in a sense he is telling her something which is quite close
to his own perception of the truth, since he believes that Kurtz experienced
a change of heart at the moment of his death: such a change might reasonably have included a revulsion from his negro mistress and regretful
recollection of his girl back in Brussels. But the reader is free to say that
the 'lie' is far more radical a departure from the truth than Marlow realizes
in that there is no 'truth', no agreed interpretation of Kurtz's last words.
This limited narrator operates within a frame. Conrad greatly admired
Wells's scientific romances of the 1890s, and the relationship between
Marlow and the anonymous outer narrator resembles that between the
Traveller and the narrator in Wells's *The Time Machine*.[44] There is a further
parallel with Wells's romance in that, as we have seen, Wells and Conrad
shared a late-Victorian preoccupation with entropy, the belief that the
planet has grown old, that the universe is winding down and that man as
a species is at the end of an evolutionary process. The setting of *Heart of
Darkness* is a yacht on the Thames estuary in the evening at the end of the
century, and the imagery suggests the desolate future in which Wells's
Time Traveller sees man's furthest descendant – a tentacled life-form
bobbing on a beach under a huge, stationary and dying sun. Conrad's
'serenity' is tinged with menace:

The day was ending in a serenity of still and exquisite brilliance. . . . Only the
gloom to the west, brooding over the upper reaches, became more sombre
every minute, as if angered by the approach of the sun. And at last, in its
curved and imperceptible fall, the sun sank low, and from glowing white
changed to a dull red without rays and without heat, as if about to go out

suddenly, stricken to death by the touch of that gloom brooding over a crowd of men (p. 46).

Marlow's remark that 'this also . . . has been one of the dark places of the earth' (p. 47) performs the essential function of linking the frame's setting (the Thames) to his narrative's setting (the Congo) and sets up Darwinian resonances which will echo throughout the novella: white civilized man is contrasted with black primitive man and it is clear that the former is further on the evolutionary path than the latter, but a question about evolution raised by Wells (will man evolve into something like the Martians in *The War of the Worlds*?[45]) pervades Marlow's narrative. Is the white man an improvement on the black man? Probably not. The black man has 'bone, muscle, a wild vitality' while the (French) white man's gunboat is engaged in the futile (and decadent?) activity of 'shelling the bush' (p. 61). The frame tells us that Marlow himself is decadent in the sense of being more sophisticated (further evolved) than other sailors (and than the Marlow who narrated 'Youth'):

> The yarns of seamen have a direct simplicity, the whole meaning of which lies within the shell of a cracked nut. But Marlow was not typical (if his propensity to spin yarns be excepted), and to him the meaning of episode was not inside like a kernel but outside, enveloping the tale which brought it out only as a glow brings out a haze, in the likeness of one of these misty halos that sometimes are made visible by the spectral illumination of moonshine (p. 48).

Terence Cave says that Marlow's narrative is like a sailor's yarn, that although the narrator 'describes Marlow's stories as enigmatic, never following the patten of the typical sailor's yarn' the 'conventions of the yarn' furnish an 'intertextual point of departure for the transformation'.[46] But I think the narrator's emphasis is on meaning rather than form: the typical sailor's story has a punch-line to reach which the narrative has to be unwrapped. Marlow's narrative has no punch-line, it has a significance which is to be observed when we stand back from the whole and appraise it.

The analogy is with a impressionist painting: when we are close to the surface we see brush-strokes, when we stand back we see (to take a famous series from Monet as an example) Rouen cathedral in 1894.[47] But there is also an association with Darwin. Marlow is free to be intuitive and flexible in his story telling, his narrative will itself be a matter of evolution rather than planning. And the central figure in Marlow's narrative seems to change as Marlow speaks. The narrative is in three parts (and first appeared in three consecutive issues of *Blackwood's Magazine*). In part I Kurtz's moral collapse seen as a more extreme instance of the moral decay which characterizes all the Belgians: 'I foresaw that in the blinding sunshine of that land I would become acquainted with a flabby, pretending, weak-eyed devil of a rapacious and pitiless folly. How insidious he could be, too, I was only to find out several months later and a thousand miles farther' (p. 65). While Marlow here lumps Kurtz together with all the other Europeans on the Congo – all flabby and weak – he later sharply contrasts Kurtz with the others.[48] Also, Marlow's focus has changed. As he travels up the Congo so he loses the terms of the earlier comparison: in part I the whites on the Congo are 'flabby' in comparison with other wicked people Marlow has known ('men', still to be admired for their virility). In part III Marlow's narrative tells us that Kurtz's wickedness is a form of strength. One way to express the difference is to return to the comparison with Wells's Martians, which are imagined as man evolved to a point where he is no longer recognizable. Kurtz is a Belgian agent 'evolved' (morally and epistemologically) to a point where the differences between his nature and that of the other agents are far more striking than the similarities. He is – obviously – strong, so strong that Marlow is radically shaken by the encounter with him.

To stand back from Marlow's narrative, as from Monet's painting, and seek the totality of its meaning in its 'glow' or 'halo' is to be struck by its generic strangeness. *Blackwood's Magazine's* readers tended to be army and navy officers and administrators of the Empire, ex-public school middle-class Englishmen who liked to have their self-esteem reinforced by stories about people like themselves: men of action doing good jobs in hazardous circumstances. Both the frame and the publication in *Blackwood's* set up expectations: this is to be a sequel to 'Youth' and a story of a white man's adventure in the bush. Part I signals that the expectations will be subverted – Marlow looks like a Buddha, a prophetic and mystical figure, and his story is untypical of sailor's yarns – and parts II and III force us to make a fundamental change in the way we read and to attend not to the subject of the tale but to the manner of the telling. I do not mean by this that I agree with Hillis Miller that the text is so elusive that one cannot locate its narrator. Hillis Miller writes: 'It is as though the story were spoken or written not by an identifiable narrator but directly by the darkness itself'.[49] This seems to me simply wrong: the narrator is always identifiable and the novella remains a dramatic work, but its focus is not where one expects it to be. It looks like a quest for Kurtz but it turns out to be 'about' Marlow. We, as readers, share the moral dislocation and recovery that Marlow undergoes and are ourselves modified by our engagement with the text.

We can break through the complexity and obscurity to a point from which meaning can be perceived.[50] We accompany Marlow through an experience which brings him to a nervous breakdown – a condition of moral and psychological collapse in which he feels wholly alone – and he then gets over this breakdown and recovers his moral bearings, but he is sadder and wiser. I am deliberately quoting *The Ancient Mariner* where the relationship between the Mariner and the wedding-guest is not unlike that of the inner and frame narrators of the told tale, and many features of Marlow's nightmare journey invite us to compare it with that undertaken by the Mariner. But the structures of the two works display an instructive contrast. Coleridge's nightmare is random in form and offers a sense of security which is then terrifyingly withdrawn. The behaviour of the moon in part IV seems to indicate the lifting of psychological torture and a re-engagement with normative experience: 'The moving Moon went up the sky/ And no where did abide:/ Softly she was going up,/ And a star or two beside.' All readers of the poem know that this remission is short-lived, that the terror returns, that the universe continues to behave in inexplicable ways and that the wedding guest's reasons for feeling sadder and wiser after hearing the tale are obscure. By comparison with that the story of Marlow and Kurtz leads from the terrifying to the normative by a more direct route: Marlow is exposed to moral relativity and disoriented by it but finally recovers from it.

Marlow learns that it is right for him, in human terms, to violate what he feels to be his moral integrity and lie to the Intended. The outer narrator makes for himself the further connection: the Thames, like the Congo, leads into 'the heart of an immense darkness' (p. 162). The experience Marlow has undergone is restricted neither to him nor to Africa: it could be undergone by any of us, anywhere and at any time, we could all be made sadder and wiser by it. It is my belief that the now unfashionable approach to the novella offered by Bernard Meyer and Frederick Crews is in fact right: that the novella is, as Crews put it in 1967, 'a clinical document, a record of persisting misery' the subject of which is 'anxiety'.[51] Conrad uses the river journey to put Marlow through a process which is like the process undergone by patients who are in psychotherapy. Marlow in his encounter with Kurtz looks into the abyss, Conrad himself is looking at the core of his depression. Going through this process unlocked Conrad's talent and permitted him to write the masterpieces which followed.

The manuscript of *Heart of Darkness* shows that Conrad made one major division – after part I – for serialisation, but that parts II and III were initially a seamless web, subsequently divided up. The manuscript of *Lord Jim* presents a more complicated picture. Conrad wrote part of the first four chapters – the omniscient narrator's account of Jim – then put it on one side to write *Heart of Darkness* and then, it seems, came back to *Lord Jim* refreshed and invigorated by the cathartic experience of writing his great novella, and ready to use Marlow again in a more extended way. Part of the manuscript of *Lord Jim* is in pencil, like that of *Heart of Darkness*, and there are indications that some of the chapter divisions were determined as Conrad composed, but on the whole the manuscript reads as a seamless web. Most of the chapter and paragraph divisions were imposed on the text retrospectively. Conrad sent a letter to Blackwood saying that he wanted the divisions between the chapters to be indicated very lightly:

> Would it not be better seeing the form of the novel (personal narrative from a third party as it were) to dispense with the word *Chapter* throughout the book, leaving only the Roman numerals. After all, these divisions (some of

them very short) are not chapters in the usual sense each carrying the action a step further or embodying a complete episode. I meant them only as pauses – rests for the reader's attention while he is following the development of *one* situation, only *one* really from beginning to end. I fear however that it may be now too late to make the alteration.[52]

He was, of course, too late: the chapters are headed 'CHAPTER ONE', 'CHAPTER TWO' and so on. Part of the extraordinary originality of *Lord Jim* lies in the fact that the apparently seamless web is 'cut up' in two different ways. In terms of its dramatic organization it has a clear division at the end of chapter 20 – the Stein chapter – where the story of Jim's jump from the Patna and his consequent attempts to hide from public disgrace is replaced by a quite different story, in which Jim makes a successful fresh career for himself as the white ruler of a Malay community: a career which is tragically truncated by Jim's misplaced clemency to an English pirate, Gentleman Brown. In terms of its narrative organization the text cuts up quite differently, into three parts of drastically uneven length: the first four chapters are spoken by a frame narrator, chapters 5 to 35 are spoken by Marlow with occasional interjections from the frame narrator, and chapters 36 to the end are written by Marlow for the 'privileged man' who has been one of the auditors of his spoken narrative. We know that the novel was originally conceived as a short story to make a third item in a volume of Marlow narratives (the first two being 'Youth' and *Heart of Darkness*): the idea of three linked narratives in a single volume may have been suggested by Flaubert's *Trois Contes*. Serial publication of *Lord Jim* began in October 1899. Conrad wrote on 25 November that he hoped that the novel would be finished by the end of the year.[53] Most of the first part of the novel – what Verleun dubs the 'Patna' part[54] – was written before the latter part, the 'Patusan' part, was planned. In February 1900 Conrad was revising the proofs of chapter 18. At that point in the composition his planning was such that the novel would have ended with what is now chapter 22.[55] A trace of this has survived into the final state of the book: at the end of chapter 21 Marlow says 'My last words about Jim shall be few' (p. 225). This should give a jolt of surprise to the reader, since from the evidence of the book that we are holding in our hands it is clear that the story is only just past its mid-point.

The many letters that Conrad wrote while he was composing *Lord Jim* display his changing perception of it as it grew from short story to novel. They also display a degree of self-knowledge. On 26 December 1899 Conrad wrote to Blackwood, 'The tale progresses and in five more days' time it will be still nearer the end which seems well in view now. I say seems, because I do suffer at times from optical delusions (and others) where my work is concerned'.[56] I think we can take this literally: he knows that he cannot trust his own state of mind and that his relationship with reality is precarious. The rest of the letter proves, as it were, the precariousness of that relationship: he still thinks of *Lord Jim* as a short story:.it 'would have hardly the lenght [sic] and certainly has not the sub[s]tance to stand alone; and the three tales, each being inspired by a similar moral idea (or is it only one of my optical delusions?) will make (in that sense) a homogeneous book'.[57] The notion that 'Youth', *Heart of Darkness* and *Lord Jim* have a similar moral idea was not, I think, a delusion.[58] But his perception of the novel's length or 'lenght' (Conrad habitually inverts the English 'th' in his manuscripts) does display 'delusion'. On 3 January 1900 he sends 'a batch of MS. Lord Jim to end Ch XVII' and says that the next batch will be the last.[59] The letters of January 1900 continue to suggest that the end of the novel will come in about chapter 20. The breeziness of his letters to Blackwood and Meldrum about *Lord Jim* contrasts sharply with the anguish and despair in his letters to trusted friends. To Ted Sanderson, 28 December 1899, he wrote 'I am at work but my mental state is very bad – and is made worse by a constant gnawing anxiety'[60] and on 19 January 1900 he wrote to Cunninghame Graham:

> The leaden hours pass in pain but the days go in a flash; weeks disappear into the bottomless pit before I can stretch out my hand and with all this there is an abiding sense of heavy endless drag upon the time. I am one of those who are condemned to run in a circle. Now and then only I have an illusion of progress but I disbelieve even illusions by this time. . . . I have lost all sense of reality; I look at the fields or sit before the blank sheet of paper as if I were in a dream.[61]

Those who are 'condemned to run in a circle' may well be a reference to Dante, *Inferno* III, the source on which Eliot drew for 'I had not thought death had undone so many' in *The Waste Land*.[62] When Garnett wrote to him in the same month praising the novel Conrad reacted with a mix of joy and anxiety, comparing Garnett's treatment of him to the temptation of Christ: 'You frighten me, because were I to let you take me up on these heights by your appreciation the fall before my own conscience's smile would be so heavy as to break every bone in my body. . . . No. I didn't know anything about *Jim*; and all I know now is that it pleases you'.[63] Are we to believe this? I think that the answer is yes and no. I think it likely that the business of writing depressed Conrad so much that he was unable to form an objective judgement and yet, being the fiercely proud and ambitious artist that he was, he cherished a hope which he could scarcely acknowledge – even to himself – that the work on which he was engaged might turn out to be the best to date. It is characteristic of him – especially when writing to Garnett – to express his anxiety and ambition through a mask of mock-despair. On 26 March 1900 he wrote to Garnett:

> I am still at *Jim*. . . . I am old and sick and in debt – but lately I've found I can still write – *it* comes! *it* comes! – and I am young and healthy and rich. The question is *will* I ever *write* anything? I've been cutting and slashing whole pars [i.e. paragraphs] out of Jim. How bad Oh! how bad! Why is it that a weary heaven has not pulverised me with a wee little teeny weeny thunderbolt?[64]

In May 1900 Conrad finally acknowledged with his conscious mind the fact of which he had been half-consciously aware for several months: that *Lord Jim* was too long to be published with the two earlier Marlow narrations. But he kept up, as a kind of noble and doomed rearguard action (reminiscent, perhaps, of the Polish nationalist movements of his childhood) the notion that the three Marlow narrations belonged together:

> It has not been planned to stand alone. *H of D* was meant in my mind as a foil, and *Youth* was supposed to give the note. All this is foolishness – no doubt. The public does not care – can not possible care – for foils and notes. But it cares for stories and *Jim* is as near a story as I will ever get. The title will have to be altered to *Lord Jim. A tale* – instead of *A sketch*. And yet it is a sketch! I would like to put it as a *simple tale A plain tale* – something of the sort – if possible. No matter.[65]

He is still thinking of it as 'A tale', not a 'novel' in the full Henry James or Ford Madox Ford sense but something small-scale, though carefully structured, like the stories in Kipling's *Plain Tales from the Hills* (Calcutta 1888, London 1890). The phrase from his letter, '*it* comes!', although triumphal in tone, still suggests half-acknowledged fear: the 'it', the flow of prose, seems to him to 'come' by a mechanism over which he has no control, so that even when writing easily and freely he is possessed by the knowledge that the process might at any moment capriciously halt itself.[66] This self-mocking element, the ability to treat his own captious and fitful relationship with his muse comically shows a surge of self-esteem. But Conrad's confidence was always fragile. Depression contributed, as we have seen, to his agonizing writer's block with *The Rescue* ('The Rescuer') early in 1898. He wrote in a letter to Garnett, 29 March, 'I sit down for eight hours every day – and the sitting down is all [. . .]. I want to howl and foam at the mouth'.[67] Depression returns to impede the progress of *Lord Jim* as he indicates in a letter to David Meldrum, 10–11 August 1899.

> I *never mean* to be slow. The stuff comes out at its own rate. I am always ready to put it down; nothing would induce me to lay down my pen if I *feel* a sentence – or even a word ready to my hand. The trouble is that too often – alas! – I've to wait for the sentence – for the word.
> What wonder then that during the long blank hours the doubt creeps into the mind and I ask myself whether I am fitted for that work. The worst is that while I am thus powerless to produce my imagination is extremely active: whole paragraphs, whole pages, whole chapters pass through my mind. Everything is there: descriptions, dialogue, reflexion – everything – everything but the belief, the conviction, the only thing needed to make me put pen to paper.[68]

The first reference in his letters to *Lord Jim* appears in June 1898, in a letter to Meldrum: he encloses the last page of 'Youth' and the first eighteen pages of 'Jim: A Sketch'.[69] It seems likely that he was working on what eventually became the first four chapters of the novel (the part preceding the Marlow narration) as early as 1896. In the 'Author's Note' of 1917 he refers to the fact that he wrote a few pages about the 'pilgrim ship episode' and then laid them aside, and got them out again when asked for a story for *Blackwood's Magazine*: it was at this point that he saw that the episode 'was a good starting point for a free and wandering tale'. The few pages he refers to must be the twenty-eight pages of ms. called 'Tuan Jim: A Sketch': these pages are in a leather-bound album which had belonged to Conrad's grandmother, Teofila Bobrowska (some of the pages had earlier been filled with Polish poetry – Conrad obviously inherited the album and used it as stationery. It is now in the Houghton Library, Harvard[70]). This early draft prepares for the disgraceful affair of the *Patna* in a way which corresponds roughly to the first two chapters of the completed novel, and it also contains a seed of the Patusan part of Jim's story. There is a reference to 'the Malays of the village where he (has fancied himself free from the intolerable).' It is these Malays who dub him 'Tuan Jim'.[71] 'Tuan Jim: A Sketch' makes no reference to Marlow. The letter of 4 June 1898 to Meldrum (referred to above) seems to indicate that Conrad was working on 'Youth' and the start of 'Lord Jim: A Sketch' at the same time, and it may well be that the use of Marlow as narrator for most of the novel was established in 1898. The writing was interrupted to write *Heart of Darkness* in 1899, and it progressed quickly – though with a good deal of agonizing – once the novel had begun to appear in serial form in *Blackwood's Magazine*.

Ian Watt suggests that *Lord Jim* was originally conceived as a 'Song of Innocence', like 'Youth', and that after the writing of *Heart of Darkness*, which he describes as 'Conrad's middle-aged Song of Experience' he came back to the writing of *Lord Jim* bringing with him an enriched Marlow, so that this novel becomes in effect 'a dialogue between the two Marlows' (with Jim as Marlow's 'innocent' self and the enriched Marlow as his 'experienced' self).[72] I think this is one of the more persuasive of Watt's comparisons between Conrad's work and that of the romantics (better than his comparison between Wordsworth's *Preface* to *Lyrical Ballads* and the *Preface* to *The Nigger of the 'Narcissus'*) though to my mind Marlow the narrator (as distinct from Marlow the protagonist) is the voice of 'experience' in all four of the Marlow narrations, 'Youth', *Heart of Darkness*, *Lord Jim* and *Chance*. Gail Fraser's study of the first three of these texts ('Youth', *Heart of Darkness* and *Lord Jim*) shows that Conrad's revisions to 'Youth' tended to enrich the significance of its frame. In Marlow's opening comment, 'You fellows know there are those voyages that seem ordered for the illustration of life, that might stand for a symbol of existence' (pp. 3–4) the phrase 'a symbol of existence' was added in the revisions that Conrad made before publication. It is clearly, as Fraser says, a critical phrase which stresses the 'universality of the *Judea*'s quest'.[73] Also, to my mind, the revision elevates Marlow's status as narrator: in 'Youth' he is already (as Ian Watt does not say) like Blake's Bard.

Fraser emphasizes the 'told-tale' device in two early stories, 'The Lagoon,' and 'Karain', as a model in his own work on which Conrad draws successfully when setting up his frame – a narrator presents Marlow who tells a story – for the Marlow-narrations.[74] In English literature the great nineteenth-century example of the told-tale is *Wuthering Heights*, but Conrad departs drastically from that novel's use of the device.[75] In Emily Brontë's novel Nellie addresses herself only to Lockwood: there is no other implied audience. In Conrad's Marlow narrations the immediate audience is the group of four other men listening after dinner or on the deck of the cruising yawl, the *Nellie*. I would think that the chime with the name of Emily Brontë's narrator is no more than a coincidence. Conrad's friend Hope owned a yacht called the *Nellie*, so this bit of the narrative is pegged down in historical reality.[76] Marlow's larger, implied audience consists of the readers of *Blackwood's Magazine* who are thought of – of course – as middle-class Englishmen, officers in the forces or civil servants in the empire. In 'Youth' the outer narrator hears the narrative, and is now imagined as writing it down: 'Marlow (at least I think that is how he spelt his name) told the story' (p. 3). The five men have between them 'the strong bond of the sea' (p. 3) and the same bond is referred to on board the *Nellie* in the fourth paragraph of *Heart of Darkness* (p. 45). I see no reason to think that the frame has changed at the end of chapter 4 of *Lord Jim*, though the outer narrator here does not refer to the bond of the sea and does not itemize the listeners. Marlow is imagined as telling his story in a continuous past, 'willing to remember Jim' on many occasions, 'at length, in detail and audibly', and the narrator is, we take it, isolating one such occasion ('Perhaps it would be after dinner'); it is 'on a verandah' and obviously in the tropics) (p. 33).

Blackwood's Magazine readers, accustomed to stories by 'Zack' and John Buchan, would have found much to relate to in the first instalment of 'Lord Jim: A Sketch' in October 1899. This instalment consisted of the first four chapters: Marlow's voice is not yet heard, but he is introduced by the frame narrator at the end of chapter 4. Readers of the late twentieth century are accustomed to think of *Lord Jim* as a study of guilt, a psychological study and a work of unprecedented narrative complexity: a novel which belongs with Flaubert, Dostoevsky and Henry James rather than with John Buchan and Robert Louis Stevenson. But it belongs to all the genres that these names evoke: it is both a sophisticated study of private experience and a story of action and adventure. It is 'about' guilt and honour; it is also 'about' friendship and work (in chapter 33 Jewel wants to know why Marlow has come to visit Jim in Patusan, and Marlow replies 'friendship, business' (p. 309)). As I have said elsewhere, I agree with Ian Watt that the emotional and dramatic centre of the novel is the Marlow-Jim relationship, a friendship which is dramatized with unprecedented wealth and particularity.[77] The friendship starts in the world of work: Jim loses his job and Marlow intervenes. Marlow finds Jim a number of jobs, but Jim's 'fine sensibilities' and 'sublimated, idealised selfishness' make him a difficult person to help. He is, as Marlow remarks, 'very fine; very fine – and very unfortunate. A little coarser nature would not have borne the strain; it would have had to come to terms with itself – with a sigh, with a grunt, or even with a guffaw; a still coarser one would have remained invulnerably ignorant and completely uninteresting' (chapter 16, p. 177). It is the egotism and sensitivity that bring Jim to the predicament in which he is encountered in the first instalment published in *Blackwood's Magazine*. The *Blackwood's Magazine* reader had the peculiar literary pleasure – as does the reader of Dante or the *Aeneid* – of entering the narrative *in medias res*.[78] The point of entry is an unspecified time during Jim's two years' wandering between the *Patna* incident and his arrival in Patusan (the dramatic dates of his wanderings must be c.1883–c.1886[79]). The omniscient voice presents Jim working as a ship-chandler's water-clerk and keeping his surname secret. His incognito, a which has 'as many holes as sieve' conceals not a personality 'but a fact'. This laconic and somewhat harsh narrator sums up Jim's predicament thus: 'He retreated in good order towards the rising sun, and the fact followed him casually but inevitably' (chapter 1, p. 5).

The bare bones of the story are simple – as Conrad says in the Author's Note, it is about 'acute consciousness of lost honour' – (p. xxxiii) but the treatment is complex. Guerard has written admirably about the coexistence of universality and complexity in the novel. He says that it is universal in that 'nearly everyone has jumped off some *Patna* and most of us have been compelled to live on, desperately or quietly engaged in reconciling what we are with what we would like to be'.[80] It is complex in that the second reading of the novel is entirely different from the first. In the first reading knowledge of Jim's disgrace and his jump from the *Patna* is withheld from us until the end of chapter 9. We would need to be preternaturally alert to pick up what has befallen the *Patna* from the clues dropped into the text before that point. But once we know the bones of the story and go back, we find on a second reading that our attention is pressed back from the content of the tale to the manner of its telling. And, specifically, we find ourselves engaging with Marlow's personality rather than with Jim's and collaborating with Marlow as he tells his tale. We share Marlow's shifting feelings about Jim, and by the time we reach the end of the text we know that the Jim/Marlow relationship is the novel's subject.

Chapter 16 of this novel tells us that the novel is about Jim, and also that it is equally about Marlow's narrative enterprise, the difficulties he encounters as he tells his story about Jim. Chapter 16 contains a paragraph which seems to me central to Conrad's perception of this novel and of all his work hitherto:

It is when we try to grapple with another man's intimate need that we perceive how incomprehensible, wavering, and misty are the beings that share with us the sight of the stars and the warmth of the sun. It is as if loneliness were a hard and absolute condition of existence; the envelope of flesh and blood on which our eyes are fixed melts before the outstretched hand, and there remains only the capricious, unconsolable, and elusive spirit that no eye can follow, no hand can grasp (chapter 16, pp. 179–80).

The artist who has been seen seeking to break out of his isolation in order to find common ground, the conviction of solidarity, with the reader or observer in the *Preface* to *The Nigger of the 'Narcissus'* is closely aligned with Marlow here seeking to break out of his loneliness in order to communicate with and alleviate Jim's loneliness, and learning from experience that it is only when we try to break down loneliness that we discover what an intractable and obdurate thing it is. The universality and centrality of loneliness, so eloquently evoked here by the dramatized narrator, can legitimately be seen as an insight into the human condition which is shared by the novelist. The whole novel, after all, displays human nature triumphing over the condition that is described here: Marlow's spoken narrative describes the way in which he befriends Jim and places him in a setting in which he can redeem his honour and fulfil himself. Marlow's written narrative, describing events which occur some two years after the close of the spoken narrative, displays the tragic aftermath of this: Jim's betrayal by the white pirate, Brown, to whom he has shown mercy, and his sacrifice of his own life for the good of his adopted people.

Lord Jim is both of the 1890s and of the first decade of the twentieth century, both decadent and Edwardian, both part of a weary European consciousness of the decline of the west and an adventure among a new young people. Two portraits of Jim, the first showing him choking back the tears in suicidal despair following his disgrace in chapter 15 and the second showing a proud and happy young man up a remote river with his Malay girl, Jewel, in chapters 28 and 29, reflect the novel's double identity. The *Preface* to *The Nigger of the 'Narcissus'* and *Heart of Darkness* as preludes to this narrative serve to enhance its decadent features in the reader's memory. Like the *Preface*, *Lord Jim* dwells on the problems of human communication, and like *Heart of Darkness* it shows western man as decadent and belonging to a historical and biological evening. Evening in the literal sense is the time of day at which Marlow in both *Heart of Darkness* and *Lord Jim* is imagined as speaking. In *Lord Jim* Marlow speaks after dinner to his circle of late Victorian gentlemen. The scene is very carefully lit, the visual effects of the waning of natural light are dwelt on 'on a verandah draped in motionless foliage and crowned with flowers, in the deep dusk speckled by fiery cigar-ends. . . . Now and then a small red glow would move abruptly, and expanding light up the fingers of a languid hand, part of a face in profound repose' (chapter 4, p. 33). This crepuscular stage on which Marlow speaks is to be imagined by us, I think, throughout his long oration so that when the spoken narrative ends, at the close of chapter 35, the draining of light from the figure of Jim on his strip of sand completes the process that has begun – for the reader's imagination – with the draining of light from the figure of Marlow. The imagery of – and indeed the title of – *Heart of Darkness* are recalled here as Marlow has his last sight of his beloved young friend:

> For me that white figure in the stillness of coast and sea seemed to stand at the heart of a vast enigma. The twilight was ebbing fast from the sky above his head, the strip of sand had sunk already under his feet, he himself appeared no bigger than a child – then only a speck, a tiny white speck, that seemed to catch all the light left in a darkened world. . . . And, suddenly, I lost him . . . (chapter 35, p. 336).

From one viewpoint this is a typical late Victorian male friendship. Ford Madox Ford clearly perceived this: his 1924 memoir of Conrad, published immediately after Conrad's death, rewrites the story of Conrad's life with himself, Ford, cast as an affectionate Conradian friend and narrator. Ford recalls Conrad unfolding one of his romantic 'schemes for sudden and unlimited wealth or for swift and undying glory'. As Conrad unfolds such a plan to a Hythe greengrocer, Mr Dan West, Ford sees the plot of *Lord Jim* being replayed. The grocer 'might have been the Stein of *Lord Jim* contemplating the hero of that wonderful work and saying within himself: "Romantic!" ', while Ford himself 'alas, alas, seems to become Marlowe [sic: it is maddeningly characteristic of Ford that he should misspell Marlow in his book]'.[81] The opening lines of Ford's memoir are written in conscious imitation of the opening lines of *Lord Jim*. Jim is 'an inch, perhaps two, under six feet, powerfully built', advancing 'with a slight stoop of the shoulders, head forward, and a fixed from-under stare which made you think of a charging bull' (chapter 1, p. 3). Ford's Conrad is 'small rather than large in height; very broad in the shoulder and long in the arm; dark in complexion with black hair and a clipped black beard', and on fresh encounters 'He entered a room with his head held high, rather stiffly and with a haughty manner, moving his head once semi-circularly'.[82] Ford Madox Ford's book is, as he says, a 'novel', a 'portrait' and a 'work of art'.[83] There is much justice in Ford's claim that he played Marlow to Conrad's Jim. *Lord Jim* is a novel about work: Jim lands himself in professional disgrace and Marlow, out of goodwill, a sense of moral responsibility and quasi-paternal affection, rescues him. The affection grows, as Jim matures, into warm reciprocal friendship. Ford Madox Ford had been Conrad's closest friend for the ten years of Conrad's highest achievement as a novelist, and, as Arthur Mizener has said, 'there was, beneath Conrad's fierce pride, a real dependence on Ford. It was never a dependence for a knowledge of his craft or for imaginative insight . . . It was psychological support – assurance that these gifts were really his – that Conrad needed'.[84] But unlike *Lord Jim*'s Marlow, Ford Madox Ford is acutely conscious that his friend is indebted to him and feels, in addition, that he has been treated ungratefully. Ford tended to blind himself to the facts, which were that the friendship foundered in 1909 because Ford tried to involve the Conrads in his matrimonial difficulties and also because of Ford's mismanagement of the *English Review*.[85] A further dissimilarity from Marlow is that Ford hated Jessie Conrad (the sentiment was, of course, vigorously reciprocated) and makes no reference at all to her in his book while Marlow gives full weight to the role of Jewel in Jim's life.

Jewel is not much admired by Conrad critics. She is a less profound invention and a less successfully drawn personality than the men in the novel, but it is important that she is there. She is part of the maturing that has been taking place in Jim. Marlow records that he sees 'very little of her' on his visit to Patusan. She is so faithful a wife to Jim that she becomes a mirror or replica of him, resembling him in 'her movements, in the way she stretched her arm, turned her head, directed her glances' (chapter 29, pp. 282, 283). As Jim talks to his friend so Marlow learns that Jewel has saved Jim's life from conspirators animated by Cornelius, and this brings him to his exclamation that his story is 'a love story' (chapter 31, p. 299). A love story *tout court*, an exemplary tale of a perfect couple. No doubt the absolute dedication, service and obedience displayed by Jewel were among the qualities that Conrad expected (and on the whole got) in his own wife.

'A love story': Conrad's great novel is uncertain about its own generic identity.[86] The serial publication was called *Lord Jim: A Sketch*, the first British edition was called *Lord Jim: A Tale*, the first American edition was called *Lord Jim: A Romance* and the first Canadian edition was called *Lord Jim: A Tale of the Sea*. In the letter quoted above (May 1900, p. 98) Conrad is thinking of it as a 'simple tale', a 'plain tale' or a 'sketch'. The generic indecisiveness indicated here carries on through the successive editions: the 1917 Dent edition, the first to carry the Author's Note, has *Lord Jim: A Romance* on the cloth cover and the dust cover but *Lord Jim: A Tale* on the title-page. The opening paragraph of the novel is itself generically equivocal. Who is speaking it? Not Marlow, who does not start to speak until chapter 5, and not 'Conrad', but someone who is a member of the audience listening to Marlow's narration – someone who has his own rule-of-thumb philosophy of solidarity to impart ('we trust for our salvation in the men that surround us', chapter 3, p. 21). Given that the whole narrative is in the past tense, this auditor has heard Jim's story, chapters 5 to 35, and has formed his own, somewhat harsh, judgement of Jim. This speaker's first paragraph establishes Jim's compromised relationship with the traditional hero. He is two inches short of heroic stature, his charging bull appearance and his from-under stare might connote stupidity rather than heroic courage and his dogged self-assertion is directed 'at himself': he may, then, be too self-absorbed to be effective. The last line of the introductory paragraph cruelly places this 'hero' by telling us that he has a precisely defined, socially restricted and somewhat demeaning job: he is a ship-chandler's water clerk. This hero, then, is also an anti-hero. The omniscient narrator has no patience with the anti-hero, who has opted for the soft life of service in the East, and become one of the self-indulgent men who 'loved short passages, good deckchairs, large native crews, and the distinction of being white' (chapter 2, p. 13). Marlow ought to be an advocate of hardness, discipline, protestant ethic, self-reliance. But he isn't: unlike the frame narrator Marlow lingers with a luxuriousness wholly appropriate to the 1890s, the decade of the decadence, over this doomed figure. There is something soft about Marlow himself. He finds Jim attractive because he is strong and also, equally, because he is weak. Marlow's sympathies are excited by Jim's pathos, the fact that he seems about to burst into tears as he makes his confession, by the bewildered and childlike shame with which he 'blurts' out (an exact verb, indicating the speaker is on the point of losing emotional control) the fact that he jumped from the *Patna*:

> He raised his hand deliberately to his face, and made picking motions with his fingers as though he had been bothered with cobwebs, and afterwards he looked into the open palm for quite half a second before he blurted out – 'I had jumped . . .' He checked himself, averted his gaze. . . . 'It seems,' he added.
> His clear blue eyes turned to me with a piteous stare, and looking at him standing before me, dumb founded and hurt, I was oppressed by a sad sense of resigned wisdom, mingled with the amused and profound pity of an old man helpless before a childish disaster (chapter 9, p. 111).

Marlow's lingering accounts for the odd – and, of course, revolutionary – shape of the novel. The question of shape gave Conrad much anguish. He depended on Ford Madox Ford and (especially) Garnett for reassurance and on *Lord Jim* Garnett let him down, complaining, according to a letter from Conrad (12 November 1900), of the 'division of the book into two parts' which Conrad described as the 'plague spot' of *Lord Jim*[87] (the *Patna* and the Patusan sections, as they have subsequently been dubbed[88]). A contemporary reviewer in the *Pall Mall Gazette* voiced a similar complaint, saying that *Lord Jim* 'is a very broken-backed narrative'.[89]

Lord Jim obviously lacks normative chronological sequence: that is the first thing that one notices about it. Lack of ordinary chronology might lead to lack of structure. As though to ensure that we sense structure the novelist has introduced a pattern of balanced and polarized scenes, images and episodes, not all of which will be noticed by the reader on his or her first encounter with the text. Tony Tanner, who is extremely sensitive to such patterns, noticed that the three Europeans who sit opposite Jim 'like three dirty owls' in the life-boat in chapter 10 (p. 123) are balanced by the three judges who have taken away his certificate at the court of inquiry in chapter 6, and that an image used to describe Jim's isolation in chapter 15 – 'he stood on the brink of a vast obscurity, like a lonely figure by the shore of a sombre and hopeless ocean' (p. 173) – becomes reality at the end of chapter 35, where Jim, 'that white figure in the stillness of coast and sea' seemed to 'stand at the heart of a vast enigma' (p. 336).[90] I disagree with Tanner's favourite polarity, in which he declares that Jim is a butterfly and Cornelius a beetle. In chapter 20 Stein makes it clear that in its beautiful adaptation to its environment the butterfly is perfect, while man – a species of which Jim, in Stein's current argument, is the exemplar – is maladapted and therefore restless.

Many symmetries in the novel press themselves on the attention of the alert reader: Jim's passive jump revealed at the end of chapter 9 is balanced by a willed jump in chapter 25, Stein's oracular and triumphal turning towards his butterflies at the end of chapter 20 is balanced by his repetition of the same gesture – but now stoical, defeated and preparing for death ('Stein has aged greatly of late') – at the end of chapter 45. The confession that Jim makes to Marlow, chapters 7 to 17 is balanced by the brief, and cryptic, confession that he makes when he stands before Doramin and takes the death of Dain Waris on his own head; the execution of Jim when he is deprived of his certificate in chapter 14 (a 'hole and corner affair', with 'no high scaffolding, no scarlet cloth', p. 157) is balanced by the formal execution of Jim at the end when Doramin shoots him.[91] Far from being in any way 'weak', the division into two settings and the multiple symmetries determine the reader's response in ways which are both strong and exquisitely skilful. The dramatic focus is deflected from Jim to Marlow and then again from Marlow to Stein. Chapter 20, the chapter in which Marlow takes the problem of finding employment for Jim to his friend Stein, is the pivot on which the whole novel turns. Before Stein's intervention Jim is subjected to narrow, professional judgement (grounded in English law and marine discipline) and is 'romantic' in the bad sense, an overdetermined, passive, weak figure. His reputation, based on his one notorious action, the jump, is that of a coward. After Stein's intervention Jim is re-evaluated in the light of universal judgement (a judgement grounded in humanist ethics, and a judgement which it takes the whole text of the novel to express) and is now seen as 'romantic' in the sense of heroic and daring, a bold and courageous figure who has rescued Patusan. Stein's readings of the words 'dream' and 'reality' mark the change. Stein says

> A man that is born falls into a dream like a man who falls into the sea. If he tries to climb out into the air as inexperienced people endeavour to do, he drowns – *nicht wahr?* . . . No! I tell you! The way is to the destructive element submit yourself, and with the exertions of your hands and feet in the water make the deep, deep sea keep you up (chapter 20, p. 214).

Immediately before this Stein has diagnosed Jim as 'romantic', as though to suggest that Jim's problem is a matter of a perceived gap between imagination and reality. After this speech 'dream' and the 'real' are merged with one another.[92] 'Romantic' is henceforth in the text a morally and dramatically positive term. The manuscript state of this paragraph indicates a crucial revision at this point in the text. In the manuscript Conrad originally wrote 'A man that is born is like a man who fall [sic] into the sea' (Rosenbach MS, p. 431). By crossing out 'is like' and altering the wording to 'falls into a dream like a man who falls into the sea' Conrad removes the distinction between reality and dream which has sustained chapter 20 hitherto. The meaning of the word 'romantic' is forced to alter by this closing of the gap between dream and reality. Hitherto, the dominant sense of the word 'romantic' as Marlow has used it has been 'unrealistic' or 'imaginative'. The *Patna* did not sink. Jim irritates Marlow by imagining how heroic he might have seemed if he had stayed with the ship: ' "My God! What a chance missed!" he blazed out . . .' Marlow sees him here as an 'imaginative beggar!' seeking an 'impossible world of romantic achievements' (chapter 7, p. 83).

Stein at first seems to use the word 'romantic' in Marlow's sense. The perfectly adapted butterfly sits still, but man (Jim) wants to be a 'saint' or a 'devil' and 'every time he shuts his eyes he sees himself as a very fine fellow – so fine as he can never be . . . In a dream' (chapter 20, p. 213). Thus far Stein seems to confirm Marlow's preconceptions about romantics. But then he reverses the argument: we live in dreams, we inhabit them from birth. The leading sense of 'dream' in the 'man that is born' passage is 'the condition in which we, man, generically contrasted with butterfly, find ourselves'. The subsidiary sense of dream, 'that which we desire', is also present, and Stein's continuation of his thought depends on us retaining this meaning: 'That was the way. To follow the dream, and again to follow the dream' (chapter 20, pp. 214–15). 'Romantic' evolves in this chapter, by its association with the mutating senses of 'dream', from referring to that which is escapist and idealistic to referring to that which is heroic and self-fulfilling. The first of these two senses remains part of Marlow's idiom throughout his narrative, as though Conrad wishes to avoid putting undue pressure on our sense of Marlow's dramatic consistency. Indeed, on the last page of the novel, it seems to be the leading sense, and we have to reflect for a moment on the following sentence before we recognize that 'heroic' as well as 'escapist' is contained in its use of 'romantic': 'He passes away under a cloud, inscrutable at heart, forgotten, unforgiven, and excessively romantic' (chapter 45, p. 416).[93]

'Shakespeare! It is enough to pronounce this name and at once a whole world of alluring visions deludes the mind.'[94] To recall Apollo Korzeniowski's essay about Shakespeare is to recall that for Conrad, as for his father, Shakespeare was both the embodiment of English heroic ideals and a romantic writer. *Hamlet* is the Shakespeare play closest to *Lord Jim*.[95] Polonius says 'For Lord Hamlet,/Believe so much in him that he is young' (I, iv, 123–4): Lord Jim and Lord Hamlet are both 'young' in terms of the world. They are in disadvantaged positions and they need help. They are also both 'Lords' in that they have a kind of natural splendour and gentlemanliness which indicates to sympathetic onlookers (Horatio and Marlow) that authority, fulfilment and love will be theirs as of right, and to jealous 'patriarch' rivals (Claudius and Cornelius) that they must be destroyed. They are mirrors of each other in that they both suffer what Conrad in the Author's Note to *Lord Jim* refers to as 'acute consciousness of lost honour' (p. xxxiii). The meaning of 'honour' is bound up with the meaning of the central chapter of the novel, chapter 20, in which Stein explores the question of the nature of Jim's identity. Jim takes a complete Shakespeare with him to Patusan ('best thing to cheer up a fellow') and Marlow would like to have 'Shakespearian talk' with him (chapter 23, p. 237) but there isn't time. There are many verbal coincidences between the play and the novel. Stein quotes the most famous of the *Hamlet* soliloquies[96] but in doing so alters its meaning. He is, as he says, *adapting* Shakespeare: ' "In general, adapting the words of your great poet: That is the question..." He went on nodding sympathetically... "How to be! *Ach*! How to be" ' (chapter 20, p. 213). The soliloquy in *Hamlet* contemplates suicide – whether to be – but Stein rightly feels that 'how to be', how to continue to live, is the central preoccupation of Shakespeare's play. Hamlet says that for right action 'the readiness is all' (V, ii, 216) and Jim refers to this at the opening of his confession to Marlow: 'It is all in being ready. I wasn't; not – not then' (chapter 7, p. 81). Hamlet is recalling his earlier failure to act, to avenge his father's murder, and recognizing that a decisive test of his personality, through action, is approaching; Jim is saying that his disastrous failure, his jump from the *Patna*, happened because he was caught off guard but next time he will be prepared. The stories of Hamlet and Jim are contrasted, of course, in that Hamlet is dishonoured by a shameful inaction – failure to avenge his father's murder – while Jim is dishonoured by a shameful action, the jump from the *Patna*. This of itself might suggest that Conrad is concerned with positive catastrophe and Shakespeare with the dramatision of negation. But in the execution they are closer to each other than one would expect. Hamlet fails to act, Jim acts, but in his account of his action he stresses his passivity. He claims in chapter 10 that the shameful act was effectively forced on him by the other white men in the life-boat: 'I told you I jumped; but I tell you they were too much for any man. It was their doing as plainly as if they had reached up with a boat-hook and pulled me over' (chapter 10, p. 123). And in describing the events leading to the jump he consistently stresses this sense of the body's actions divorced from the mind's control. Honour in *Lord Jim* and *Hamlet* is related both to Greek shame-culture whereby he who strikes hardest gains most honour, and to Stoicism, whereby it is honourable to endure. In Shakespeare's England the revival of classical learning had brought with it the notion that it was proper to be passive in the presence of suffering, but that suicide was nevertheless a permissible extreme response. Hamlet displays stoic virtue; his soliloquy reflects the fact that suicide is a sin in Christian terms but that in some Renaissance writers about stoicism (Montaigne, for example) it is honourable. Hamlet's reasons for seeking death – psychological agony and public humiliation (having been usurped) – are among those that the Stoics found permissible.

The stoic alternatives – endurance or suicide – confronting Hamlet are present throughout Conrad's novel and at the end Jim does, of course, in effect kill himself by surrendering to Doramin for execution. Suicide is

rare in the English novel but common in Conrad (there are fifteen suicides in his fiction): Jim and Heyst in *Victory* are the heroes of two major
tragic novels who voluntarily end their own lives.[97] Brierly, as far as we can
tell, commits a Stoic's suicide: he opts for death rather than dishonour.
The nature of the dishonour remains concealed from us, but the way
Brierly's story is dramatized indicates that it must have analogies with Jim's
story. For much of the novel Jim himself chooses endurance, exposing
himself to the inquiry; this brings his form of Stoicism into direct conflict
with Brierly's. Brierly wants Jim to hide, for shame reasons: 'The fellow's
a gentleman if he ain't fit to be touched,' and he ought not stick it out
at the inquiry, giving evidence 'that's enough to burn a man to ashes with
shame' (chapter 6, p. 67). Brierly urges Marlow to offer money to Jim to
get him away from the inquiry, but Marlow resists because he is positive
in his mind 'that the enquiry was a severe punishment to that Jim, and
that his facing it – practically of his own free will – was a redeeming
feature in his abominable case' (chapter 6, p. 68).

Hamlet and *Lord Jim* are both written at the ends of their respective
centuries (1599–1600 in the case of *Hamlet*[98] and 1899–1900 in the case
of *Lord Jim*), they both deal with an anguished and divided anti-hero, they
both take an existing form – revenge tragedy and the story of imperial
adventure – and adapt it so drastically that the mould is broken and a new
literary form is created. *Hamlet* is both the first major tragedy since the
Greeks and the first modern tragedy, *Lord Jim* is both a masterpiece in a
high Victorian tradition (as practiced by Stevenson and Haggard) and a
psychodrama in a new form: a work which involves the reader with the
narrator and the protagonist in unprecedented ways. In the careers of
Shakespeare and Conrad these two early works are consciously innovative.

There is a strong argument for the view that *Lord Jim* is a self-portrait.
Jim's short life coincides almost exactly with the period of Conrad's early
manhood; Jim was born in 1859 or 1860 (and died in 1889 or 1890),[99]
Conrad was born in 1857 and nearly died (from illness in the Congo) in
1890. Conrad was disabled by a falling spar on the *Highland Forest* in 1887
and hospitalized in Singapore in 1887 (as Jim is hospitalized in 'an Eastern
Port' as a result of a similar accident). Both Conrad and Jim are suicidal;
Conrad shot himself in Marseille in 1878, Jim contemplates suicide at least
twice (once by drowning, immediately following his jump from the *Patna*,
and once by throwing himself from the window in Marlow's hotel room)
and his death is itself, of course, suicide in that it is voluntary. Also Conrad,
like Jim, had 'jumped': he had taken, as we have seen, a 'standing jump'
out of Poland (see above p. 23). Gustav Morf believed that *Lord Jim* was
essentially a confessional novel in which Conrad sought to express, and
cope with, the guilt that he felt over having left Poland. In this reading
much of the novel is to be understood as an expression of Conrad's own
anguish, a dramatized personal confession in which the circumstances of
Jim's story up to his jump are modelled on those leading to Conrad's
naturalization as a British subject. He is 'Lord Jim' just as Conrad was 'Pan

Jozef' to the servants in Poland when he was a child.[100] The sinking ship
is itself Poland, *Patna* being an adaptation of *Patria*. Norman Sherry points
out that a ship called the *Patna* visited Singapore during the 1880s, and
it seems clear that this must have been Conrad's immediate source, but
there is still some force in Gustav Morf's ingenious observation that at a
distance the *r* and the *i* of *Patria* could easily look like the *n* of *Patna*, thus
assisting the identification of ship with country.[101] Given Conrad's known
distress about the article written by Eliza Orzeszkowa attacking him in
April 1899[102] it seems very likely indeed that guilt over leaving Poland is
part of the fuel for the novel: in her attack Orzeszkowa noted that Conrad
'bears the same name and may even be a very close descendant of Józef
Korzeniowski, whose books brought tears to my eyes when I was a teen-
ager'.[103] This Korzeniowski was an early nineteenth-century patriotic writer,
no relation of Conrad; but the suggestion that he had betrayed his country
and besmirched a famous name would have struck deep. It is an important detail of the dramatization of Jim in the novel that he has no surname,
he is a deracinated man in relation to his family as well as to his country.

But *Lord Jim* is not all guilt and it is not all Jim: I see it in a way as a triple
self-portrait, with Conrad as Marlow and Stein as well as Jim. Jim is his
younger self's youthfulness, uncertainty, guilt, ambition and idealism;
Marlow is, as we have said, the Englishman that Conrad would have liked
to have been; and Stein is, in a sense, Conrad as he actually was. Stein is
a projection of the aspects of his social identity that he acknowledged
(reluctantly) to be seen in him by his English friends: not 'one of us' but
an exotic stranger speaking broken English, a wise foreigner with an
adventurous past. Certainly Conrad was fêted by younger men as a sage,
and the oracular quality of Stein's utterances and the way Marlow hangs
on his words and Jim's life is determined by his actions displays the foreignness of which Conrad was always painfully conscious in a flattering
light.

> 'He is romantic – romantic . . . And that is very bad – very bad. . . . Very
> good, too,' he added. 'But *is he?*' I queried.
>   '*Gewiss*', he said, and stood still. . . . 'Evident! What is that by inward pain
> makes him know himself? What is it that for you and me makes him –
> exist?' . . .
>   'Perhaps he is,' I admitted. . . . 'But I am sure you are.' . . . 'Well – I exist,
> too,' he said (chapter 20, pp. 216–17).

It is his inner awareness of himself, qualified by Stein as romantic, that
gives Jim his knowledge of his own identity. Marlow doubts this but
acknowledges, with a surprising access of tenderness for the somewhat
defended figure of Stein, that Stein himself is romantic. In recognizing
this Marlow implicitly acknowledges a degree of romanticism in himself:
each of these three figures, Jim, Marlow and Stein, relates to the word
'romantic' in a slightly different way. The shifts of meaning taking place

between these reiterations cause the word to be stressed by the text in two senses, both emphasised and subjected to modulating pressure. 'Romantic' unites these three men, reinforcing my sense of them as a triple self-portrait, three aspects of the Conradian identity seeking 'solidarity', the re-integration of the suffering and depressed artist.

Marlow first talks to Jim as a result of a misunderstanding outside the courthouse which causes Jim to think that Marlow has called him a 'wretched cur' (chapter 6, p. 70). Marlow has in fact embraced Jim (metaphorically) from his first sight of him, acknowledging him as a fellow professional, 'one of us' (chapter 6, p. 43). At the time of his spoken narrative, chapters 5 to 35, Marlow believes that he is telling a success-story: Jim has redeemed his honour and become a ruler of a native state on a remote island in the far east, like his real life namesake, Sir James Brooke of Sarawak (one of Conrad's acknowledged sources, whom I have discussed fully elsewhere;[104] Conrad wrote to the Dowager Ranee of Sarawak, the widow of Brookes' nephew, on 15 June 1920 to say that the novel had been 'inspired in great measure by the history of the first Rajah's [Brooke's] enterprise'[105]). In his warmth and generosity Marlow refuses to blame Jim, seeing him after his disgrace as a 'dear good boy in trouble' (chapter 16, p. 180), recalls being distressed by the thought that the 'solidarity of our lives' might be upset by Jim becoming a derelict drunkard as a result of his disgrace, and happily – and, of course, prematurely – expresses his pleasure in what he believes to be Jim's present security in Patusan, 'The time was coming when I should see him loved, trusted, admired, with a legend of strength and prowess forming round his name as though he had been the stuff of a hero' (chapter 16, p. 175). *Lord Jim* completes the process embarked on in the *Preface* to *The Nigger of the 'Narcissus'*: the depressed novelist, isolated, feeling unable to communicate and denied 'solidarity' with his readers, has found in this triple self-portrait a model of solidarity, community and integration.

Conrad tended to be defensive about *Lord Jim*. Ian Watt thinks that his readiness to change its subtitles ('A Sketch', 'A Tale', 'A Romance') indicates 'a tendency to take it rather lightly'.[106] It seems to me that absolutely the reverse of this is true: the change of titles, the distance and defensiveness that Conrad displayed over *Lord Jim*, are marks of his intensely high ambition for the work and his corresponding anxiety that it might not attain that ambition. In these respects Conrad is very like his creation: Conrad's pride, ambition and vanity are Jim's pride, ambition and vanity. As we have seen, these qualities account for the defensiveness and ambivalence of his letters to friends describing the novel's progress,[107] and in his letters to Meldrum (who was serializing *Lord Jim* in *Blackwood's Magazine*) once the writing was finished. On 3 April 1900 Conrad wrote to Meldrum that 'Jim is very near my heart' and 12 April he write to say that *Lord Jim* could be cut for *Blackwood's Magazine* if Meldrum so wished, but that Conrad could not bear to make the changes himself: 'I am . . . in such a state of mind about the story – so inextricably mixed up with it in my daily life – that I feel unequal to doing the cutting myself'.[108] If Conrad had really felt *Lord Jim* to be shapeless he surely would have risen to the responsibility of the creator to impose shape, when given the opportunity by his publisher to do so?

Conrad's forty-third birthday, 3 December 1900, was a high point of his career. *Lord Jim* had been published in book form and was selling well, and he had made a start on *Typhoon*. *Lord Jim* was a work of extraordinary modernity, standing at the end of the nineteenth century and at the beginning of the twentieth as a kind of milestone. As Ian Watt remarks, it is a paradox that the works that he wrote during the reign of Queen Victoria should have been his most modern.[109] In just five years of writing he had established himself as a modern master.

To speak of the ending of *Lord Jim* is to speak of something which Conrad both wanted and did not want. Writing the novel was agony to him, he desperately desired to finish it, but equally he did not want to relinquish it until the subject had exhausted all its riches. This tension is reflected in the text. From the Stein chapter – chapter 20 – to the end it becomes increasingly valedictory in tone and expression, repeatedly referring to its own 'last words': 'the last word is not said – probably shall never be said', 'My last words about Jim shall be few'. Those quotations are from the last paragraph of chapter 21 (p. 225). Arbitrary though Conrad's chapter divisions often are, a discernible pattern is emerging whereby the last paragraph of each chapter, from chapter 21 to the end, is valedictory in tone and frames Jim as though the narrative is shortly to take leave of him. At the end of chapter 22 Jim pronounces on his own future, which is to be as though he 'Never existed – that's it, by Jove!' (p. 232). Chapter 23 is a self-contained poem of friendship, starting with Stein's friendship with Doramin, of which the ring is an emblem 'promising eternal friendship' (p. 253). It shows the mixed feelings with which Marlow helps Jim prepare for his adventure in Patusan (he lends Jim a tin trunk and thus catches a glimpse of Jim's Shakespeare as it is tumbled in with his other possessions). The friendship reaches a point of painful tension as they take leave of each other: Jim goes to Patusan, they do not know when, or whether, they will meet again, and the chapter ends with Jim's arrogant and ambivalent cry 'You-shall-hear-of-me' (p. 241). These could well have been Jim's last words, but they are not, of course, because two years later, as we know, Marlow sails to Patusan to inform Jim that Stein is effectively making him a gift of the agency: the last line of chapter 25 sees Jim welded into Patusan by this gift, 'received . . . into the heart of the community' (p. 258). Chapter 26 tells the story of Jim's successful attack on Sherif Ali which is contributing to the apotheosis of Jim: Marlow closes the chapter by saying 'I don't know why he should always have appeared to me symbolic' (p. 265). Similarly valedictory, though less final, phrases haunt the closing paragraphs of the chapters telling the story of his relationship with Jewel, leading to the climactic moment at which Marlow tells Jewel that Jim will not return to England 'Because he is not good enough' (p. 318). The valediction at the end of chapter 35 is a huge and moving set piece: Jim has spoken his last words to Marlow, which are characteristically terse and inarticulate – 'Tell them ... No-nothing' (p. 335), and Marlow in his extended apotheosis of Jim – the passage in which he describes Jim as 'white from head to foot' – provides all that is unspoken at this moment of parting. The friendship and the reputation of the friend are deeply entwined. The last words of all to come from Jim to Marlow appear after his death, in chapter 36; they are written, and Marlow cannot even be sure that they are addressed to him: 'An awful thing has happened ... I must now at once. . . .' (p. 340). Jim's last recorded utterance is addressed to the people he has betrayed and is a clear request for punishment: 'I am come ready and unarmed' (chapter 45). The point of listing these instances is to show that since at least chapter 21 the novel has been hugging its valedictory gestures, reiterating its last lingering looks at Jim to a point where in the hands of any lesser craftsman they could be tedious or risible. The novel clings to the nineteenth century and its values – honour, loyalty, manhood – but knows itself to belong to the twentieth. The slow, reluctant slide away from the figure of Jim marks Conrad's knowledge that he is a modernist caught in a richly generative paradox: his method belongs to the future while his deepest convictions and sympathies belong to the past.

5

From *Typhoon* to *Nostromo*, 1900–1904

Some harbours of the earth are made difficult of access by the treachery of sunken rocks and the tempests of their shores. Sulaco had found an inviolable sanctuary from the temptations of a trading world in the solemn hush of the deep Golfo Placido as if within an enormous semi-circular and unroofed temple open to the ocean, with its walls of lofty mountains hung with the mourning draperies of cloud.

From the first paragraph of *Nostromo*

Lord Jim had critical acclaim, the collaboration with Ford gave Conrad much-needed personal support and (by contrast with his miserable struggle in the last years of the old century with the intractable *Rescue*) the year 1900 was a good one for him. He felt optimistic and 'professional', and it is a mark of this new optimism that he had the confidence to put his career in the hands of a literary agent: in October, 1900, he went to London with Ford Madox Ford to meet J. B. Pinker who was to become for him 'the indispensable Pinker' (letter to H. G. Wells, 20 October 1905[1]), the literary agent who would guide and nourish Conrad's writing and publication for the next twenty years. Pinker began his working life as a clerk in Tilbury Docks before becoming a journalist (his last post in journalism was with *Pearson's Magazine*). In 1896 he started up his own literary agency in Arundel Street. He was not the first literary agent in London – A. P. Watt and Curtis Brown had both started up earlier – but he was the best, with an extraordinary instinct for cherishing 'difficult' writers who would in due course become recognized and successful; his clients included H. G. Wells, Stephen Crane, Henry James, Ford Madox Ford and Conrad.[2] He was the recipient of a huge number of letters from Conrad (which are now in the Berg collection, New York Public Library). These show the extraordinary degree to which Conrad was dependent on him. Pinker advanced Conrad very considerable sums of money and also was required by Conrad to intervene for him in his personal and domestic affairs; bills for such things as school fees, servants' wages and coal were sent to be settled by Pinker. In 1910 there was a quarrel, brought on by Conrad's depression, and thereafter for about six months Conrad saw himself as 'not on speaking terms' with Pinker (Pinker, for his part, never allowed himself the luxury of such *hauteur* in his dealings with Conrad, but he was sometimes provoked into giving the neurotic and prodigal novelist a brisk ticking-off). In due course the quarrel was made up and they became close friends (and were to remain so until Pinker's early death in 1922).

Between 1900 and 1904 Conrad continued to live at Pent Farm as Ford Madox Ford's tenant, and the relationship between the two men continued to be close, producing in fairly rapid succession (as we have seen) the two collaborative publications: *The Inheritors* (June 1901) and *Romance* (October 1903; May 1904 in America). (Once they had finished *Romance* (March 1902) Conrad missed collaboration, as we have seen,[3] and found the writing of *Nostromo* an appalling solitary struggle.)

Lord Jim was completed at 6.00 in the morning on the 14 July 1900. The process had been exhausting and agonizing, but ended in triumph.[4] In the euphoria following this Conrad took a holiday in Belgium with Ford and their two families to work on *Romance*. The euphoria soon evaporated: the two-year old Borys Conrad became ill with dysentery and Conrad himself became gripped by gout and depression. After his return home in later August work on *Romance* continued, but Conrad showed impatience with it: he wrote to Galsworthy, 19 September 1900, saying 'I am drooping still. Working at Seraphina [*Romance*]. Bosh! Horrors!'[5] Conrad escaped from *Romance* into work on 'Typhoon', which was completed shortly before the death of Queen Victoria (January 1901) and published between January and March 1901 in the *Pall Mall Magazine*. In the first six months of 1901 Conrad wrote 'Falk' and 'Amy Foster'. Pinker had trouble placing these pieces for serial publication (which was always desirable because it paid well). In March 1902 *Blackwood's Magazine* refused to publish 'Falk' because of its cannibalism. 'Amy Foster', the theme of which was suggested to him by Ford Madox Ford, was published in the *Illustrated London News* later in December 1901. Too much of 1901 and 1902 was devoted to *Romance*, but in March 1902 Conrad started (at Ford's suggestion) 'The End of the Tether'; this story was to mark his return to *Blackwood's Magazine*.[6]

'Typhoon', 'classed' as Conrad puts it 'by some critics as a deliberately intended storm-piece' (p. vi), is also – often – a comic work. MacWhirr has no rhetorical devices: Jukes says 'I feel exactly as if I had my head tied up in a woollen blanket' to which MacWhirr responds 'D'ye mean to say, Mr Jukes, you ever had your head tied up in a blanket?' (chapter 2, p. 25). This joke – MacWhirr takes metaphors literally – becomes part of the narrative strategy when metaphors become concrete in the text, as when Jukes seeks the ear of his commander. This idiomatic phrase, deploying a metaphor so familiar that it has become inert, is disconcertingly and

comically animated by Conrad's text: Jukes 'poked his head forward, grop-
ing for the ear of his commander. His lips touched it – big, fleshy, very
wet' (chapter 2, p. 44). Jukes and his skipper, MacWhirr, go in for 'solidarity' in the same concretising way: 'Jukes felt an arm thrown heavily over
his shoulders; and to this overture he responded with great intelligence by
catching hold of his captain round the waist. They stood clasped thus in
the blind night, bracing each other against the wind, cheek to cheek and
lip to ear, in the manner of two hulks lashed stem to stern together'
(chapter 2, pp. 45–6). Jukes's ironic intelligence permits both the narrative voice and the readerly mind grazing in the text to feel at one with
him. There is a passing resemblance to the narrative structure of *Lord Jim*:
as Marlow ends *Lord Jim* with a written testament, so Jukes ends *Typhoon*
with his long witty letter to his friend. He closes his letter quoting MacWhirr
as saying 'There are things you find nothing about in books,' and he adds:
'I think that he got out of it very well for such a stupid man' (chapter 6,
p. 102).

Jukes' judgement is callow. MacWhirr certainly makes a mistake when
he chooses to sail the *Nan-Shan* through a typhoon, but this mistake is not
outrageous, given the season – the storm takes place on Christmas day
which is not the typhoon season in the China seas – and the confusing
instructions given by the seamanship manual that MacWhirr consults. To
face the storm for MacWhirr is to act on his deeply held conviction that
'there's just so much dirty weather knocking about the world' and that
'the proper thing is to go through it'; this, the omniscient narrator remarks,
is MacWhirr's 'confession of faith' (chapter 2, pp. 34–35). Having made
this mistake he displays courage, tenacity, practical good sense and administrative skill in dealing with the successive ensuing crises: damage to the
ship, near-revolt from the engineers, loss of nerve on the part of the second officer, fighting between the Chinese passengers when their boxes
of money are broken open by the storm. He requires that the fighting
between the Chinamen shall be stopped and that their money shall be
redistributed as equitably as possible out of a practical moral conviction:
'Had to do what's fair, for all – they are only Chinamen. Give them the
same chance with ourselves – hang it all. She isn't lost yet' (chapter 5, p.
88). The limitations of unexamined late Victorian assumptions about race
('they are only Chinamen') coexist in MacWhirr with exemplary moral
integrity and judgement. The model, whom Conrad encountered in the
1880s, may have had some of these qualities. John McWhir [sic], of County
Down, was master of the iron barque (sailing-ship) *Highland Forest* on which
Conrad served as first mate on a single voyage, from Amsterdam to
Samarang in Java, 18 February to 20 June 1887. In *The Mirror of the Sea*
Conrad refers to this man patronizingly as 'good Captain McW-' and remarks that he was reclusive and eccentric, seldom came out of his cabin
and communicated with his officers 'through the keyhole, as it were' but
always 'in a mild and friendly tone' (pp. 5–6). For his story Conrad keeps
the name, the taciturnity and the Northern Irish origins of the original

McWhir but has aged him considerably. The younger Conrad who wrote *The Mirror of the Sea* is like Jukes in that they both patronize McWhir, or 'MacWhirr', and they are both wrong. Jukes's wit rebounds on him: he judges MacWhirr as 'stupid' but we recognize that MacWhirr lives on a level plain of experience which ensures an achievement of which Jukes is clearly incapable, the restoration of good order on a damaged and threatened ship.

Typhoon is thus a witty work which dramatizes the confounding of wit. The owners of the *Nan-Shan* find it expedient to register it under the Siamese rather than the British flag and young Jukes's patriotic sentiments are outraged. He exclaims 'Queer flag for a man to sail under' and MacWhirr takes him literally, looks up the Siamese flag in a reference work and finds that it is correct and correctly flown, and thus heads off Jukes who is harbouring the thought that he might strike an attitude and resign: as he confesses later, 'I might just as well fling my resignation at this bulkhead. I don't believe you can make a man like that understand anything' (chapter 1, pp. 10–12). Whether he understands or not is not revealed, but it is unanswerably the case – despite the ironic tone – that 'every ship Captain MacWhirr commanded was the floating abode of harmony and peace' (chapter 1, p. 4). When MacWhirr has read on his barometer 'the lowest reading he had even seen in his life' (chapter 5, p. 84) the text itself behaves in a MacWhirr-like way by refusing to imagine the unimaginable. The great typhoon is not described. It takes place in the gap, so to speak, between chapters 5 and 6, and is referred to only by an extreme laconic utterance from MacWhirr: 'Before the renewed wrath of winds swooped on his ship, Captain MacWhirr was moved to declare, in a tone of vexation, as it were: "I wouldn't like to lose her". He was spared that annoyance' (chapter 5, p. 90). By this device *Typhoon* declares itself MacWhirr's tale.

The Inheritors is a poor product of the Conrad/Ford collaboration (and is almost entirely Ford's work) but it is of interest as a political novel which can be seen as a grotesque prelude to Conrad's first great political novel, *Nostromo*. *The Inheritors* is largely a political *roman à clef* whose main figures represent Arthur Balfour, the Prime Minister, set against the imperialists, Joseph Chamberlain and Leopold II, King of Belgium. It would appear that Conrad wrote only twenty thousand words of the total, mainly concentrated in the final episodes, although Ford said that Conrad gave other scenes a 'final tap'. Conrad announced the completion of the novel to Blackwood on 12 April 1900. He explained that he had not offered the novel to Meldrum for 'two and even three reasons'. These reasons show the complexity of Conrad's professional situation:

> First of all I did not wish to offer you a work in its nature necessarily tentative – an initial experiment, in fact. The second reason was my running actually singlehanded in Maga and of course my partner and myself are very anxious for serial publication. The third reason for you not having had the

refusal of these first-fruits is that you have (virtually) a book of mine while poor Heineman[n] (who has been awfully decent to me) has nothing to show for his decency but a few receipts for moneys paid out and half a novel which is hung up, to ripen – I trust.[7]

The 'half a novel' referred to was *The Rescue*, at this stage known as 'The Rescuer', which was not completed until 1919; Heinemann had been 'awfully decent' in publishing *The Nigger of the 'Narcissus'* and in paying an advance on *The Rescue*. In the course of the letter Conrad spoke of their intentions concerning Seraphina: 'If [*The Inheritors*] goes down well with the public we shall try our hand at an adventure story of which the skeleton is set up – with some modelling here and there already worked up.'[8]

If Conrad was being truthful in saying that only the 'skeleton' of the story had been written then the collaboration, first arranged in September 1898, had produced little by the spring of 1900. *The Inheritors* is interesting for its obliqueness and its use of satire. Ford's writing here makes us aware of one of his least attractive characteristics, his capacity for covert spite, which is directed in this instance at those whom he perceived as successful writers and publishers (the figures satirized as Callan – possibly Henry James – and Polehampton – probably Unwin – in the novel). It owes much to *Heart of Darkness*. The Duke De Mersch – Leopold of Belgium – is opening up Greenland, with extreme brutality. The development of Greenland involves the building of a railway and for much of the text the Greenland of Ford's novel feels surprizingly, and absurdly, like an African country: at one point we are told that it is De Mersch's practice to have 'the blacks murdered' in Greenland.[9] *Heart of Darkness* and *Nostromo* both deal with politics, and *The Inheritors* is a kind of conduit between these two texts, showing Ford digesting Conrad's political perceptions and reflecting them back to Conrad. I think that the fact of having collaborated (however little) on *The Inheritors* helped Conrad to write *Nostromo* (see below p. 138). Conrad despised *The Inheritors*. It was accepted for publication by Heinemann, for whom Garnett was working as a reader, and Conrad wrote to Garnett a somewhat callous letter (26 March 1900):

What a lark! I set myself to look upon the thing as a sort of skit upon the political (?!) novel, fools of the Morley Roberts[10] sort do write. This in my heart of hearts. And poor *H* was dead in earnest! O Lord. How he worked! There is not a chapter I haven't made him write twice – most of them three times over. . . . And . . . in the course of that agony I have been ready to weep more than once. Yet not for him. Not for him. You'll have to burn this letter. . . . I suppose you've scornfully detected whole slabs of my own precious writing in that precious novel?[11]

Garnett did not burn the letter: in 1928 he published it, and Ford was desperately hurt to see how Conrad had used and disparaged him.[12] *The Inheritors* and *Nostromo* have an intriguing detail of imagery in common. In the Conrad/Ford collaboration the protagonist, in conversation with his 'sister', the woman from the Fourth Dimension who is one of the Wellsian 'Inheritors' of the title, notes this: 'It was as if the controlling powers were flitting, invisible, just above my head, just beyond my grasp. There was obviously something vibrating; some cord, somewhere, stretched very taut and quivering' (p. 188). The image reappears later in the text: 'There was a tension somewhere, a string somewhere that was stretched tight and vibrating' (p. 232) and in terms of its function (though not – obviously – its literary quality) it relates to the image associated with Decoud's suicide in *Nostromo*: 'The solitude appeared like a great void, and the silence of the gulf like a tense, thin cord to which he hung suspended by both hands, without fear, without surprise, without any sort of emotion whatever' (Part 3, chapter 10, p. 498). The cord stretched across the gulf remains the image which gives Decoud his sense of his own fragile identity until he shoots himself: 'The stiffness of the fingers relaxed, and the lover of Antonia Avellanos rolled overboard without having heard the cord of silence snap in the solitude of the Placid Gulf, whose glittering surface remained untroubled by the fall of his body' (p. 501).

Blackwood's Magazine's rejection of 'Falk' had come at a bad time: Conrad's finances were in very low water, *Romance* was proving exhausting and unrewarding and he became increasingly frustrated as the year wore on. In May 1902 he tried to raise cash by attempting to sell the copyrights of *Lord Jim* and of *Youth: a Narrative; and Two Other Stories* outright to William Blackwood. Blackwood declined to buy and told Conrad that he was a loss to the firm. Conrad responded with a letter which is in part a personal cry of pain, displaying his accelerating paranoia about the contrast between the big sales of popular authors like Conan Doyle, Stevenson, John Buchan and Hall Caine and his own pitiful sales, and in part a new declaration of his convictions and practice as an artist. In this respect it can be regarded as an extended coda to the *Preface* to *The Nigger of the 'Narcissus'*:

I am emboldened to say that ultimate and irretrievable failure is *not* to be my lot. I know that it is not necessary to say to You but I may just as well point out that I must not by any means be taken for a gifted loafer intent on living upon credulous publishers. Pardon this remark – but in a time when Sherlock Holmes looms so big [*The Hound of The Baskervilles* was published in 1902] I may be excused my little bit of self-assertion.

I am long in my development. What of that? Is not Thackeray's penny worth of mediocre fact drowned in an ocean of twaddle? And yet he lives. And Sir Walter, himself, was not the writer of concise anecdotes I fancy. And G. Elliot [sic] – is she as swift as the present public (incapable of fixing its attention for five consecutive minutes) requires us to be at the cost of all honesty, of all truth, and even the most elementary conception of art? But these are great names. I don't compare myself with them. I am *modern*, and I would rather recall Wagner the musician and Rodin the Sculptor who both had to starve a little in their day – and Whistler the painter who made

Ruskin the critic foam at the mouth with scorn and indignation. They too have arrived. They had to suffer for being 'new'. And I too hope to find my place in the rear of my betters. But still – my place. My work shall not be an utter failure because it has the solid basis of a definite intention – first: and next because it is not an endless analysis of affected sentiments but in its essence it is action (strange as this affirmation may sound at the present time) nothing but action – action observed, felt and interpreted with an absolute truth to my sensations (which are the basis of art in literature) – action of human beings that will bleed to a prick, and are moving in a visible world.

That is my creed. Time will show. (To William Blackwood, 31 May 1902)[13]

The 'Author's Note' to *Typhoon and Other Stories* seems to echo this letter of 1902. He refers, somewhat loftily, to the year in which the stories were written as that 'which follows on my connection with *Blackwood's Magazine*' (as though severing that connection had been his decision; p. v), and proceeds in the consciousness that time had indeed 'shown', and that the Conrad who is creating his notes for his collected edition had undoubtedly secured his 'place': 'in everything I have written there is always one invariable intention, and that is to capture the reader's attention, by securing his interest and enlisting his sympathies for the matter in hand, whatever it may be, within the limits of the visible world and within the boundaries of human emotions' (pp. vii–viii). He refers obliquely to the cannibalism in 'Falk' at which *Blackwood's Magazine* had baulked: 'certain peculiarities of its subject' had upset some readers, but his intention was certainly 'not to shock anybody. As in most of my writing I insist not on the events but on their effect upon the persons in the tale' (p. vii).

'Falk', 'Amy Foster', 'To-morrow' and 'The End of the Tether' were all written fairly close together, but the range of achievement that they display is considerable: 'Falk' and 'Amy Foster' are clearly major pieces, while the other two remind us that Conrad's writing could become slack and (by his best standards) commonplace when he was off form or writing purely for money. *Youth: a Narrative; and Two Other Stories* was initially planned, as we have seen, as a group of three stories narrated by Marlow ('Youth', *Heart of Darkness* and *Lord Jim*) but after *Lord Jim* had grown too big for the volume and been published separately 'The End of the Tether' was written to complete it. Some readers see a similarity of dramatic pattern between 'The End of the Tether' and *Heart of Darkness* in that both end ironically.[14] But for me 'The End of the Tether' is like 'The Black Mate', a thinly disguised expression of a middle-aged man's fear of failure. Captain Whalley goes blind and is driven to lies and expediency for the sake of his daughter.[15] *Heart of Darkness* obviously eclipses the other two tales in the *Youth* volume: *Youth: A Narrative; and Two Other Stories* is a thoroughly misleading title. The next volume of short stories, *Typhoon and Other Stories* (1903) comprises 'Typhoon', 'Amy Foster', 'Falk' and 'To-morrow'; it is better balanced than the *Youth* volume, though 'To-morrow' is less strong than the other stories (it is of biographical interest, which I discuss below pp.

123–4). 'Falk' (completed by May 1901) and 'Amy Foster' (written in May and June 1901) have autobiographical roots: the first is one of the four narratives based on Conrad's command of the *Otago* in 1888 (the others are *The Shadow-Line*, 'The Secret Sharer' and 'A Smile of Fortune'; it also figures briefly in chapter 19 of *Lord Jim*), the second tells us what it felt like to be a young Pole coming to live in the Kentish countryside.

'Falk' concerns the skipper of a tugboat who previously has been the principal player in a what the narrator tolerantly refers to as 'a case of "Cannibalism and suffering at sea"' (p. 226). Adrift in a helpless steamer which had lost its propeller, Falk arms himself with a revolver and shoots and eats his fellow crew-members as they approach the ship's water-supply until he is the only man left alive. He thus embodies a recently discovered late Victorian truth: 'Only the best man would survive. It was a great, terrible, and cruel misfortune.' The narrator makes the connection with popularized Darwinism of the 1890s: 'He had survived! I saw him before me as though preserved for a witness to the mighty truth of an unerring and eternal principle' (p. 235; the connection is reinforced by the 'Author's Note': 'Falk obeys the law of self-preservation without the slightest misgivings as to his right', p. viii). Falk is disliked by the story's Germans, Schomberg the hotel-keeper (who reappears in *Victory*) and Captain Hermann, master of the *Diana*, whose niece Falk loves. Conrad here – as surprisingly often (remember the German skipper of the *Patna* in *Lord Jim*) – uses familiar Edwardian dramatic stereotypes: the Germans are thickset, stupid and aggressive, Falk himself is a well set-up Scandinavian hero who could easily be as English as Jim. Later Conrad protested that he was not (as a naturalized Englishman) guilty of adoptive partisan national feeling. He wrote to Kazimierz Waliszewski, 16 December 1903: 'Quand à "l'infériorité des races, je me permets de protester..." Je prends mes personnages oú je les trouve. Hermann est un Allemand, mais Stein l'est aussi. J'ai pris grand soin de donner une origine cosmopolite à Kurtz.' ['As to the "inferiority of the races", I mean to protest... I take my characters where I find them. Hermann is a German, but Stein is too. I took great care to give Kurtz a cosmopolitan origin'].[16] But as far as 'Falk' is concerned, the charge sticks (and Conrad's reference to Hermann in the above letter makes it fairly clear that he was aware of that): Schomberg splutters with rage because Falk will not eat meat at his hotel – 'A white man should eat like a white man, dash it all. . . . Ought to eat meat, must eat meat' (p. 174), 'what satisfaction is that for a well-educated young fellow to feed all alone in his cabin – like a wild beast?' (p. 175) – and Hermann, using the words 'Mensch' and 'Fressen', warns his niece not to marry Falk (p. 221). The narrator looks up 'Fressen' in the dictionary to find that it means 'devour'. It is also, as his dictionary seems not to say, a verb used of animals (and thus, colloquially, rough humans), reflecting Hermann's view that Falk is 'a beast, an animal' (p. 221). He is right, of course, in that the Darwinian Falk is a heroic animal and is related to the myth of the centaur. The narrator dwells elaborately and playfully on this:

It seems absurd to compare a tug-boat skipper to a centaur: but he reminded me somehow of an engraving in a little book I had as a boy, which
represented centaurs at a stream, and there was one especially, in the fore-
ground, prancing bow and arrows in hand, with regular severe features and
an immense curled wavy beard, flowing down his breast. Falk's face reminded
me of that centaur. Besides, he was a composite creature. Not a man-horse,
it is true, but a man-boat (p. 162).

His man-beast's literal hunger for other men has been replaced by a beast-
man's metaphorical hunger for the huge, silent, goddess-like niece, 'a very
nymph of Diana the Huntress' (p. 208), for whom Falk displays heroically
violent sexual need: 'He was a child. He was as frank as a child, too. He
was hungry for the girl, terribly hungry, as he had been terribly hungry for
food. Don't be shocked if I declare that in my belief it was the same need,
the same pain, the same torture' (p. 224).

'Falk' and *Heart of Darkness* deal with abominations, but 'Falk' does so
in a disconcertingly polite manner and is told by a narrator in whom
Marlow's agonized need to know is replaced by an amused knowingness
(it is slightly odd that having taken on the profound moral subversiveness
of *Heart of Darkness, Blackwood's Magazine* wouldn't print 'Falk' because of
its cannibalism). Cedric Watts says that the urbanity of 'Falk' is subtler than
it looks because it challenges our expectations.[17] This is over-generous:
the story's tone of world-weariness and condescension, marking a gap
between the sophistication of the author and the rough vigour of his subjects, is one into which Conrad can fall rather easily when he gets into
his Gentleman of Letters mode (what in Ford Madox Ford is the Grand
Manner) and his interest in the interior lives of his figures becomes relaxed. The *Preface* to *The Nigger of the 'Narcissus'* has shown us that Conrad
is at his most honest with (and most likely to do justice to) his own talent
when he conceives of the artist as an isolated figure urgently seeking to
communicate his unique discoveries. The narrator of 'Falk' is by contrast
too securely a member of a club, too comfortably part of a collective
Edwardian literary voice.[18]

'Amy Foster', the story of a young immigrant, Yanko Goorall, who is
misunderstood and ill-treated by the English villagers among whom he
finds himself, certainly reflects some of Conrad's fear for himself as a Pole
in England. As Cedric Watts says, Jessie Conrad's recollection of Conrad
being ill on their honeymoon in 1896 can be taken as an indirect commentary on the tale:

For a whole long week, the fever ran high and for most of the time J. C. was
delirious. To see him lying in the white canopied bed, dark-faced, with
gleaming teeth and shining eyes, was sufficiently impressive, but to hear him
muttering to himself in a strange tongue (she thinks he must have been
speaking Polish), to be unable to penetrate the clouded mind or catch one
intelligible word, was for a young inexperienced girl truly awful . . .[19]

Ford Madox Ford claimed that the story was one of his which Conrad rewrote[20] while Jessie Conrad said that the figure of Amy Foster herself was based on one of the servants whom the Conrads employed.[21] The story is narrated by a doctor who is called to Yanko's deathbed: where the villagers have displayed hostility the cultivated and educated doctor feels sympathy, but he is as much mystified by Yanko as anyone else, thus intensifying our perception of his loneliness. Yanko, bewildered, asks why his wife has ill-treated him: 'She has left him – sick – helpless – thirsty. The spear of the hunter had entered his very soul. "Why?" he cried, in the penetrating and indignant voice of a man calling to a responsible Maker. A gust of wind and a swish of rain answered. And as I turned away to shut the door he pronounced the word "Merciful!" and expired' (p. 141).

The suggestion that this short story about sex war in which a man is tortured like an uncomprehending animal by a woman was initially Ford's story seems to me quite plausible. The love that Etchingham Granger in *The Inheritors* feels for his 'sister', the 'fourth Dimensionist', is like a variant of the plot of 'Amy Foster' in that Etchingham is all warm messy passion, the girl is all cold inhuman efficiency. Ashburnham, the tortured hero of *The Good Soldier* (1915) can be seen as a development of this figure: Ashburnham is tormented literally to death. In this novel as in all his work Ford displays a self-flattering self-portrait. Ashburnham is the kind of aristocratic Englishman that Ford would have liked to have been. Dowell, the American narrator (and therefore an outsider) is as it were erotically drawn to this emblematic figure. And the title, 'The Good Soldier' (forced on Ford, because the publisher felt that 'The Saddest Story' was not an appropriate title to use in war-time) is itself a good title, indicating claims to social status which are drained of significance by the novel's dramatic action (it and 'Lord Jim' are both ironic titles, using the labels of status in parallel ironic ways).

The plot of 'To-morrow', final story of the *Typhoon* volume, came from Ford. Conrad wrote to Ford, 10 January 1902, saying that the story is '*All your* suggestion and *absolutely my* conception' (the tone of this letter is placatory because Conrad was pursuing his own work instead of getting on with his share of *Romance*).[22] Jessie Conrad played down 'To-morrow', saying 'The last story in that volume we neither of us liked very much'.[23] We should bear in mind here Jessie's tendency to deprecate retrospectively anything with which Ford had been associated. Conrad himself was professional about the story, describing it to Pinker (16 January 1902) as '"Conrad" adapted down to the needs of a magazine' but 'By no means a pot-boiler'.[24] The periodical for which it was 'adapted down' was the *Pall Mall Magazine*, where it appeared in August. Conrad thought enough of 'To-morrow' to adapt it for the stage, as *One Day More*, in 1905 (see below p. 149).

'To-morrow' tells the story of a Captain Hagberd who has not seen his son since the boy was fourteen, but expects his return 'to-morrow'. The old man lives in a world of mild delusion, dressing himself in a home-made suit of sail-cloth and filling his house with unopened boxes of furnishings for the imminent return of this son, who is to marry, he believes, Bessie Carvil, the daughter of his blind neighbour (and tenant) in the cottage adjacent to his own. The son, Harry, does return, but the old man's delusions are too strong for him to recognize the son. The son, for his part, is an adventurer who goes back to the sea, leaving his father secure in his delusions and Bessie condemned to perpetual imprisonment with her blind father. Hagberd has been the skipper of *The Skimmer of the Seas*, a coaling ship which barely left the coast. Old Hagberd is a sailor by necessity who hates the sea and whose instincts are all for the land-based security embodied in the two cottages that he has built; young Hagberd is a wild, unsettled man for whom the sea is the perfect environment. Conrad is going back to his early days with British ships: we have seen that *The Skimmer of the Sea* [sic] was an East Coast coal schooner sailing between Newcastle-upon-Tyne and Lowestoft on which Conrad served in 1878 (p. 29). Captain Hagberd may be based on the skipper of one of these early ships, although two small details of his characterization link him with Captain Ellis, the Harbour-Master or 'Master-Attendant' at Singapore who told Conrad of his appointment as skipper of the *Otago* in 1888, In *Lord Jim*, where he appears as 'Captain Elliot' (Captain Ellis was still alive at the time of writing *Lord Jim*), the Master-Attendant has unmarried daughters who 'resembled him amazingly' and the unmarried son of Captain Hagberd also, in the identical phrase, 'resembled him amazingly' (p. 248). In *The Shadow-Line*, where Captain Ellis (dead by the time this novel was written) appears without disguise, he is described as a 'divine (pagan) emanation' and a 'deputy-Neptune' (pp. 29–30). The domesticated Captain Hagberd with his 'beard of Father Neptune' is described as a 'deposed sea-god who had exchanged the trident for the spade' (p. 253). Captain Ellis was ferocious and bullying but also capable of great generosity, a dominant figure who made enough impact on the young Conrad to appear in several of the fictions. The ambivalence of a young man's feelings about an old man in authority surfaces here, and it may be that young Hagberd's behaviour towards his father embodies something of Conrad's interaction with the father-figures of his early years, and that his feelings about Ellis are being mapped onto his far deeper and more complex feelings about Bobrowski. Young Hagberd's pained sense of being misunderstood and rejected by his parents, whom he left at the age of fourteen, could reflect one aspect of the myth that Conrad constructed for himself about turning his back on Bobrowski's protection, at the age of fifteen, and leaving Poland: 'They were so afraid I would turn out badly that they fairly drove me away'.[25]

Nineteen-hundred and three and the first half of 1904 was a miserable period for Conrad. He was depressed, he had no faith in his own work, he felt the business of proof-reading *Romance* was a time-wasting chore and he found the writing of *Nostromo* excruciatingly difficult. He wrote to J. M. Barrie (31 December 1903): 'My work which has no delicacy, no felicity, no inspiration has gone on lamely – but still it has gone on; and I've learned during the last disastrous Year to be very thankful for small mercies. As long as something gets itself written one needn't grumble'.[26] But he did grumble, of course. He and Ford kept up a brave face over *Romance*, but beneath the cordiality Conrad was aware that the collaboration on *Romance* had been wasteful expenditure of time on a second-rate enterprise. Tension surfaced when Ford Madox Ford wanted to print the dates '1896–1903' at the end of *Romance*. Conrad feared that to appear to have worked on this minor piece for so long would expose them to mockery from the reviewers: 'The apparent want of proportion will be jumped upon. Sneers at collaboration – sneers at those two men who took six years to write "this very ordinary tale" – whereas R.L.S single handed produced his masterpieces etc etc.' With more sensitivity than he sometimes displayed in his dealings with Ford he saw that Ford wanted to give these dates for personal and emotional reasons: he was out to show that he and Conrad, friends and partners, had come a long journey together. But 1896 was misleading by any computation (the collaborators had not met before 1898) and Conrad was right to say that the truth of the situation would be more accurately expressed by a note indicating that Ford's 'Seraphina', written in 1896, had been re-written jointly between 1900 and 1902.[27] The outcome was that they agreed not to print any note of the dates of composition.

The plot and the characters of *Romance* are Ford's: Conrad's contribution was to try to get some impetus and realism into the action.[28] The enterprise was misconceived from the outset, because Ford's real talent was for passivity, urban consciousness and modern sexual suffering, not for historical romances about pirates. The protagonist, John Kemp, is a passive anti-hero (a familiar type from popular romantic fiction, including Scott's Waverley, Stevenson's Jim Hawkins and John Buchan's Davie Crawfurd): 'It was, I suppose, what I demanded of Fate – to be gently wafted into the position of a hero of romance, without rough hands at my throat' (p. 30). Kemp is adopted by Don Carlos, a 'Byronic' consumptive (the novel is set in the first decade of the nineteenth century) as heir to his South American estate and husband-designate of his cousin, Seraphina. (Conrad had earlier treated a similar pattern in Lingard's relationship with Almayer.) Kemp's weakness is compounded by his post-adolescent hero-worship of Don Carlos marked in this scene of leave-taking between the two men:

'I shall come for you one day.' He looked at me and smiled. It stirred unknown depths of emotion in me. I would have gone with him, then, had he asked me. 'One day,' he repeated, with an extraordinary cadence of tone. 'His hand was grasping mine; it thrilled me like a woman's; he stood shaking it very gently . . . He leaned over and kissed me lightly on the cheek, then climbed away. I felt that the light of Romance was going out of my life' (p. 51).

Using Kemp as first-person narrator adds to the novel's difficulties, because as well as being unintentionally spineless he is required by the method to be implausibly stupid in that key facts have to remain hidden from him though the reader can easily discern them (Don Carlos's attraction to Kemp's sister Veronica, for instance, is apparent to the reader quite early in the novel but comes as a surprise to Kemp as part of the dénouement). To compare the narrative awkwardness and embarrassing emotional explicitness of *Romance* with the narrative control and reticent dramatization of friendship in *Lord Jim* is to wonder (as with *The Inheritors*) that Conrad allowed *Romance* to appear with his name on it.

Much of Ford's work suffered from unreality. He wrote very fast and was usually unwilling or unable to assimilate and synthesize information (*The Fifth Queen* is an exception to this): hence his habitual defensive assumption of superiority to mere facts and his excessive reliance on impressions. When trying to improve Ford's work Conrad could see these weaknesses clearly enough, but with *Nostromo* he felt that his own work was similarly afflicted and he was too close to it to judge it objectively. Also *Romance*, like *Nostromo*, is set in South America. It may be that writing something which was intended to be commercial and popular in a South American setting unsettled Conrad's sense of his own literary standards when it came to using a similar setting in his own work, and contributed to his doubts and agonies over the writing of *Nostromo*. To Cunninghame Graham (8 July 1903) he writes: 'I am dying over that cursed Nostromo thing. All my memories of Central America seem to slip away. I just had a glimpse 25 years ago – a short glance.[29] That is not enough pour bâtir un roman dessus. And yet one must live. When it's done I'll never dare look you in the face again [because Cunninghame Graham knew South America well]'.[30] Lamentation over the difficulty of writing *Nostromo* features in many of his letters for the rest of 1903: to Galsworthy he complains dismally of inefficiency and 'powerlessness' (10 or 17 July 1903)[31] and to Henry-Durand Davray on 22 August he writes: 'La solitude me gagne: elle m'absorbe. Je ne vois rien, je ne lis rien. C'est comme une espèce de tombe, qui erait en même temps un enfer, ou il faut écrire, écrire, écrire. On se demand si cela vaut la peine, – car enfin on n'est jamais satifait et on n'a jamais fini.' ['Solitude overpowers me; it absorbs me. I see nothing, I read nothing. It is like a kind of tomb, at the same time a hell, where one has to write, write, write. One asks oneself if that's worth the trouble – because in the long run one is never satisfied and never finished'].[32] The many letters to Galsworthy complain of anxiety about money (Galsworthy made regular loans or gifts to alleviate that) and the agony of writing the book in 'belittling' and 'demoralising' circumstances. To Pinker he writes an extraordinary letter (22 August 1903) saying that *Nostromo* has been the most difficult of all his novels, but plans for serializing it can nevertheless go ahead because if Conrad gets behind 'you know that at the very worst H[ueffer] stands in the background (quite confidentially you understand)'.[33] Conrad was thus incorporating into his professional calculations for *Nostromo* that fact that Ford would write some of his novel for him if called upon (this was to happen, as we have seen,[34] early in 1904). The agony went on unabated: to Wells, 20 November 1903, he writes: 'Things are bad with me – there's no disguising the fact. Not only is the scribbling awfully in arrear but there's no "spring" in me to grapple with it effectually.'[35]

There were some alleviations of the gloom. Roger Casement, whom he had encountered in the Congo in 1890, came back briefly into Conrad's life. Casement, then working in the British consular service, wrote a report on King Leopold's atrocities in the Congo and tried to interest Conrad in a newly established 'Congo reform association'.[36] His risk-taking man-of-action qualities, which resembled Cunninghame Graham's, were of the kind to help Conrad believe in the reality of his current novel. He writes a pleased schoolboyish letter to Cunninghame Graham commending this friend (26 December 1903):

> He's a protestant Irishman, pious too. But so was Pizarro. For the rest I can assure you that he is a limpid personality. There is a touch of the Conquistador in him too; for I've seen him start off into an unspeakable wilderness swinging a crookhandled stick for all weapons, with two bull-dogs: Paddy (white) and Biddy (brindle) at his heels and a Loanda boy carrying a bundle for all company. A few months afterwards it so happened I saw him come out again, a little leaner a little browner, with his stick, dogs, and Loanda boy, and quietly serene as though he had been for a stroll in a park.[37]

The detail about the adventurer looking virtually untouched by physical hardship as though in a (presumably English) park recalls Charles Gould's appearance, looking 'in his English clothes and with his imported saddlery as though he come this moment to Costaguana at his easy swift *pasotrote*, straight out of some green meadow at the other side of the world' (*Nostromo*, I, chapter 6, p. 48). Cunninghame Graham later objected to the '*pasotrote*' (which is the equivalent of 'walk' but Conrad took it to mean 'canter'[38]). Casement visited the Conrads in January 1904 and the two remained on cordial terms (with occasional meetings) thereafter: but when Casement was on trial for his life in 1916 Conrad declined to sign a petition for clemency.[39]

Early in 1904 Conrad sank to a new depth of depression, writing to Galsworthy about the relief that early death would bring.[40] External circumstances conspired against him: in January 1904 Jessie fell heavily and hurt both her knees, damaging one of them for life. Henceforth she was to have persistent trouble, requiring recurrent surgery, was partially immobile and in constant pain. For the rest of their lives together – twenty years – she tended to make light of her trouble in order not to increase his anxieties. Jessie had her faults but one has to admire her stoicism.

In the first few months of 1904 Ford mounted (as he saw it) a rescue operation to support Conrad during the struggle with *Nostromo*. Both of them were under severe strain: in June and July Conrad's letters speak of exhaustion and despair ('I am tired, tired, as if I had lived a hundred years'[41]). The symmetry between Conrad's and Ford's crises often makes it appear, as we have noticed,[42] that they were unconsciously competing with each other for attention and sympathy. At the end of July 1904 Ford collapsed completely with a nervous breakdown. *Nostromo* was therefore finished without his help or knowledge. The completion of *Nostromo*, like the completion of *Lord Jim*, was a matter of high drama; wracked by trouble with his teeth (he had a tooth extracted on 26 August) Conrad went to stay with the Hopes and wrote day and night until he finally completed the novel at 3.00 a.m. on 30 August 1904, after which, as he writes to Galsworthy, he collapsed.[43] But work on *Nostromo* was by no means finished: the last episodes were botched and rushed, and although it sufficed for serial publication Conrad rewrote the ending completely for book publication.[44]

Like many of Conrad's major works, *Nostromo* was originally conceived as a short story. He was referring to it as a story in October 1902, and in January 1903 he envisaged it as a 35,000 word story to be finished by the end of the month. Conrad's insouciant reference to the writing of *Nostromo* as a mode of rest and recreation looks painfully ironic in the light of the agony the novel was to cause him: 'Since Xmas day I've for relief been writing a story called (provisionally) *Nostromo* which will do for the Kendal people.[45] Half or so of the MS. you shall have by the *15th inst* and the balance end of the month. About 35,000' (to Pinker, 5 January 1903).[46]

The sources for *Nostromo* include the voyage that Conrad made with the *Saint-Antoine*, as 'steward', in 1876:[47] the ship arrived in Martinique on 18 August. In the 'Author's Note' to *Nostromo* Conrad says that in 1875 or -6 'in the West Indies or rather in the Gulf of Mexico' his 'contacts with land were short, few, and fleeting' (*Nostromo*, p. xl). Conrad may have visited ports in Colombia and Venezuela but the *Saint-Antoine* itself did not leave Martinique before sailing for St Pierre; it was back in St Pierre on 16 September, sailed to the Virgin Islands later in the same month, and on 12 October set out with a cargo of coal for Port-au-Prince, and left St Pierre for Marseille on 25 November.[48] Thus Conrad's South America is based not on direct observation but almost entirely on reading.[49] The books that Conrad used included his friend Cunninghame Graham's *A Vanished Arcadia*, G. F. Masterman's *Seven Eventful Years in Paraguay*, Garibaldi's autobiography, Edward B. Eastwick's *Venezuela*, Ramon Paez's *Wild Scenes in South America* and Frederick Benton Williams's *On Many Seas*.[50] Williams's *On Many Seas* gives the outline of the episode in which Nostromo steals the silver. In the Author's Note Conrad says that on his voyage to the West Indies as a young man he heard of the theft of a whole lighter full of silver, and that he came across the same story, 'the very thing in a shabby volume [Williams's book] picked up outside a second-hand book-shop' (in 1902, presumably) (pp. xl–xlii). It was when he saw that he could *invert* this source that he became interested in Nicolo's story as the subject of a novel. The thief need not be a simple rascal, as Williams's Nicolo was:

> It was only when it dawned upon me that the purloiner of the treasure need not necessarily be a confirmed rogue, that he could be even a man of character, an actor and possibly a victim in the changing scenes of a revolution, it was only then that I had the first vision of a twilight country which was to become the province of Sulaco, with its high shadowy Sierra and its misty Campo for mute witnesses of events flowing from the passions of men short-sighted in good and evil (p. xlii).

In *On Many Seas* the captain of a lighter, 'Nicolo', a 'swarthy, piratical-looking fellow', tells the story of his life. He comes to Panama (from Italy, presumably) at the age of sixteen and becomes so well trusted that 'on the breaking out of one of the usual revolutions, he was chosen to take charge of a lighter containing a large and valuable consignment of silver bullion, and his orders were to get it out of Panama as quickly as possible.' He murders his two negro crew, scuttles the lighter full of silver near a beach, and thereafter uses the silver to live on over the years: 'I mus git reesh slow, don you see?' is his comment on this procedure.[51]

Conrad's other reading saturates *Nostromo*, but particular episodes can be picked out. The torture of Hirsch by the strappado comes from Garibaldi's autobiography. Garibaldi describes the effect of the torture as comparable with burning: 'All the weight of my body hung by my bleeding wrists and my dislocated shoulders. My whole body burned like a furnace; at every instant I begged for water'. Like Hirsch, Garibaldi spat in the face of his torturer, one Don Leonardo Milan. Thereafter the thought of this man filled him with terror (as the thought of Father Beron demoralizes Dr Monygham).[52] Another source for Dr Monygham's torture is Masterman's account of the tortures he underwent in Paraguay: he focuses particularly on the fact that a priest was seeking to force him to confess (as Father Beron seeks to force Monygham to confess).[53] Many of the names used in the novel come from these sources: from Masterman, Conrad takes Decoud, Padre Corbelàn, General Barrios, Gould, Captain Fidanza, Mitchell, Monygham and Don José: from Eastwick he takes Guzman Bento, Antonia, Ribiera and Sotillo. A woman called Antonia Ribiera who seems strongly to resemble Antonia Avellanos appears in Eastwick's book described thus: 'She was very unlike the other Creole ladies I had seen. Her dress and manner were rather those of an aristocratic English beauty than of a Creole. . . . She talked like a bookworm, like a politician, like a diplomatist, like a savant'.[54]

Not all of *Nostromo* comes from reading, of course. One of its most robust and nourishing roots, as I have indicated, was Conrad's friendship with Cunninghame Graham.[55] He and Conrad were so different from each other, in their histories, political affiliations and literary claims that friendship with him could be breezily competitive and full of displays of mutual bravura without threat to the well-being of either party. His personality has contributed much to the personality of Charles Gould in *Nostromo*. Charles Gould looks and behaves like Graham: he was an excellent horseman, he had experience of South America, he was a political idealist, he had a courageous wife who accompanied him (and made sketches) on his adventures. Also, Graham's writings about South America – and, of course, those conversations which are the core of a friendship and of which no record can survive – contributed to Conrad's material for the invention of Costaguana. On 14 January 1898 Conrad wrote to Graham 'What don't you know! From the outside of a sail to the inside of a prison![56] When I think of you I feel as tho' I had lived all my life in a dark hole'.[57] On 16 February 1905 the admiration was still generous and unabated: 'You seem to know more of all things that (sic: for 'than') I thought it possible for any man to know, since the Renaissance swells (who knew everything about everything)'.[58] With Ford such communications would have been part of the power-struggle. With Cunninghame Graham they were happy acknowledgements of mutually rewarding complementary qualities.

We have seen that Conrad wrote sceptical letters to Cunninghame Graham.[59] The most sceptical of his letters are written in the 1890s, when such a tone and outlook were fashionably part of the *fin de siècle* and it is never quite clear how far Conrad believed in his own attitudes, or indeed how consistently he held them. After 1899 – after, that is, the publication of *Heart of Darkness* – Conrad's writings seem to indicate that human beings have it in them to attain some degree of (limited and secular) redemption: by the recovery of lost honour in *Lord Jim*, by loyalty to love – though not necessarily sexual love – in *Nostromo*, by belief in liberty in *Under Western Eyes*, by generous self-surrender in *Chance*. Richard Curle said of them, much later, 'In each other's company they appeared to grow younger; they treated one another with that kind of playfulness which can only arise from a complete, unquestioning, and ancient friendship. I doubt whether the presence of any man made Conrad happier than the presence of Don Roberto'.[60]

In his conversations about his experiences of South America Cunninghame Graham gave Conrad a number of items which found their way into *Nostromo*. He had personally witnessed tortures like those experienced by Dr Monygham, and in 1873 in Paraguay he met an Italian who is one of the sources for Giorgio Viola. The Italian was one Enrico Clerici, a former member of Garibaldi's Italian Legion who had set up as a bartender in Encarnacion.[61] In 1894 Cunninghame Graham set out on a characteristically wild and romantic expedition. Having inherited Gartmore, the family estate in Scotland, he was heavily encumbered with debt. He was stimulated by reading Pliny to set out in search of a goldmine in Northern Spain (there was, of course, no gold).[62] It may well be that two features of Charles Gould's relationship with his father's silver-mine stem from this. The mine, his father's legacy, looks as though it is nothing but an embarrassment and a drain on his resources (as Gartmore was for

Graham), but Charles Gould has a romantic faith – which is of course vindicated – that it can be worked.

Graham was taking a great deal of interest in South American affairs between 1897 and 1903 (and thus during the period 1901–3 when Conrad was working on *Nostromo*) and Conrad read two of his accounts of the Spanish conquest of South America (*A Vanished Arcadia*, 1901 and *Hernando de Soto*, 1903) before and during the writing of *Nostromo*. Watts and Davies point out that Graham's A *Vanished Arcadia* displays the same kind of ambivalence about the progress achieved by the Jesuits in Paraguay in the seventeenth and eighteenth centuries as Conrad's novel does about the modernizing effect of British and American economic imperialism in Costaguana. At the end of his book Graham writes that despite the Jesuit's achievements, 'The self-created goddess Progress was justified by works, and all the land left barren, waiting the time when factories shall pollute its sky, and render miserable the European emigrants, who, flying from their slavery at home, shall have found it waiting for them in their new paradise beyond the seas'.[63] He thus anticipates Conrad by writing about the effect that *nineteenth* century economic progress will have on this arcadia.[64] Gould's personality is powerfully dramatized for us within the brilliant fragmentariness of *Nostromo*'s narrative structure, and I shall return to this. But I want to ask: why is the novel called *Nostromo*? The first popular edition (Dent, 1918) has a dust-jacket which adds urgency to this question: 'NOSTROMO. A MOVING TALE OF HIGH ADVENTURE – OF REVOLUTION, ROMANCE, HIDDEN TREASURE, AND A HERO OF THE MOST VIVID PERSONALITY. 5s.' As though the anonymous designer of the dust-jacket felt uneasily that that might not have done full justice to the novel the inner flap urges us not to throw the text away: 'CONRAD'S NOVELS ARE WORTH KEEPING. The work of this author are [sic] literature, and invite reading again and again.' Whatever one may think of the tone of this, its counsel is fair enough. And the jacket reminds us of the familiar problem of genre in Conrad: with *Nostromo* we do indeed have a 'moving tale of high adventure' with the listed ingredients present. And if we feel that more than 'high adventure' is involved then re-reading may lead us in the right direction. As in *Lord Jim*, action and adventure disconcertingly co-exist with narrative and dramatic complexity. But what about the 'Hero of the most vivid personality'? Ford Madox Ford says that the working title of *Nostromo* was '*The Silver of the Mine*' (five words that Ford Madox Ford tells us that he came to hate as he tried to help Conrad through the agonizing business of writing *Nostromo*[65]) but there is no evidence for this in Conrad's letters or in the manuscript of the novel. He seems to have thought of it as *Nostromo* from the beginning, so that the story of Nicolo, the sailor who has stolen the lighter full of silver taken from Williams's *On Many Seas* is, indeed, the source for the novel as the author's note indicates.

I have said that like most of Conrad's major works *Nostromo* started as a short piece and then grew. It was initially conceived – as he wrote to

Ford, 2, January 1903 – as a 'silly and saleable' *novella*, comparable with 'Youth'.[66] The situation fell into a by-now-familiar pattern. It was Conrad's obvious duty to get on with *The Rescue*. A short narrative about the theft of the silver presented itself as a refreshing alternative to, and escape from, that obvious duty, and it grew and grew, as *Lord Jim* had, under the novelist's hand. The Author's Note refers to the 'Nicolo' episode in Williams's book, remarks that it is very short ('about three pages . . . Nothing to speak of') and adds that it then 'evoked the memories of that distant time when everything was so fresh, so surprising, so venturesome, so interesting. . . . Perhaps, perhaps, there still was in the world something to write about' (*Nostromo* p. xlii). The letters of 1903–4 show the text steadily growing. The manuscript shows that the narrative procedure was very like that of *Lord Jim*. Captain Mitchell, 'Fussy Joe', is introduced early as a narrator. We have an ironic perspective on him from the start (as we do in the novel's final state, of course). The manuscript is relatively clean when presenting Fussy Joe's direct speech, while elsewhere it is characterized by masses of erasure and revision. It is as though the same narrative trick that had rescued Conrad from his writing block in the Marlow narrations was being tried again here: Conrad was using a straightforward, confident and somewhat obtuse English sailor and thereby releasing his own congested narrative into fluency.

Like the manuscripts of *Heart of Darkness* and *Lord Jim*, the manuscript of *Nostromo* shows that Conrad did not think in chapters. The chapter divisions and many of the paragraph divisions tend to be added later. But the manuscript does indicate that as the narrative grew Conrad came to think of it as three parts: 'The Silver of the Mine', 'The Isabels' and 'The Lighthouse' are present as working titles. Some of Conrad's best inventions came to him in his first draft as visionary experiences: for example, the eye is led by Old Giorgio's action as he burns his onions to this clumsy round-shouldered figure holding a frying-pan, and then outward and upward to the landscape. This beautiful moment is virtually clean and unrevised between the first draft and the final printed state. Giorgio burns the onions, his wife emerges and tells him that he will make himself ill in the sun:

At her feet the hens made off in all directions, with immense strides; if there were any engineers from up the line staying in Sulaco, a young English face or two would appear at the billiard-room occupying one end of the house; but at the other end, in the *café*, Luis, the mulatto, took good care not to show himself. The Indian girls, with hair like flowing black manes, and dressed only in a shift and short petticoat, stared dully from under the square-cut fringes on their foreheads; the noisy frizzling of fat had stopped, the fumes floated upwards in sunshine, a strong smell of burnt onions hung in the drowsy heat, enveloping the house; and the eye lost itself in a vast expanse of grass to the west, as if the plain between the Sierra overtopping Sulaco, and the coast range away there towards Esmeralda had been as big as half the world (I, chapter 4, p. 24).

Comic domestic misadventure focuses the eye and then leads us out to the landscape, establishing the relationship between the individuals and the political scene which will obtain throughout the novel: we will be aware, constantly, that the individual is performing his actions on a stage which confers on them large political significance. This technique is beautifully exemplified by this chapter of the novel: Giorgio looks out, a few paragraphs beyond the one that I have quoted, at the plain, and the reader shares his vision:

> His eyes examined the plain curiously. Tall trails of dust subsided here and there. In a speckless sky the sun hung clear and blinding. Knots of men ran headlong; others made a stand; and the irregular rattle of firearms came rippling to his ears in the fiery, still air. Single figures on foot raced desperately. Horsemen galloped towards each other, wheeled round together, separated at speed. Giorgio saw one fall, rider and horse disappearing as if they had galloped into a chasm, and the movements of the animated scene were like the passages of a violent game played upon the plain by dwarfs mounted and on foot, yelling with tiny throats, under the mountain that seemed a colossal embodiment of silence. Never before had Giorgio seen this bit of plain so full of active life; his gaze could not take in all its details at once; he shaded his eyes with his hand, till suddenly the thundering of many hoofs near by startled him (I, chapter 4, pp. 26–7).

This activity, witnessed with dispassionate neutrality by Giorgio, is subjected to judgement by Emilia Gould in chapter 6: she sees the violence of political events in Costaguana as 'a puerile and bloodthirsty game of murder and rapine played with terrible earnestness by depraved children' (I, chapter 6, p. 49). This judgement is, of course, the product of personal feeling: the political life of the country is chilling her marriage. But for most of the novel's length the emphasis will be on showing rather than telling, or 'story' rather than 'history,' to use a distinction that Guerard makes in his chapter on *Nostromo*.[67] The politics will not be interpreted or conceptualized for us; unless by obviously unreliable narrators like Fussy Joe, all of whose judgments must be questioned and modified. And I think that this relationship between the foregrounded figure and the large political action indicated in this paragraph helps to explain why the title of the novel is and remains *Nostromo*. Nostromo himself, Captain Fidanza, has a symbolic relationship with the fate of Costaguana. Like it, he moves from the prelapsarian, innocent condition indicated by the opening paragraph to the fallen, commercially and economically compromised condition indicated in part III, chapter 10 where Fussy Joe's confident narrative invites our scepticism and suspicion. The opening of *Nostromo*, part of which forms the epigraph to this chapter, is one of the best beginnings of any novel in the language:

> In the time of Spanish rule, and for many years afterwards, the town of Sulaco – the luxuriant beauty of the orange gardens bears witness to its

antiquity – had never been commercially anything more important than a
coasting port with a fairly large local trade in ox-hides and indigo. The
clumsy deep-sea galleons of the conquerors that, needing a brisk gale to
move at all, would lie becalmed, where your modern ship built on clipper
lines forges ahead by the mere flapping of her sails, had been barred out of
Sulaco by the prevailing calms of its vast gulf. Some harbours of the earth
are made difficult of access by the treachery of sunken rocks and the tempests
of their shores. Sulaco had found an inviolable sanctuary from the temptations
of a trading world in the solemn hush of the deep Golfo Placido as if within
an enormous semi-circular and unroofed temple open to the ocean, with
its walls of lofty mountains hung with the mourning draperies of cloud
(I, chapter 1, p. 3).

A great deal is going on in this opening paragraph. Ironic prolepses bris-
tle: this 'inviolable' place is shortly to be violated by American and British
economic imperialism (Holroyd's investment in the silver mine and Sir
John's investment in the railway respectively). This 'unroofed temple' has
been sacred to systems of belief which will soon become obsolete. The
'draperies' mourn the mythical past of the country which is to be taken
over by the vulgar energies of the economic present. To take this first
paragraph and the final incident of the first part of the novel, 'The Silver
of the Mine', is to see prelapsarian Nostromo at his most splendid against
the background of the prelapsarian Golfo Placido. The barbaric figure of
Nostromo on horseback – silver buttons, silver plates on headstall and
saddle, an embroidered silk sash – proclaims primitive vanity, energy and
confidence. And the ensuing scene is itself primitive: his current girl re-
proaches him for failing to give her a present and this prompts in him a
prodigal and flamboyant gesture – he cuts the silver buttons from his coat
(I, chapter 8, pp. 125, 129–130). Nostromo is there for us to admire and
applaud. His heroic actions ensure Sulaco's successful secession from
Costaguana – he takes the lighter of silver out over the Placid Gulf, thus
protecting it from Sotillo, and he performs the remarkable ride to Cayta,
bringing Barrios and his reinforcements to rescue Gould and Monygham.
But heroic action coexists with his fall from a paradisal to a guilty state:

> Nostromo woke up from a fourteen hours' sleep, and arose full length from
> his lair in the long grass. He stood knee deep amongst the whispering
> undulations of the green blades with the lost air of a man just born into the
> world. [*] Handsome, robust, and supple, he threw back his head, flung his
> arms open, and stretched himself with a slow twist of the waist and a leisurely
> growling yawn of white teeth, as natural and free from evil in the moment
> of waking as a magnificent and unconscious wild beast. Then, in the sud-
> denly steadies glance fixed upon nothing from under a thoughtful frown,
> appeared the man (III, chapter 7, pp. 411–12).

At the point marked [*] in the above paragraph (after 'a man just born
into the world') the serial publication has: 'But quickly the look of recognition came into his eyes'. Cedric Watts thinks that to restore this sentence

would restore the paragraph's sense.[68] I disagree: I think the 'look of recognition' in this sentence comes too early and that Conrad successfully heightens his effect by removing it. In its final state this paragraph beautifully sustains Nostromo's innocence until the punch line in the last sentence destroys it. In the penultimate sentence he emerges from drowsiness still 'unconscious' and 'free from evil' and the paragraph packs its shocking knowledge of Nostromo's fallen state into the final sentence's reference to Nostromo's 'steadied glance', which points up the contrast between the 'beast' (last word of the penultimate sentence) and the 'man' (last word of the whole paragraph).

Nostromo, 'our man,' who, as Teresa says, has a name which is not a real name – a name conferred on him by the English – is an exemplary figure. He is exemplary in that he embodies the fate of his country. Greed undoes him. He conceals the silver from the lighter on the Great Isabel and recognizes – in the phrase taken from Williams's Nicolo – that he must 'grow rich very slowly' (III, chapter 10, p. 503). From his mythical identity – the proud horseman who cuts off his silver buttons for his girl (it is important, of course, that the buttons are silver and that by thus scornfully disposing of them he is displaying his freedom from cupidity) he is transformed, by greed, into the figure whose supposed 'fabulous good luck in trading' makes him look as vulgar and suburban as (say) Arnold Bennett:

> Fiercely whiskered and grave, a shade less supple in his walk, the vigour and symmetry of his powerful limbs lost in the vulgarity of a brown tweed suit . . . Captain Fidanza was seen in the streets of Sulaco attending to his business, as usual. . . . Nostromo, the miscalled Capataz de Cargadores, had made for himself, under his rightful name, another public existence, but modified by the new conditions, less picturesque, more difficult to keep up in the increased size and varied population of Sulaco (III, chapter 12, p. 527).

In the first part of the novel Nostromo is seen defending his adoptive family, the Violas, at the height of the civil war (I, chapter 4). Giorgio is confidently proud of this sturdy young man who is the same age as his own son would have been, had he lived. At the close of the novel the adopted son, the beloved Gian' Battista, is shot by Giorgio in error for Ramirez, the philanderer who is thought to be paying unwelcome respects to Giselle, the old man's daughter. The story of Nostromo's relationship with the Viola family is thus a frame surrounding the more complex stories, those of Gould, Decoud and Monygham. 'Nostromo' as title points to the allegory embedded in the Nostromo-plot. In the Morenita scene the Nostromo who disregards silver is a supremely confident male, capable of vigorous sexual conquest; 'our man' in the sense of having the kind of freedom that we would all like to enjoy. In the final scene he has been effectively unsexed by the silver that he has stolen. He comes to the island to collect from his hoard, and pays court to Linda as his pretext for his visits, but is actually attracted to Giselle. The silver has cut across his sexuality just as it has destroyed the Gould marriage. Nostromo's dying dialogue with Emilia Gould underlines this symmetry: he tells her that 'the silver has killed me' and she replies that 'I, too, have hated the idea of that silver from the bottom of my heart' (III, chapter 13, pp. 559–60).

Jacques Berthoud remarks that 'For all its imaginative appeal Nostromo has acquired some notoriety as a novel that one cannot read unless one has read it before'.[69] I sympathize with this: I think that Conrad plunges us into the historical complexity of Costaguana and the psychological complexities of Gould, Decoud and Monygham so that we are as bewildered and exhausted as we would be if we were ourselves participating in the revolution and civil war in Costaguana. But I think the title and the story it refers to are designed to help us. Nostromo's own story is not a narrative which one cannot read unless one has read it before, and vindicates, to some extent, the engaging description of the novel offered by the hack who wrote the cover-note for Dent ('A MOVING TALE OF HIGH AD-VENTURE,' etc[70]). If we attend to the Nostromo narrative on its own we see him in three distinct stages of clearly delineated dramatic development: as the protector and adoptive son of the Violas, as the hero who ensures that Sulaco's secession will succeed, and, finally, as the corrupted thief who is ironically killed by the man who has consistently loved and admired him.

This leads us into the more complex stories: the stories of Gould, Decoud and Monygham. As I have said, Gould is substantially based on Cun-ninghame Graham. As a young man Gould is free and adventurous, look-ing on in pitying dismay at his father, caught in a merciless trap. As an adult he willingly enters that same trap – the San Tomé concession – intent on converting his father's failure into success. This seems to work: the mine becomes both a profitable enterprise and the one source of stability in Costaguana. In the political crisis which occupies much of the text it is the major source of strength of those seeking secession for Sulaco. Yet as it displays the Gould marriage the novel makes it clear that the mine is, in the end, as much a trap for Charles Gould as it had been for his father. Emilia Gould sees his possession by the mine with horrible clarity: 'A man haunted by a fixed idea is insane' (III, chapter 4, p. 379). This insight of hers is offered to us at a fairly late point in the reader's engagement with the text; much earlier, we have been shown that Gould's supposed freedom is an illusion. The narrative consciousness has more access to Gould in his young manhood than anywhere else in the text. His ambition is hard and fine: he is resolved to make the mine profitable; he is also passionately in love with Emilia, but the mine comes first, and the later tragedy of the Gould marriage is glanced at proleptically in the scene in which she agrees to marry him: 'The only thing he wanted to know now, he said, was whether she did love him enough – whether she would have the courage to go with him so far away? He put these questions to her in a voice that trembled with anxiety – for he was a determined man. She did. She would. And immediately the future hostess of all the

Europeans in Sulaco had the physical experience of the earth falling away from under her' (I, chapter 6, p. 63). A dark shadow lingers ironically behind this high moment for Charles Gould: at his moment of erotic triumph the trap is beginning to close. And it is shortly shown that his freedom is illusory: he is *owned* by Holroyd, the American millionaire:

> It interested the great man [Holroyd] to attend personally to the San Tomé mine; it interested him so much that he allowed this hobby to give a direction to the first complete holiday he had taken for quite a startling number of years. He was not running a great enterprise there; no mere railway board or industrial corporation. He was running a man! (I, chapter 6, p. 81).

Although Charles Gould is born and bred a Costaguanero he is educated in England '(The Gould family, established in Costaguana for three generations, always went to England for their education and for their wives)' (I, chapter 6, p. 46), and we are regularly reminded that his style is that of a displaced Englishman: 'He looked more English than a casual tourist. . . . He looked more English than the last arrived batch of young railways engineers, than anybody out of the hunting-field pictures in the numbers of *Punch* reaching his wife's drawing-room two months or so after date. . . . [He] went on looking thoroughly English even on horseback' (I, chapter 6, pp. 47–8). But his 'accent had never been English' (I, chapter 6, p. 48). Surely Conrad, whose own accent never sounded remotely English, is working out some of his feelings about social displacement in England here.

Part of Gould's tragedy is that he allows himself to be dominated by an inferior. As an American, Holroyd is by definition the child of emigrants – but then so is Gould. To establish the difference between them Conrad has to have Holroyd the child of many European countries: 'His parentage was German and Scotch and English, with remote strains of Danish and French blood, giving him the temperament of a Puritan and an insatiable imagination of conquest' (I, chapter 6, p. 76). Conrad the purebred Pole looks down with aristocratic disdain at the hybrid vigour of this aggressive mongrel, and at the extraordinary crass arrogance of his expression of America's wealth and power: 'Time itself has got to wait on the greatest country in the whole of God's Universe. We shall be giving the word for everything. . . . We shall run the world's business whether the world likes it or not. The world can't help it – and neither can we, I guess' (I, chapter 6, p. 77).

Gould is known to us as a schoolboy and as a young man. As his ambition for Sulaco and for the mine hardens, so he is perceived not by the omniscient narrative voice having direct access to his consciousness, but by the consciousnesses of others – Emilia, Monygham. As his portrait becomes externalized and is seen in terms of his actions, so Martin Decoud's becomes internalized. The lover of Antonia Avellanos, the Paris-oriented Costaguanero of the Boulevards, becomes a sufferer from psychological illness at the moment of his suicide. Conrad uses Decoud's death to point to what he clearly perceives as universal truths about the human condition. Decoud is clinging to a thin cord which crosses the Placid Gulf, which, as I have said above, resembles the tight vibrating cord which is associated with psychological anguish in *The Inheritors*.[71] Cedric Watts imagines the cord to be vertical, like the cord used to torture Hirsch with the strappado,[72] but to me it seems to be a horizontal cord, crossing the Gulf like a tightrope, Decoud hanging from it by his hands like a tightrope walker who has slipped: 'the solitude appeared like a great void, and the silence of the gulf like a tense, thin cord to which he hung suspended by both hands, without fear, without surprise, without any sort of emotion whatever' (III, chapter 10, p. 498). The cord in *The Inheritors* is horizontal, and the cord in *Nostromo* is described in similar language and has a similar function. It is important that Decoud is imagined as 'hanging', by both hands, from the stretched cord. He is not imagined as tied to it, nor, as far as I can see, as swinging at the end of it.

I agree with Cedric Watts that there is a puzzle in the Decoud story in that Conrad is unduly harsh on Decoud. It may be, as Watts suggests, that in punishing Decoud Conrad is punishing his own depressive temperament,[73] but I would not want to understate Decoud's representative status. This passage invites us to see Decoud as a type or exemplar, from whose predicament arises a resonant generalization which embodies one of Conrad's major convictions about the human condition:

> Solitude from mere outward condition of existence becomes very swiftly a state of soul in which the affectations of irony and scepticism have no place. It takes possession of the mind, and drives forth the thought into the exile of utter unbelief. After three days of waiting for the sight of some human face, Decoud caught himself entertaining a doubt of his own individuality. It had merged into the world of cloud and water, of natural forces and forms of nature. *In our activity alone do we find the sustaining illusion of an independent existence as against the whole scheme of things of which we form a helpless part* [my italics]. (III, chapter 10, p. 497).

It is relevant, of course, to remember that Conrad shot himself through the chest at the age of twenty when we see Decoud shoot himself before he topples out of the boat:

> The great gulf burst into a glitter all around the boat; and in this glory of merciless solitude the silence appeared again before him, stretched taut like a dark, thin string.
>
> His eyes looked at it while, without haste, he shifted his seat from the thwart to the gunwale. They looked at its fixedly, while his hand, feeling about his waist, unbuttoned the flap of the leather case, drew the revolver, cocked it, brought it forward pointing at his breast, pulled the trigger, and, with convulsive force, sent the still-smoking weapon hurtling through the air. His eyes looked at it while he fell forward and hung with his breast on

the gunwale and the fingers of his right hand hooked under the thwart. They looked –

'It is done,' he stammered out, in a sudden flow of blood. His last thought was: 'I wonder how that Capataz died.' The stiffness of the fingers relaxed, and the lover of Antonia Avellanos rolled overboard without having heard the cord of silence snap in the solitude of the Placid Gulf, whose glittering surface remained untroubled by the fall of his body (III, chapter 10, pp. 500–1).

There is a delicate metaphorical irony here. The cord stretching across the gulf has until this moment existed in Decoud's mind. Now, suddenly, it is imagined as snapping, or as having the capacity to snap, *outside* the consciousness of Decoud at the moment of his death (the text seems to leave open the question of whether the cord actually snaps or not; all we know is that Decoud hasn't heard it do so).

At the heart of the novel is Dr Monygham, one of Conrad's subtlest and most complex characterizations, the man who is strong because he understands his own weakness. His life and that of Nostromo are displayed in contrary motion by the text. At first the reader sees Monygham through the eyes of the general, and hostile, public gossip of Sulaco: 'At his worst people feared the open scornfulness of his tongue. Only Mrs Gould could keep his unbelief in men's motives within due bounds' (I, chapter 6, p. 44). He is disliked and feared as a foreigner who is 'loco' – mad – and whose precarious standing in Sulaco is sustained only by Emilia Gould's unaccountable friendship for him. In part III, chapter 4 we are suddenly given full access to Monygham's mind. He was tortured, during the reign of Guzman Bento, by one Father Beron. The core of his self-mistrust is the fact that although Father Beron is now dead he still haunts Monygham's dreams and would be a source of terror to him if encountered in the street. Many readers, including A. J. Guerard and Robert Penn Warren[74] think that Monygham has in reality betrayed friends under torture. But this is wrong, I think. The popular view, held in Sulaco and expressed in chapter 6, is this: 'Years ago, in the time of Guzman Bento, he had been mixed up, it was whispered, in a conspiracy which was betrayed and, as people expressed it, drowned in blood' (p. 45). But this is *only* the popular view. Under the pressure of Beron's tortures Monygham *invented* his confessions; the general belief that he betrayed a conspiracy is in fact mistaken, he betrayed nobody: 'His confessions, when they came at last, were very complete. . . . Sometimes on the nights when he walked the floor, he wondered, grinding his teeth with shame and rage, at the *fertility of his imagination* [my italics] when stimulated by a sort of pain which makes truth, honour, self-respect, and life itself matters of little moment' (III, chapter 4, p. 373).

The torture unmans Monygham not by forcing him to crack under it but by doing him lasting psychological damage. A terror of Father Beron, the torturer, becomes ingrained and continues to haunt him long after Father Beron's death. Once Sulaco has seceded and Monygham is appointed the Inspector-General of State Hospitals, he becomes psychologically stronger. He looks more smartly dressed, and this reflects an increase in his 'self-respect' which is marked by 'the almost complete disappearance from his dreams of Father Beron' (III, chapter 11, p. 508). He will never be happy, because his love for Emilia is not the 'most splendid of illusions' of literary tradition but 'an enlightening and priceless misfortune' (III, chapter 11, p. 513). All he gains from this honourable love is wisdom: the clearsighted ability to witness Emilia's unhappy and childless marriage with despairing compassion. As he grows in confidence and self-knowledge so his declared enemy, Nostromo, sinks. Nostromo is as completely a victim of 'material interest' as is Charles Gould: 'A transgression, a crime, entering a man's existence, eats it up like a malignant growth, consumes it like fever. Nostromo had lost his peace; the genuineness of all his qualities was destroyed. He felt it himself, and often cursed the silver of San Tomé' (III, chapter 12, p. 523).

In his simplicity Nostromo never understands the Doctor. The novel's finest irony is found in part II, 'The Isabels', where Nostromo fails to see that he is being manipulated into playing two crucial roles in the struggle for the secession of Sulaco. Conrad dramatizes power-struggles which are contained within, and which illustrate, the political pressures at work in Costaguana. The Holroyd/Gould relationship, the Decoud/Nostromo relationship and (finally) the Monygham/Nostromo relationship are power-relationships in which the stronger, more self-possessed and more self-knowing figure manipulates and controls the other. Coleridge, in one of his most painful and embarrassing acts of hero-worship, speaks of his friend Wordsworth inhabiting 'the dread watch-tower of man's absolute self'[75]. Nostromo explores a web of relationships between men who are passionate and men who have cold self-possession. Decoud, for much of the text, seems to be such a person: a calculating ironist, a dilettante who comes to Costaguana initially in the spirit of a tourist, and then engages in the campaign for the secession of Sulaco in a spirit which seems very like that of Wildean paradox. He declares to Mrs Gould that he involves himself in Sulaco's bid for secession from Costaguana solely because of his love for Antonia Avellanos. He congratulates himself on what he sees as the French intellectual clarity of his position:

'I am not deceiving myself about my motives. She won't leave Sulaco for my sake, therefore Sulaco must leave the rest of the Republic to its fate. Nothing could be clearer than that. I like a clearly defined situation. I cannot part with Antonia, therefore the one and indivisible Republic of Costaguana must be made to part with its western province' (II, chapter 6, p. 215).

Decoud sees himself as an ironist working with sentimentalists: the sentimentalists are Charles Gould and his master, Holroyd. To be a sentimentalist, in Decoud's formulation, is to endow one's 'personal desires with a shining robe of silk and jewels' (II, chapter 6, p. 218). Yet the novel

systematically undercuts Decoud's position and finally kills him. I have
referred to Cedric Watts' suggestion that in the death of the sceptical
Decoud Conrad is punishing – by execution – the sceptical aspects of his
own temperament.[76] I do not think that Conrad is punishing himself, but
I do think that he is exploring the dynamics of two relationships that he
knew in life. With Cunninghame Graham, Conrad could see himself as
the cosmopolitan ironist and his friend as the headlong man of action –
in that coupling Graham was the more 'male' partner. With Ford, Conrad
himself was the more mature, the more seasoned (his life in the merchant
navy looked very macho indeed compared with Ford's closeted aesthetic
young manhood) and the more 'male'. Because his intellect is much more
subtle Decoud seems to be the stronger partner as he and Nostromo take
the lighter out over the gulf with its cargo of silver. He and Nostromo are
working to sustain the 'sentimental' illusions of the two 'idealists', Gould
and (especially) Holroyd, 'who attached a strangely idealistic meaning to
concrete facts' (II, chapter 6, p. 219). But Hirsch's over-civilized terror
can be taken as an expression of something that could happen to Decoud
himself, while Nostromo is upheld, as Decoud sees, by his fierce and
primitive vanity, 'that finest form of egoism which can take on the aspect
of every virtue' (II, chapter 7, p. 300). Each of the supposedly strong figures in the novel is undone, apart from Monygham who never imagines
himself to be strong in the first place. Decoud's irony ceases to serve him
when he is alone. Conrad's omniscient narrator displays Decoud's in-
sufficiency: 'The brilliant "Son Decoud," the spoiled darling of the family,
the lover of Antonia and journalist of Sulaco, was not fit to grapple with
himself single-handed. Solitude from mere outward condition of existence
becomes very swiftly a state of soul in which the affectations of irony and
scepticism have no place' (III, chapter 10, p. 497). After his death Gould
and Nostromo in turn are undone, as we have seen: it is as though there
are to be no victors in these partnerships and power-struggles. But Conrad
himself emerges victorious, looking on from a great height at the cruel
ironic world in which his figures are trapped.

Guerard thinks that the first two parts of *Nostromo* are excellent and that
the last part is unsuccessful. He says this in the context of his observation
about the omniscient narrator's relationship with the reader, and anyone
thinking about Guerard's discussion has to be forgiven for concluding
that his adverse opinion of the last part of the novel is not unrelated to
his sense of the narrative technique as vexatiously taxing: he says that 'the
common reader's notorious general aim – to enter into the book and
become one of its characters – is carefully and austerely baffled. The
novelist (shifting scene, time, emphasis, focus, post of observation) mali-
ciously chops at his [or her] hands'.[77] Guerard thinks that Nostromo's
'grand-opera' conclusion is 'unworthy of the novel that has gone before'.[78]
I find that I want to relate that to an intriguing point raised by Robert
Penn Warren's essay in which he suggests that we ought not to speak of
'character' in Conrad 'for Conrad, in one sense, had little concern for

character independently considered. He is no Dickens or Shakespeare, with relish for the mere variety and richness of personality. Rather, for him a character lives in terms of its typical involvement with situation and theme: the fable, the fable as symbol for exfoliating theme, is his central fact'.[79] But is this right? In *Nostromo* I find that the personalities of Gould, Decoud and Monygham are powerfully present to me at the points of the text that I have indicated: that is, at the points at which the reader is permitted to have full access to them. Nostromo himself is dramatized in a rather different way. Many of the scenes are at pains to display him to us as a kind of icon, a perfect man, balanced, intelligent, self-possessed, quiet: a man who embodies force and energy *for others*. The scene in which he visits the Padrona Teresa on her death-bed takes place nearly half-way through the text, but displays Nostromo to us as though we are meeting him for the first time: he is given an operatic entrance, carefully lit:

> Nostromo slowly crossed the large kitchen, all dark but for the glow of a heap of charcoal under the heavy mantel of the cooking-range, where water was boiling in an iron pot with a loud bubbling sound. Between the two walls of a narrow staircase a bright light streamed from the sickroom above; and the magnificent Capataz de Cargardores stepping noiselessly in soft leather sandals, bushy whiskered, his muscular neck and bronzed chest bare in the open check shirt, resembled a Mediterranean sailor just come ashore from some wine or fruit-laden felucca. At the top he paused, broad shouldered, narrow hipped and supple, looking at the large bed. . . . The Capataz had a red sash wound many times round his waist, and a heavy silver ring on the forefinger of the hand he raised to give a twist to his moustache (II, chapter 7, p. 252).

The Padrona has sought to annex him as a husband for Linda, the older and more responsible of her daughters, because of his quiet steadiness: 'He had seemed to her courageous, a hard worker, determined to make his way in the world' (II, chapter 7, p. 253). Now as she dies she is disappointed in him: he seems to have surrendered his ambition to vanity, to be content with a name given to him by the English, 'Nostromo', rather than his real, Italian name, Gian' Battista Findanza. These fellow-Italians should be Nostromo's family. The novel is clearly at pains to make a point of this: Ian Watt remarks that there are very few families anywhere in Conrad and that most of the major figures in *Nostromo* are alone or childless (Monygham, Decoud, Nostromo himself and the Goulds), so this Italian group of two elderly parents and two adolescent children is conspicuous.[80] (The Avellanos are another fairly conspicuous family group: Decoud's love for the daughter, Antonia, and respect for the father, Don José, contribute to his death.) The Violas lost a son, who would now be roughly Nostromo's age if he had lived. In their emotional logic the admired Gian' Battista should replace that dead son. But Nostromo refuses to fetch a priest to hear Teresa's last confession and turns away from the tight-knit Italian unit to unite himself with the much larger group, the political activists who are working for the plan devised by Decoud to achieve Sulaco's independence from Costaguana. Nostromo's usual affectionate address to old Giorgio is 'Vecchio', Italian for 'old man', and it is an odd and intriguing detail that at the end of this scene he says '*Adios, viejo*'; he takes leave of old Giorgio in Spanish, the language of their adopted country, Costaguana, and not Italian, their mutual family language. It may be that this marks the difference that I've described: his relationship with these old Italians is not, after all, familial, they do not own him, Teresa's reading of him has been mistaken, he is more Costaguanan than Italian, he is his own man. But it is hard for us to say this with confidence as he is presented externally, here; the scene gives no access to his thoughts. He is dramatized in a different way later in the novel.

He 'was on the point of jumping overboard.' He 'looked suicide deliberately in the face.' The phrases sound as though they are part of Jim's struggle with his lost honour at the end of *Lord Jim*, but they are not: this is Nostromo, having stolen the silver and buried it on the Great Isabel, confronting the appalling fact that a lighthouse is being built close to the site of his buried treasure and that he therefore faces exposure and disgrace. Jim inhabits a guilt culture. Nostromo, a more primitive being, inhabits a shame culture: it is this that links the barbaric and self-possessed 'incorruptible' figure of the earlier part of the story to this furtive criminal, resorting to desperate expedients, in the latter part. It is the self-image, the public esteem, that is in danger of being destroyed, as we see by restoring the above phrases to their context:

> The incomparable Nostromo, the Capataz, the respected and feared Captain Fidanza, the unquestioned patron of secret societies, a republican like old Giorgio, and a revolutionist at heart (but in another manner), was on the point of jumping overboard from the deck of his own schooner. That man, subjective almost to insanity, looked suicide deliberately in the face. But he never lost his head. He was checked by the thought that this was no escape. He imagined himself dead, and the disgrace, the shame going on. Or rather, properly speaking, he could not imagine himself dead. He was possessed too strongly by the sense of his own existence, a thing of infinite duration in its changes, to grasp the notion of finality. The earth goes on for ever (III, chapter 12, pp. 525–6).

The figure who has performed the two heroic actions which have ensured the secession of Sulaco – the rescuing of the lighter-load of silver from the mine, which is to be shipped North to Holroyd, and the ride to Cayta to bring Barrios to the defence of Sulaco – has now, in the 'vulgarity' of his brown tweed suit, become a thief who looks like a businessman.

Conrad's desire to dress Nostromo in appropriate costumes and give him operatic entrances remains a feature of his dramatization right to the end. On the Great Isabel, in a scene of emotional torment in which Nostromo is torn between his formal commitment to Linda and his sexual attraction to Giselle, the narrative draws attention, again, to his costume:

The incorruptible Nostromo breathed her ambient seduction in the tumul-
tuous heaving of his breast. Before leaving the harbour he had thrown off
the store clothing of Captain Fidanza, for greater ease in the long pull out
to the islands. He stood before her in the red sash and check shirt as he
used to appear on the Company's wharf – a Mediterranean sailor come
ashore to try his luck in Costaguana (III, chapter 12, p. 537).

His clothes point up the irony of the situation. In order to row out
comfortably to the island where he has persuaded 'Fussy Joe' to establish
Giorgio Viola and his daughters as lighthouse keepers (thus providing
cover for Nostromo's clandestine visits to his hoard of silver) Nostromo
has taken off his brown suit and resumed his earlier costume. He looks
like the pre-lapsarian, self-possessed hero, but the inner man has fallen,
morally hollowed out by the silver. Giorgio shoots him, mistaking him for
Ramirez the seducer of Giselle, and the novel offers a final, and powerfully operatic, tableau in which Emilia Gould hears Nostromo's last words.
Nostromo would not call a priest to hear the confession of Teresa, his
surrogate mother: now a mother- figure, wearing quasi-religious costume,
bends over Nostromo at his death:

> Mrs Gould . . . cloaked and monastically hooded over her evening cos-
> tume . . . full of endurance and compassion, stood by the side of the bed on
> which the splendid Capataz de Cargadores lay stretched out motionless on
> his back. The whiteness of sheets and pillows gave a sombre and energetic
> relief to his bronzed face, to the dark, nervous hands, so good on a tiller,
> upon a bridle and on a trigger, lying open and idle upon a white coverlet
> (III, chapter 13, p. 558).

The symmetry is incomplete, of course: Mrs Gould plays the role of
confessor but declines to hear Nostromo's full confession. Instead she
makes a confession of her own, bringing in another, surprising symmetry
– she and he are equally victims of the mine. She declares her hatred for
the silver and refuses to be told where Nostromo has hidden it: 'No one
misses it now. Let it be lost for ever.' And when Monygham – moral centre
of the novel and Emilia Gould's platonic lover – asks her for Nostromo's
last words she refuses to disclose them.

The scene recalls an earlier symmetry, also perceived by Monygham and
involving three families, the Violas, the Goulds, and the family of Basilio,
the Goulds' servant. Monygham is reporting trouble in the Viola family to
Mrs Gould; he has seen Ramirez raging at Linda (Ramirez has deduced,
accurately, that Giselle is being seduced by Nostromo, despite the latter's
engagement to Linda). The narrative again sets up a piece of operatic
staging for us: ' "It was a strange sight, Mrs Gould [says Monygham]: the
long jetty, with this raving Cargador [Ramirez] in his crimson sash and the
girl all in black, at the end; the early Sunday morning quiet of the harbour
in the shade of the mountains; nothing but a canoe or two moving between
the ships at anchor". . . .' (III, chapter 11, p. 517.)

Mrs Gould regards it as her duty to solve the Viola family problems: she declares, peremptorily, that Nostromo must 'put an end to all this by marrying Linda at once.' This is immediately juxtaposed with a little scene which forces on us another irony: Emilia Gould can see the solution to the Violas' problems but cannot cope with her own. Basilio appears with a message from Charles Gould. Basilio is holding a baby, 'his own and Leonarda's last born'. His message is that Gould is not coming home: 'The master remains to sleep at the mountain to-night.' Emilia Gould replies 'Very well, Basilio,' and watches her servant return to his quarters holding his child. Monygham 'pours mental imprecations on Charles Gould's head'. Emilia Gould does not have children and never will have, and this is experienced by Monygham at this moment as tragedy. The narrative then enters Emilia's own consciousness and confirms that she is indeed suffering: 'for life to be large and full, it must contain the care of the past and of the future.' For her there is no future to care for, and she receives 'a great wave of loneliness that swept over her head' (III, chapter 11, pp. 519–21). These little scenes register and enact what we already know, that the Gould marriage is loveless and childless because Charles is wedded to the mine. He 'sleeps' with it, not with his wife. The effect of these scenes is to put Nostromo and Gould side by side; in each case the emotional life has been corrupted and destroyed by the 'material interests' which Gould, in an imaginary letter to Holroyd, identifies as dictating his actions:

> Charles Gould imagined himself writing a letter to San Franciso in some such words: '. . . The men at the head of the movement are dead or have fled; the civil organization of the province is at an end for the present; the Blanco party in Sulaco has collapsed inexcusably, but in the characteristic manner of this country. But Barrios, untouched in Cayta, remains still available. I am forced to take up openly the plan of a provincial revolution as the only way of placing the enormous material interests involved in the prosperity and peace of Sulaco in a position of permanent safety. . . .' That was clear. He saw these words as if written in letters of fire upon the wall at which he was gazing abstractedly (III, chapter 4, p. 379).

Jan Verleun remarks that from this point in the novel Gould 'can no longer follow the dictates of his moral sense'.[81] We may add that it is here that Emilia Gould, witnessing his abstraction, reflects that 'A man haunted by a fixed idea is insane.' 'Insane' may not be the right word: but whatever his state of mind, she is right to intuit disaster in that her marriage is henceforth doomed. The final scenes of the novel display Nostromo's death as a kind of victory: over Gould and Monygham (Mrs Gould is more loyal to Nostromo than to either her husband or her friend) and over the Viola family. Linda's bereft cry of love for him is described in the novel's final paragraph as the greatest of Nostromo's 'triumphs'. But the triumphal and tragic tone here is ironic in relation to the novel's dramatic organization. Nostromo has been the frame, the flourish or arabesque with which the novel surrounds itself by taking his name as its title. He is the central instrument in the political story and also, in the novel's final chapters, the dominant figure on stage. When we have finished reading *Nostromo* we know that material interests have destroyed him, reducing him from an 'incorruptible' mythic to a corrupted bourgeois identity, and that the shape of his story is an allegory of the history of Costaguana and thus of mankind.

6

Towards Verloc, 1904–1907

One fell to musing before the phenomenon – even of the past – of South America, a continent of crude sunshine and brutal revolutions; and of the sea, the vast expanse of salt waters, the mirror of heaven's frowns and smiles, the reflector of the world's light. Then the vision of an enormous town presented itself, of a monstrous town more populous than some continents and in its man-made might as if indifferent to heaven's frowns and smiles, a cruel devourer of the world's light. There was room enough there to place any story, depth enough there for any passion, variety enough there for any setting, darkness enough to bury five millions of lives.

From the 'Author's Note' to *The Secret Agent*.[1]

People don't want intelligence. It worries them – and they demand from their writers as much subserviency as from their footmen if not rather more.

Conrad to Norman Douglas, 18 October 1905[2]

If 1900 had been a peak, 1904–6 was a trough. For a good deal of the time in these two years Conrad seems, as far as his writing goes, to lack direction and dissipate his energies on timewasting and minor projects (and the blind alley of theatrical ambition). The completion of *Nostromo* had been a shattering business, 'a fact' as Conrad put it to Edward Garnett, 'upon which my friends may congratulate me as upon a recovery from a dangerous illness' (3 September 1904).[3] And the torture was prolonged: he was 'half dead' and told Elsie Hueffer that 'the last few nights I felt my brain going' but he still had 'a lot to do to the *book text* of N' (2 September 1904);[4] he spent several more weeks expanding and revising the ending of *Nostromo* for book publication.[5] There is no doubt that the exhaustion was real and that lassitude and depression followed, reinforced by the fact that *Nostromo* had disappointing reviews: he wrote ruefully to Pinker 'I am afraid Nostromo had a bad sendoff. I receive magnificent letters from unexpected quarters; I know well enough that the book is no mean feat – but what about the public?' (31 October 1904).[6] This sums up the problem as Conrad saw it: *Nostromo* was a masterpiece but people would not buy it and he had to *sell* his work. The need was desperate before *Nostromo* was finished and, as we have seen, provoked him early in 1904 to resort to his taxing regime of writing *Nostromo* during the day and dictating *The Mirror of the Sea* to Ford late at night: in a letter to Wells, 7 February 1904, he acts tough about the commercial spirit in which he is working: 'I've started a series of sea sketches and have sent out P on the hunt to place them. This must *save* me. I've discovered that I can dictate that sort of bosh without effort at the rate of 3000 words in four hours. Fact! The only thing now is to sell it to a paper and then make a book of the rubbish. Hang! So in the day *Nostromo* and from 11pm to 1am dictation'.[7] This letter is a fine instance of Conrad as epistolary chameleon: Wells himself adopted a similar tone in many of his letters about the literary market place, especially in his correspondence with Bennett. But Wells *believed* in the market-place, Conrad patently did not.

Part of the problem was Jessie's incapacity. Her injury forced Conrad to go to Pinker and Galsworthy for money for the medical expenses. She could no longer help with his work, and Pinker hired for Conrad a secretary, Lilian Hallowes, who came into his service in March 1904 (and stayed for twenty years): she took the last part of *Nostromo* from Conrad's dictation. But Conrad's state of mind was deteriorating: on 5 April 1904 he writes to Galsworthy 'Pain and trouble are the only incontrovertible [sic] realities of existence. . . . This is hell. I suppose I am near enough to insanity.' And on the same day to Meldrum, Blackwood's London agent 'Half the time I feel on the verge of insanity. The difficulties are accumulating around me in a frighful manner'.[8]

When the struggle with *Lord Jim* was at its height Conrad had been able to take refuge from poverty in the fact of the book itself: the sense of achievement alone made him feel 'young and healthy and rich' (to Garnett, 26 March 1900).[9] By 1904 the sensation of being rich could no longer be afforded by the knowledge that he had written great books. Actual money was needed. Anxiety about money began to affect his relationships, producing cringing prostration with close friends (especially Galsworthy, who always responded with 'loans' which were understood by both parties to be gifts) and evasiveness and mendacity with Pinker, to whom he was deeply and increasingly in debt. He was in debt to others, notably Ford. who was no better at managing his affairs than was Conrad. During this period Ford regularly asked for repayment and Conrad repeatedly put him off. Jessie seems never to have known how desperate their circumstances were during these years. Conrad could probably have managed better, and would certainly have been less worried, if he had confided in her, especially in the early days. She was capable, she understood poverty and Conrad's required lifestyle did not really suit her (she got bored if there were too many servants) but after her injury early 1904 she could do less (and her medical expenses added to the debts). Conrad's behaviour indicated that it was as a consequence of some fault in the arrangement of the universe that he was not rich. He lived expensively as a way of forcing reality to conform to his wishes. Early in 1905 we find him writing to Pinker to 'refute the charge of mad extravagance which your perfectly friendly remarks as to my expenditure did in fact contain'[10] and preparing for a four month visit to Capri. The idea was that he could rest from financial anxiety and that he would be able to write fluently in a pleasant climate, but it turned out to be financially disastrous and artistically barren. Conrad himself soon came to see that the trip was an absurd mistake: on 21 January 1905 he wrote to Galsworthy begging urgently for funds and saying that 'the whole expedition is a mad thing really for it rests upon what I am not certain of – my power to produce some sixty thou: words in 4 months'.[11] On Capri Conrad befriended Norman Douglas, whose work he would loyally promote for the next few years, and Count Zygmunt Szembek, who gave him the idea of 'Il Conde'. By April Conrad was in despair as far as his writing was concerned though Jessie's improved health was some compensation: 'As far as my plan of keeping the pot boiling is concerned the last three months are gone to waste in a way which would be nothing short of miserable if it were not for the very great advantage to my wife's health'.[12]

One of the projects for keeping the pot boiling was his dramatization of 'To-morrow'. This was written early in 1904 with a great deal of help from Ford – there is a forty-three page draft of the play in Ford's handwriting[13] – and send to Arnold Bennett and J. M. Barrie for their opinions. It was understandable that Conrad should wish to write for the stage. Much money was to be made by a novelist who could successfully turn his hand to playwriting – the success in the theatre of his friend John Galsworthy was an immediate demonstration of this fact. Conrad's play was called *One Day More* (the phrase is a quotation from the text of 'To-morrow', a cry of despair from old Hagberd locked in his delusions). Like Henry James, whose agonizing failure with *Guy Domville* (1895) was a fairly recent memory, Conrad was a man of great dramatic imagination who somehow could not write for the theatre. In a later letter to Pinker he was to protest, rightly, that 'the bulk [of my work] *is* dramatic', and that writing for the stage was only a matter of acquiring some technical skills.[14] But he never gained those skills. *One Day More* is better than his later dramatizations, *Laughing Anne* and *Victory*; better perhaps because it is, in effect, a collaboration with Ford (Galsworthy – an experienced playwright and a good judge – wrote in 1924 that he regarded it as the best of Conrad's stage adaptations[15]). It was not taken on by a commercial company but had three performances from the Stage Society, 25–27 June 1905. Conrad wrote to Galsworthy afterwards (30 June 1905) a bit ruefully, saying that the audiences had clearly not liked his play but that Shaw had been 'extatic [sic]' about it. He went on: 'I don't think I am a dramatist. But I believe I've 3 or even 5 acts somewhere in me.' His verdict on this adventure in the theatre was 'Loss of time. A thorough unsettling of the writing mood. Added weariness'.[16]

In 1905 Conrad wrote his great political essay 'Autocracy and War' and the start of a narrative, described to Pinker as 'a short story something in the style of Youth – about a dynamite ship'[17] and provisionally known as 'Explosives' (later *Chance*). He kept going with this during 1905 (the title *Chance* began to be used in October of that year, and Conrad began to refer to it as a 'novel' rather than a story[18]) but half-heartedly, and with impatient digressive forays which produced short, marketable narratives: 'An Anarchist' was finished by the end of the year in this way as were 'The Informer' (by 11 January 1906) and 'The Brute' (probably also written in January: completed by 21 February).

'The Brute' is a pot-boiler about a dangerous ship, written for the (substantial) audience which liked Conrad's Old Salt narratives. The political themes of the other two stories have a bearing on Conrad's major political novels, *The Secret Agent* and *Under Western Eyes*. 'An Anarchist' tells the story of a workman, Paul, on a South American cattle ranch. This man has been since his young manhood a victim of political forces. Imprisoned in Paris for shouting 'Vive l'anarchie' he received the maximum prison sentence because an unscrupulous lawyer sought to make a political martyr of him; subsequent violent events include the murder of those responsible for his arrest. He is now enslaved by the manager of the cattle ranch where he works and has arrived at a kind of quietism: it is still imprisonment, but he will die here away from the political forces which destroyed him. Like Michaelis and Winnie Verloc he is a bewildered victim.

In 'The Informer', subtitled 'An Ironic Tale' we have another anarchist, this time the narrator, telling a story which demonstrates the futility of anarchist enterprise. An upper-class young woman allows an anarchist group to use her house as a safe base from which to publish seditious leaflets. The recurrent failure of all the anarchist plans suggests that there is a police informer in the group, and the informer is found to be the young woman's lover, Sevrin. In outline Sevrin's role resembles those of Verloc and of Razumov in *Under Western Eyes*, and there are further links: the respectable house resembles that of Ford's relations, the civil servant William Michael Rossetti and his gifted teenage children who had an anarchist printing press in their father's basement, and the rich girl falling in love with the stateless anarchist recalls the feelings that Olive and Constance Garnett had for Stepniak, the Russian revolutionary to whom they gave sanctuary. We shall see that the adolescent Rossettis' anarchist press lends colour to the opening of *The Secret Agent* while Stepniak is an important source for aspects of both Haldin and Razumov in *Under Western Eyes*.[19]

The trip to Capri had been a disaster, but Conrad seemed unable to learn from his mistakes. A year later, early in 1906, we find him taking Jessie, now pregnant, to Montpellier for two months (the long-suffering Pinker was, of course, again expected to pay). Conrad was disgusted with his own lack of progress over the last two years and was trying to break out of stagnation, but still felt blocked in Montpellier: he wrote to Galsworthy, 9 April 1906: 'I have always that feeling of loafing at my work, as if powerless in an exhaustion of thought and will. Not enough! not enough! And yet perhaps those days without a line, nay, without a word, the hard, atrocious, agonizing days are simply part of my *method* of work, a decreed necessity of my production.'[20]

Events were to show that this was right, because one of the things on which he had been working since 13 January was a short story, 'Verloc', which in due course became *The Secret Agent*. Conrad was at last on the right track. The story's progress was delayed by family preoccupations: Borys had a series of illnesses during this year, and on 2 August John Conrad (named after John Galsworthy) was born. This did not lift Conrad's mood. On 15 August he wrote to Galsworthy about his listless and depressed work on 'Verloc':

I manage to write something nearly every day but it is like a caged squirrel running in his wheel – tired out in the evening and no progress made. It's very mysterious that thing. I feel as if I should like to sit down for a couple of years and meditate. Sisyphus was better off. He did get periodically his stone to the top. That it rolled down again is a mere circumstance – and I wouldn't complain if I had his privilege. But I roll and roll and don't seem to gain an inch up the slope. And that is distinc[t]ly damnable (15 August 1906).[21]

Anguish, travel and concomitant expense to Pinker continued to set the pattern in 1907, in the first month of which Conrad took his family once more to Montpellier, which they had found they liked, in search of ease for his writing. Montpellier was beautiful but the writing was no better, as he wrote to Ford Madox Ford (8 January 1907) extolling the beauty of the place but adding: 'Work at a standstill. Plans simply swarming in my head but my English has all departed from me.'[22] Short saleable stories such as 'Il Conde', 'Karain' and 'The Duel' continued to distract him from what was supposed to be the major work in hand (*Chance*). Borys had measles in February and then in March developed an intractable lung infection and the Conrads were advised to take him to Switzerland. Conrad himself became ill with gout and depression: he writes to Galsworthy, 6 May 1907, 'I am sinking deeper and deeper. The state of worry in which I am living – and writing – is simply indescribable. It's a constant breaking strain.'[23] But the move to Switzerland went ahead, and there Conrad tried to correct (and revise) the proofs of *The Secret Agent*. He was worried about the reception of that novel because it broke new ground: 'Preconceived notions of Conrad as sea writer will stand in the way of its acceptance,' he told Pinker.[24] In Geneva everything got worse: Borys and John got whooping cough, the problem of money became acute (Pinker had, of course, been subsidizing this travelling) and Conrad wrote a graphic account to Galsworthy, 6 June 1907, of himself trying to revise *The Secret Agent* in a hotel room surrounded by invalids:

Borys is very plucky with the pain. . . . Now and then I steal an hour or two to work at preparing the Secret Agent for book form. And all this is pretty ghastly. I seem to move, talk, write in a sort of quiet nightmare that goes on and on. I wouldn't wish my worst enemy this experience. Poor little Jack has melted down to nothing. . . . From the sound next door (we have three rooms) I know that the pain has roused Borys from his feverish doze. I won't go to him. It's no use. Presently I shall give him his salicylate take his temperature and shall then go to elaborate a little more the conversation of Mr Verloc with his wife. It is very important that the conversation of Mr Verloc with his wife should be elaborated – made more effective, don't you know – more true to the situation and the character of these people. By Jove I've got to hold myself with both hands not to burst into a laugh which would scare wife, baby and the other invalid – let alone the lady whose room is on the other side of the corridor. To day completes the round dozen of years since I finished Almayer's Folly![25]

Pinker did not always take Conrad's demands on his purse lying down: in April 1905 he had displayed one of his rare bursts of impatience and refused to pay £120 to settle Conrad's Capri expenses. Conrad replied with a magnificent air of logical calm (not unlike that of Dickens's Skimpole) to point out that whereas Pinker had money he, Conrad, had no money:

> I don't know what to say for if your position is difficult in the face of my exigencies, mine in the face of Your Non Possumus ['we cannot'] is absolutely without issue. . . . Your right in the matter is undeniable. The question is whether you will exercise it now. What I feel is the suddenness. It seems to me you might have given me a warning with the last remittance. For even from the point of view of the business that concerns us most, the prospect of being abruptly chucked (in debt) into the street in Capri . . . is not likely to get the story finished in time. . . . Don't imagine I beg you to reconsider it; I am only waiting till the 28th to see whether you will do so. . . . A certain amount of pressure may do to bring a drunkard to his bearings but it must fail with my temperament (24 April 1905).[26]

Here as elsewhere Conrad's tone in his communications with Pinker suggests a prince in straitened circumstances dealing with a shop-keeping creditor who has unaccountably forgotten his manners. It must have been hard for Pinker to swallow but swallow it he did. Conrad had a fine nose for the degree of abuse that Pinker's tolerance would stand, and could and did at any time invoke the bargaining chip of his incontrovertible talent to suggest that if Pinker cut off the funds he would kill the goose that laid the golden egg (not that Conrad's eggs had yielded much gold to date, though they did later: see below pp. 214–15). The expenses in Capri were part of a pattern of expenditure which had become a psychological necessity. To spend money gave the sensation of being rich and helped to lift the depression. It seems that at the back of his mind, as during all those years when Uncle Tadeusz was alive, was the calculation – or at least the unexamined conviction – that there would always be some protector to rescue him. And this was justified: Pinker and Galsworthy *were* there, however much Pinker might baulk at some of Conrad's demands, and they were joined by such figures as William Rothenstein, the artist and lithographer, who secured £200 for Conrad from the Royal Literary Fund in June 1904. In March 1905 the Royal Bounty Fund awarded him £500, to be administered by Rothenstein jointly with John Henry Newbolt, the naval historian and poet. Welcome and urgently needed though it was this award caused further trouble. Conrad assumed that the sum would be paid in full and at once, and became indignant when it was made clear that his debts would be looked into and paid off in order: he felt that he was being treated as a bankrupt. His predicament merited such treatment but Newbolt did his best to preserve Conrad's dignity.

In 1906 Conrad formed an important new friendship, with Arthur Marwood. Marwood was probably Conrad's closest friend between 1908 and Marwood's death in 1916. He was the younger son of a Yorkshire baronet, educated at Clifton and Trinity College Cambridge. He was an able mathematician. He was too ill (with tuberculosis) to seek a career for himself and lived quietly in the country in Kent. Ford greatly admired him (for snobbish reasons, partly). From Ford's view-point it was a mistake to introduce his two most admired friends to each other because after 1909 they united to exclude him. It was largely Ford's fault: he quarrelled with Conrad over Conrad's contributions to the *English Review* (which Marwood helped to found), but the worst offence was that Ford and his wife tried to implicate Marwood in the break-up of their marriage: in April it was alleged that Marwood have been making advances to Elsie Hueffer while Ford was having an affair with Violet Hunt (it is possible that Marwood *did* have an affair with Elsie, although he denied it and Conrad believed him and took his part). Tietjens in Ford's *Parade's End* tetralogy, published in the 1920s, is based partly on Marwood. For all that he was regarded as a genius and a model of gentility Marwood has left little written evidence of himself, and it is hard to reconstruct his friendship with Conrad. Conrad certainly admired him to end: on 30 April 1915 he wrote him to thank him for comments on *Victory* and hails him as a sage, the 'real Wise Man of the Age'.[27]

Living in the country gave Conrad a good viewpoint from which to display his ironic perception of London's moral squalor in *The Secret Agent.* Conrad explores the position of the ironist in Decoud (in *Nostromo*) and finds it wanting, but in *The Secret Agent* the method and the voice are themselves – throughout – ironic. The Author's Note invites us to see a close, but antithetical, connection between this novel and the one that preceded it. In the paragraph quoted as an epigraph to this chapter he says goodbye to his previous novel and greets the new one, and he congratulates himself, rightly, on the consistency with which he employs the ironic method:

Personally I have never had any doubt of the reality of Mrs Verloc's story; but it had to be disengaged from its obscurity in that immense town, it had to be made credible, I don't mean so much as to her soul but as to her surroundings, not so much as to her psychology but as to her humanity.... The purely artistic purpose, that of applying the ironic method to a subject of that kind, was formulated with deliberation and in the earnest belief that ironic treatment alone would enable me to say all I felt I would have to say in scorn as well as in pity. It is one of the minor satisfactions of my writing life that having taken that resolve I did manage, it seems to me, to carry it right through to the end (p. 7).

As with the composition of *Lord Jim* the way out of the *impasse* was presented by a short story which grew into a novel, 'Verloc'. The manuscript grew and grew until it became the short version of the novel, *The Secret Agent: A Novel Dealing with the Anarchists of London*, which was published in *Ridgway's: A Militant Weekly for God and Country*, 6 October 1906–15 December 1907. The serial was arranged in only six chapters: the first four coincided with the book chapters, but chapters 5 and 6 were much longer and took up most of the last seven issues. The manuscript, which is in the Rosenbach Museum in Philadelphia, has 'Verloc' as its working title throughout. It starts with large, confident handwriting, double spaced: much less erasure than in the manuscript of *Lord Jim* and much less revision, recension (or redaction) and sheer agony than in the manuscript of *Nostromo*. The confidence is conferred on the writer from the outset, I think, by the irony: the sense that he is at a securely established distance from his material. He looks down on Winnie (or 'Minnie,' as she is throughout the manuscript) Verloc and her mother from an intellectual and social height which seems neither to waver nor to cause him embarrassment. One cannot help thinking that Conrad is dealing with hostile feelings towards Jessie and her mother. We know that he found Mrs George extremely irritating and that his distaste for his mother-in-law was reciprocated. She had been one of the three witnesses of Conrad's marriage to Jessie.[28] That was probably the high point of the relationship with Conrad. Borys Conrad disliked Mrs George ('Grandmama') as much as Conrad did, describing her in his memoir as grim-featured, disapproving, and as sour in character as in appearance. He gives a lively account of one of the skirmishes (not dated, but probably some time in 1902) in the war between Conrad and his mother-in-law. Mrs George, staying with the Conrads at the Pent, had to visit the outdoor privy – the Pent's only sanitation – very early one morning:

The toilet facilities at the Pent were housed in a separate building of considerable size; having been designed by the architect, if any, upon what one might describe as social and family lines inasmuch as it provided adult accommodation for two and, at an appropriately lower level, juvenile accommodation for one. It also possessed a heavy oak door fitted with two iron hasps through which the occupant, or occupants, were supposed to pass a piece of wood, thus forming a crude bolt. It was towards this building that Grandmama directed her steps, but her movements attracted my Father's attention as he sat writing at his desk. He immediately seized his rifle and rushed out of the front door at about the same moment as Grandmama emerged from the back entrance. Seeing no sign of an intruder, he proceeded to make a reconnaissance. Grandmama must, it her turn, have heard the noise of his approach and fled, with the result that they would appear to have made one or more circuits of the house before Grandmama recovered her wits sufficiently to run for shelter in the toilet building. Unfortunately, she omitted to make use of the wooden bolt and my Father, having as he thought, run the intruder to earth, burst into the building shouting: 'Come out you – Damn you.'[29]

Consigning Winnie's mother to the almshouses in chapter 8 of *The Secret Agent* probably fulfils a stifled and resentful desire on Conrad's part to get his mother-in-law out of sight and out of mind.

Bernard Meyer explores the autobiographical question: he notes that Conrad was writing the novel during Jessie's second pregnancy and again after the birth of the baby (John) and he suggests that Conrad's jealousy of the baby is felt in the dramatic structure. Stevie is effectively Winnie's son rather than her brother: 'Thus in spite of the thin disguises employed, the family group concerns a father, a mother, and their child. Moreover, in being responsible for killing the boy, Verloc becomes an appropriate substitute for the child's murderous real father'.[30] Verloc, Winnie and Stevie can in a way be identified with Joseph, Jessie and John. The whole manuscript proceeds with apparent ease: large, legible handwriting and clear chapter divisions. A sense that the work was changing from a short story into a novel develops with chapter 4, which is headed in the manuscript 'The Agent'. Later in the course of this chapter, though, the heading 'Verloc' reappears in instructions to the typist (Jessie). Chapter 4 in the manuscript comprises chapters 4–9 of the finished novel (in book form), with some chapter divisions indicated retrospectively by instructions to the typist such as 'Drop 3 lines here' at the end of what in due course became chapter 7 (manuscript page 428) and 'Leave a space here' at the end of what in due course became chapter 8 (manuscript page 520). Clearly after the start of chapter 4 Conrad chose to indicate the chapter divisions in the typescript rather than in the manuscript. To help his imagination Conrad does drawings, the most striking of which are three comic sketches of a glum-looking middle-aged man in profile, with long moustaches (p. 367 of the Rosenbach manuscript). This relates to what the Assistant Commissioner sees when he looks at Heat in chapter 6 of the novel in its final state:

The Assistant Commissioner watched the bullet head; the points of the Norse rover's moustache, falling below the line of the heavy jaw; the whole full and pale physiognomy, whose determined character was marred by two much flesh; as [sic] the cunning wrinkles radiating from the outer corners of the eyes – and in that purposeful contemplation of the invaluable and trusted officer he drew a conviction so sudden that it moved him like an inspiration (chapter 6, p. 91).

Conrad in the Author's Note to the novel refers lightly to conversation with a 'friend' who gave the basis for the story of Verloc and Stevie in 'a casual conversation about anarchists' (p. 4). The friend was Ford Madox Ford. In Conrad's account he and Ford referred to an attempt to blow up the Greenwich observatory in the 1890s, and Ford had remarked in his characteristically casual and omniscient manner: ' "Oh, that fellow was half an idiot. His sister committed suicide afterwards" ' (p. 5). Conrad's note tends to play down Ford's contribution. Ford's memoir rebukes Conrad for this, and gives an amended version: 'What the writer [Ford's habitual, and annoyingly mannered, way of referring to himself] really did say to Conrad was: "Oh that fellow was half an idiot! His sister murdered her husband afterwards and was allowed to escape by the police. I remember the funeral. . . ." ' The suicide was invented by Conrad. And the writer knew – and Conrad knew that the writer knew – a great many anarchists of the Goodge Street group, as well as a great many of the police who watched them'.[31] Inquiry into the history of this vindicates Ford.[32] The anarchist group that he knew centered on his young cousins, the children of William Michael Rossetti, who published *The Torch: A Revolutionary Journal of Anarchist Communism* from their father's house, 3 St Edmund's Terrace, in the 1890s. Conrad was in close touch with Ford in 1905 and 1906, and drew on his knowledge for 'The Informer', 'An Anarchist' and some details of *The Secret Agent*.[33] The Verloc's shop in the first chapter sells 'a few apparently old copies of obscure newspapers, badly printed, with titles like *The Torch, The Gong* – rousing titles' (p. 9). The immediate source – as for *Lord Jim* – was an event which had attracted wide publicity in the newspapers. On the 15 February 1894 one Martial Bourdin was blown to pieces by his own bomb as he approached Greenwich observatory. Sherry shows that Bourdin's family circumstances are like those of Stevie: the bomb he is carrying has been furnished by his sister's husband, one Samuels. This Samuels was believed to have been in league with the police and working to bring the anarchist movement into disrepute. As Sherry says, 'Vladimir's decision that Verloc should bomb the observatory stems directly from Samuels's attempt to discredit the anarchists in England. Conrad did not find a prototype for Verloc's character in Samuels, but he did find a prototype of the double agent and the *agent provocateur*. The sinister double agent behind the death of Bourdin was his brother-in-law, Samuels.'[34] Norman Sherry's careful research showed a number of other sources: he suggests that Karl Yundt is based on Michael Bakunin and Johann Most, that Michaelis is based on two Fenians – a man called Condon, who was involved in an attack on a police van in Manchester in 1867 and Michael Davitt, a famous political prisoner of the day, sentenced to fifteen years in 1870 but released on 'ticket-of-leave' in 1877 – that the Professor is based partly on another Fenian, Luke Dillon, that Heat is based partly on one Inspector Melville, that Verloc is based on a half French, half Irish 'mongrel' called Coulon, who worked for Inspector Melville, and that Sir Ethelred is based on the Home Secretary, Sir William Harcourt.[35] Some of these sources are more direct, and more interesting, than others. The Cambridge University Press editors of the novel (1990) emphasise the fact that Michael Davitt – undoubtedly one of the sources for Michaelis – published a book about his experiences: *Leaves from a Prison Diary, or Lectures to a Solitary Audience* (1885).[36] Michaelis himself, of course, writes a book: the lady Patroness installs him in a cottage which strongly resembles The Pent, ir order that he can write. Conrad was often happy working from and with texts: in this case, newspaper reports and possibly an anarchist pamphlet called *The Greenwich Mystery*,[37] certainly Sir Robert Anderson's *Sidelights on the Home Rule Movement* (1906). There is a complication here: much of the ironic portrayal of the forces of law and order – Sir Ethelred's resentment of the Assistant Commissioner's secrecy, and his resentment, in turn, of Heat's secrecy – comes from Sir Robert Anderson's book, yet that book wasn't published until Conrad had written the first three chapters of the tale.[38] Other texts in the background of the novel are spy stories, including *The Scarlet Pimpernel* (1905), E. L. Voynich's *The Gadfly* (1897) and Erskine Childers's *The Riddle of the Sands* (1903).[39] The sense that menace underlies seemingly normal life, and that this menace can indicate the activity of an enemy agent, is certainly something that Conrads' and Childers's novel have in common.[40]

It is important, though, that Conrad dedicates his novel to H. G. Wells, the 'chronicler of Mr Lewisham's love' and the 'biographer of Kipps'. Lewisham and Kipps are both lower-middle-class anti-heroes in comic novels, set in the moral and economic squalor of modern London. Conrad seems to indicate that Wells's dramatization of such figures is helplessly euphoric, and that the lives of such people are in fact caged lives, like that of Winnie Verloc: locked in with a husband whose life is largely closed to her, and trapped by economic and social circumstance; she has sold herself sexually to Verloc in order to protect Stevie. The great source for Wells's work in turn was, of course, Dickens, and Dickens can be felt everywhere in this novel. The dramatization of Heat owes a great deal to the presentation of Bucket in *Bleak House*, and the name of Toodles, Sir Ethelred's private secretary, comes from the family of Paul Dombey's wet-nurse in *Dombey and Son*; and his role, as a 'nice and privileged child' (chapter 7, p. 105) is like that of the Barnacles in *Little Dorrit*. Sir Ethelred (to return to *Bleak House*) is like a less intelligent and more powerful Sir Leicester Dedlock, and The Professor resembles Smallweed. The richly mythologized London in *Oliver Twist*, *Bleak House* and *Our Mutual Friend* seems to be revisited in the London of Conrad's novel. It must also owe something – though it is hard to tell how much – to Henry James's novel of terrorist conspiracy and mobility between the upper and criminal classes of modern London, *The Princess Casamassima* (1886).

The novel was initially called 'Verloc', as we have seen, but in due course the focus changed. In its final state it has two subjects: the story of the Winnie/Stevie/Verloc household and the story of the monstrous power system that Verloc is employed to defend. *Lord Jim* was a moving dramatization of guilt, *Nostromo* urgently displays the lack of – and the need for – self-knowledge (in Gould and Nostromo) and the winning of partial self-knowledge (in Monygham and Decoud). In both those novels the narrative voice is emotionally engaged, to varying degrees, with the dramatic material, while the narrator of *The Secret Agent* is icily detached from Verloc and Winnie. To return to the Author's Note: the novelist has no 'doubt of the reality of Mrs Verloc's story' but felt that 'the ironic method . . . would enable me to say all I felt I would have to say in scorn as well as in pity' (p. 7). He deliberately keeps narrative at a distance from mimesis. The quest for knowledge which animates Marlow in *Lord Jim* and the narrative voices of *Nostromo* is replaced here by a disgusted omniscience. The narrator is in full possession of all the facts and the novel's art consists of the way in which the voice chooses to reveal these facts to the reader. The novel's subject is evil. London is another heart of darkness. If *Lord Jim's* story is that of Kurtz turned outwards, Verloc's is that of Gould turned inwards; Verloc is a curdled anti-entrepreneur, springing from the entrepreneurial class but inverting their values – an ironic instance of social Darwinism: 'Born of industrious parents for a life of toil, he had embraced indolence from an impulse as profound as inexplicable and as imperious as the impulse which directs a man's preference for one particular woman in a given thousand' (p. 16).

Stevie has a true insight in chapter 8, that part of the novel in which the moral categories are allowed to relate to norms that we understand (only to be inverted the more savagely later) when he says 'Bad world for poor people' (p. 132). Stevie's relationship with his brother-in-law is one of naive hero-worship: a kind of ironic variant of the relationships with his disciples (figures like Ford and Garnett) that Conrad liked to establish in his life (Conrad always needed to be worshipped – in a way he plays Kurtz to Ford's Marlow). Norman Sherry shows that Martial Bourdin had such a relationship with his brother-in-law, Samuels: an eye-witness recalled 'little Bourdin sitting at the feet of Samuels, and looking up into his eyes with loving trust. To the little man he was evidently a hero to be loved and revered'.[41] Stevie inverts categories in his belief that Mr Verloc, who is to kill him, is 'good' (p. 135). This belief has been established in him as part of an elaborate fictional edifice constructed by the women to deceive Verloc and Stevie equally: as Barbara Melchiori says, Verloc's downfall takes place when his private life and his employment as an agent for the Russians intersect and the death of Stevie is brought home to his door, Verloc 'never having realised that all his comforts depended on the fact that the two women saw him as the provider for Stevie'.[42] Stevie lives in a world largely dominated by Verloc. Verloc is his moral touchstone: 'His father's anger, the irritability of gentlemen lodgers, and Mr Verloc's predisposition to immoderate grief, had been the main sanctions of Stevie's self restraint. Of these sentiments, all easily provoked, but not always easy to understand, the last had the greatest moral efficiency – because Mr Verloc was *good*' (p. 135). Verloc is the most powerful of the 'sanctions' in Stevie's life, but the trusting child is willing to put faith also in Winnie – 'who was good' (p. 132). – and in the police. We thus have a sense of an authority system, perceived by Stevie, which starts with Verloc and Winnie and radiates outward to include the authoritarian system – embodied in Heat and the Assistant Commissioner – which is one of Verloc's employers. Stevie, distressed by the spectacle of the cabbie beating his horse 'had his moments of consoling trust in the organized powers of the earth' (p. 132) and says that the police should look after the cabbie. Winnie instantly disabuses him. She knows that all the police do is protect property: 'They are there so that them as have nothing shouldn't take anything away from them who have' (p. 133).

Stevie and Winnie are both humanists in that they both find the highest value in another human being: Stevie in Verloc, Winnie in Stevie. In early Dickens good and evil tend to be vested in human beings rather than in institutions (compare the function of Fagin in *Oliver Twist* with the function of money in *Our Mutual Friend*) and this novel takes that mode of literary procedure and extends it: for Stevie and Winnie the good is invested in Verloc and Stevie respectively. For Winnie, after the dreadful revelation of Stevie's death and a correspondingly violent reversal of values, evil is invested in Verloc ('He took the boy away from me to murder him!' (chapter 11, p. 186)). Once she has freed herself of Verloc by killing him she can express her moral view forcibly (to Ossipon): 'He was a devil!' (chapter 12, p. 207). For Verloc evil is embodied in Vladimir, who forces him to take action in order to justify his payments from the Russian embassy; Vladimir is both a dangerous stranger, a 'Hyperborean swine' and 'a gentleman' (like Gentleman Brown from *Lord Jim* or Mr Jones from *Victory*, he embodies the undoing of the protagonist) (chapter 9, p. 160) Verloc is quite intelligent, but is a man of feeling and personality rather than of analysis: he never sees that it is the organizations behind Vladimir and the Assistant Commissioner, not the men themselves, who are undoing him. The Professor – the most isolated individual in the book – sees clearly that evil exists in a *class*, not an individual, and that that class is the weak: ' "The source of all evil! They are our sinister masters – the weak, the flabby, the silly, the cowardly, the faint of heart, and the slavish of mind. They have power. They are the multitude. Theirs is the kingdom of the earth. Exterminate, exterminate!" ' (chapter 13, p. 226).

The Professor here takes on the role of Kurtz in *Heart of Darkness*, seeking to control by terror. The final paragraph of the novel operates magnificently, displaying the Professor both as he sees himself and as he is seen from without by the omniscient voice. He is 'incorruptible' and 'had no future. He disdained it. He was a force': 'He walked frail, insignificant, shabby, miserable – and terrible in the simplicity of his idea calling madness and despair to the regeneration of the world. Nobody looked at him. He passed on unsuspected and deadly, like a pest in the street full of men' (chapter 13, p. 231)

Verloc becomes the focus of evil in the mind of Winnie. It may be that Winnie's disillusionment with Verloc follows a parallel disillusionment in the pattern of Conrad's friendships. It has been suggested that Adolf Verloc may be based on Adolf Krieger, Conrad's long-standing friend who, as we have seen, had lent him money and then pressed for repayment of the debt: this caused cooling of the friendship and finally a breach.[43] Conrad's response to Krieger's perfectly correct request for the return of his money was to behaved as though he had been outraged and betrayed. In a letter to Garnett, 5 December 1897, he wrote about Krieger:

> I am going through the awful experience of losing a friend. Hope [G. F. W. Hope, friend and neighbour when Conrad was living at Stanford-le-Hope, Essex] comes every evening to console me but he has a hopeless task. Death is nothing – and I am used to its rapacity. But when life robs one of a man to whom one has pinned one's faith for twenty years the wrong seems too monstrous to be lived down.[44]

The fact that he is blamed by Krieger for taking Krieger's money is translated into a somewhat lofty scenario in which Krieger has sinned against honour and the code of gentlemen. I am not suggesting that Conrad consciously misrepresented Krieger. Conrad genuinely saw the situation this way.

Krieger was of German origin but born in the USA.[45] They seem to have met when they were sharing digs in 1880. The friendship was essentially the friendship of two lonely men thrown together by circumstances. Krieger became less lonely when he married in 1881, and during the 1880s he had a number of slightly low-grade jobs (foreign correspondent, commercial clerk and continental carrier). He may have been in reality a 'secret agent' – a spy working for the American Fenians – and his many absences on the continent may have contributed to Verloc's mysterious and sudden continental trips.[46] His wife had a child who had suffered from meningitis and who thus might be a source for Stevie. The Kriegers took lodgers, and it is possible that Conrad himself rented lodgings with them between 1881 and 1885.[47] The Kriegers, then, belonged to a phase of Conrad's life when he had no polite English friends and no claim to literary recognition but was simply the obscure and rootless Captain Korzeniowski, a not very successful officer of the merchant marine. They were associated, in other words, with a decade of frustration and displacement, a period of his life which Conrad very understandably preferred, later, to put behind him. The Kriegers were the kind of people whom Conrad would have chosen to drop once he had established himself with grander friends; it may well be that the quarrel over the debt was in part a convenient way of turning his back on this undesirable connection. Though Conrad seems also to have felt guilty over the breach: *Tales of Unrest*, published in 1898, was dedicated to Krieger 'for the sake of old days'. It has been suggested that the volume was thus dedicated to placate Krieger.[48] But it was more a graceful gesture of farewell than an attempt at *rapprochement*: it was necessary to break with this particular friend while at the same time continuing to express loyalty to the ideal of friendship. It seems quite possible, as I have suggested, that some aspects of Verloc are taken from Krieger, or rather from Conrad's feelings about Krieger once the friendship was over. If that is true then the failed friendship has been recast in a pattern which offers the consolation of indicating that the friend was not worth having. An ostensible benefactor – '*good*' in Stevie's idealizing perception, *reliable* to Winnie's custodial and manipulative view of marriage – is revealed as lazy, shabby, greedy, incompetent and (of course) treacherous.

In the Author's Note to the novel Conrad speaks of his many solitary walks round the streets of London as having contributed to the writing of the novel: 'I had to fight hard to keep at arms-length the memories of my solitary and nocturnal walks all over London in my early days, lest they should rush in and overwhelm each page of the story' (p. 7). He evokes London in a state of love-hate relationship with his material. The younger self who walked the streets of London was the displaced and (often) socially humiliated foreigner looking for a job among the English. As he writes his novel Conrad turns his back on all that: the Polish gentleman is on his way to establishing the status which he knows is his due. He enjoys the freedom to express some degree of contempt for his adopted country by displaying the hateful urban lifeforms that England generated in the 1880s (the dramatic date of the novel – from the date on Winnie's wedding-ring – is 1886) when he was an unhappy young man wandering in London's unfriendly streets.

This novel is even handed: while it disparages the English lower-middle class it is also hearteningly reluctant to be daunted by the upper-class. The Lady Patroness of Michaelis is socially impressive but she is reassuringly stupid. She supports – vaguely and decorously – the ambition of the anarchists like Michaelis because their hopes are not for 'utter destruction' but for 'the complete economic ruin of the system'. She is quite unable to see that her own position in the system is sustained by economic and social forces: she dislikes parvenus and believe that 'with the annihilation of all capital they would vanish too' but that universal ruin 'would leave the social values untouched. The disappearance of the last piece of money could not affect people of position' (chapter 6, p. 88). And at the heart of power Sir Ethelred, the Home Secretary, is almost as stupid in his way as is the Lady Patroness: he is comically unable to take in any 'detail' and cannot in any case attend properly to the bomb outrage because he is wholly preoccupied with his fisheries (chapter 10, p. 162).

The change of direction represented by *The Secret Agent* expresses a need in Conrad's life. Suresh Raval contrasts the Professor with Lord Jim; both are egotists, but Jim after his failure seeks to redeem himself by declaring his allegiance 'to the legitimizing values of society' while the Professor is so enclosed in his egotism that 'society's legitimacy depends on whether or not it recognizes its worth', and its failure to do so condemns it: for the Professor 'the very concept of legitimacy has lost its meaning'.[49] Raval could have added that Jim and the Professor are dramatically parallel in that their titles ironically express the way status has been withheld from them: Jim is not a Lord, the Professor is not a Professor. Taking his lead from Fredric Jameson[50] Raval notes that resentment is 'at the origin of the Professor's radical posture'.[51] Resentment – destructive envy which cannot express itself in direct action and is thus wholly different from the aggressive competitiveness of the man of honour – marks the change of direction to which I have referred. Jim in the second, Patusan, part of *Lord Jim* and Gould in *Nostromo* are seeking to translate their aggressiveness and self-esteem into effective political action, they are powerful men visibly imposing order on their communities and earning honour for it. The settings are exotic places carefully made real for the civilian English reader, and the notion of heroic and valiant endeavour is itself made real.

Resentment proceeds secretly. The setting is familiar to the civilian English reader – he sees it every day, and he has had it fully displayed for him in literature by Dickens, James, Gissing and Wells – and is here set out for his contempt and loathing. And in this setting furtive human beings seek their objectives by stealth. The Professor seems to be the epitome of this, but he is also – as Raval fails to say – the exception to it , since he is the only anarchist who is not secretive: he is open about his ambition (the destruction of what is) and his instrument (the bomb attached to his person, which makes him immune from arrest by Inspector Heat). In the battle of egos with Inspector Heat in chapter 5 – 'a meeting in a side corridor of a mansion full of life' (p. 68) – the Professor is able to say, truthfully, 'I am doing my work better than you're doing yours' (p. 77). But it is a Pyrrhic victory: he leaves the scene 'miserable' because there is too much life to destroy. The meeting contains a long analepsis recounting Heat's inspection, earlier in the day, of the remains of Stevie: 'what might have been an accumulation of raw material for a cannibal feast' (p. 70). Competitiveness and power feature here, too: it is important that Heat should not be sick in front of his inferior, the constable (who enjoys the fact that one of the park keepers did not have the stomach for the scraping up of Stevie and was 'as sick as a dog'). Heat must remain imperturbable 'with a calm face and the slightly anxious attention of an indigent customer bending over what may be called the by-products of a butcher's shop with a view to an inexpensive Sunday dinner' (p. 71). The fact remains that the Professor is in his limited way effective – he made the bomb round which the whole novel is organized – and that the novel is to some extent aligned with his view of society: both Conrad and the Professor despise what they see. His will to power is an inverted expression of ambition which in another novel would be honourable: he has 'genius' but lacks recognition – 'His struggles, his privations, his hard work to raise himself in the social scale, had filled him with such an exalted conviction of his merits that is was extremely difficult for the world to treat him with justice' (chapter 4, p. 62). I think Raval is right to say that he is like Jim. He is also – alarming thought – like the unhappy, angry, unrecognized Conrad of the 1880s.

The writing of *The Secret Agent* marks a new professionalism in Conrad. Experience is enabling him to appraise his own work with detachment and accuracy. These qualities are found both in his letters written during composition (especially during the period of revision from periodical to book form) and in his reaction to *The Secret Agent's* fate in the market place. He writes to Pinker, 18 May 1907 'The *S.A.* approached with a fresh eye does not strike me as bad at all. There is an element of popularity in it. By this I don't mean to say that the thing is likely to be popular. I merely think that it shows traces of capacity for that sort of treatment which may make a novel popular'.[52] And on 30 July 1907 he writes an important letter to Pinker about his own present standing, now that he has completed *The Secret Agent*, in relation to other writers:

> It will not be on popular lines. Nothing of mine can be, I fear. But even Meredith ended by getting his sales. Now, I haven't Meredith's delicacy and that's a point in my favour. . . . I don't get in the way of established reputations. One may read everybody and yet in the end want to read me – for a change if for nothing else. For I don't resemble anybody; and yet I am not specialised enough to call up imitators as to matter or style. There is nothing in me but a turn of mind which, whether valuable or worthless can not be imitated.[53]

Ian Watt remarks that *The Secret Agent* dashes all our expectations: 'Picking up a book about a secret agent we expect to find a hero who, happily unlike ourselves, knows both how the social mechanism works and how to manipulate it for his own gratification. Instead Conrad gives us someone who understands even less than we do; and instead of perfectly engineered encounters with ruthless killers and beautiful spies, we are given a married man who hardly notices that his wife is murdering him.' Watt expresses the distinctiveness of this novel among Edwardian political novels thus: '*The Secret Agent* seems modern in the way that Yeats, Eliot and Joyce are. All of them assume that it is the artist's voice alone which can impose some order on the vulgar folly of the modern world'.[54] Conrad himself knew that the virtue of his novel was that it was a tightly controlled work of art imposing order on chaos. He wrote to Methuen, 7 November 1906, to say that he had not sanctioned American publicity which called his novel 'A Tale of Diplomatic Intrigue and Anarchist Treachery'. He plays down the subject and stresses the form and the method: 'it is a fairly . . . successful piece of ironic treatment applied to a special subject . . . otherwise it is *purely a work of imagination*. It has no social or philosophical intention'.[55]

Conrad then resists comparison with other writers and denies political

significance in his novel. On neither of these fronts were the commentators deterred: an absurd review by Anderson Graham in *Country Life*
compared *The Secret Agent*'s realism unfavourably with Scott and Thackeray,
said that the dramatic method was modelled on Zola and that Verloc and
the Professor were grotesques from a Gilbert and Sullivan opera.[56] The first
of these comparisons reminds us that Conrad himself, when depressed,
had felt that his *style* (as against the dramatic method) suffered from resemblance to Zola. As he wrote on 12 September 1906 to Galsworthy: 'The
beastly trick of style . . . is Zola jargon simply.'[57] On the political front many
of the reviewers – including Edward Garnett in the *Nation*, 28 September
1907[58] – felt it relevant that Conrad attitudes to Engand and Russia were
determined by his 'Slav' origins. This always enraged Conrad. Garnett
wrote another piece correcting the earlier emphasis on Conrad as a Slav,
and Conrad wrote to thank him, 28 August 1908 saying 'is my earnestness
of no account? Is that a Slavonic trait?'[59] Galsworthy, writing the first
extended piece of literary criticism on Conrad in 1908 said that *The Secret
Agent* displayed Conrad's latent radical sympathies in that he was willing
to write about bourgeois rather than upper class lives[60] while Thomas Mann,
writing in 1926, took a very clear and simple political view of *The Secret Agent*:
'It is an anti-Russian story, plainly enough, anti-Russian in a very British
sense and spirit. Its background consists in politics on the large scale, in
the whole conflict between the British and the Russian political ideology;
I think it possible that this conflict has always formed the background –
I will not say the motive – of the Pole's passionate love of England'.[61] That
the London displayed in *The Secret Agent* might be felt to communicate
Conrad's 'passionate love' of his adopted country is an odd claim, but
Mann is surely right on balance to stress the feelings about Russia that
lurk beneath *The Secret Agent* and link it to the next great novel, *Under Western
Eyes*.

1 The young Joseph Conrad in Warsaw in 1862. The Mansell Collection, London.

2 The two towers of the fourteenth-century Church of Our Lady, Cracow. Reproduced by kind permission of The Mansell Collection, London.

3 The adolescent Joseph Conrad in Cracow in 1873.
Reproduced by kind permission of The Mansell
Collection, London.

4 Marseilles, c.1895. Reproduced by kind permission of The Mansell Collection, London.

5 The *Tilkhurst* at San Francisco. Conrad served in this sailing ship as second mate, voyaging to Singapore. He said of her captain that he was: 'One of the best seamen whom it has been my good luck to serve under.' Reproduced by kind permission of Mr Philip Conrad.

6 A. P. Krieger and his wife. Krieger was one of Conrad's earliest English friends.

7 Jessie George in 1896, the year of her marriage to Conrad. Reproduced by kind permission of Mr Philip Conrad.

8 Augustine Podmore Williams, first mate of the *Jeddah* and the main source for *Lord Jim*, with his young wife in Singapore, c.1883.

9 Captain John Snadden, who preceded Conrad as Master of the *Otago* and whose spirit vitally informs Conrad's *The Shadowline*, was buried at sea, probably off Cape St Jacques on the coast of Cochin/China.

10 The *Otago*, in 1888 Conrad's first command.

11 Stanley Falls, 1896.

12 John Galsworthy (left) and Edward Sanderson on board the *Torrens*, 1893. 'The first mate is a Pole called Conrad and is a capital chap, though queer to look at: he is a man of travel and experience in many parts of the world, and has a fund of yarns on which I draw freely' (Galsworthy).

13 Edward Garnett with his son David in 1897. It was in October 1894 that Garnett, one of the readers for Fisher Unwin, advised acceptance of Conrad's first novel, *Almayer's Folly*. Garnett's support for Conrad and his critical appreciation of his work was to outlast the writer's life. Reproduced by kind permission of Mr Richard Garnett.

14 Conrad and H. G. Wells together. Their friendship resulted from Wells's review of *An Outcast of the Islands* in 1896. Conrad wrote at the time, 'He descended from his "time machine" to be kind as he knew how.' Reproduced by kind permission of Mr Frank Wells.

15 Pent Farm, near Hythe in South West Kent. Conrad lived here from 1898 to 1907, a period in which he wrote some of his best works.

16 R. B. Cunninghame Graham dressed as a gaucho, probably soon after his return from South America in the late 1870s. Conrad's friendship with him lasted from 1897 until Conrad's death in 1924. In a letter to Graham in 1920, Conrad wrote: 'May you ride firm as ever in the saddle, to the very last moment, et la lance toujours en arret, against The Enemy whom you have defied all your life!' Reproduced by kind permission of the R. B. Cunninghame Graham Estate (John Johnson, Authors' Agents).

17 Stephen Crane. Reproduced by kind permission of The Mansell Collection, London.

18 Conrad's wife, Jessie, with their eldest son, Borys, at Pent Farm, in 1900. Reproduced by kind permission of Mr Philip Conrad.

19 Ford Madox Ford. Reproduced by kind permission of The Mansell Collection.

20 J. B. Pinker and Conrad at Pinker's home in 1922. Pinker approached Conrad in 1899 and later acted as his literary agent until Pinker's death in the year this photograph was taken. Pinker was agent for many leading writers of the day. When he recognized talent he was generous with his financial aid, as Conrad and Arnold Bennett knew from experience. Reproduced by kind permission of Mr Philip Conrad.

21 Joseph Conrad with his son Borys and Edmund Oliver on the occasion of Borys's joining *HMS Worcester* in 1911. Edmund Oliver was owner of Capel House. Reproduced by kind permission of Mr Philip Conrad.

22 Capel House, Conrad's residence from June 1910 to March 1919.
Reproduced by kind permission of Mr Philip Conrad.

23 Mr and Mrs Joseph Conrad and
their son John. Reproduced by kind
permission of The Mansell
Collection London.

24 Joseph Conrad, c.1911. Reproduced by kind permission of The Mansell Collection, London.

25 Oswalds, Bishopsbourne, near Canterbury. This was Conrad's last home, where he lived from 1919. Reproduced by kind permission of Mr Philip Conrad.

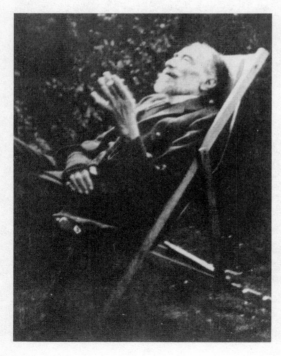

26 Conrad in the garden at Oswalds, June 1924, shortly before his death.

7

From Verloc to Razumov, 1907–1911

His good looks would have been unquestionable if it had not been for a peculiar lack of fineness in the features. It was as if a face modelled vigorously in wax (with some approach even to a classical correctness of type) had been held close to a fire till all sharpness of line had been lost in the softening of the material. But even thus he was sufficiently good-looking.

Under Western Eyes, Part First, Introduction, p. 5.

Then stillness again, with the great shadow gliding closer, towering higher, without light, without a sound. Such a hush had fallen on the ship that she might have been a bark of the dead floating in slowly under the very gate of Erebus.

'The Secret Sharer', p. 292.

A restless desire to change his working environment is characteristic of a writer who feels that his work is going badly. In Conrad it was to become persistent and obsessional: his sons recall constant weekend outings to look at houses which might be to let, even when Conrad knew that the terms of his rental agreement did not make such a move practicable. The expensive and unproductive visits to Capri and Montpellier were part of the same quest. Yet anyone looking dispassionately at Conrad's life during these years will be struck by the fact that it was precisely the Kentish farmhouse from which he was seeking to escape – the Pent – that had provided the environment for the composition of four masterpieces, *Heart of Darkness*, *Lord Jim*, *Nostromo* and *The Secret Agent* (as well as a number of important tales including 'Typhoon', 'Falk' and 'Amy Foster'). It had been sublet to Conrad by Ford who had entered into the arrangement, as we have seen, with his characteristically impulsive generosity because he knew that the Pent was a good place in which to work. Clearly he was right. But there were things against the house: the sanitary arrangements were primitive (an outdoor earthcloset, as we have seen), there were rats, and Conrad felt – mistakenly – that it would be possible to live more cheaply

elsewhere ('The Pent is damnably expensive to live in. The idea is to have
no bills. One spends always more than one intends to'[1]). In August 1907
he came to an arrangement whereby Pinker would pay £600 for the coming year provided that Conrad wrote 80,000 words of a novel. This was
extraordinarily advantageous, from Conrad's viewpoint, but was to add to
rather than decrease the pressures on him. Conrad had not paid his debts
to Ford and this caused increasing friction between the two friends.
In September the Conrads moved to another rented house called Someries,
at Luton Hoo, where he hoped to feel closer to literary London. Conrad
wrote to Henry James expressing something of his disenchantment with
the Pent (20 September 1907). 'We have abandonned [sic] the Pent to its
green solitudes – to its rats. Here's a chapter closed. The new one opens
much nearer London'.[2] There was a quarrel with Ford over the unpaid
debts just before the move. He felt guilty about his treatment of Ford
and half-heartedly entertained a scheme whereby Ford would sue him for
the money owed, thus forcing Pinker to pay it (nothing came of this).
Conrad wrote to Galsworthy, 15 September 1907, in an attempt to vindicate
his behaviour: 'My conduct to Ford is not so base as it looks. . . . Five
months I *could not* work.' He goes on to say that without the 'fatal
[financially] excursion' to Montpellier he would have collapsed psychologically, and 'I've come back ruined again for a time. I am too weary for
words. And again there is writing under pressure pumping for dear life –
before me. I would rather die than be ill again but as a matter of fact I
can't afford either. I will have to pump till the handle breaks or the ship
goes down under me'.[3] Writing is back-breaking labour like the most arduous jobs facing an Ordinary Seaman, and Conrad feels (as Marlow says
in *Lord Jim*) that 'loneliness' is 'a hard and absolute condition of existence' (chapter 16, p. 179). One is struck, as often before, by the contrast
between his perception of his predicament – penniless, alone, heroically
discharging his duty against overwhelming odds – and one possible objective judgement of it, which is that he was spongeing off willing and loyal
friends to finance an unnecessarily luxurious life-style. But such a judgement only expresses part of the truth: however self-induced his sufferings,
the anguish was real.

It soon became clear that moving to Someries was a mistake. Within a
year Conrad was trying to find somewhere else to live, and early in 1909
he was living in the worst of all his homes, rooms over a butcher's shop
in Aldington, where he stayed for nearly a year until in June 1910 he took
up the tenancy of Capel House, Orlestone, Kent; a small attractive farmhouse remembered by his sons as the most agreeable of all his homes. It
was not long before the arrangement with Pinker was violated by Conrad
who found that 'Razumov', or *Under Western Eyes*, grew on him while he
was supposed to be writing *Chance*. On 2 January 1908 he speaks of
'Razumov' as a story of 14,000 words ('two inst: of 7,000 each') while on
7 January he pleads for patience over *Chance*: 'Do not take a gloomy view
of my work on that book. It *is* going on. But a big conception can't be

kept going like a shorter work'.[4] He is writing constantly to both Galsworthy and Pinker during this month: the letters to Galsworthy are euphoric and triumphant, the letters to Pinker guarded and evasive – the contrast, of course, marks the difference between a friend in whom Conrad had utter trust and his agent whom he felt to be a nagging authority figure. A sense of being persecuted by Pinker surfaced in a very long and extremely impatient letter of 14 January 1908. He complains that Pinker thinks he is a lazy 'literary man', and he protests that he is 'not a literary man', meaning that he has plenty of experience of other work and that Pinker must *stop nagging him.* 'I know what all sorts of work mean. It is extraordinary that people who understand that a carpenter can't make a box if somebody keeps on jogging his elbow will say that no jog of any sort shall matter to a mind.' Conrad was anxious about (and easily annoyed by) R. L. Stevenson's reputation for fluency, and he suspected Pinker of comparing him adversely with Stevenson. Stevenson had referred to himself in print as a 'sedulous ape': hence Conrad's 'I have no charm, no flow of wit or of facetiousness or mere patter to fill in chinks with. . . . I have no literary tradition even which will help to spin phrases. . . . I am not a "Sedulous Ape"'.[5] It may have been in an attempt to demonstrate fluency and saleability that he dashed off the short story, 'The Black Mate', in the last ten days or so of January 1908. We have seen that this story is possibly a revision of a story submitted to *Tit-Bits* in 1886.[6] It is not a distinguished piece but its theme – an ageing man who dyes his hair in order to keep himself employable in a young man's profession, the merchant marine – reflects Conrad's current anxiety about the passage of time and the slow rate of his achievement, an anxiety compounded by the fact that he was a month or so past his fiftieth birthday (3 December 1907).

For the first few months of 1908 his letters indicate that he thinks of his Russian story as a novella, 'Razumov'. He sent a very important letter of 6 January 1908 to Galsworthy outlining the plot of the novella as he then conceived it:

The Student Razumov (a natural son of Prince K-) gives up secretly to the police his fellow Student Haldin who seeks refuge in his rooms after com[m]itting a political crime (supposed to be the murder of de Plehve) [A reference to the Russian Minister of the Interior who was murdered by a bomb thrown at his carriage, 15 July 1904]. First movement in St Petersburg. (Haldin is hanged of course). [in margin] 'done'

2d in Geneva: The Student Razumov meeting abroad the mother and sister of Haldin falls in love with that last, marries her and after a time confesses to her the part he played in the arrest and death of her brother. [in margin] 'to do'
   The psychological developments leading to Razumov's betrayal of Haldin, to his confession of that fact to his wife and to the death of these people (brought about mainly by the resemblance of their child to the late Haldin) form the real subject of the story.

At this time, then, it was conceived as a neat two-part structure, with a highly melodramatic plot in the second part providing retribution for the moral crime of the first part. The focus on Razumov's 'psychological development' supports the suggestion that at this stage it was a Razumov-centred work and thus a tragedy. This letter supports the notion that the writing of short stories was truancy from Pinker and from his duty to get on with the big job in hand, which at the moment was *Chance*: 'I had to write [Razumov]. I had to get away from *Chance* with which I was making no serious progress.' Pressure to escape from novel-writing into short-story writing was reinforced by the fact that *The Secret Agent* had had a disappointing reception: it 'may be pronounced by now an honourable failure' says Conrad in the same letter. 'It brought me neither love nor promise of literary success. I own that I am cast down. I suppose I am a fool to have expected anything else. I suppose there is something in me that is unsympathetic to the general public'.[7] The short story called 'Razumov' grew much as *Lord Jim* grew, and like *Lord Jim* it was at an early stage seen as the third item in a volume of three short stories. We can see Conrad moving beyond this conception in a letter to Pinker of 7 January 1908. Conrad wrote saying that there would be no room in one volume for 'three big machines like *Strong Man* ["Gaspar Ruiz"] *the Duel* and *Razumov*'. Razumov is seen as 'the nucleus of another vol.' because it is 'altogether on another plane'.[8] By the middle of March 1908 he was writing about Razumov as a novella, telling Pinker that it will be '43,000 words'.[9] This was a length that Conrad liked. *An Outcast of the Islands, Lord Jim, Nostromo* and *The Secret Agent* had all gone through a stage of being seen as novellas, 'the form I like best (30–40,000 words)' as Conrad had written to John Watson on 26 November 1902.[10] On 23 March 1908 Conrad writes to Pinker saying that he has taken against the name 'Razumov' partly because it resembles *Rezanov*, by Gertrude Atherton (published in 1906), and partly because the subject is bigger than the working title indicates: 'My story deserves a better title than a man's name'.[11] On 28 August, writing to Edward Garnett, he speaks of 'a long spell of heavy pulling at the novel without a name'.[12] The final title comes into being early in 1910: on 10 January Conrad writes to Pinker still referring to the novel as 'Razumov' but on 12 January he writes: 'What do you think of the tittle [sic] to give the book. Would *Under Western Eyes* do at all – or something of the kind?'[13] So we can date, approximately, the point at which the fiction finally ceased in Conrad's mind to be Razumov-centred. The process was not sudden, of course: the large structure that we have was already substantially written (indeed, as I have shown, more of it was written than was in due course published). Conrad's question – 'Would *Under Western Eyes* do?' – is a rhetorical sounding out of Pinker. There is justifiable pride behind the question. The novel is no longer a monodrama but an ambitious political novel, his most ambitious to date.

Conrad had to renegotiate his obligations to his own writing schedule (and to Pinker) twice during this year. The first stage was to decide that

Under Western Eyes was a novel rather than a story, and that it was to take precedence over *Chance* (to which Conrad was still referring, in the early months of 1908, as 'the big book' – as contrasted with *Under Western Eyes* which was presumably still thought of as a little book). The second stage was to support Ford Madox Ford in the founding of the *English Review*, in August of 1908: Conrad's reminiscences, later *A Personal Record*, were to figure importantly in the *English Review*'s early issue. Ford claimed that he took down the reminiscences from Conrad's dictation. Najder remarks that 'neither the style nor the fact that several sections were translated from Bobrowski's *Memoirs* support Ford's claim; besides, collaboration would have been difficult, since during most of the time when the text was being written the two authors lived in different places'.[14] Conrad and Marwood were closely involved in the planning of the new periodical's first number: there was an editorial meeting at the Conrad's house, Someries, in October 1908. Jessie Conrad recalls the excitement of putting the first edition to bed:

> That final operation took the whole of one night. Mr F. M. Hueffer arrived late in the afternoon, accompanied by his secretary and his sub-editor, all carrying parcels of papers and very little other luggage. Each took possession of a single room, and that night nobody slept a wink except the baby and the servants. . . . The consumption of oil and candles was prodigious. But I like to remember that period of excitement, if only for the reason that one of Conrad's most precious books, the 'Personal Record', owes its existence to the *English Review*.[15]

When he founded the *English Review* Ford's ambition was to furnish a prestigious vehicle for major writers and to foster new talent. The writers he published included an impressive array of names: Hardy, Wells, Bennett, D. H. Lawrence. The first number contained Hardy's poem 'A Sunday Morning Tragedy', Henry James's 'The Jolly Corner', the first instalment of H. G. Wells's *Tono-Bungay* and pieces by Galsworthy, W. H. Hudson, Cunninghame Graham, W. H. Davies and Arthur Marwood. The last of the Conrad/Ford collaborations, *The Nature of a Crime* (almost entirely written by Ford), was serialized in the *English Review*. Ford saw himself as a gentleman patron of the arts who was above business matters. He saw himself as helping out indigent men of genius, and in this role paid some contributors, including Conrad, over-generously. Although he was undoubtedly an editor of genius, the power and importance (as he saw them) of his position went to his head. In the long-term, the *English Review* can be seen as a tragedy for Ford. It was a subsidiary cause of his quarrels, in 1909, first with Marwood and then with Conrad. As we have seen, he quarrelled with Marwood (because his wife Elsie alleged that Marwood had made sexual advances to her) and tried to involve Conrad in the quarrel. Ford's motivation was complex. Marwood had advanced money for Elsie to have some surgery in 1907, and her illness and the fact of her estrangement from Ford may well have prompted Marwood into making what was from his point of view a gallant old-fashioned offer of emotional comfort. Ford was concurrently involved in a sexual liaison with the novelist Violet Hunt. H. G. Wells was a former lover of hers and she consulted Wells about her difficult sexual relationship with Ford. Frederick Karl aptly remarks that this displayed 'some indelicacy' on her part since Wells and Ford had worked closely together on the founding of the *English Review* and Wells was initially very pleased to have his most ambitious work to date, *Tono-Bungay*, serialized there.[16] (Ford's mismanagement of the publication of *Tono-Bungay* was later to provoke a quarrel with Wells.)

Conrad was distressed when control of the *English Review* passed into the hands of Ford's brother-in-law, David Soskice ('that horrible Jew' as he called him to Galsworthy, 17 July 1909: it seems that his real objection to Soskice was that he was Russian), and became so disturbed by the unsatisfactory state of the *English Review* that contributions of his reminiscences dried up. Ford Madox Ford published a notice saying 'We regret that owing to the serious illness of Mr Joseph Conrad we are compelled to postpone the publication of the next instalment of his Reminiscences'.[17] Conrad sent a furious letter, 31 July 1909, protesting that ending his reminiscences where the did had not 'discredited' Ford and the *Review* and that he had not left the Reminiscences 'ragged'. On 4 August he poured out his rage with Ford in a letter to Pinker saying that Ford was blaming him for the collapse of the *English Review* and that 'His conduct is *impossible*. All this will end badly. He's a megalomaniac who imagines he is managing the universe and that everybody treats him with the blackest ingratitude.' Conrad was angry, but he knew Ford well and the next bit of his letter reads true: 'A fierce and exasperated vanity is hidden under his calm manner which misleads people ... I do not hesitate to say that there are cases, not quite as bad, under medical treatment'.[18] It is likely that Ford was indeed psychologically unbalanced at this time. Conrad too was under great strain, made worse by the Russian novel which was forcing him to revisit his childhood. The quarrel with Ford created a breach which was never healed.

Involvement with the *English Review* seriously delayed Conrad's work with *Under Western Eyes* and put heavy pressure on the relationship with Pinker. The writing of 'Razumov'/*Under Western Eyes* displays Conrad's love-hate relationship with writing ('ce vrai métier de chien') in its most acute form. Writing his Russian story was both an emotional necessity and a source of anguish, because the material recalled his unhappy childhood: the result was that he alternated between energetically committing himself to it and taking flight from it. The writing of *A Personal Record* and the time taken up by the *English Review* can be seen as holidays from *Under Western Eyes*. Conrad's behaviour over this book, together with his inability to control his expenditure, infuriated Pinker. By July 1910 Conrad's debts to Pinker were £2,225. This was at a time when a servant would be paid £30 a year and middle-class family could maintain a comfortable lifestyle on £500 a year: in other words it was a big investment, and from Pinker's viewpoint the return on it was steadily diminishing. Once he was free from the *English Review* Conrad made rapid progress with *Under Western Eyes*, and wrote to the end of Part Third by the end of the year. On 17 December Conrad wrote to Will Rothenstein about his misery with *Under Western Eyes*. He has been beset by illness, delay, and the 'terrible moral stress' of unburdening himself that the book's content caused him.[19] Meanwhile Pinker had lost patience with Conrad and written to him protesting that 'The Secret Sharer' and *A Personal Record* (of which Pinker is quoted as saying '*I can do nothing with that*') were not what he was paying for, and threatening to cut off the funds if he did not receive the end of *Under Western Eyes* within two weeks. Conrad felt that his honour was impugned and was stung into a furious reply: 'Had you answered simply I can't or I won't do what you ask for there would have been nothing to be said. But in a manner which is nothing short of contemptuous you seem to be holding out a bribe – next week forsooth! – as though it were a bone to a dog to make him get up on his hind legs.'[20]

To his friends he was able both to strike an exhilarating attitude and to dump his predicament entirely on Pinker's shoulders. To Perceval Gibbon (whose memories of Russia he had been drawing on for *Under Western Eyes*) he wrote (19 December 1909) about Pinker's threat to cut off the funds: 'If he does that I shall fling the MS of Raz in the fire – and see how he likes that. He positively writes as if [I] had done nothing. You imagine how charming it is to be following the psychology of Mr Razumov under these conditions. It's like working in hell.'[21] And to Galsworthy, on 22 December, he wrote enclosing Pinker's letter: 'I think I have the right to resent it, as I could not have a plain refusal which would have been the assertion of strict right or of plain impossibility. You write like that to a loafer who wants spurring. It's casting a distinct aspersion.' Conrad knew that in Galsworthy he had an auditor whose devotion and sympathy were guaranteed. This letter is a long and well-written performance in which Conrad vilifies the tone of Pinker's threat, repeats the complaint about being treated like a dog and the threat to burn the manuscript, and makes an oblique threat of suicide: 'By Jove all the moral tortures are not in prison-life. I assure you I feel sometimes as if I could drop everything and beat at the door – you understand. . . . I am at the present moment unable to write a line. One must secure a certain detachment which is beyond me. I can hardly sit still. If it wasn't for dear Jess – well I don't know'.[22] The late adolescent Conrad who shot himself in 1878 has come to the surface here. The anguish is – again – real. He feels that his personal and social insecurity have been touched on the raw, but at the same time it is hard not to see this as a self-serving tantrum, a form of acting-out at which, as we know, Conrad was both experienced and skilled.

Pinker had calculated correctly, though: his threat did in fact spur Conrad to finish *Under Western Eyes* early in 1910 at great speed. He seems to have written fifty pages in three days, between 19 and 22 January, and another twenty-five pages of revision to the last chapter by 26 January. He took the

finished manuscript to deliver to Pinker on 27 January.[23] There he and
Pinker had an explosive quarrel; its substance is not known, but in the
course of it Pinker seems to have touched on one of Conrad's most acute
anxieties by telling him that he 'did not speak English'. As a result of the
quarrel Conrad transferred his literary affairs to Robert Garnett, a lawyer
(and Edward's elder brother) for several months. Conrad wrote to Pinker
on 23 May, addressing him as 'Dear Sir' and referring to the quarrel on
27 January in his best *de haut en bas* manner: 'As it can't have escaped your
recollection that the last time we met you told me that I "did not speak
English" to you I have asked Robert Garnett to be my mouth-piece – at any
rate till my speech improves sufficiently to be acceptable'.[24] The years 1909–
10 had thus seen major quarrels with the two men on whom Conrad had
most depended, Ford Madox Ford and Pinker. While Ford was largely
to blame for the first quarrel, Conrad was undoubtedly to blame for the
second, though it should be noted that his psychological illness was a
major contributory factor. The breach with Pinker lasted some two years,
but after that Pinker's patience and good sense ensured that normal relations were restored. In the later years of their association Conrad's reservations about Pinker's social standing, evinced by the air of 'not dealing
with a gentleman' which pervades his earlier letters to Pinker, were to be
abate and the letters of 1912 onwards (most of which are still – at the time
of writing, 1993 – unpublished)[25] display increasing trust and intimacy. By
the time of Pinker's death in 1922 Conrad regarded him as a close friend.

The strain of completing *Under Western Eyes* had taken a severe psychological toll. When he got home after his quarrel with Pinker, Conrad
collapsed. He was ill for many weeks and lay in bed raving in Polish. It
seemed to Jessie that he had lost all grip on reality and was talking to the
characters in his novel. She wrote to a friend: 'Conrad has had a complete
nervous breakdown and gout. Gout everywhere, throat, tongue, head'.[26]
And in a letter to David Meldrum, 6 February 1910:

> Poor Conrad is very ill and Dr Hackney says it will be a long time before he
> is fit for anything requiring mental exertion. . . . There is the M. S. [of *Under
> Western Eyes*] complete but uncorrected and his fierce refusal to let even I
> [sic] touch it. It lays [sic] on a table at the foot of the bed and he lives mixed
> up in the scenes and holds converse with the characters.[27]

The great novelist lay prostrate and agonized, covered in inexplicable and
humiliating swellings. No wonder Jessie was terrified. *Under Western Eyes*
clearly focuses a crisis for Conrad. What were the constituents of this
crisis? It must be the case that writing a novel about Russia, the country
which had imprisoned and effectively killed his parents, reopened childhood grief for Conrad, and that painful relationships in the present
were being emotionally linked for him to this pain in the past by the re-
examination of so much buried experience. Garnett, in a letter now lost,
seems to have said that Conrad expressed hatred of Russia in *Under*

Western Eyes, and in a review of *Under Western Eyes* in the *Nation*, 21 October 1911, Garnett uses (in contexts which offer only slight qualification) terms like 'vindictive', 'vitriolic' and 'scathing' to describe Conrad's writing.[28] On 20 October 1911, the day before this review appeared, Conrad wrote to Garnett (presumably in answer to the lost letter) responding to the charge that *Under Western Eyes* expresses hatred of Russia:

> There's just about as much or as little *hatred* in this book as in the Outcast of the Islands for instance. Subjects lay about for anybody to pick-up. I have picked up this one. And that's all there is to it. I don't expect you will believe me. You are so russianised my dear that you don't know the truth when you see it – unless it smells of cabbage-soup when it at once secures your profoundest respect. I suppose one must make allowances for your position of Russian Embassador [sic] to the Republic of Letters . . . but it is hard after lavishing a 'wealth of tenderness' [this presumably refers to a phrase in Garnett's letter] on Tekla and Sophia, to be charged with the rather low trick of putting one's hate into a novel. If You seriously think that I have done that then my dear fellow let me tell you that you don't know what the accent of hate is. Is it possible that You haven't seen that in this book I am concerned with nothing but ideas, to the exclusion of everything else, with no arrière pensée of any kind.[29]

A. J. Guerard says that *The Secret Agent* is a comedy whilst *Under Western Eyes* is a tragedy.[30] This distinction has more than neatness in its favour, though I am not sure that 'comedy' is quite the right word for *The Secret Agent* since comedy invites us to think of Shakespearean closure with its characteristic double burden of judgement and celebration. Zdzisław Najder is nearer the mark when he calls it realistically treated melodrama.[31] *The Secret Agent* judges, unsparingly, but it refuses to celebrate anything and its closures – the deaths of Stevie, Verloc and Winnie – resemble the closures of tragedy. Conrad's own dominant word for *The Secret Agent*, 'irony', seems to be the right one. *Under Western Eyes* is undoubtedly a tragedy, although Razumov himself, as we see below (p. 181), experiences the web of misunderstanding in which he finds himself enmeshed among the Geneva revolutionaries as a kind of comedy.[32] *Lord Jim* was a tragedy and so, I think, is *Victory*, though the subversive energy with which that novel resists our desire for generic neatness means that such a statement is bound to be qualified.[33] *The Secret Agent* is an ironic fiction which has an inverse and adversarial relationship with these works, especially with *Under Western Eyes*. Guerard's 'comedy'/'tragedy' distinction does alert us, though, to Conrad's use of dramatic stereotypes. Conrad's theatrical imagination is somewhat conventional: the good tend to be handsome and the bad ugly. This convention is used in a direct way in *Lord Jim* (compare Jim and the German skipper) but it is also overlaid by sophistication – the first sentence of *Lord Jim* tells us that Jim is of less than heroic stature and Marlow when he first sees Jim is distressed by the split between Jim's good looks and his culpability. But the convention doesn't vanish: Jim could be said to grow into his physical beauty so that when he redeems his honour by sacrificing his life to Doramin he has become, in his moral nature, as heroic as he looks. In *Nostromo* the pattern is adapted: Gould and Nostromo have physical splendour but become morally corroded, while integrity remains the possession of the physically unimpressive Monygham. I would wish to stress my word 'adapted': although *Nostromo* works against the convention the pattern that I have described has to be implicitly present behind the text for the novel to resist it. *Under Western Eyes* restores the pattern in an almost naive form: the Haldin family have wide brows and distinguished features and look noble and highly bred, while Razumov's good looks are blurred (as shown in the passage that I quote as an epigraph) in a manner appropriate to his oblique and unfocussed genealogy. In *The Secret Agent*, by contrast, the major male figures are heavily or pathetically ugly (Verloc, Heat and Stevie) and Winnie and her mother have the plain frumpishness that Conrad thinks characteristic of women of their class. Ossipon, on the other hand, is sexually presentable – he causes a stir in Winnie – though his features, because 'flattened' and 'negroid' indicate moral weakness (note Conrad's schematic use of Lombroso here). I think he resembles Razumov in this respect. A tiny early scene in Conrad's Russian novel could have come out of his London novel: Razumov is out in the streets, shaking with terror because of Haldin's revelation, and has a near sexual encounter:

> He noted . . . the sidelong, brilliant glance of a pretty woman – with a delicate head, and covered in the hairy skins of wild beasts down to her feet, like a frail and beautiful savage – which rested for a moment with a sort of mocking tenderness on the deep abstraction of that good-looking young man (*Under Western Eyes*, Part First, Section 2, p. 40).

Compare chapter 2 of *The Secret Agent* where Verloc sees passing carriages 'with here and there a victoria with the skin of some wild beast inside and a woman's face and hat emerging above the folded hood' (p. 15). Both instances stress the Darwinian kinship of woman and beast.

'Part First' of *Under Western Eyes* is characterized throughout by careful scene-setting and theatricality. Close attention is paid to the physical appearance of each figure as it is presented. The narrative convention involves a limited narrator using a written record – the English teacher of languages using Razumov's journal – and we can take it that the foci of attention displayed in the narrative reflect Razumov's own preoccupations. Razumov has no family. He is the most deracinated of Conrad's heroes, 'officially and in fact without a family' and 'as lonely in the world as a man swimming in the deep sea' (Part First, Section I, p. 10). He is a self-possessed outsider who finds it difficult to make contact with other human beings. The only emotionally significant older male in his life is Prince K., Razumov's father (whom he is not permitted to acknowledge publicly) whose identity becomes in a sense fetishized by the synecdoche of his side-whiskers: he is a 'tall, aristocratic-looking personage with silky, grey side-whiskers' whose only indication of parentage is a quasi-masonic handshake ('a light pressure like a secret sign', p. 12) and who is further fetishized by Razumov by the use of the monosyllable 'He!' ('it was by this monosyllable that Mr Razumov got into the habit of referring mentally to the stranger with grey silky side-whiskers', p. 13). His self-esteem is bound up with his Western ambition to become a civil servant or a professor: 'A celebrated professor was a somebody' (Part First, p. 13).[34] But the ideal up to which he should seek to live is embodied in the figure (sculpted by an artist, Spontini, whom Conrad seems to have invented) which stands in the corner of General T-'s room: 'Filling a corner, on a black pedestal, stood a quarter-life-size smooth-limbed bronze of an adolescent figure, running' (Part First, p. 43). This heroic posture is imitated by Haldin when he leaves Razumov's room: 'Haldin, already at the door, tall and straight as an arrow, with his pale face and a hand raised attentively, might have posed for the statue of a daring youth listening to an inner voice' (Part First, p. 63).

The dramatic device of the double is a recurrent feature of Conrad's work. The *Doppelgänger* of romantic fiction is both the opposite of the protagonist (the many doubles in Dostoevsky, Wringhim and Gil-Martin in Hogg's *Confessions of a Justified Sinner*, Jekyll and Hyde in Stevenson's famous romance) and his mirror-image, who may also embody the Jungian 'shadow' – the part of the self that the conscious mind seeks to split off and deny (the painting in *The Picture of Dorian Gray*, the maimed spectre encountered in New York in James's 'The Jolly Corner'). In Conrad, Leggatt in 'The Secret Sharer' is a mirror-image figure who carries some of the young skipper's 'shadow' (properly to command his ship the young skipper needs to display some of the aggression that has got Leggatt into trouble), Haldin in *Under Western Eyes* embodies the selfless moral courage that Razumov lacks, Jones in *Victory* acts out the fear of women which, in Heyst, is unacknowledged but has chilled his capacity to love.

Razumov needs to arrive at self-knowledge by bonding powerfully with another person. In his deracinated state he needs affirmation from contact with a significant other: he feels the need of 'some other mind's sanction' (Part First, Section II, p. 39). This need reflects the emotional hunger of Jim which prompts Marlow, as we have seen, to think that 'loneliness' is 'a hard and absolute condition of existence' (*Lord Jim*, chapter 16, p. 180) though it is, of course, a feature of Jim's predicament that he is not, in fact, lonely but is surrounded by potentially helpful people, starting with Marlow himself.[35] It also reflects the epigraph to *Lord Jim*: 'It is certain my Conviction gains infinitely, the moment another soul will believe in it.' Razumov seeks a leader, 'not the conflicting aspirations of a people, but . . . a man – strong and one' (Part First, Section II, p. 33). After Haldin has taken Razumov into his confidence and confessed to the murder of de P-, Razumov envisages for a moment a dramatic reconciliation and *éclaircissement*:

He embraced for a whole minute the delirious purpose of rushing to his lodgings and flinging himself on his knees by the side of the bed with the dark figure stretched on it; to pour out a full confession in passionate words that would stir the whole being of that man to its innermost depths; that would end in embraces and tears; in an incredible fellowship of souls – such as the world had never seen (Part First, Section II, pp. 39–40).

When I say 'dramatic' I mean that Conrad's imagination is staging this as a scene in the theatre, as it does much of the 'Part First' of this novel. Razumov seeks in other men the mirror to his own nature, seeks to understand himself by anxious contemplation of Haldin, contemplation so anxious that it causes him to hallucinate and to see the figure of Haldin, whom he has determined to betray, laid out on the snow. Love and hatred are close to each other: with part of his mind – and, more importantly, his emotional being – Razumov knows that Haldin himself is the man, strong and one, who could serve as hero and model and could release Razumov from his isolation and queasy selfishness.

The doubling here is destructive and thus reverses the liberating and redemptive doubling of 'The Secret Sharer' which Conrad wrote in 1908. This story has the same kind of relationship to *Under Western Eyes* as 'Heart of Darkness' does to *Lord Jim*. If we think in each case of the novel as the planet and the tale as its satellite a symmetrical patterning of the relationships between the male protagonists in the four works emerges: in 'Heart of Darkness' and *Lord Jim* the satellite reveals by contrast and the planet by comparison, and in 'The Secret Sharer' and *Under Western Eyes* the position is reversed, the satellite reveals by comparison and the planet by contrast. The interactions of Marlow and Kurtz, Razumov and Haldin are deployed dramatically to display the profound contrasts between these figures: those of Marlow and Jim, the skipper and Leggatt are deployed to show comparisons. Jim becomes somewhat like Marlow – the emotionally significant older male in his life – when he redeems his honour, and the young skipper becomes somewhat like Leggatt, morally as well as physically, when he takes command of his ship. Cutting across this is the presence of strong feeling between the males in three of these four works: Marlow's feeling for Jim (and Jim's for Marlow, though this is harder to show), the skipper's for Leggatt and Razumov's for Haldin.

The emotional content of 'The Secret Sharer' has been acknowledged by other commentators: Cedric Watts, for instance, speaks sensitively of the way in which the skipper's 'sense of intuitive comradeship modulates, very reticently, towards love' for Leggatt.[36] It is important that all this is in the narrator's – the unnamed young skipper's – temperament or consciousness. Leggatt is a mirror – the skipper sets the scene, directing it for an imagined audience: if the mate were to see them together 'he would think he was seeing double, or imagine himself come upon a scene of weird witchcraft; the strange captain having a quiet confabulation by the wheel with his own grey ghost' (p. 255). There is no reason to think that Leggatt is as powerfully attracted to the young skipper as the latter is to

Leggatt: for the skipper Leggatt is a forceful embodiment of a romantic cliché, an unjustly condemned fugitive whose life is in danger, while to Leggatt the young skipper is less interesting as a man than as an instrument of escape. When they part, Leggatt takes his hand in a 'steady, motionless clasp' (p. 290) out of gratitude, presumably, rather than erotic feeling, in a powerful Edwardian variant of the manly handshake. The skipper is dramatized as immature, and there is no doubt that the emotional immaturity, registered by his need to engage strenuously with a strong exemplary male, will be left behind when he overcomes his professional immaturity and takes command of his ship.

Razumov is also immature. His face looks incomplete, like an unfinished sculpture, contrasting sharply with Haldin's strong and finely modelled features, and his erotic nature is ambivalent. He is attracted to Nathalie Haldin partly because she has a 'masculine' handshake and bearing. Reflecting both *Hamlet* and Calderón's *Life is a Dream*, and thus aligning himself with that earlier tragic protagonist, Jim in *Lord Jim*,[37] Razumov thinks to himself that life is both a 'dream' and a 'fear' (Part Fourth, Section II, p. 316). By juxtaposing him with the figure of Rousseau the novel emphasises the contrast between the security of the Swiss bourgeois intellectual and the tragic terror which is in store for the young Russian. The teacher of languages looks on at him and notes both his conformity to the good-looking protagonist stereotype and the fact that for Razumov at this moment life is a dream. The teacher of languages here is a bit like Marlow looking on at the unconscious Jim in chapter 6 of Lord Jim:

> He was crossing the Rue Mont Blanc with every appearance of an aimless stroller. He did not recognize me, but I made him out at some distance. He was very good-looking, I thought, this remarkable friend of Miss Haldin's brother. I watched him go up to the letter-box and then retrace his steps. Again he passed me very close . . . he had the expression of a somnambulist struggling with the very dream which drives him forth to wander in dangerous places. . . . There was something shocking in the expression of that face (Part Fourth, Section II, p. 317).

The teacher of languages then switches his thoughts to Miss Haldin and makes her explicitly a participant in a tragic drama: 'She was one of those natures, rare enough, luckily, in which one cannot help being interested, because they provoke both terror and pity' (Part Fourth, Section II, p. 318). Conrad is writing in a period which was accustomed to think of tragedy as the dominant dramatic genre – A. C. Bradley's hugely influential *Shakespearean Tragedy* was published in 1904. Conrad borrowed this book from Richard Curle in late 1913 or early 1914.[38] Did he read it for the first time in 1913, or had he perhaps borrowed it from Curle to refresh his mind, having read it, or read in it, when it was first published? He would certainly have been aware of it in 1904–5 since it had received major reviews indicating its great importance and the transforming impact that it had had on contemporary thinking about Shakespeare.[39] Bradley takes Aristotle as the model on which Shakespeare is building and Conrad would have been aware of this.[40] I cannot see anything in a recent suggestion that he is writing 'Bergsonian comedy' in both *The Secret Agent* and *Under Western Eyes*.[41] It is true that there is a good deal of emphasis on gesture in both novels, but this is because Conrad is thinking in terms of the theatre – which means, obviously, that he could be thinking in terms of tragedy as much as of comedy. I think an observation of work-in-progress on the novel makes it clear that tragedy was the dramatic genre in his mind, but he was not clear whether he should commit himself wholly to it. The manuscript had the working title 'Razumov', inviting us to focus our dramatic attention on the protagonist, but the manuscript also contains long scenes excluding Razumov himself, scenes which are cut from the serial and the book publications. These scenes include a dialogue between Nathalie and Peter Ivanovitch and a long and interesting restaurant contest between Peter Ivanovitch and the teacher of languages.[42] In other words the manuscript is less Razumov-centred and more Russia-centred – less of a tragedy, more of a political novel – than the text in its final state.

'Razumov' would have been a good title. Like *Lord Jim* it is partly ironic, in that Razumov is a man without a father and therefore without a name to which he is properly entitled; the novel never explains the source of the name Razumov, nor does it tell us explicitly how he came by his Christian name, Kirylo, and his patronymic, Sidorovitch. (The Prince's surname may have been 'Sidor', hence 'Sidorovitch'. The 'K-' in 'Prince K-' would be a family name.[43])

The sources of *Under Western Eyes* have been much discussed. It has long been recognized that the novel must owe something to Dostoevsky's *Crime and Punishment*. The names of Razumov and Raskolnikov have an assonance which cannot be accidental and their respective stories show a number of parallels. In both the novels the protagonists suffers physical and psychological illness brought on by guilt. In each novel a seemingly perfect alibi presents itself (in *Crime and Punishment* a housepainter is thought guilty of the crime, which deflects suspicion from Raskolnikov; in *Under Western Eyes* that role is given to Ziemianitch the sledge-driver, who deflects suspicion from Razumov). As a result of this plotting Razumov and Raskolnikov find themselves in closely similar final situations at the end of their respective novels, and in each case the confession, when it comes, is made of the protagonist's own free will. And each is cared for by a self-sacrificing woman (Tekla and Sonia respectively). In addition to these parallels there are, of course, important differences: Dostoevsky's novel is Christian, broadly, in its outer assumptions and in its frame of reference, while Conrad's novel is wholly secular – indeed existentialist – in its frame of reference.[44]

There was also a biographical source, indicated by Cedric Watts and Thomas Moser (and briefly noted above, p. 150).[45] Sergey Stepniak, a Russian political refugee who was a friend of the Garnett family at a time when Conrad was very close to Edward Garnett, may well have been one of the sources both for Haldin and for Razumov. Conrad met the Garnetts in 1894, when Edward Garnett read *Almayer's Folly* for Unwin (see above, p. 48). As Moser points out, Conrad became friendly with the Garnetts at a time when the Garnett world was intensely Russian. Olive Garnett, Edward's sister, was in love with Stepniak and Constance Garnett, Edward's wife, the famous translator of Tolstoy, Dostoevsky, Turgenev and Chekhov, embarked on this career partly because she was encouraged to do so by Stepniak. Indeed, it seems likely that she, too, was in love with him.[46] Moser points to several features of the Olive Garnett-Stepniak relationship which anticipate features of *Under Western Eyes*:

> A young Russian revolutionist assassinated a hated Tsarist official; a young Russian revolutionist escaped to a Western capital; he there involved himself in political activity; an idealistic young woman fell in love with him; subsequently she discovered a shocking fact about his past; the relationship ended with the young man being struck down on railway tracks; the young woman went to Russia, remained unmarried, and led a life of self-denial.[47]

Like Haldin, Stepniak was a killer. In 1878 he had murdered General Mezentsev, the Russian Chief of Police.[48] Like Razumov's, his career was brought to an end by a collision: Stepniak was run down by a train and killed on 23 December 1895, while walking from his house in Bedford Park to visit his fellow refugee Volkhovsky in Shepherd's Bush; the driver of the train testified that Stepniak seemed not to hear his whistle.[49] Conrad met Constance Garnett in 1896, two months after Stepniak's death. It is not known whether Conrad had read any of Stepniak's revolutionary writings, but he would certainly have known about his friendship with the Garnetts, his political life and his violent death. Moser suggests that Conrad would have identified with Stepniak as a fellow Slav in exile but this is at odds with what we know about Conrad's attitude to 'Slavs'. It annoyed him to be called a 'Slav' by his friend Garnett. Like other Poles, Conrad saw himself as belonging to Western civilization, not to the Slavs. (Najder points out that Russian revolutionaries would also have resisted being described as 'Slavs' because the term was exploited for political purposes by the Tsarist regime.[50])

While Stepniak is probably a source for Haldin and Razumov there is no need to identify him with Conrad as well; the novelist is very aware, in *Under Western Eyes*, of the gap between himself (as Western consciousness) and his doomed young Russians. Conrad's Russian novel draws on both the terror and the political rightness of Stepniak's revolutionary actions: both are felt in Haldin's anguished self-defence, following the death of de P-. Haldin sounds at times, when he is in Nietzschean and Messianic mode, like the Professor from *The Secret Agent*, who drinks a toast 'To the destruction of what is':[51] 'You suppose that I am a terrorist, now – a destructor of what is. But consider that the true destroyers are they who destroy the spirit of progress and truth. . . . Men like me are rare' (*Under Western Eyes*, Part First, pp. 19–20).

The arrogance of this last line compares with the Professor's 'To deal with a man like me you require sheer, naked, inglorious heroism'.[52] Elsewhere Haldin sounds like Jim in chapters 15 and 16 of *Lord Jim*. Jim chokes back the tears as he makes his great confession to his friend Marlow, and Haldin weeps – more openly, as is appropriate to a more emotionally expressive Russian male – after he has unburdened himself to Razumov:

> 'I respect your philosophical scepticism, Razumov, but don't touch the soul. The Russian soul that lives in all of us. It has a future. It has a mission, I tell you, or else why should I have been moved to do this – reckless – like a butcher – in the middle of all these innocent people – scattering death – I! I! . . . I wouldn't hurt a fly!' . . . Haldin sat down abruptly, and leaning his head on his folded arms burst into tears. He wept for a long time. The dusk had deepened in the room (*Under Western Eyes*, Part First, p. 22).

Razumov is also a murderer in that he betrays Haldin, and in Moser's view Razumov, too, is drawn from specific features of Stepniak; he notes that it makes sense to connect Haldin and Razumov to the same historical figure because Conrad habitually links the two characters in *Under Western Eyes*.[53] Stepniak had a capacity to make himself literally *deaf* to anything other than his own thoughts, and it seems to have been this capacity for insulating himself from the outside world that led to his death; he was run over by a train, vividly foreshadowing Razumov's drastic destiny as he staggers, deafened by Nikita, in the streets of St Petersburg and is run down and crippled by a tram.[54] Stepniak's funeral in 1895 (Conrad didn't attend it, but it was widely reported in the press) may have sparked off recollections for Conrad of his father's funeral, where Conrad aged eleven marched at the head of the procession.[55] Both funerals were major political manifestations. And *Under Western Eyes* brings together guilt, psychological anguish, political considerations and recollection of Conrad's childhood. As Conrad remarks in his famous letter to John Galsworthy, the 'psychological developments' in Razumov's story furnish the novelist with his focus of interest.[56] In a brilliant study of the *Doppelgänger* as a literary topos Karl Miller explores the dramatic doubling in *Under Western Eyes* and 'The Secret Sharer', noting that such doubling is a way of dealing with the neurotic and romantic pressures that swirl beneath his work:

> The romantic Conrad has been undervalued in comparison with the achievements of the moralistic Conrad which are set out as canonical in Leavis's *[The] Great Tradition*. If Conrad was suspicious of romance, he was also suspicious of morality, and the distinction is in any case, in its relation to his work, somewhat chimerical. There is a great fund of romance in the novels Leavis loves. In *Under Western Eyes*, for instance. This is a book about a betrayer who finds on one occasion that he has 'another self, an independent sharer of his mind'.[57]

The phrase that Miller refers to comes after Razumov's dialogue with Peter Ivanovitch and Madame de S- in the Chateau Borel: 'He felt, bizarre as it may seem, as though another self, an independent sharer of his mind, had been able to view his whole person very distinctly indeed' (Part Third, Section II, p. 230). Narrative method and dramatic organization are made here to intersect by the device of the doubling. Later in the novel, when Razumov learns that the revolutionaries believe that Haldin was betrayed by Ziemianitch he compares the plot in which he finds himself to Shakespeare's archetypal structure of doubling and disguises: this is 'no tragedy' but 'a comedy of errors' (Part Third, Section IV, p. 285). The teacher of languages as narrator is himself, in a sense, the secret sharer looking on as he reads Razumov's document, his diary, and translates and adapts it into the English narrative which gives access to the reader's Western eyes. The teacher of languages compares Razumov's relationship with his own diary to a man confronting his own mask or image in a mirror, a central *topos* of romanticism and of the *Doppelgänger* motif. Given the roles he is forced to play as a secret agent Razumov uses the diary as the one place in which he can speak the truth, and the teacher of languages asks whether this may not be failing him. At the end of his interview with Madame de S- Razumov has a brief moment in which to 'make sure that his face did not betray his angry curiosity and his mental disgust':

> These sentiments stand confessed in Mr Razumov's memorandum of his first interview with Madame de S-. The very words I use in my narrative are written where their sincerity cannot be suspected. The record, which could not have been meant for any one's eyes but his own [certainly not for our Western eyes], was not, I think, the outcome of that strange impulse of indiscretion common to men who lead secret lives, and accounting for the invariable existence of 'compromising documents' in all the plots and conspiracies of history. Mr Razumov looked at it, I suppose, as a man looks at himself in a mirror, with wonder, perhaps with anguish, with anger or despair. Yes, as a threatened man may look fearfully at his own face in the glass, formulating to himself reassuring excuses for his appearance marked by the taint of some insidious hereditary disease (Part Third, Section I, p. 214).

Doubling and splitting become powerfully associated with Razumov's psychological collapse following the dialogue – one of the best scenes in the whole of Conrad – in which Mikulin sadistically and skilfully plays his man, like a fish, until Razumov is reduced to the state in which we see him at the start of Part Four – the state in which he is ready to serve the Russian autocracy as a secret agent. As he goes home from this interview Razumov displays symptoms of depression, that illness so well known to Conrad: 'He had to stop several times; all his strength seemed to run out of his limbs; and in the movement of the busy streets, isolated as if in a desert, he remained suddenly motionless for a minute or so before he could proceed on his way' (Part Four, Section I, pp. 297–8).

Here and elsewhere in this novel, as in *Lord Jim*, guilt is associated with a sense of unbearable isolation. The teacher of languages as narrator asks:

Who knows what true loneliness is – not the conventional word, but the naked terror? To the lonely themselves it wears a mask. The most miserable outcast hugs some memory or some illusion. Now and then a fatal conjunction of events may lift the veil for an instant. For an instant only. No human being could bear a steady view of moral solitude without going mad (Part One, Section II, p. 39).

Surely the narrator here is speaking for the novelist. In a similar way, as we have seen, Marlow as narrator speaks, on Conrad's behalf, about the universality of loneliness in chapter 16 of *Lord Jim* (see above, pp. 101–102).

For Marlow his beloved Jim is 'one of us', and the same phrase appears in a horribly ironic context in *Under Western Eyes*, reinforcing our sense of Razumov's isolation. He is penetrating the Geneva revolutionaries in order to betray them, he is believed (by them) to have been the closest friend and ally of the dead Haldin, and (supreme irony) he is regarded by the despicable parasite Peter Ivanovitch as a 'revolutionary' who is at heart an aristocrat, and can thus in this highly specialized sense be regarded as 'one of us' (Part Third, Section I, p. 208). Embraced by Peter Ivanovitch both as a fellow-parasite and as a fellow-revolutionary Razumov is thus praised for qualities to which he is diametrically opposed. The crisis in Part First has forced him to codify his own sense of his political allegiance:

History not Theory.
Patriotism not Internationalism.
Evolution not Revolution.
Direction not Destruction.
Unity not Disruption

(Part First, Section II, p. 66)

In its large structure, then, the novel sets up lovers – for Razumov discovers, to his anguish, that he loves Nathalie – who are politically polarized. Razumov is cautious, 'English' in outlook and style (when Haldin confides to Razumov that he has killed de P- he adds 'I cannot expect you with your frigid English manner to embrace me'; Part First, Section I, p. 16), intent on his Prize Essay, his silver medal, and his career as a professor or a civil servant. As a schoolboy in Cracow Conrad must have noted the great gulf between his own wayward and negligent attitude to his studies and that of his more conventional schoolfellows, eager to pursue their ambitions however horrible the political system within which they would have to make their careers. Nathalie is a fervent revolutionary, whose credo is simply and passionately expressed: 'I would take liberty from any hand as a hungry man would snatch at a piece of bread' (Part Second, Section III, p. 135). The teacher of languages perceives Nathalie ironically. In his struggle with Razumov's document he seeks to express the nature of his task thus:

The task is not in truth the writing in the narrative form a *precisé* of a strange human document, but the rendering – I perceive it now clearly – of the moral conditions ruling over a large portion of this earth's surface; conditions not easily to be understood, much less discovered in the limits of a story, till some key-word is found; a word that could stand at the back of all the words covering the pages, a word which, if not truth itself, may perchance hold truth enough to help the moral discovery which should be the object of every tale (Part First, Section III, p. 67).

The teacher of languages thinks that this key word is 'cynicism' (*ibid.*). And in his inconclusive argument with Nathalie about the respective English and Russian attitudes to political liberty he explains her expression of her beliefs, which he finds alien and rebarbative, in terms of 'cynicism':

I suppose one must be a Russian to understand Russian simplicity, a terrible corroding simplicity in which mystic phrases clothe a naïve and hopeless cynicism. I think sometimes that the psychological secret of the profound difference of that people consists in this, that they detest life, the irremediable life of the earth as it is, whereas we westerners cherish it with perhaps an equal exaggeration of its sentimental value (Part Second, Section I, p. 104).

E. M. Forster's great liberal novel, *Howards End*, published in 1910, takes a phrase by one of its female characters, Margaret Schlegel, and quotes it as the epigraph on the title-page, 'Only Connect'. The same unusual procedure is adopted by Conrad here in his final and major political novel, and it may well be that he is consciously following Forster's example. The teacher of languages substitutes 'cynicism' for 'mysticism'. Nathalie's cry, 'I would take liberty from any hand as a hungry man would snatch a piece of bread' is, by virtue of its position on the title page, given greater authority than anything said by the teacher of languages. His narrative frames Razumov's story but Nathalie's formulation in turn frames his narrative and is privileged in relation to it. The teacher of languages gets its wrong. Nathalie's faith in freedom is neither cynical nor mystical, it is severely practical.

The Garnetts were, of course, as we have seen, closely associated with and warmly sympathetic to Russian revolutionaries, and also immersed in and powerfully influenced by Russian literature. Conrad always professed to dislike Dostoevsky and must have been annoyed to read (in Garnett's review in the *Nation*) this: 'The sinister force of the last twenty pages has the effect of a thunderbolt cleaving the brooding, sultry air. Here Mr Conrad is at his best, and many of his pages may be placed by the side of notable passages in Turgenev and Dostoievsky [sic], to both of which great masters Mr Conrad bears affinities and owes a debt.'[58] When he read Constance Garnett's translation of Dostoevsky's *The Brothers Karamazov* Conrad wrote to Edward Garnett as follows:

It [*The Brothers Karamazov*]'s an impossible lump of valuable matter. It's terrifically bad and impressive and exasperating. Moreover, I don't know

what D. stands for or reveals, but I do know that he is too Russian for me.
It sounds to me like some fierce mouthings from prehistoric ages. I understand the Russians have just 'discovered' him. I wish them joy (27 May,
1912).[59]

The Brothers Karamazov was not the only Dostoevsky text which Conrad
held in abhorrence. He professed himself able to bear none of Dostoevsky's
work, and a bit later in this letter he indicates that Turgenev and Tolstoy
(in that order), were the Russian novelists with whom he felt in sympathy.[60] Garnett wrote a study of Tolstoy, and a further exchange between
the friends shows that Garnett interpreted Conrad as saying that he disliked Tolstoy. Conrad replied, 23 February 1914, to say that 'dislike' was
the wrong world but that Tolstoy's 'anti-sensualism' (Conrad doesn't explain what he means by that) is unsympathetic to him and that 'the base
from which he starts – Christianity – is distasteful to me.' It was not always
distasteful: in his later years, as we shall see, he was to display more sympathy with Christianity and occasionally referred to the Catholicism of his
childhood as though it was still an active force in his life.[61] But in relation
to Tolstoy Christianity was a target for spirited comic attack:

> I am not blind to its services but the absurd oriental fable from which it
> starts irritates me. Great, improving, softening, compassionate it may be but
> it has lent itself with amazing facility to cruel distortion and is the only
> religion which, with its impossible standards, has brought an infinity of
> anguish to innumerable souls – on this earth.... Why I should fly out like
> this on Xtianity which has given to mankind the beautiful Xmas pudding I
> don't know, unless that, like some good dogs, I get snappish as I grow old.[62]

Conrad's argument with Garnett needs to be read, of course, in the light
both of Garnett's passionate commitment to Russian life and literature
and of the warm friendship between the two men. Throughout their correspondence Conrad kept up the fiction that he was a child and Garnett
his literary father: in a letter of 12 January 1911 (referring to *Under Western
Eyes* and 'Freya of the Seven Isles') Conrad says, affectionately and playfully, 'it is a far cry from 1894 when this literary child was born to
you.... You are responsible for my existence'.[63] This enabled Conrad to
feel that he himself was somehow *not* responsible for his own existence.
The pattern of dependence ran deep. But the hatred of Russia was real
enough. In 'Autocracy and War', the essay written in 1905 for the *Fortnightly
Review* following Russia's war with Japan, Conrad speaks of Russia's power
as a 'dreaded and strange apparition, bristling with bayonets, armed with
chains, hung over with holy images' and notes the way in which the war
with Japan has brought Russia to the attention of Europe: 'Never before
had the Western world the opportunity to look so deep into the black
abyss which separates a soulless autocracy posing as, and even believing
itself to be, the arbiter of Europe, from the benighted, starved souls of its
people' ('Autocracy and War', *Notes on Life and Letters*, p. 89).

In addition to the Russian content of the novel and Conrad's feelings about it there were immediate reasons for Conrad's psychological collapse in 1910. He had worked with great intensity on the final stage of the writing. This was typical: he had written the endings of earlier great novels that had given him trouble, *Lord Jim* and *Nostromo,* in long drags of twenty hours or more continuous writing. So he was physically and mentally exhausted. Also, he quarrelled with Pinker on 27 January which clearly removed one of his sources of support, and he had earlier quarrelled with Ford, which removed another. And, as we have just noted, he was disagreeing with one of his most trusted friends, Garnett, over the central matter of sympathy with Russia. Sherry points out that Conrad always needed the support of a young man, and that as a result of the disagreement with Garnett the dependency there cooled, and Conrad was soon to transfer his affection to a new young man, Richard Curle.[64]

Razumov in his isolation and anguish doubts his own identity. So does Conrad as he writes. The manuscript of *Under Western Eyes* has a number of doodlings and marginalia, and one of these becomes obsessively frequent in the latter part of the manuscript. It is the letter 'K', sometimes elaborately ornamented, sometimes much underlined, usually capitalized: K for Korzeniowski, K for Kyrilo, K for Prince K- and K – of course – for Konrad, as Conrad's name was spelt in his childhood. K stands for the dead father and the displaced son in Conrad's life and for the absent, hidden father and the displaced son in his novel. As obsessively as Kafka (and using the same initial) Conrad erects textual barriers against psychological collapse. When he finished writing his text collapse overtook him.

Jeremy Hawthorn asks why it is that Conrad does not use Marlow as narrator of *Under Western Eyes.*[65] The immediate answer is that Marlow knew no Russian (he sees the Russian annotations to Towson's *Seamanship* in *Heart of Darkness* as notes in cypher) and has never visited Russia. Also, Marlow is a warm personality who seeks contact with the subjects of his narratives – especially Jim in *Lord Jim* and Flora in *Chance,* and even with Kurtz in *Heart of Darkness.* Haldin and Razumov are on their own in the dramatic economy of *Under Western Eyes.* We have seen that when Jim believes himself to be isolated he is in fact wrong; Marlow and others offer him support. Razumov by contrast is accurate about his own isolation: he has literally no one to go to, as he exclaims to Nathalie in the climactic and appalling scene of his confession to her (Part Four, Section 3, p. 354). Uncomprehending, emotionally insufficient, embarrassed by his own narrative enterprise and declaring his incompetence, the teacher of languages is the narrator to leave his subjects in their hapless solitude.

The stories in *A Set of Six* (1908) display some connection with the themes of *Nostromo, The Secret Agent* and *Under Western Eyes.* They are commercial, some of them are based on observation, and they are not Conrad at his best. In terms of chronology this volume and *'Twixt Land and Sea,* 1912, frame the great achievement of *Under Western Eyes.* In each case the reviewers tried to come to terms with these obviously minor collections by comparisons: Robert Lynd in the *Daily News* compared *A Set of Six* with Turgenev[66] and *'Twixt Land and Sea* with Kipling.[67] John Masefield made a rather forced comparison between *'Twixt Land and Sea* and Conrad's own earlier volume, *Youth,* a comparison based on the fact that each volume contains three stories (Masefield's scheme forces him to say that 'A Smile of Fortune' is like *Heart of Darkness,* that 'The Secret Sharer' is like 'Youth', 'a second "Youth", beautiful like that fine tale' and that 'Freya of the Seven Isles' is like 'The End of the Tether').[68] One may as well acknowledge that Conrad was capable of churning out short stories of variable quality. Of the six stories in *A Set of Six* 'The Duel', 'Gaspar Ruiz', 'The Brute', 'An Anarchist' and 'The Informer' all display themes and preoccupations which overlap with themes and preoccupations of the great political novels of this period.[69] The historical narrative 'The Duel' contains a secret agent. 'The Duel' is a long and ambitious account of archaic dedication to honour, displaying the fidelity with which two of Napoleon's officers maintain a life-long quarrel. As a foil to these guileless warriors Conrad invents the figure of Fouché, whose duplicity and cynicism are comparable with those of Vladimir or Nikita: Fouché is 'traitor to every man, to every principle and motive of human conduct' (p. 224). 'Gaspar Ruiz' is not a major work but its interest in the strong man Gaspar, who 'used his strength honourably' (p. 18) and whose strength is 'like an enormous stone lying on the ground, ready to be hurled this way or that by the hand that picks it up' (p. 27) is like *Nostromo*'s use of its folk-hero, whose force and enterprise are energies to be harnessed by subtler minds (Monygham and Mrs Gould). The source for Conrad's story is an episode about adventures in Chile from the published journal of one Captain Basil Hall.[70] The scene in which Gaspar Ruiz is supposedly executed and his neck is slashed with a sword, but he survives, is based on a real event in the life of a bandit called Benavides. Like Ruiz, Benavides has extraordinary courage and physical endurance, but, unlike him, is treacherous and murderous. The name 'Gaspar Ruiz' comes from one of Benavides' victims. Kirschner thinks that Conrad was drawn to Benavides's story because his life of guilt and treachery made Conrad think of his own guilt over leaving Poland, but this seems to me unlikely.[71] I think that Conrad was drawn to a figure of huge and gentle strength for reasons similar to the reasons for which he chooses elemental hero figures, such as Singleton, Falk or Nostromo, in his other fictions. In a minor work like this the writing about such a man readily spills over into sentimentality and romantic cliché, which enables us to appreciate the more fully the virtuosity of *The Nigger of the 'Narcissus'* and *Nostromo.*

For the volume *'Twixt Land and Sea,* Conrad depends heavily on his titles. *'Twixt Land and Sea* is presumably an echo of the phrase "Twixt the devil and the deep blue sea' and is chosen because it sounds nautical but is not too specific; he then seeks to lend cohesion to the group of stories by giving them subtitles, 'Harbour Story', 'An Episode from the Coast' and 'A Story of the Shallow Waters' which draw attention to their common setting. For these stories he has gone back to his earliest literary stimulus, the Malay archipelago. Interest in this early source was stirred up for him by a visit from Captain C. M. Marris, who has recently worked in the Malay Seas. Conrad wrote to Pinker that 'It was like the raising of a lot of dead – dead to me, because most of them live out there and even read my books and wonder who the devil has been around taking notes. . . . The best of it is that all these men of 22 years ago feel kindly to the Chronicler of their lives and adventures. They shall have some more of the stories they like'.[72] Marris's visit triggered the writing of these three stories, the first to be written from personal experience since 'The End of the Tether'. As he says in the Author's Note to the volume, the common setting is the only bond that may be said to unite the three tales. 'A Smile of Fortune' and 'Freya' were makeweight works which offer support to the view that Conrad couldn't write about women. The need to dramatize Alice in 'A Smile' and Freya in 'Freya' seems to paralyse Conrad's imagination. Garnett disliked 'Freya', and Conrad defended it in a letter in which he says that Marris's visit had stimulated him to write the tale and that it was based on an actual incident: the source for Jasper Allen was an Englishman called Sutton whom Conrad had heard about in Singapore. Sutton's ship, the *Costa-Rica*, was marooned on a reef 'by the commander of a Dutch gun-boat whom he had managed to offend in some way' (4 August 1911);[73] and Sutton, like Allen, became derelict on the beach of Macassar and didn't marry his girl. Later Conrad despaired of 'Freya' and acknowledged to Garnett that it was no good: 'I daresay *Freya* is pretty rotten. On the other hand the *Secret Sharer*, between you and me, is *it*. Eh? No damned tricks with girls there. Eh? Every word fits and there's not a single uncertain note. Luck my boy. Pure luck. I knew you would spot the thing at sight. But I repeat: mere luck' (5 November 1912).[74]

'The Secret Sharer' towers above the other short stories of this period. Our sense that it is a masterpiece is reinforced by the knowledge that in inspiration and source material it has common ground with *Lord Jim*. Leggatt and the young skipper learn that they were both '*Conway* boys'; that is to say, both trained on the *Conway*, a training-ship for cadets moored in the Mersey at Liverpool. The *Conway* boys were encouraged to be fiercely loyal to their training-ship. The training-ship that Lord Jim attends in his novel resembles the *Conway* and underpins the 'one of us' sensation, the knowledge that loyalty is a desirable and binding thing, which underpins so much of that novel. Like Leggatt, Jim is a parson's son, became a fugitive from a maritime scandal and was sympathetically treated by a sailing-ship captain.[75] But the dramatic relationship is reversed in 'The Secret Sharer' since *Lord Jim*'s Marlow is, of course, the stronger partner in the friendship while the young skipper is the weaker. There is a further point of contact between the two texts in chapter 18 of *Lord Jim* where Jim takes passage with Marlow on a ship sailing (as does the ship in 'The Secret Sharer') from Bangkok, and he skulks below as though – like Leggatt – he needs to conceal his guilt from view. Also, both *Lord Jim* and 'The Secret Sharer' are based on events reported in the newspapers in 1880: in the case of 'The Secret Sharer' the scandal was that of a murder on board the famous tea clipper, the *Cutty Sark*. John Anderson, the first mate, killed a disobedient and incompetent black sailor, John Francis. The skipper enabled Anderson to escape from the ship (the skipper subsequently drowned himself: a source for the death of Brierly in *Lord Jim*). Anderson was arrested later in London and sentenced to seven years' penal servitude for manslaughter.[76]

Another source for 'The Secret Sharer' is noted in *The Mirror of the Sea*. Charles Born, first mate of the *Otago*, Conrad's first and only command (sailing from Bangkok and a source for *The Shadow-Line*) received an 'unforgettable scare' from Conrad's manoeuvring in the Gulf of Siam. Cedric Watts comments that Conrad's motives for his adaptation of his two sources seem to include: 'A mixture of psychological compensation and vicarious (imaginative) atonement. At one level, the story says to the Charles Born of memory, "What you deemed to be reckless manoeuvring had a very good reason, though one that I, the young captain, could not reveal to you at the time." '[77] The 'erotics' of 'The Secret Sharer' coexists with a comedy of misunderstanding. The young skipper, feeling protective – almost maternal – towards Leggatt in a Marlow-like way offers Leggatt his hat. A comic struggle ensues: 'I snatched off my floppy hat and tried hurriedly in the dark to ram it on my other self. He dodged and fended off silently. I wonder what he thought had come to me before he understood and suddenly desisted. Our hands met gropingly, lingered united in a steady, motionless clasp for a second. . . . No word was breathed by either of us when they separated' (p. 290). 'Erotics' is the wrong word for this, of course. It is intense bonding, all the more intense for being fleeting, surreptitious and wordless. It owes much to the tender and unsurpassed delineation of friendship in *Lord Jim*. It also unmistakably resembles the odd quality of the impersonal sexual encounter found in Genet and other male homosexual writers, but the resemblance is in the oddness, the surreptitiousness and the intensity rather than in the sexuality.

Conrad almost spoils his story by overwriting the appearance of Kohring, the mountain which 'seemed to hang right over the ship like a towering fragment of the everlasting night' (p. 291). The same mountain looms equally in *The Shadow-Line*, 'a great, black upheaved ridge' (p. 84). The mountain rears up and is at first a source of terror, later a source of strength. The pattern reminds me irresistibly of Wordsworth's account of Black Crag, at Ullswater, which admonishes the truant boy in the stolen boat and is a source of moral teaching to him in Book I of *The Prelude*:

> From behind that craggy steep, till then
> The bound of the horizon, a huge cliff,
> Upreared its head. I struck, and struck again,
> And, growing still in stature, the huge cliff
> Rose up between me and the stars, and still

> With measured motion, like a living thing
> Strode after me.[78]

Conrad's odd 'upheaved' seems to echo Wordsworth's 'upreared'. Other literary echoes cluster round the end of 'The Secret Sharer'. *The Ancient Mariner* seems to be present in the negatives and the sense of living death, while 'Erebus' is carefully chosen, a region of terrifying dislocation and not-being. In Milton it is the lowest imaginable part of hell, but Milton's sources allow latitude: in Hesiod Erebus is nonspecific, 'From Chaos sprang Erebus and black Night', while in Virgil, *Georgics IV*, it is the land of the dead from which they are startled by the song of Orpheus.[79] the distinguishing features of Erebus for Conrad are that it is dark and that it is associated with the gates of hell. (This reinforces the probability that Conrad has *Paradise Lost* at the back of his mind here. As Sin opens the gates of hell the grating of their hinges creates 'Harsh thunder, that the lowest bottom shook/of Erebus'[80].) 'The Secret Sharer' ends with imagery which vigorously recalls – of course – *Heart of Darkness*, but also recalls the end of chapter 35 of *Lord Jim*, where Jim is the white speck in a darkening world. The white hat, left by Leggatt, the Jim-like disgraced young hero, keeps the nameless skipper out of the gates which enter into the final darkness:

> Walking to the taffrail, I was in time to make out, on the very edge of a darkness thrown by a towering black mass like the very gateway of Erebus – yes, I was in time to catch an evanescent glimpse of my white hat left behind to mark the spot where the secret sharer of my cabin and of my thoughts, as though he were my second self, had lowered himself into the water to take his punishment: a free man, a proud swimmer striking out for a new destiny (p. 295).

As so often in Conrad, this final paragraph behaves like a carefully balanced stanza in lyric poem. In the structure of this stanza the white hat is the exceptional item – small, fragile but intensely visible by contrast with its setting – and it is the pivot between two sets of elements. The first of these sets is the associated 'death' group: the actual darkness, the actual mountain and the metaphorical gateway to hell. The second is the associated 'life' group: free, proud, swimmer, destiny. The rapid unravelling of the words following the colon is itself an enactment of Leggatt's self-command.

8

The Problems and Paradoxes of *Chance*, 1911–14

I can't tell you how relieved I am to be done with the book [Chance]. *I have been very anxious – but I am so no longer. It's the biggest piece of work I've done since* Lord Jim. *As to what it is I am very confident. As to what will happen to it when launched – I am much less confident. And it's a pity. One doesn't do a trick like that twice – and I am not growing younger – alas! I will vanish in the ruck.*

Conrad to Pinker, 2 June 1913[1]

A critic [*of* Chance] *has remarked that if I had selected another method of composition and taken a little more trouble the tale could have been told in about two hundred pages.*[2] *I confess I do not perceive exactly the bearings of such criticism or even the use of such a remark. No doubt that by selecting a certain method and taking great pains the whole story might have been written out on a cigarette paper. For that matter, the whole history of mankind could be written thus if only approached with sufficient detachment. The history of men on this earth since the beginning of ages may be resumed in one phrase of infinite poignancy: They were born, they suffered, they died. . . . Yet it is a great tale! But in the infinitely minute stories about men and women it is my lot on earth to narrate I am not capable of such detachment.*

Author's Note to *Chance*

For Conrad 1910–12 was a period dogged by illness and writing block. After the nervous breakdown early in 1910 he spent three months in bed. In June 1911 he was slowly recovering, with much support from his friends (Arthur Marwood visited every Thursday). The move to Capel House at Orlestone raised his spirits enough for him to resume communication with friends. He wrote to Norman Douglas, 28 June 1910, to say that he has lost four months of his life: 'I am all of a shake yet; I feel like a man returned from hell and look upon the very world of the living with dread'.[3] As he emerged from his nervous breakdown he tried to pick up his interrupted writing, and in August was debating – often in conversation with

Arthur Marwood and Perceval Gibbon, who seem to have been the most trusted friends during this dark period – whether to press on with *Chance* or to try to resurrect *The Rescue*. At this date he still regarded the breach with Pinker as permanent and was seeking to discharge his debt to Pinker and free himself from dependence on him. In September 1910 he finished 'A Smile of Fortune' and wrote 'Prince Roman', reworking the latter tale from an earlier draft which had been composed as part of *A Personal Record* in 1908.

'A Smile of Fortune' is a story of the initiation of a young skipper on his first command, sharing common ground with 'Falk', 'The Secret Sharer' and *The Shadow-Line*. The young skipper, docking at Mauritius, becomes involved with Alfred Jacobus, a ship's chandler who uses his daughter, Alice, to ensnare and compromise the skipper and thus force on him purchases he does not need. The purchases include a huge cargo of potatoes. The smiling fortune of the title refers to the turn of events which enables him to sell this unwanted cargo at a profit, and he retreats from the relationship with Alice. The story was published in the *London Magazine* and it has been pointed out that the dark aspects of its theme – the destructiveness of sexual desire and the connections between economic and sexual impotence – were unsuitable for that essentially light and breezy periodical, and that as it stands the story is one of unrealized potential.[4] The comic figure of Mr Burns, the first mate, reappears in *The Shadow-Line*.

'Prince Roman' is the only Conrad narrative to make direct use of Polish history. It is based, as we have seen, on the true story of a hero of the 1830 uprising against the Russians, Prince Roman Sanguszko.[5] The Sanguszko estates, where the first part of the story is set, were in Byelorussia, but it seems likely that Cunninghame Graham, writing in 1925, was right to suggest that parts of this narrative may be drawn directly from Conrad's childhood memory of Uncle Tadeusz's house in the Ukraine[6] (the narrator recalls that at the age of eight he was staying 'in the country house of my mother's brother in our southern provinces' (p. 97) accompanied by his little girl cousin, who is not named but is presumably Józefa, Bobrowski's only child). He sees a guest arrive at night: 'The big travelling carriage on sleigh-runners harnessed with six horses, a black mass against the snow, going off to the stables, preceded by a horseman carrying a blazing ball of tow and resin in an iron basket at the end of a long stick swung from his saddle bow' (p. 99). He escapes from his lessons in the schoolroom: 'I found myself in the great stone-paved hall, warmed by a monumental stove of white tiles, a much more pleasant locality than the school-room which for some reason or other, perhaps hygienic, was always kept at a low temperature' (p. 98). More generally, the story displays Conrad's powerful capacity for conveying landscapes (the reference to the Lithuanian forest locates the following passage in Byelorussia).
Prince Roman rides over the

countryside where he had been born and had spent his happy boyish years. He knew it well – every slight rise crowned with trees amongst the ploughed fields, every dell concealing a village. The dammed streams made a chain of lakes set in the green meadows. Far away to the north the great Lithuanian forest faced the sun, no higher than a hedge; and to the south, the way to the plains, the vast brown spaces of the earth touched the blue sky (pp. 112–13).

After the tormented and oblique account of a Pole's anguished relationship with Russia in *Under Western Eyes*, 'Prince Roman' seems a direct, lyrically evocative elegy for Poland's thwarted hopes and for the lost generation of which Prince Roman is a representative. The story looks back with contained sorrow at the futility of the 1830 uprising:

> The year 1831 [the year of the defeat of the uprising] is for us an historical date, one of these fatal years when in the presence of the world's passive indignation and eloquent sympathies we had once more to murmur 'Vae Victis' and count the cost in sorrow. Not that we were ever very good at calculating, either in prosperity or in adversity. That's a lesson we could never learn, to the great exasperation of our enemies who have bestowed upon us the epithet of Incorrigible . . . (p. 91).

In most of his writing about politics – in his fictions, at least – Conrad's posture is ironic. Here he is direct, indeed triumphal, in his dramatization of the heroism with which Prince Roman faces the Commission that tries him for joining the insurrection, and brings punishment on himself by presenting them with a written statement (thus denying himself the clemency that his captors were prepared to show) saying: 'I joined the national rising from conviction' (p. 147). The presence of three officers conducting the examination and the management of the narrative voice remind me of the trial of Jim by the Court of Inquiry in *Lord Jim*:

> Within those four sinister walls shutting out from him all the sights and sounds of liberty, all hopes of the future, all consoling illusions – alone in the face of his enemies erected for judges – who can tell how much love of life there was in Prince Roman? . . . . Nearing the supreme moment of his life the Prince could only have had the feeling that it was about to end. He answered the questions put to him clearly, concisely . . . with the most profound indifference (pp. 144–5).

Roman is condemned for life to the Siberian mines, and the Tsar adds a personal instruction in his own handwriting:[7] 'The authorities are severely warned to take care that this convict walks in chains like any other criminal every step of the way.' In Conrad's story the Prince is declared legally dead but is released from Siberia, after twenty-five years, stone deaf, and now lives in a house belonging to his daughter who has inherited his estates. In old age he has become valued for his sanity and wisdom. The detail of his deafness links him to Razumov: in the deafness which follows their active lives both these figures become revered sages.

Towards the end of 1910 Conrad took a break from his own writing and read work by his friends – Galsworthy's *The Inn of Tranquillity* (1910) and Douglas Goldring's *The Country Boy and Other Poems* (1910). The suffragette movement's 'Black Friday' (18 November 1910) may have stimulated Conrad's interest in feminists (which is then used in *Chance*). In December the serial of *Under Western Eyes* began to appear simultaneously in the *English Review* and in the *North American Review*. Early in 1911 he worked on 'Freya of the Seven Isles' (using material gleaned from Captain Carlos Marris's visit in September 1909) but still felt enervated after his nervous breakdown. He wrote to Edward Garnett, 12 January 1911, to say that he feels that he has changed. Garnett reported that he had kept Conrad's letters: Conrad writes as though the man who wrote those letters is now dead: 'And so you've kept my letters! Have you! Ah my dear you'll never meet the man who wrote them, again. I feel as if I had somehow smashed myself. But do come over and look at the pieces. The only thing You'll find uninjured will be my affection for you'.[8] March and April 1911 were marked by another writing block, during which he read Galsworthy's *The Patrician* (1911) and the manuscript of Edward Garnett's *The Trial of Jeanne d'Arc* (1912). On 4 May 1911 he wrote to Galsworthy about his prostrating writing blocks: 'Three weeks in Dec[ember 1910] without writing a line; and now again seven weeks – the most horrible nightmare of an existence – from March 5th to April 29th with not a page – not half a page in all that time! How I came out of it with my sanity unimpaired I don't know'. The depression comes like a physical attack: 'this may happen to me again any day, any time, like being bludgeoned from behind'.[9] In May Conrad surfaced and found himself able to make progress with *Chance*. He wrote quite quickly for two months but then became blocked again for the whole of August and September. Part of the problem seems to have been simple distaste for the novel. On 11 December 1911, Conrad wrote to Arthur Symons to say 'I am trying to finish a beastly novel which ought to have been done with last Oct[ober]. I am sick of the pen'.[10]

Chance had been on the go, on and off, since 1906 and one would have expected it therefore to show powerful continuity with the great novels of Conrad's major decade. But, notoriously, it does not, and this is partly because the novelist who completed *Under Western Eyes* in 1910 was rather different from the novelist who completed *Chance* in 1913. He recovered from his illness after *Under Western Eyes* to find the circle of his friends reduced (by the two-year breach with Pinker and the long-term breach with Ford). Until he was fifty-three Conrad had been in a sense a 'young man', that's to say a striving and ambitious figure struggling for success and buoyed up in his struggle by like-minded friends with similar ambitions. It should never be forgotten that in their hey-day he and Ford had supported each other with a strength and loyalty which it is now hard for us to recapture: hard because the record is muddied somewhat by such things as the friends' quarrel, Ford's mendacity and Jessie's hatred of Ford. After 1912 Conrad was no longer a *primus inter pares* but a sage, surrounding himself with young admirers and courtiers: Richard Curle, Francis Warrington Dawson, Józef Retinger, André Gide and Jean-Aubry. Of these only Gide could be regarded as an equal, and he was not a rival because he wrote in French. It suited Conrad to be undisputed King of his little world.

André Gide was brought to Capel House (by Agnes Tobin and Arthur Symons) to meet Conrad on 17 July 1911.[11] Thus began a friendship which was as momentous for the latter part of Conrad's career as had been the friendship with Ford earlier. Gide was drawn to Conrad's work by the divided nature of Conrad's heroes: the guilt displayed by Jim and Razumov spoke directly to Gide's own view of the nature of man. In his own work, especially in *L'Immoraliste* and *Les Caves du Vatican*, Gide explores the notion of a hero who performs a relatively unwilled action which alters the direction of his life, the *acte gratuit*. For Gide, *Lord Jim* was the great masterpiece. In a 1914 notebook entry on the novel Gide writes: 'The despair of the man who thinks he is a coward because he yielded to a momentary weakness – when he hoped he was courageous (*Lord Jim*).' He finds a relationship between this novel and *Under Western Eyes*: 'Much interested by the relationship I discover between *Under Western Eyes* and *Lord Jim*. (I regret not having spoken of this with Conrad.) That *irresponsible act* of the hero, to redeem which his whole life is subsequently engaged. For the thing that leads to the heaviest responsibility is just the *irresponsibilities* in a life. How can one efface that act?' This insight remained with Gide the central truth to be drawn from his readings of these two novels. In 1930 he writes: 'Noteworthy that the fatal *irresponsible* acts of Conrad's heroes (I am thinking particularly of *Lord Jim* and *Under Western Eyes*) are involuntary and immediately stand seriously in the way of the one who commits them. A whole lifetime, afterward, is not enough to give them the lie and to efface their mark.' Gide and Jean-Aubry supervised the translation into French of Conrad's work: Gide gave himself to the project with selfless energy and dedication (and personally translated 'Typhoon').[12]

Another friend, Norman Douglas, was a direct impediment to the progress of *Chance*. In the summer of 1911 Conrad was desperately trying to make headway with the novel when Norman Douglas descended on him (12 August), prostrate with fever, and effectively turned the house into a hospital.[13] Conrad wrote frantically to Galsworthy about this development (18 August 1911):

> Today he does not recognize anybody, his temp after most appalling ups and downs has reached 105°. – and here we are. . . . He can't be moved and indeed where could one move him? One can hear him moaning and muttering all over the house. . . . Should he die I shall have to bury him I suppose. But even if he recovers (which we still hope for) it will be a matter of weeks. All my work, all our plans and our little pitiful hopes seem knocked on the head. I have seen and tended white men dying in the Congo but I have never felt so abominably helpless as in this case. As Jessie said last night – this is like a nightmare.[14]

Everything was wrong for Conrad this summer. Even the good things, such as the award of a Civil List pension, of which he received notice in July, were seen as part of the living hell in which he found himself. Ford had sent congratulations and Conrad replied (possibly in October – the letter is undated):

> I was touched by your congratulatory telegram and yet it might have been ironic too! That sort of recognition is the consecration of failure, for even talent must be appreciated by the standards of the world we live in. On receiving the gift I glanced back and what I said most clearly then is that there hasn't been a book published for 3 years! . . . I am living in a state of savage exasperation with myself, unfit to talk, unfit to write . . . I am writing, however, spasmodically, with long intervals of absolute dumbness. *Quel enfer!*[15]

He was in hell, but this did not prevent him from writing copiously to the friends – such as Galsworthy – with whom he still felt intimate, and it is a mark of his unrelenting coolness to Ford that Conrad seems not to have responded to Ford's telegram of congratulation for three months. Ford had irrevocably fallen from favour. The recurrent despair is expressed in a letter to Galsworthy of 28 July 1911 in which he described all of his life as a 'dead pull': a life of continuous, unrelenting strain, devoid of pleasure or variety. 'I am beginning to get used to it'.[16]

The pension that he received early in July was felt as a double-edged benefit: he needed the money, but as on earlier occasions when he received financial assistance (in 1905 and 1909) he did not like to be reminded that he was unable to support his family from his writings alone. He was able to feel unreservedly pleased, though (for the moment) with another financial windfall, the discovery that he could sell the manuscripts of his work to John Quinn, the American collector. At the end of August 1911 Quinn bought the manuscripts of *An Outcast of the Islands* and 'Freya of the Seven Isles'. Quinn paid good prices: £40 for a story (a year's salary for a servant) and £100 to £150 for a full-length work.[17] Conrad was not being exploited, and he was to derive steady additional income from such sales to Quinn for the next ten years.

In September Borys Conrad joined the H.M.S. *Worcester,* a nautical training ship (like those attended by Jim in *Lord Jim* and Leggatt in 'The Secret Sharer'). It was not a satisfactory remedy to the continuing problem of Borys's education: Borys was short-sighted so a career in the navy was not open to him and the *Worcester* took him as a favour to Conrad. But it was better than nothing.

A personal digression is permissible here: my father, Aubrey Batchelor, born in 1896, was a fellow trainee on the *Worcester*. He remembered (and liked) Borys Conrad, who was two years his junior. My father was a similar 'problem' child: he had poor eyesight and no prospect of a career in the navy, but he was incapable of making progress in ordinary boys' schools and the *Worcester* was willing to take him. My father's impression of Conrad was that he seemed arrogant: he remembered Conrad 'striding about the

deck with his beard sticking out' looking as though he 'was in command
of the ship'.

It has been pointed out that Conrad's farewell to Borys, which he records
in a letter to Galsworthy (23 September 1911), is like Marlow's farewell to
Jim in *Lord Jim:*[18]

> Poor Mons. B looked to me a very small and lonely figure on that enormous
> deck in that big crowd where he didn't know a single soul. It is an immense
> change for him. Yes. He did look a small boy. I couldn't make up my mind
> to leave him and at last I made rather a bolt of it. I can't get him out of my
> eyes. However there are over twenty new boys and all their hammocks are
> slung together aft on the port side of the lower deck so he shall have some
> companions in the first few days of misery. I went ashore in the 14 oared
> second cutter and I have never seen a nicer boat's-crew. Having more than
> an hour to wait in Maidstone I wrote a letter to B which I am certain it must
> have comforted him to receive this morning.

He closes the letter with lamentation over his unproductiveness, a sense
that 'time is running out', and apprehension about another *soi-disant* child,
Under Western Eyes, which was to be published on 5 October.[19]

The reception of *Under Western Eyes* contributed to the depression. Conrad
wrote to Galsworthy ten days after publication (15 October 1911) saying
that he had been so ill that he made cuts in *Under Western Eyes* that were
errors: 'There are passages which should have remained. I wasn't in a fit
state to judge them'.[20] He pretended to ignore the reviews but the dis-
ingenuousness of this assumed detachment is painfully apparent: 'Well-
it's done now and let the critics make what they can of it. I have ordered
no press-cuttings, not because I am afraid of them but that I am really
indifferent to what may be said'.[21] The reviews were respectful but in many
cases obtuse. The *Pall Mall Gazette*'s reviewer was plainly baffled: he resorted to bland superlatives, saying that 'the book startles one by its amazing
truth and by the intimate knowledge of the human heart that it reveals',
and ended with a comparison which was unwittingly calculated to enrage
Conrad, saying that the clanking of Peter Ivanovitch's chain was 'almost as
unforgettable as the tapping of blind Pew's stick'[22] ('Blind Pew' is, of course,
a character in Stevenson's *Treasure Island*; Conrad passionately resented
Stevenson's fluency and commercial success and hated being compared
with him). The reviewer for the *Morning Post* thought that the professor
of languages must be a Jew, 'holding the balance between the West and
the East' (Conrad's appearance sometimes led people to think that he was
Jewish: another source of irritation). Some reviews, including one by Edward
Garnett, annoyed Conrad by stressing his foreignness. In the *Nation,* as we
have seen, Garnett suggested that Conrad was influenced by Dostoevsky.
This is obviously true but since, as we know, Conrad always denied any
sympathy with Dostoevsky, he was bound to resent both the close dramatic
resemblance to Dostoevsky and the putative stylistic debts to Dostoevsky
and Turgenev attributed to his work by Garnett's review (see above, pp.

183–184).[23] (We have also seen how irritated Conrad was by a letter from Garnett indicating that he thought *Under Western Eyes* demonstrated hatred of Russia.[24]) None of these reviews was of the kind that help books to sell, and sales of *Under Western Eyes*, as of all Conrad's novels to date, turned out to be disappointing.

The relationship with Pinker had been patched up by this time. We have seen that following the row in January 1910 correspondence had resumed in May 1910, with Conrad addressing Pinker, chillingly, as 'Dear Sir'. Presumably Pinker's balanced, commonsense ability to deal with emotions on a level plain soon restored Conrad's confidence in him, since the threat to break with Pinker permanently was now forgotten. The pattern of the former relationship with Pinker – debt, tactful pressure from Pinker to speed up the work, agonized protestation from Conrad about his illnesses and depressions – was resumed, but was soon to become warmer, and by December 1912 he was trusting Pinker with confidences about the problems he had writing *Chance*. On 12 December 1911 he wrote to Pinker: 'I *see* my end right enough but the putting it down with some effect is the very devil'.[25] But the process of writing speeded up in the first few months of 1912, largely because the novel was due to begin serialization (on 21 January) in the *New York Herald*.

Conrad finished *Chance* on 25 March 1912. Plans for publication in England were not yet firm and it is an interesting footnote to Conrad's relationship with the *English Review* that he tried to persuade Austin Harrison, the new editor of the *English Review*, to serialize it. As part of the attempt to persuade Harrison Conrad stressed that *Chance* was more popular in its appeal than an earlier work such as *Lord Jim*, and since *Lord Jim* had been successful in a periodical with a broad readership (*Blackwood's Magazine*) *Chance* could do well in a consciously highbrow vehicle like the *English Review*:

[*Blackwood's Magazine*] accepted my *Lord Jim* a much closer knit and more complicated work with a remote psychology – sailors, Malays, and so on – whereas *Chance* is English in personages and locality, much easier to follow and understand. It was a very new form then; and yet old Maga had the audacity to take it up when we all were much less advanced than we are now and Conrad was a practically unknown writer.[26]

Despite Conrad's professed hatred of David Soskice, the *English Review*'s new backer, and his ostentatious coolness towards the whole venture, the fact that he negotiated with Harrison in this way indicates that the real quarrel was not with the *English Review* but with Ford. He was willing to be flexible towards others associated with the *English Review*. And he very much wanted *Chance* to be serialized in England.

Once he had finished *Chance* he was instantly plunged into what we can now recognise as a recurrent pattern: depression, insomnia, intense anxiety. This began to be dispelled somewhat towards the end of April by a familiar creative pattern. The work which was ostensibly on the stocks was *Suspense*, but Conrad turned aside from that (at the end of April, 1912) to write another 'short story', called 'Dollars', which in due course grew to be *Victory*. Nineteen-thirteen was a rather better year for Conrad, especially in the summer: he was increasingly becoming accepted by the very grandest kind of English people, which included Ottoline Morrell and Bertrand Russell. Henry James introduced Lady Ottoline to Conrad, but he seems to have been reluctant: Lady Ottoline records (with some exaggeration, one guesses) James's snobbish reaction to the proposal that she should call on the Conrads: ' "But, dear lady. . . . He has lived his life at sea – dear lady, he has never met 'civilized' women. Yes, he is interesting, but he would not understand you. His wife, she is a good cook. She is a Catholic as he is, but . . . No, dear lady, he has lived a rough life" '.[27]

One guesses that James felt it his duty to convey – however obliquely – that Jessie was working-class ('a good cook') and that the excuse for Conrad's socially disastrous marriage was that being foreign and nautical he knew nothing about the English social system. Undaunted, Lady Ottoline called and was shrewd about Jessie's role in the marriage, finding that she was indeed a good cook, as James had said, and that she was in all respects an excellent wife for Conrad. She saw that it required a very particular kind of woman to cope with Conrad's temperament, and she judged (as we have seen) that Jessie was 'a good and reposeful mattress' for the neurotic author.[28]

Lady Ottoline introduced Bertrand Russell to Conrad. Russell's reaction was extraordinary. The piece in which it is recorded is often quoted as an instance of the instant and noble affinity between the two men. But is that likely? Both were grand, arrogant and competitive: I suspect that behind Russell's fulsomeness and adulatory prostration lurks a degree of competitiveness which is being vigorously 'denied':

> At our very first meeting, we talked with continually increasing intimacy. We seemed to sink through layer after layer of what was superficial, till gradually both reached the central fire. It was an experience unlike any other that I have known. We looked into each other's eyes, half appalled and half intoxicated to find ourselves together in such a region. The emotion was as intense as passionate love, and at the sime time all-embracing. I came away bewildered, and hardly able to find my way among ordinary affairs.[29]

At one level, of course, this is a commonplace view of Conrad taken to extremes: as his young group of disciples assembled around him so he was increasingly venerated as one of the two grand old men of English letters (the other was Hardy) and reports of personal contact with him tended to be hushed and worshipping in tone. Russell is outdoing the other disciples by claiming an intimacy not granted to others, the intimacy of 'lovers'. And Russell was competing not only with the other disciples but also with his mistress. Owen Knowles shows that Russell's contemporaneous correspondence with Lady Ottoline Morrell indicates that the Conrad-Russell-Lady Ottoline relationship becomes a triangle in which Conrad is in a sense being used by the other two. On his way back to Cambridge from the visit to Conrad, Bertrand Russell wrote to Lady Ottoline:

My Darling
   Here I am on my way back from Conrad. It was *wonderful* – I *loved* him & I think he liked me. He talked a great deal about his work & and life & aims, & about other writers. At first we were both shy & and awkward – he praised Wells and Rothenstein & Zangwill and I began to despair. Then I asked him about Arnold Bennett, & found he despised him. Timidly I stood up for him, & he seemed interested. Then I got him on to Henry James, & he began to expand – said he likes his middle period better than the novels from the Golden Bowl onwards — attributes the falling off to the practice of dictating. Then we went for a little walk, & somehow grew very intimate. I plucked up courage to tell him what I find in his work – the boring down into things to get to the very bottom below the apparent facts. He seemed to feel I had understood him; then I stopped & we just looked into each other's eyes for some time, & then he said he had grown to wish he could live on the surface and write differently, that he had grown frightened. His eyes at the moment expressed the inward pain & terror that one feels him always fighting. Then he said he was weary of writing & felt he had done enough, but had to go on & and say it again. Then he talked a lot about Poland, & showed me an album of family photographs of the 60's – spoke about how dream-like all that seems, & how he sometimes feels he ought not to have had any children, because they have no roots or traditions or relations. He told me a great deal about his sea-faring time & about the Congo & Poland and all sorts of things. At first he was reserved even when he seemed frank, but when we were out walking his reserve vanished & he spoke his inmost thoughts. It is impossible to say how much I loved him. He spoke very nicely about you, & had been evidently *very* glad of your appreciation. He said he valued a woman's appreciation, as he had thought his novels were not the kind women liked. I realized as he spoke that he had hardly known any cultivated or intelligent women.[30]

That last sentence suggests that Russell's 'love' for Conrad has a whiff of slumming about it: that part of the pleasure that these two aristocrats take in their relationship with Conrad is the pleasure of bridging the social gulf between themselves and this exotic foreigner.[31] Frederick Karl quotes (from memory) Russell, aged ninety-three, saying of Conrad: 'Conrad was a very strange man, as you may know. When he spoke rapidly he became extremely volatile, and his speech was unintelligible. He ranted. He considered himself a raconteur and was amusing, if unpredictable, company. But as I say, we saw very little of each other'. This testimony seems cool by comparison with the relationship 'intense as passionate love' that Russell recalled for publication. In justice to Russell, though, it should not be forgotten that he wrote one of the most evocative and memorable formulations of Conrad's attitude to human affairs: 'I felt, though I do not know whether he would have accepted such an image, that he thought of civilized and morally tolerable human life as a dangerous walk on a thin crust of barely cooled lava which at any moment might break and let the unwary sink into fiery depths'.[32]

I have noted that Jeremy Hawthorn asks why it is that Conrad uses the teacher of languages, rather than Marlow, as the narrator of *Under Western Eyes*. *Chance*, which resurrects Marlow as narrator, appears as the next novel in Conrad's sequence almost as though in answer to this question. The Marlow of *Chance* is sometimes regarded as unaccountably misogynist and difficult compared with the Marlow who loves Jim and seeks to understand Kurtz. A typical approach sees Marlow as an 'unintentional caricature of his former self' and the whole text as an 'unintentional parody of the self-conscious narrator that was perfected by James, Ford and Conrad'.[33] One can counter this by pointing out that the circumstances within which Marlow and the outer narrator tell the stories of Roderick Anthony and Flora de Barral are different from the circumstances in which Marlow told the story of Jim. For *Lord Jim* the situation is one of work – professional disgrace in a professional situation, and the male bonding within the profession which goes some way to redeem the disgrace – while in *Chance* the situation is more like the domestic situations that one finds in Henry James: loving innocents whose relationship is blocked by wicked and scheming sophisticates. The Marlow who tells Jim's story is dealing with an area of human experience about which he feels confident and in charge. The Marlow who tells the story of Flora, the Fynes and the wicked governess sounds different because he is dealing with different things. Mrs Fyne's feminism, for example, is detested by Marlow (and presumably by Conrad). The Marlow who speaks and writes *Heart of Darkness* and *Lord Jim* would probably have detested feminism equally: we can't know because the issue doesn't arise in those books. Mrs Fyne's feminism is brutal and ruthless: 'No consideration, no delicacy, no tenderness, no scruples should stand in the way of a woman (who by the mere fact of her sex was the predestined victim of conditions created by men's selfish passions, their vices and their abominable tyranny) from taking the shortest cut towards securing for herself the easiest possible existence' (p. 59).

Mrs Fyne's ideas are dangerous: their effect is to turn her 'girl-friends' into the terrorists of sexual politics. She puts a 'salad of unprincipled notions' into their heads and they are already predisposed to unscrupulous political operation because, being female, they have no honour:

> As to honour – you know – it's a very fine mediaeval inheritance which women never got hold of. It wasn't theirs. Since it may be laid as a general principle that women always get what they want, we must suppose they didn't want it. In addition they are devoid of decency. I mean masculine decency. Cautiousness too is foreign to them – the heavy reasonable cautiousness which is our glory.... All the virtues are not enough for them; they want also all the crimes for their own. And why? Because in such completeness there is power – the kind of thrill they love most.... (p. 63)

The interlocutor, the outer narrator, interrupts him at this point, saying 'Do you expect me to agree with all this?' (p. 63). Marlow says that 'it isn't necessary' to agree with him, but he is obviously fixed in his attitudes. There is something in women which acts 'both as restraint and as in-spiration' which prevents them from 'coming on deck and playing hell with the ship' (p. 63), he says. But one may feel that in his heart he thinks that they *will* play hell with the ship. And it seems to me that in Conrad at a deep level the same instinct is operating: if women get power they will upset the chain of command, they will destroy what is good in civilization as Conrad knows it.

Marlow in *Lord Jim* listens to Jim's confession. Marlow in *Chance* listens to Flora's confession, and harks back to his earlier self as he does so: the continuity between the stages of the dramatization of Marlow, arching over four of Conrad's works, is clearly felt here. In chapter 7 of *Chance*, 'On the Pavement', Flora is confessing to Marlow that she thought of commit-ting suicide by throwing herself from a cliff, and was deterred by her sense of responsibility for the Fyne's dog. (Jim contemplates suicide in the open boat immediately after his jump from the *Patna* and in Marlow's hotel room – Marlow thinks that he may jump from the window – and, of course, surrenders his life to Doramin at the end of the novel.) With Flora as with Jim Marlow feels that he has been brought into intimacy-with-distance by the confession: 'We had nothing to say to each other; but we two, stran-gers, as we really were to each other, had dealt with the most intimate and final of subjects, the subject of death. It had created a sort of bond be-tween us' (p. 209).

Negotiation with Flora is more difficult than was negotation with Jim because of the difference between men and women. He can't ask Flora intimate questions about her relationship with Roderick Anthony because 'you can't buttonhole familiarly a young girl as you would a young fellow'. Equally, though, a woman will not trust another woman as a man will trust another man: 'There is not between women that fund of at least condi-tional loyalty which men may depend on in their dealings with each other. I believe that any woman would rather trust a man' (p. 209).

However much one may feel doubt about these observations as gen-eral truths about human nature, they have a point for this narrative. Jim confessed to Marlow. Flora has done – it emerges – something parallel but unwise, by writing a letter of confession to Mrs Fyne (her first name, not much used in the novel, is 'Zoe' – a wonderfully horrible indication that she is by Edwardian standards 'advanced'). In her letter Flora indicates that she is marrying Roderick Anthony, Mrs Fyne's brother, out of des-peration, believing that he could not love her and that she did not love him. She writes this letter partly in deference to Mrs Fyne's teaching – this is an example of Mrs Fyne's theory making an impact beyond anything she could anticipate. In *Lord Jim* Marlow has described a confession as an appalling lack of discretion, with the tacit implication that Jim was very lucky that he chose Marlow, and not a shallower and less kind, and less discreet, personality to confess to. In *Chance* Marlow sets up a general observation about the unwisdom of confessions:

> There's nothing like a confession to make one look mad; and . . . of all confessions a written one is the most detrimental all round. Never confess! Never, never! An untimely joke is a source of bitter regret always. Sometimes it may ruin a man; not because it is a joke, but because it is untimely. And a confession of whatever sort is always untimely. The one thing which makes it supportable for a while is curiosity. You smile? Ah, but it is so, or else people would be sent to the right-about at the second sentence. How many sympathetic souls can you reckon on in the world? One in ten, one in a hundred – in a thousand – in ten thousand? (p. 212)

Here Marlow stresses both the rarity of the appropriate vocation – the priestlike qualifications, referred to in *Lord Jim,* that equip the listener to hear confessions – and the effect that a confession has on the hearer. As in *Lord Jim,* the impact of the victim on the listener becomes part of the narrative: we press back from the tale to the manner of the telling. 'For a confession, whatever it may be, stirs the secret depths of the hearer's character. Often depths that he himself is but dimly aware of. And so the righteous triumph secretly, the lucky are amused, the strong are disgusted, the weak either upset or irritated with you according to the measure of their sincerity with themselves' (p. 212). This Marlow, like the Marlow of *Lord Jim,* is the kind of person to whom people easily make confessions, people like his unnamed suicidal acquaintance who abruptly 'came to my rooms one evening' in search of some 'graceful way of retiring out of existence' (p. 213).

The two halves of *Chance* invite us to see it as a mythical work about polarities. The 'Knight' and the 'Maiden' are the simple polarity; the sea and the land are the complex polarity. The sea people are lovable and the land people, led by the governess and closely followed by Mrs Fyne, are detestable.

Chance is a romantic work, full of chapter headings which reinforce this romanticism for us. The most romantic of its chapter headings, perhaps, is the one which ushers in the love that Roderick and Flora do, eventually, feel for each other. This is part 2, chapter 6: the title is 'A Moonless Night, Thick with Stars Above, Very Dark on the Water.' (The chapter heading is a quotation from the chapter itself, p. 406.) The quotation doesn't do very much for the chapter and cannot divert our attention from the fact that the writing of this scene is self-consciously solemn:

> Standing firm and still [Roderick Anthony] gazed with sombre eyes at Mr Smith [i.e. de Barral]. For a time the low convulsive sobbing of Mr Smith's daughter was the only sound to trouble the silence. The strength of Anthony's clasp pressing Flora to his breast could not be doubted even at that distance, and suddenly, awakening to his opportunity, he began to partly support her, partly carry her in the direction of her cabin (p. 430).

The sombre eyes, the strength of his clasp, the breast with an inescapable hint of 'manly' about it and the split infinitive ('to partly support') all indicate that the novelist was both tired and uneasily aware that what he was doing at this point was not his best. This is an isolated weak patch, though. It is easy for literary criticism to become impatient with *Chance*. Much commentary on the novel testifies to that impatience; to a feeling – first put about by Henry James, and endorsed by critics such as A. J. Guerard[34] that the novel's narrative method is over-ingenious while its vision of Roderick Anthony as hero is naive. Yet if *Chance* were Conrad's only novel we would read it as a major post-Edwardian achievement. And if *Chance* were Conrad's only Marlow narration – if 'Youth', *Heart of Darkness* and *Lord Jim* didn't exist – we would revalue *Chance* as Conrad's reworking of the themes of *The Secret Agent* and *Under Western Eyes*, with particular reference to the comedy of mutual incomprehension.

Conrad was sensitive to the charge that *Chance*'s narrative method was excessively oblique. The quotation from the Author's Note given as epigraph to this chapter shows his reaction to Robert Lynd, who had said that 'if Mr Conrad had chosen to introduce us to his characters in the ordinary way, he could have told us their story in about 200 pages instead of the 406 pages of the present book'.[35] The hostile criticism of *Chance* that really hurt Conrad was not was not Lynd's largely adulatory review, but the long discussion by Henry James in the *Times Literary Supplement*, 'The Younger Generation' (March and April 1914). Conrad had regarded James as a friend and master and had published a laudatory article about him,[36] and he was hurt by James's remarks. After James's death Conrad wrote to Quinn (14 May 1916) showing just how hurt he was:

> The only time he did me the honour of speaking of me in print (about 2 years ago) he confined himself to the analysis of method which he rather airily condemned in relation to the method of two young writers. I may say, with scrupulous truth that this was the *only* time a criticism affected me painfully. But in our private relations he has been always warmly appreciative and full of invariable kindness. I had a profound affection for him. He knew of it and he accepted it as if it were something worth having. At any rate that is the impression I have. And he wasn't a man who would pretend.[37]

In 'The Younger Generation' James may be said to be firing from both barrels: he begins by attacking the young writers like Wells and Bennett who don't give enough attention to narrative method[38] and then turns to attack Conrad for giving too much attention to it. There is something self-regarding and territorial about James's attack on Conrad: as the only artist who can compare with him in terms of complexity Conrad is to be 'seen off'. James mocks the indirect narrative method of *Chance* as 'wanton':

> What concerns us is that the general effect of *Chance* is arrived at by a pursuance of means to the end in view contrasted with which every other

current form of the chase can only affect us as cheap and futile; the carriage of the burden or amount of service required on these lines exceeding surely all other such displayed degrees of energy put together. Nothing could well interest us more than to see the exemplary value of attention, attention given by the author and asked of the reader, attested in a case in which it has had almost unspeakable difficulties to struggle with – since so we are moved to qualify the particular difficulty Mr Conrad has 'elected' to face; the claim for method in itself, method in this very sense of attention applied, would be somehow less slighted if the difficulties struck us as less consciously, or call it even less wantonly, invoked.[39]

This is wounding stuff. James is out to expose vulgar ostentation and absence of literary tact in the narrative method of *Chance.* He proceeds to deliver what amounts, for all its guarded circumlocution, to a stinging rebuke:

His genius is what is left over from the other, the compromised and compromising quantities – the Marlows and their determinant inventors and interlocutors, the Powells, the Franklins, the Fynes, the tell-tale little dogs, the successive members of a cue from one to the other of which the sense and the interest of the subject have to be passed on together, in the manner of the buckets of water for the improvised extinction of a fire, before reaching our apprehension: all with whatever result, to this apprehension, of a quantity to be allowed for as spilt by the way.[40]

Graham Hough is surely more accurate about *Chance*'s method when he says 'The complexities of his narrative method are . . . layers of protective covering to an essentially simple heroic vision'.[41] James misreads *Chance* because he is over-attuned to its complexity (which resembles his own) and deaf to its concomitant simplicity. The interplay between the narrators in the opening chapter of *Chance* establishes these contrasts for us. Charles Powell is straightforward, honest and open, Marlow is ironic and subversive. It is Charles Powell's qualities that prevail, in collusion with the honesty of that other Powell, 'Old' Powell, who in this opening scene has the openness of somebody much younger, a schoolboy indeed: as he helps his younger namesake he has the demeanour of a little boy up to what are known in Dickens's *Great Expectations* as 'Larks': 'All the time with one knee well up he went on swinging his other leg like a boy on a gate and looking at me very straight with his shining eyes' (I, chapter 1, p. 15). Captain Anthony, when he enters, has the same frank and open qualities of appearance: a tall, active man with a very red face – 'You could see at once he was the skipper of a big ship' (p. 16).[42] Old Powell is *not* of course frank and open in that he is deceiving Anthony (allowing him to think that Charles Powell is his nephew) and breaking a law (against helping seamen to berths); this demonstrates that the code of the sea, the solidarity that springs up between sailors, is of greater validity and is more vigorously sanctioned than any land-based code. Marlow, ironist and cynic, seeks to detect irony in Old Powell's avuncular kindness to young Powell, thus establishing the distance between these two narrators. Marlow believes that 'mediocrity is our mark' and that there was 'malice' in Old Powell's eagerness to help: 'He managed to make you uncomfortable. You wanted to go to sea, but he jumped at the chance of accommmodating your desire with a vengeance. I am inclined to think your cheek [in approaching Old Powell to angle for a berth] alarmed him. And this was an excellent occasion to suppress you altogether. . . . You might have had to decline that berth for some very valid reason. . . . The notice was too uncommonly short' (p. 24). We as readers are free to disbelieve Marlow, and to adhere to the initial dramatic impact of Old Powell and Charles Powell, whose heartening loyalty to the solidarity of sailors lingers in the reader's mind as an index of human excellence as the novel addresses itself to the distasteful task of displaying the cruelties and mendacities of the land-based people. As so often, Conrad uses a surprisingly elementary mode of moral characterization: the good look virtuous, the mean look mean. The insolent clerk encountered by Young Powell in the basement of the shipping office belongs to the same body of Dickensian caricature as the grotesques in *The Secret Agent* (and the gas-light is a *Secret Agent* prop):

A gas bracket hung from the middle of the ceiling over a dark, shabby writing-desk covered with a litter of yellowish dusty documents. Under the flame of the single burner which made the place ablaze with light, a plump, little man was writing hard, his nose very near the desk. His head was perfectly bald and about the same drab tint as the papers. He appeared pretty dusty too. . . . His dungeon was hot and musty; it smelt of gas and mushrooms, and seemed to be somewhere 120 feet below the ground (p. 11).

This character turns out to be mean-spirited and suspicious, as does the clerk in Old Powell's office, who looks like Stevie the Lombrosan degenerate, 'with a thin, long neck and sloping shoulders' (p. 12). Old Powell, by contrast, has clear boyish eyes but also looks like an old sea-dog turned Greek philosopher: 'a full unwrinkled face and such clear-shining eyes that his grey beard looked quite false on him, stuck on for a disguise' (p. 13).

Conrad takes away with one hand what he gives with the other. Charles Powell's idealism and his tendency to sentimentalize the virtues of others (Old Powell's altruism, Anthony's steadfastness) are balanced by Marlow's scepticism. The novel takes great care to establish the contrast between these two principal narrators in the opening scenes and the dramatic method that I've referred to is strikingly deployed here as the novel gives us the physical characteristics of these two men: Marlow is 'lanky, loose, quietly composed in varied shades of brown, robbed of every vestige of gloss' and 'had a narrow veiled glance, the neutral bearing and the secret irritability which go together with a predisposition to congestion of the liver', while Charles Powell 'compact, broad and sturdy of limb, seemed extremely full of sound organs functioning vigorously all the time in order to keep up the brilliance of his colouring, the light curl of his coal-black hair and the lustre of his eyes, which asserted themselves roundly in an open, manly face' (p. 32). Powell's sound organs functioning vigorously and Marlow's congested liver: idealism and irony, innocence and experience. The unnamed omniscient narrator, holding the ring between these two figures, tends towards detachment and non-commitment; but his background and training ensure that he is attuned to the sea: 'The men of the sea understand each other very well in their view of earthly things, for simplicity is a good counsellor and isolation not a bad educator. A turn of mind composed of innocence and scepticism is common to them all, with the addition of an unexpected insight into motives, as of disinterested lookers-on at a game' (p. 33). This could be read as a schematic account of the roles of the three narrators, with Powell as the innocent, Marlow as the sceptic and the omniscient voice as the disinterested looker-on who has insight into motives. For his most ambitious urban novel Conrad is establishing for himself a generous breadth of narrative perspective. James was thus quite wrong to complain about the method: a novel which comprises the innocence and purity of the Anthonys, the compromised moral dwarfism of the Fynes and the dedication to evil of such figures as de Barral and the governess requires as flexible and wide a narrative approach as can be achieved.

I have referred above to Anthony's frank and open appearance. In the manuscript of *Chance* (now in the Berg collection, New York Public Library) the account of Anthony's first appearance and of his motivation is fuller:

> [The] door came open with a bang and a tall big man rushed in with great strides. His face looked very red and rough below his high silk hat. A large gold pin stuck in a black scarf, such as people used to wear then, glittered through his thin brown beard. His hands were large and hairy. You could see at once he was a big ship skipper – not one of your famous crack ships but a solid comfortable ship belonging to a respectable firm (*Chance* MS p. 60, relates to p. 16 of the published text).

He is worried about his volatile cargo of which, again, more detail is given: 'It was all arranged for next day. The stuff would be waiting for him in barges. Such a lot of explosives couldn't be left kicking about on the river. There would be no end of a fuss' (MS p. 65, relates to p. 17 of the published text).

He can't go to sea without a second officer: again, the manuscript gives more detail:

> [He couldn't go to sea without a] second officer and these explosives couldn't be kept waiting twenty four hours while he was looking for somebody more suitable. Forty tons of dynamite, hundred and twenty tons of gunpowder, and fourteen cases of detonators. The detonators were the most dangerous of all. 'I shall be glad when I am rid of that sweet lot, I know!' says he excitedly (MS p. 72, relates to p. 19 of the published text).

The narrator finds the skipper's anxiety 'surprising and amusing' and thinks to himself: 'Well! If you are in such a stew already what will it be when your explosive stuff is actually under hatches. But I thought this as if it hadn't anything to do with me' (MS p. 73).

These details build up to the dénouement of 'Young Powell's' story in the first chapter (Old Powell says 'I guess it's that shipment of explosives waiting down the river which has done most for you. Forty tons of dynamite have been your best friend to-day, young man', p. 22), but they are also relics of an earlier scheme of the story in which the explosives detonate and the ship is destroyed (a similar scheme is used in the published text of *The Rescue*). They are reminders that the novel began as a long short story called 'Explosives'. When he sold the manuscripts to Quinn Conrad added a note in which he said that he was enclosing five batches of pinned pages (numbered 1 to 152) which were written in the year 1906 and that the work was taken up again in June 1911. The manuscript has two titles: 'Explosives: A Ship-Board Tale' (deleted) and 'Chance: A Tale with Comments'.

The narrative situation at the beginning of the manuscript is broadly the same as that of the published text – Powell is joined at his unsatisfactory meal by a group which includes Marlow – but is much longer and more detailed, and is linked by the name 'Nellie' directly to the beginning of *Heart of Darkness*, where a group of friends aboard the *Nellie* listen to Marlow's story. In the manuscript of *Chance* the 'Nellie' seems to belong to 'Archie' Powell, whereas in the published text of *Chance* the (unnamed) yawl belongs to Marlow; it will be recalled that in *Heart of Darkness* the *Nellie* belongs to a director of companies (and in life it belonged to Conrad's friend G. F. W. Hope). The mansucript opens with an unnamed narrator asking a group of friends if they know Archie [not Charles] Powell. They have been seen 'out of the window come off in a crowd of four overloading the dinghy of the "Nellie" the 14 ton yawl belonging to our friend and skipper who with his usual good nature was himself pulling us ashore' (MS p. 2). The dinner that they eat is disgusting. A lot of space is given to this in the manuscript: a reminder of Conrad's own gourmet tastes and his tyrannical fussiness over food. From a literary point of view it displays interesting parallels with the theme of 'Falk'; men eating are primitives reverting to an early stage in the history of human evolution. The vegetables are badly cooked, the waiter is 'a greasy dingy savant in a tailcoat' (MS p. 9) and 'we used our teeth without grace and amenity like ill natured savages with no language as yet but grunts and monosyllables, devouring in a cavern the product of the common chase. And man's superiority [in] thought, profound, speculative thought, survived only in the gaze of our casual President [Powell] fixed pensively upon the cruet stand' (MS p. 10).

The *Chance* manuscript is considerably longer than the published novel and the cuts that Conrad made have several functions. One of them is to change the identity of the outer narrator: in the manuscript he is a novelist and he has a number of extended reflections about the nature of novel-writing. Though not valuable artistically some of these are of great interest biographically. In 'The Governess' (I, chapter 4) Marlow describes the governess's dreadful frustrations with such skill that the outer narrator jocularly congratulates him on his virtuosity: ' "You have a ghastly imagination," I said with a cheerfully sceptical smile' (p. 102). This is followed in the manuscript by a cancelled passage about the difference between the sailor's imagination, which is fresh, and the novelist's which is strained and jaded:

> 'Ghastly – is it?' he retorted with a no less affected disdain. 'I'll tell you what is the matter with my imagination. It can rise to the demands of a situation, because it is fresh. It isn't foundered and winded hunting after situations as the "imagination" of you professionals is bound to be. Fancy a man sitting down at a table for the purpose of imagining situations. Heavens! What an occupation! What a corrupt use of natural faculties . . .'
>
> 'I didn't know you were a moral creature' I interposed quickly.
>
> 'Well, I am' he returned unabashed. 'My situations come to me unmasked; and then I am like a puzzle-headed chief mate we had once in the dear old *Samarcand* when I was younger' [etc.] (MS 186–7).

Here Conrad is reflecting painfully on his own circumstances in middle age, the former sailor become agonised novelist: the fresh direct observations he made a sailor are denied to him now that he lives the unnatural life of the novelist. In terms of the novel's moral scheme the novelist is a reluctant member of the corrupt group, the land people, as against the innocent group, the sea people. The fact that some much of his narrative is about women prompts the novelist narrator to think that he would have liked to have had, like Tiresias of the *Metamorphoses*, the opportunity to experience a woman's emotions and sexuality from within. In part II, chapter 3, Marlow has been describing to the narrator how Young Powell and Flora first got to know each other aboard the *Ferndale* ('How he first got in touch with his captain's wife', p. 315). In a long cancelled passage Marlow tries to imagine what it would be like, being Flora, to find oneself falling in love with Powell, and says: 'It is true that he [Powell] is no longer in his fresh twenties and that I having never been a young girl can't tell how . . .' (MS 759). The narrator then embarks on this reflection, based on the Tiresias myth: 'There was once in the ages of dim legend a Greek who had that extraordinary experience. It would be very curious being a man to remember the time when one was a woman. What an enlargement of view and depth of insight it would give one' (MS 761). Later in this long passage he reflects that the 'legendary ages are over' and the one 'can't have that in the modern world'.

Another change effected by the cuts is to reduce Marlow's sententiousness. In the manuscript Marlow is very garrulous and has a great deal to say about the evils of the land people. There are parallels in the published text between England and a ship: for example Powell says with contempt of the land people that however they misconduct themselves 'this tight little island won't turn turtle with them or spring a leak and go to the bottom with their wives and children' (I, chapter 1, p. 4). In the manuscript there is a great deal more of this, mostly in Marlow's narrative. The simile is extended to the whole earth, which is imagined by Marlow as a space-ship which needs to be managed with the same skill as a ship on the sea (similar images occurred in letters to Cunninghame Graham written in the 1890s). On page 32 of the published text Marlow says 'A sailor finds a deep feeling of security in the exercise of his calling.' In the manuscript this is followed by a long passage, some of which I quote here:

> It is certain that once in the keeping of the sea you are not distracted by the hammering of innumerable hot irons and are not jostled by the elbows of other craftsmen. You become the inhabitant of a world which is not over-populated and that holds no rewards. . . . Theirs [sailors'] is a moral calling. One thought, one aim, one duty, one penalty, bind you to your fellows. At sea you dare not say – or even think to yourself: devil take the hindmost. You've got to be moral whether you like it or not for this reason that you have no other welfare but the welfare of your little world which depends on the faithful discharge of their trust by all the ship's company. It's a pity the earth is not more like a ship sent out on a voyage; it's a pity that it won't be steered and handled and navigated and kept fit to meet the dangers of space. There is something pleasing to my imagination in the conception of the succeeding generation informed and faithful taking over the duty with the course to be steered and the responsibility to be borne, from their greyhaired predecessors leaving the deck for a long watch below. It would make better men of her population if the earth were more like a ship that had got to be brought in a port of final discharge safely some day. But she isn't. She merely drifts.' 'More like a raft with castaways' suggested our new friend [Powell. Marlow says no to this:] 'She resembles more a rudderless and unrigged hull launched helpless upon the deep for no interesting purpose. . . . [The] crowd on board [are] . . . fighting among themselves for the stores and the accomodation [sic] and clambering over each other ever since they learned to balance themselves on their hindlegs. . . . The earth makes no call upon their fidelity and their vigilance and oppressed by an infinite idleness they turn their attention upon the uneasiness of their thinking souls which clamour for intellectual certitude and the misery of their tender bodies hungering for food. . . . [They are] crafty, violent, fearful, overbearing subtle and unhappy (MS 124–8).

The manuscript shows Conrad casting about uneasily to find a satisfactory perspective on Marlow. These huge speeches, prosy, sententious and heavily moral, are clearly endorsed to some extent by the novel's shape, but at the same time in the manuscript they are treated ironically. Reference in the manuscript to 'our new acquaintance [Powell] whose attention was beginning to flag a little' (MS 130) shows Conrad becoming uneasily aware as he writes that Marlow is boring. The narrator in the manuscript takes an ironic perspective on Marlow and a few pages later that ironic perspective includes Powell as well: Marlow says that on a ship 'the rule of life is hard but clear' while the earth is as 'unmanageable as Noah's old ark' (MS p. 135) and the narrator remarks that 'this facile comparison appealed to the fancy of Mr Charles Powell[43] ex-sailor' (MS p. 136). Conrad was right to cut all this: if we take it that the general dramatic scheme of the novel was already in Conrad's mind the irony seems both tediously drawn-out and misdirected: misdirected in that the novel clearly *endorses*, in the end, the simple heroic view of sea-life that Marlow and Powell share.

The problem recurs in Marlow's extended commentary on the dockside police who enabled Powell to get to the *Ferndale* despite the thieves who tried to deprive him of his luggage: Marlow delivers about two thousand words of ironical stuff about the cowardice and expediency of land-based authority. I give a small excerpt from this huge speech: 'They founded their honesty upon the force and plenitude of the rare wisdom that knows itself: no nerve. No muscle. They knew it and what's more they were faithful to their knowledge. It's immense!' (MS p. 150). Powell is exhausted by Marlow's rhetoric. His mouth is open as he tries to absorb Marlow's eloquence 'by the gullet' and finally he rebels: ' "Get along with you! Who are you trying to get at" he apostrophized Marlow suddenly in slangy tones and with a knowing wink' (MS 151–2).

A third set of cuts in the manuscript is of link passages between scenes. The *Chance* manuscript has in common with some of the earlier manuscripts (notably much of *Lord Jim*) a lack of chapter divisions. The narrator goes on and on, seamlessly reminiscing and reporting, and the novelist creates the divisions that we have in the published text by a method which seems oddly wasteful: large chunks of narrative are simply excised and the scenes thus marked off are then given the elaborate chapter headings that we have in the published text. Reading the *Chance* manuscript as a whole makes one marvel that the published novel is as good as it is. Much of the manuscript is so loose, prolix, tedious and undirected that it reads as though it is being 'churned out' in a spirit of grinding duty. The fact that some of it is in Jessie Conrad's handwriting is consistent with this: when Conrad's gout prevented him from writing he resorted to dictation, which inevitably resulted in a further loosening of his prose. We may surmise that Conrad was responding both desperately and cynically to Pinker's persistent demands for steady production of copy.

Having said all that, some of the cancelled manuscript material is interesting and should have been retained, notably the description of Powell's cabin in the Ferndale. This cancelled passage relates to p. 31 of the published text where Powell has a 'dazzling glimpse of my berth'. The manuscript then continues:

'There were no furnishings ["fixtures" deleted] whatever in it except a close washstand and a narrow bench with a shabby oil cloth cushion as thin as a pan cake, for a couch of ease. Four bare white bulkheads a deck above with a beam also painted white and the swept planking of the deck under my feet enclosed a space eight feet by fourteen about. It would be my portion of space for purposes of rest and privacy for a period of time not exceeding two years and between the latitudes 70 north and sixty south back to a final port of discharge in the United Kingdom etc etc – as the ship's articles I had signed only eight hours ago had it' (MS 117–18).

The austerity of his cabin matches and amplifies Powell's straightforward masculine virtue, and provides an expressive contrast with the weary frippery with which the Captain's cabin has been tricked out in order to provide a home at sea for his new wife and her wicked father. It lends particularity to the 'peace of the sea', recognized by both Powell and Marlow as their leading sensation on setting out on a long voyage. It adds to the rather meagre details that Conrad gives us in his autobiographies, *A Personal Record* and *The Mirror of the Sea*. And it anticipates the fine scene in *The Shadow-Line* in which the unnamed young skipper – the closest figure to a self-portrait in all Conrad's fiction – takes possession of the Captain's cabin and thinks about his little kingdom and his place in the dynasty of skippers; with the additional interest, for us, of knowing that the spartan accommodation of a junior officer could be just as satisfying a kingdom as the Captain's grander accommodation. Conrad should have kept this passage.

The Marlow of the *Chance* manuscript is so unfocused that it is not surprising that the 'new' Marlow of the published text into whom this ironist evolves gives Conrad some trouble: he 'had the habit of pursuing general ideals in a peculiar manner, between jest and earnest'. What has given him this 'peculiar manner'? Why, the old – and obsolescent – Victorian life of sailing-ships: 'He was patient and reflective. He had been at sea many years, and I verily believe he liked sea-life because upon the whole it is favourable to reflection. I am speaking of the now nearly vanished sea-life under sail. To those who may be surprised at the statement I will point out that this life secured for the mind of him who embraced it the inestimable advantages of solitude and silence' (p. 23).

I have referred to the possibility that Henry James's dislike of *Chance* was a matter of threatened territoriality. It may be that this extended not only to the narrative methods of *Chance* but also to its dramatic content. It has been pointed out (by Mrs Duncan-Jones) that Flora is an intensely Jamesian heroine, probably owing both her name and her dramatic interaction with an evil governess to James's 'The Turn of the Screw'.[44] She is also like the eponymous narrative focus of James's *What Maisie Knew*, an innocent limited narrator registering the sexual misbehaviour of furtive adults for the aware reader; and like Millie in *The Wings of the Dove* she is passive and punished but in the end a touchstone of virtue. But another great urban novelist, the first English novelist that Conrad had read – Dickens – has contributed to the making of Flora. At the end of chapter 6 of the novel

Marlow recalls what Mrs Fyne has told him 'of the view she had years ago of de Barral clinging to the child at the side of his wife's grave and later on of these two walking hand in hand the observed of all eyes by the sea. Figures from Dickens – pregnant with pathos' (p. 162). The Dickens novel he has in mind must be *Dombey and Son* (1848), where Mr Dombey the heartless business man is subjected to chastisement and moral education firstly by the deaths of his wife and son and secondly by a plot which forces him to recognize the virtues of his daughter, Florence. Florence becomes her father's saviour and companion: the dark business premises in London are contrasted with Brighton, where Florence Dombey, finally reconciled with her father, walks by the sea on his arm.

We have seen that Conrad was aware of the philosopher Henri Bergson[45] and refers to him obliquely in Chance. Marlow laughs at the misadventures of Flora, the anonymous outer narrator rebukes him for his laughter and Marlow replies: 'Don't you know that people laugh at absurdities that are very far from being comic? Didn't you read the latest books about laughter written by philosophers, psychologists? There is a lot of them . . .'(p. 283). The mutual misunderstandings are Chekhovian: the figures proceed from positions which must be unpacked. Failure to acknowledge their differences lead to mutual detonation. The great misunderstanding, of course, is that between the lovers: Roderick is convinced (by Flora's letter to Zoe Fyne) that Flora does not love him, Flora is convinced that Anthony has married her out of 'magnanimity' – an extreme instance of gentlemanly behaviour. The sexual impasse between the two, which so many critics have found it impossible to accept, is a natural extension of the code of honour operating in *Lord Jim*. One of de Barral's venomous complaints about Roderick Anthony ironically points up that code of honour:

> 'What induced that man to marry you? Of course he's a gentleman. One can see that. And that makes it worse. Gentlemen don't understand anything about city affairs – finance. Why! – the people who started the cry after me were a firm of gentlemen. The counsel, the judge – all gentlemen – quite out of it! No notion of . . . And then he's a sailor too. Just a skipper –'
> (p. 385).

Like those of Brown in *Lord Jim* and Jones in *Victory*, the judgements of de Barral must be inverted before they will make any kind of moral sense. Gentlemen and sailors are to be trusted. Franklin, first mate of the *Ferndale*, calls de Barral a 'devil', a word reinforcing the resemblance to Jones and Brown (and recalling Kurtz). Franklin is one of a group of figures who are caught up in the comedy of misunderstanding. He, Powell, Roderick Anthony and de Barral embody different meanings of the work 'love'. Franklin's love for Roderick Anthony is a mixture of unthinking hero-worship and doglike loyalty and possessiveness (Powell remarks that Franklin has the faults of a spoilt 'pet old dog', p. 399). The only other love in his life, at forty-eight, is his mother and he has never thought of marriage (though he is heterosexual). Conrad may have changed his mind about Franklin's age in the course of writing: late in the narrative he is 'thirteen years older' (p. 303) than Roderick Anthony, who is thirty-five (p. 155): but earlier Franklin's age is described as being merely 'over forty' (p. 268).[46]

Conrad displays great skill (*pace* Henry James) in his deployment of the figure of Franklin. Franklin's judgements of Flora and de Barral must at first seem to us obtuse: the innocent hostility of a man with no experience of relationships other than the undemanding male bonding that characterizes the working life of sailors: 'I have heard tell of women doing for a man in one way or another when they got him fairly ashore. But to bring their devilry to sea and fasten on such a man!' (p. 305). The point of the Franklin story is that his suspicions, as far as de Barrall is concerned, turn out to be well-founded. He thinks of Roderick as 'engaged in an active contest with some power of evil' (p. 305). The good-natured Powell pooh-poohs such an idea: but Franklin is, of course, right. The occasional over-writing – for example, that of the scene in which Powell sees de Barral's murderous intentions for himself (p. 417) – would be much less acceptable were it not prepared for by Franklin's judgements (so spectacularly vindicated) and by the dark hints of the steward, who has learnt from his wife that the Anthonys' marriage has not been consummated (p. 390). Powell loves Anthony and Flora, and is almost as innocent and obtuse as Franklin in relation to Anthony's inner anguish. Powell sees the Anthony marriage as a fairy-tale relationship, with Roderick (by virtue of his office as Captain) as its prince, 'alone of his kind, depending on nobody' (p. 288), and assumes that Roderick must be 'happy' in his marriage, until a strained dialogue with Anthony – beautifully observed by the novelist – brings it inescapably to Powell's attention that Anthony seems to have 'forgotten the meaning of the word' (p. 313). The sustained dramatic irony of these chapters, in which Roderick's male friends and colleagues, both qualified by epithets which indicate their limited perception ('sentimental' Franklin, 'young' Powell) blunder towards knowledge of the sexual and emotional torment in which he lives, is admirably controlled. And the impasse itself – the 'psychological cabin mystery' as Marlow quaintly terms it – is believable. Marlow understands it better than Powell does, the outer narrator understands it better than Marlow does, and we, as late twentieth century readers, must look over the shoulders of these embarrassed male narrators who back away, in their English Edwardian middle-class reticence and decency, from the spectacle of Roderick's suffering. Marlow judges that Anthony has several fatal characteristics. Marlow should know as he has met these characteristics before, in Jim: they are generosity, pride and lawlessness (p. 351). Marlow could, but doesn't, add narcissism to this list: a fixed and self-regarding obstinacy which makes Anthony loyal to his own gentlemanly gesture – giving poor Flora her 'liberty' from sexual obligations (p. 335) – and prevents him from seeing the suffering human being in front of him. As with the earlier Marlow narrations, the novelist is subtler than his narrators.

Conrad had dramatized women interestingly before – Emilia Gould in *Nostromo*, Winnie in *The Secret Agent*, Nathalie in *Under Western Eyes* – but the sustained energy with which he creates his villainesses in *Chance* indicates hard reading of James, Flaubert and Maupassant. We have seen that the governess traumatizes Flora in a way which recalls the psychological sadism displayed by another governess towards another Flora in Henry James's famous ghost story: 'It was like having the mask torn off when you don't expect it. . . . "What are you screaming for, you little fool?" she [the governess] said advancing alone close to the girl who was affected exactly as if she had seen Medusa's head with serpentine locks set mysteriously on the shoulders of that familiar person' (p. 118). Flora is totally unprepared: she has no defence against the governess's vindictive onslaught. Conrad is good on the psychology of repression. In a decent profession the governess might have been a fulfilled person, but working as a governess, with the 'practice of hypocrisy' (p. 119) that that involves, the 'restraint, the iron, admirably mannered restraint at every moment' and the 'never-failing correctness of speech glances, movements, smiles, gestures' (p. 120) has turned her, in the moment of throwing off her repression, into a violent and vindictive extremist. The effect on Flora is very well-observed: shock followed instantly by paralysis: 'She only caught her breath in one dry sob and said nothing, made no other sound, made no movement. When she was viciously assured that she was in heart, mind, manner and appearance an utterly common and insipid creature, she listened without indignation, without anger' (p. 119). Conrad is ahead of his time. A victimized woman turns into a psychopath; an opinionated feminist (Mrs Fyne) who is also a crypto-lesbian spreads political views which destroy individuals. The individuals destroyed – almost – by the activity of these two women are, of course, Roderick and Flora. (The attack is not restricted to women: the novel spreads its focus to say that all land-people, with their abominable laws sanctioned by the most abominable of institutions – the prison that perverts and dements Flora's father – are to blame.)

Why did *Chance* sell so well? Conrad himself would not have had an answer. He was pessimistic about the chances of *Chance*, and when he knew that it was a commercial success he was pessimistic about it from the literary point of view. If he had had sales like those of *Chance* at the beginning of his career the creation of the masterpieces would have been eased: as it is, he knows that his best work is in the past: '*Chance* had a tremendous press. How I would have felt about it ten or eight years ago I can't say. Now I can't even pretend I am elated. If I had *Nostromo, The Nigger, Lord Jim*, in my desk or only in my head, I would feel differently no doubt', (letter to John Galsworthy, 19 March 1914).[47] *Chance* of course transformed his fortunes. The earlier works – which he wished he had yet to write – were to enjoy new sales and a wider audience as a result of the sales of *Chance.* Conrad had arrived, at last.

Conrad's relationship with cities was ambivalent. As a young man he had been in some respects a conventional sailor; throughout his life he was a sensualist – this is particularly marked with regard to food – and we can assume that when not suffering from depression he had a normal sexual appetite. Marseille was the place in which, as a young man, he had enjoyed himself, had affairs, spent money, got into scrapes (whether there was a 'Rita' or not). London, also, where Conrad belonged to two clubs (the RAC and the Athenaeum) and enjoyed visiting music-halls, was a place for the somewhat queasily luxurious pleasures of an Edwardian gentleman. It has been pointed out[48] that the topography of cities in Conrad's later novels is very precise. In *The Secret Agent* and *Chance* we have a clear map of London, and in *Under Western Eyes* we have a clear map of Geneva.[49]

The London of the early story, 'The Return' (*Tales of Unrest*) is airlessly unspecific, but the other Londons of Conrad's novels have a lot of particularity. A detail of *Lord Jim* anticipates the contrast between cityscape and seascape in *Chance.* At the start of chapter 36 of *Lord Jim* the 'privileged man', the member of Marlow's audience who has listened most carefully to Marlow's spoken narrative and is rewarded for his care by becoming the chosen recipient of the written narrative which takes up the last ten chapters of the novel, is in:

> the highest flat of a lofty building [it is with an effort that we remind ourselves that these events are taking place in the 1880s], and his glance could travel afar beyond the clear panes of glass, as though he were looking out of the lantern of a lighthouse. The slopes of the roofs glistened, the dark broken ridges succeeded each other without end like sombre, uncrested waves, and from the depths of the town under his feet ascended a confused and unceasing mutter (p. 337).

As at the end of *The Nigger of the 'Narcissus'*, the narrator makes sense of the city to himself by expressing its appearance as though it were the sea. The land, to course, is stable, will not give way under you, and therefore will tolerate the kinds of moral fraily which would immediately cause damage to a ship: when Egstrom in *Lord Jim* says to Jim 'This business ain't going to sink' (*Lord Jim*, p. 195) Jim interprets this – quite wrongly – as meaning that Egstrom is making the same kind of point about Jim's moral nature that Marlow in *Chance* makes about 'the shore gang' who can see that 'no matter what they do this tight little island won't turn turtle with them or spring a leak and go to the bottom with their wives and children' (p. 4). It is interesting to know that the urban settings of *The Secret Agent*. *Under Western Eyes* and *Chance* are carefully mapped: but it is not, in the end, important. We learn that the Château Borel in *Under Western Eyes* is based on the Villa la Grange, a large property on the lake to the North of the main city of Geneva.[50] Paul Kirschner discusses the question of whether this villa was dilapidated or not: but does it matter? Conrad's imaginative transformation of it is what we remember.

We may stand back from *Chance* and ask: how good is it? What is its place in Conrad's canon? I have compared *Lord Jim* with *Hamlet*[51] and I would compare *Chance* with the next (chronologically) of Shakespeare's great tragedies. *Hamlet* was written 1599–1600, exactly three hundred years earlier than *Lord Jim*. Hamlet the prince gives way to *Othello* the soldier, but the horizon narrows: *Othello* accentuates the sexual anguish that has already found a place in the earlier play, and restricts the political themes to a point where the agony of the bedroom almost obscures the larger world of responsibility, honour and action. A similar pattern emerges in the two longest Marlow narratives, *Lord Jim* and *Chance*: Jim in Patusan is a prince governing a community, a prince whose downfall caused by Brown's treachery will have repercussions on his people (Jim's decision to take full responsibility for Dain Waris's death is, from one view-point, a supreme act of statesmanship: by surrendering his own life he prevents civil war in Patusan). Roderick Anthony is an excellent skipper and a courageous man of action, but once his wife is on board the *Ferndale* the ship ceases to be a microcosm of the state (as it had been in earlier works such as *The Nigger of the 'Narcissus'* and *Typhoon*) and becomes instead a sexual torture chamber. *Hamlet* had furnished Conrad with a model of a tragedy, *Othello* is useful to him because it can be adapted to the preoccupations of the novel of sensibility and sexual intrigue as practiced by Henry James. *Chance* has a double ending which seems to align it with both comedy and tragedy: the wicked father, de Barral, is exposed by young Powell and takes his own life, but Roderick later drowns with the *Ferndale*. As far as Roderick is concerned the novel looks like a tragedy, but formally it declares itself to be a comedy by closing with the promise of another marriage, that of Young Powell and Roderick's widow, Flora.

I have raised above (chapter 7, pp. 177–8) the question of Conrad's reading of A. C. Bradley's *Shakespearean Tragedy*, and in particular the question of whether Conrad had read Bradley's book earlier than 1913. The *Othello* transmitted by *Chance* seems to be an *Othello* transmitted by Bradley, or, at least, an *Othello* read in the climate created by Bradley. Bradley emphasizes his belief that the force of the human passions in Shakespeare have to be experienced in reading, not in the theatre, and that in *Othello*'s case the emphasis is on 'mere suffering.'[52] Especially interesting for my purpose is a passage in which Bradley notes the 'influence of accident' on the plot of *Othello*:

> This influence of accident . . . is incessant and terrible. The skill of Iago was extraordinary, but so was his good fortune. Again and again a chance word from Desdemona, a chance meeting of Othello and Cassio, a question which starts to our lips and which anyone but Othello would have asked, would have destroyed Iago's plot and ended his life.[53]

With its iteration of the word 'chance' this passage is bound to alert the interest of a reader of Conrad's novel. It would be nice to be able to show that Conrad changed his title from 'Explosives' to 'Chance' on the day that he read that bit of Bradley's book, but it seems unlikely. He could, of course, have been led to his title by *Othello* without Bradley's help: Iago is at every point an opportunist. There is no one equivalent of Iago in *Chance*, but Young Powell is seen by some commentators as a kind of benign or reverse Iago because he too is an opportunist: he gets his first commission on the *Ferndale* with Roderick Anthony (in the chapter called 'Young Powell and his Chance') because his name happens to be the same as that of the shipmaster, Old Powell, and the kindling of love for Flora and the saving of Roderick's life are both the consequences of chance (Flora helps him to light a flare because she is sleeping in what should be the skipper's side of the ship, and Powell has inadvertently alerted her to the danger of a collision with another ship; Powell happens to be by a broken window reglazed with clear glass when de Barral poisons Roderick Anthony's brandy and water). But if Powell is an adapted Iago, de Barral is an unreversed Iago: like his prototype, his satisfaction has been that of controlling and destroying other people's lives. On board the *Ferndale* he seeks to control (Flora) and to destroy (Anthony), driven by the wholly understandable Iago-like rancour of a defeated man who is accustomed to giving orders. At the moment of his defeat he continues to behave like Iago, refusing – as he takes his own life – to explain his actions.

Roderick has many Othello features. He is hugely attractive to Flora because he is mature (thirty-five), has lived adventurously and comes from a different place – not Ethiopia but (simply) the sea. The contrast between the Moor's blackness and Desdemona's pallor – a matter much discussed by Bradley, who labours the point that the Moor is imagined as black, not brown (despite the convention among late Victorians of playing him as though he were an English gentleman with a suntan), recurs at the climax of *Chance*, where Roderick Anthony heroically seeks to protect his wife from the knowledge that her father is a would-be murderer as well as an embezzler. Young Powell relates the scene:

> Mrs Anthony had on a dressing gown of some grey stuff with red facings. . . . She looked a child; a pale-faced child with big blue eyes . . . Captain Anthony had moved towards her . . . I had never seen them so near to each other before, and it made a great contrast. It was wonderful, for, with his beard cut to a point, his swarthy, sunburnt complexion, thin nose and his lean head there was something African, something Moorish in Captain Anthony (pp. 423–4).

Although *Chance* is usually considered apart from the other Marlow narrations, in an important way it follows directly from *Lord Jim*. Roderick has one set of Jim's qualities: courage, leadership, honour, stoicism and romanticism. In Jim these qualities lead to honourable death. In Roderick they lead to impasse, fulfilment and another honourable death. Young Powell has many of the foregoing qualities together with another set of Jim qualities: the good looks, the boyish eagerness (and unconscious arrogance), the young man's gentlemanly 'readiness' which elicits warm 'one of us' sympathies from older men. When Marlow leaves Jim in Patusan, at the start of the upward curve of Jim's fortunes, at the end of chapter 24 of *Lord Jim,* Jim calls 'You-shall-hear-of-me' (Marlow comments 'Of me, or from me, I don't know which', p. 241). At the end of *Chance* Young Powell, now looking very like Jim, says goodbye to Marlow with the words 'You shall hear from me before long' (p. 446).

9

Victory and Defeat, 1914–1915

There is every schoolboy knows in this scientific age a very close chemical relation between coals and diamonds. Not being a schoolboy any longer I have no very clear notion of its nature. It seems to be – that if you take a lot of coals and melt, or roast, or evaporate it, or destroy it in some such way, if in short you do anything but cook or warm yourself with them you may obtain (so they say) out of a ton of coals (with luck) a diamond rather smaller than the usual pin-head. It is the reason I believe why some pecular [sic] people allude to coal as black diamonds. Mankind is prone to exaggeration of language but the commodities represent wealth. But coals are a much less portable form of property. There is from that point of view a deplorable lack of concentration in coals. Now if a coal mine could be put into one's waistcoat pocket – but it can't. At the same time there is a fascination in coals, the supreme commodity of the age we are camped in like bewildered travellers in a garish, unrestful hotel. And I suppose those two considerations, the practical and the mystical prevent Berg, Augustus Berg, from going away. He called himself Berg but I suspect that it was not the whole of his name. I don't mention this surmise . . . found it more handy in that form. More portable – hm. Well – Berg.

The Archipelago Coal Syndicate went into liquidation . . . I am truly distressed. I must apologise for the clumsiness of my proceedings. Here I begin as though I were going into chemistry and then I seem to be putting my foot into finance now. Nothing is further from my thoughts than to either attract or frighten away my readers by a show of science. But necessity knows no law and I must wear the false mantle of erudition for a little while longer. The world of finance then is a mysterious world in which incredible as the fact may appear, evaporation precedes liquidation. First the capital evaporates and then the company goes into liquidation. Those are very unnatural physics, but they account for the persistent inertia of the body called A. Berg; an inertia at which we 'out there' used to laugh amongst ourselves – but not inimically. . . .

Manuscript state of the opening of *Victory*.[1]

The novelist who wrote *Victory* was the beneficiary of the great commercial and critical success of *Chance*. Conrad's relationship with his public had changed, permanently – from 1914 onwards anything that he wrote was certain to be valued. The reception of *Chance* was ecstatic. Almost all of the reviews were adulatory: 'One may well declare the latest to be the best of his books', 'Mr Conrad is a great architect of novels, and this book is wonderfully and ingeniously planned', 'One of the most gifted and original writers of our time', '*Chance* leaves on the mind the impression of a work of genius in the full sense', '*Chance* is one of the best works which Mr Conrad has written comparable with *Lord Jim* and *Nostromo*', 'The whole thing is much nearer wizardry than workmanship'.[2] Early 1914 was, then, a wonderful period for Conrad: recognition and substantial sales had come at last. The only hostile account of the book was in James's essay in the *Times Literary Supplement* in March 1914. Conrad was worried by this, as we have seen, but he needn't have feared any adverse effect on his sales. The future was assured.

Conrad is capable of self-parody. His letters about some of his stories – especially 'Freya of the Seven Isles' – are almost embarrassingly frank acknowledgements of this: 'Quite good magazine stuff, quite Conradesque (in the easier style), – "no blush to the cheek of the young person" sort of thing. Perfectly safe. Eastern sea setting, but not too much setting'.[3] 'Conradesque', 'Conradese': by allowing himself to prostitute his capacity for creating 'exotic' and highly wrought prose Conrad dulls his own ear, and this permits the somewhat vulgar extravagance of some of his later writing. He was aware that the collection called *Within the Tides*, published in January 1915, was more commercial than literary. He seems to have distinguished clearly in his practice between *nouvelles*, consciously serious short works on the Flaubertian and Jamesian models, and *contes*, saleable episodes for magazines. It was a mark of his new prestige that all the stories in *Within the Tides* were favourably reviewed, even 'The Inn of the Two Witches'. It is likely that the pace and garishness of this story were dictated by its publication in *Pall Mall Magazine*. This periodical favoured what Lawrence Graver calls 'rococo romance' and 'virile optimism' (Anthony Hope's *The Prisoner of Zenda* was serialized in *Pall Mall Magazine* in 1894).[4] Conrad's contributions to it were 'Typhoon' (January–March, 1902), 'To-morrow' (August 1902), 'Gaspar Ruiz' (July–October 1906), 'The Duel' (January–May, 1908) and finally 'The Inn of the Two Witches' (March 1913). 'Typhoon' and 'The Inn of the Two Witches' were illustrated by Maurice Greiffenhagen.

Within the Tides was dedicated to two recent friends, Ralph Wedgwood, a railway administrator and a member of the famous industrial and political family) and his wife Iris. Conrad was introduced to the Wedgwoods by Richard Curle in 1912, and in July 1914 stayed with them at their house in Yorkshire, Stonefall Hall (near Harrogate), where he wrote part of *Victory*. It is a mark of Wedgwood's importance in Conrad's later life that he was one of the executors of Conrad's will. By calling the stories in the dedication 'this sheaf of care-free ante-bellum pages' Conrad draws attention to the fact that they are relatively straightfoward narratives (I saw 'relatively' because, as I shall show, 'The Partner' in fact displays – in this company – a surprisingly high level of narrative sophistication and self-consciousness). When he came to write the 'Author's Note' to *Within the Tides* in 1920 Conrad was somewhat apologetic about all the stories (he remarks that 'The Planter of Malata' was the most ambitious, 'a nearly successful attempt at doing a very difficult thing' p. viii). Innocence, romanticism and a taste for stage-Gothic certainly characterize 'The Inn of the Two Witches', a story which is set in the romantic period (it has to do with a British sailor murdered in Spain in 1813) and has latent within it – as do the Gothic romances of the period (I am thinking especially of Mary Shelley's *Frankenstein* and James Hogg's *The Confessions of A Justified Sinner*) – energies which seem not to be fully realized on the dramatic surface. In this tale 'Cuba Tom', the murdered sailor, has the 'finest pigtail for thickness and length of any man in the Navy. This appendage, much cared for and sheathed tightly in a porpoise skin, hung half way down his broad back to the great admiration of all beholders and to the great envy of some' (p. 134). The pigtail, potent emblem of Cuba Tom's 'manly qualities' (which inspire in the young officer, Edgar Byrne, 'something like affection') is the subject of vigorously detailed writing early in the narrative and then seems to vanish and is not mentioned at all in the account of the death of Tom (crushed and suffocated by thieving inn-keepers, the witches of the title, who lower the weighted canopy of an ornate bed onto him while he is asleep). A roguish and deviant element has been at play and is left unaccounted for in the dénouement of this tale, perhaps because it is too strong for the story's essentially light structure.

In the 'Author's Note' Conrad says that in retrospect he feels that the emotions of Felicia Moorsom and Geoffrey Renouard in 'The Planter of Malata' (1914) were over-explicit, but otherwise writes about the story as though it were a well-chosen subject which has not fulfilled its promise. To the reader much of its content, as well as its style, seems alien to Conrad's temperament: the characters are too urban, articulate and sophisticated for Conrad. Renouard the journalist, Professor Moorsom the 'famous' philosopher (G. E. Moore?) and his frustrated daughter Felicia seem to have strayed into Conrad's Malay archipelago from Edwardian Bloomsbury, as though Conrad had worked up some discarded notes for an unwritten episode of Forster's *Howards End* (a novel Conrad certainly knew). The sexual dialogue between Renouard and Felicia is certainly unconvincing, as Conrad notes, but other features of the action – not least Renouard's suicide – are no less stagy and improbable. There are connections to other parts of Conrad's oeuvre: Renouard's French name, sexual fixation and lack of principle distantly recall *Nostromo*'s Decoud, and his death recalls the way in which Leggatt intends to swim until he dies at the beginning of 'The Secret Sharer'. Renouard dies by swimming out to sea until he drowns – he 'set out calmly to swim beyond the confines of life' (p. 85).

And there are links to the major novel of these years: the bullying philosopher parent and the sexual failure of the protagonist look like rehearsals
for the full developments of these themes in *Victory*.

One feature 'The Planter of Malata' (1914) and 'The Partner' (1911)
have in common is that the working experience of a professional writer
gets into the narrative. The same was true of the early drafts of *Chance*,
where, as we have seen, the outer narrator was a novelist. 'The Planter' is
framed by 'the Editor', and the frame narrator of 'The Partner' is a
professional writer, quizzed by a story-teller, a stevedore [docker] and an
'impressive ruffian', about his method. 'The Partner' is an interesting and
under-regarded narrative experiment. The 'ruffian' who engages the professional writer in conversation in a public bar wants to know 'the process
by which stories – stories for periodicals – were produced' (p. 90) and
proceeds to offer the material for such a story. The ruffian's narrative
describes how the Yankee Cloete, partner of George Dunbar, schemes
with a villainous sailor, Stafford, to scuttle a ship for its insurance value
in order to invest in a patent medicine (the plan miscarries, and in the
confusion Stafford murders Dunbar's brother, heroic Captain Harry). 'The
Partner' is a sophisticated narrative enterprise in that the question about
narrative technique raised at the outset is answered by quoting the 'impressive ruffian' *verbatim*. 'It would have been too much trouble to cook'
the narrative 'for the consumption of magazine readers. So here it is raw,
so to speak – just as it was told to me' (p. 128). It contains glances at
popular serial fiction of the day, especially Wells's *Tono-Bungay* (1910).
Wells's title refers to a quack patent medicine which makes the fortunes
of the Ponderevo brothers. George Dunbar fails to invest in a medicine
which has subsequently boomed and would have made his fortune: 'Nothing
less than Parker's Lively Lumbago Pills. Enormous property! You know it;
all the world knows it' (p. 126).

The last story in *Within the Tides*, 'Because of the Dollars' (1914), arises
directly out of the writing of *Victory*: it concerns Davidson, the same Davidson
as in *Victory* but here in the story he has an unsympathetic wife and a
wholly innocent relationship with a prostitute known as Laughing Anne.
Davidson's goodwill is prominent, as it is in *Victory*. The plot turns on his
attempt to help Anne and the conspiracy of Bamtz, Anne's lover, and his
villainous accomplices, to rob a cargo of government dollars which Davidson
is carrying on his steamer. As Graver points out 'the parallels with *Victory*
are obvious: an isolated hero is set upon by a theatrical band of robbers
and, after a savage dénouement, a befriended woman dies for him.' He
adds that 'Davidson's dilemma . . . suggest[s] a familiar Conradian theme:
the perils of simpleminded altruism'.[5] This is the least effective of the
volume's stories, using as its sensational murderous villain a Frenchman
who has no hands and batters people to death with the aid of a seven-
pound weight tied to his stump. Conrad was curiously attached to this
story: he dramatized it as *Laughing Anne*, a play which was never performed probably because the sets Conrad demanded were very elaborate

(requiring several scene changes and a ship onstage: the technical requirements resemble those of *Peter Pan*) and because the brutal figure of
the Man Without Hands would have required an appropriately maimed
actor (while Barrie's maimed villain is allowed – of course – to wear the
hook from which he takes his name).

He began writing *Victory*, as we have seen, in April 1912: it was described
to Pinker as a short story called 'Dollars'; 15,000 words, forty or fifty
printed pages. The theme of the story had been with him since late in
1911. *Heart of Darkness* had been a satellite to *Lord Jim*, 'The Secret Sharer'
had been a satellite to *Under Western Eyes* and *Victory*, envisaged as 'Dollars'
in 1912, was a satellite to the big Napoleonic novel that Conrad had been
reading for and thinking about since 1904. A paradox of Conrad's working
life is that for so prodigal a man he disliked waste, and part of the rationale
for the Napoleonic novel (eventually published as *Suspense*) was that it might
harvest some of the otherwise wasted observations of Mediterranean life
that Conrad had made during the ruinous trip to Capri that he and the
family had made early in 1905. After further negotiation with Harrison
Conrad thought he had a promise to serialize 'The Dollars' in the *English
Review* and he wrote to Pinker, 13 May 1912, that the novel was still of
story length but was threatening to grow (to the novella length – Conrad's
preferred length – that of *Heart of Darkness* and 'The Secret Sharer'):

> What if the story grows beyond say 12 or even 15 thou? This is what stumps
> me. The story now in hand is of that kind which may grow even to 30,000.
> Short serial. What *can* you do if the story should get beyond the 12 thou.
> words. . . . In this case (Dollars) the E.R. is safe for serial on this side. I am
> reading for the novel [*Suspense*] meantime. It's going to be done round
> Napoleon in Elba and it may turn out a biggish thing. I am still in doubt
> about the form. Whether a narrative in the first person or a tale in the third.

The story of the growth of 'Dollars' resembles the story of the growth of
Lord Jim between 1898 and 1900; he writes to Pinker on 3 September 1912
that he is still working on *Suspense* but that 'Dollars' is growing and 'I
suppose this thing must be allowed to grow. I understand that the E.R. is
still keen on having it and it will make a small vol. We must reckon on
40,000 w. but no more. Short serial. Meantime the long novel simmers in
my head. This is the only possible way to go on, tho' of course it would
have been better if I had been able to get away to the Mediterranean for
a month of musing and looking at the scene'.[6] Note the way in which
Conrad seems to stand back from, and disown responsibility for, his own
creation: 'Dollars' is growing of its own volition; the *English Review* is
pressing for it; Conrad's *real* current enterprise is *Suspense*; he would like
Pinker to finance another Mediterranean trip in the interests of this novel
(recalling the Capri fiasco of 1905, Pinker must have blanched).

There is a good deal of manipulation going on here, and manipulation
not only of Pinker (who in any case was used to it by this time). Conrad
had a standing agreement with Methuen to write three substantial novels

(over 75,000 words each). On 7 October he wrote to say that Methuen could have no claim on 'Dollars' since it is still a short work, although he now acknowledges that it is a 'novel certainly'. To make it palatable for serial publication in America he gives a synopsis, stressing the saleable features of its plot:

> It has a tropical Malay setting – an unconventional man and a girl on an island under peculiar circumstances to whom enters a gang of three ruffians also of a rather unconventional sort – this intrusion producing certain psychological developments and effects. There is philosophy in it and also drama – lightly treated – meant for cultured people – a piece of literature before everything – and of course fit for general reading. Strictly proper. Nothing to shock the magazine public.

I don't think this is disingenuous, though by focusing on the 'general reader' Conrad ignores some of the more sensational material in the novel: prostitution, homosexuality, fetishism, masochism and suicide. On 2 November 1912 he was still describing 'Dollars' as a 'short novel' which he planned to submit by the following March: on 17 December he wrote that it was over 50,000 words and would be submitted in February, on 26 January 1913 he wrote that he was thinking of a new title – 'The Man in the Moon'[7] – and on 20 February he wrote that it would be completed in another two weeks. On 13 April 1913 he wrote that 'The D novel is drawing to an end.' Yet he was to work on the novel for another fourteen months: it is likely that he had written about half of the text by this time. The novel went more slowly during the summer. On 4 May 1913 he wrote to Pinker 'Here's the usual instalment. Will I ever be able to pick up the lost time? – for I have not averaged that much per week since last June.' He was still unrealistically optimistic about the imminence of the novel's conclusion: 'I may yet be done in a month's time with Mr Berg and his girl and all the rest of them'.[8]

The summer of 1913 saw a developing quarrel with Methuen, with whom Conrad had a contract. He supposed it to be for three novels, Methuen supposed it to be for four: Conrad thought the contract fulfilled when he delivered *Chance*. His letter of 28 March 1913 demonstrates, if read from the point of view of the recipient, how difficult Conrad was capable of being: he was trying to disengage himself from the contract with Methuen on the (spurious) grounds that he misunderstood his work and was expecting him to produce 'sea' novels. He bitterly attacks Methuen for his persistence in demanding what was (after all) agreed:

> After the confession of your deceived hopes and in view of the fact that the novel I am writing has no more sea in it than the ordinary citizen can enjoy from the end of Brighton pier it could be only for the grim satisfaction of holding by the neck a man who has not given you what you expected for your money, who does not share you view of his writings and of the public's attitude to them [Methuen was inclined to market Conrad as an exotic

foreigner and ex-sailor], and whose only sin is that he insists on the freedom to dispose of his work to which he now feels morally entitled.

He tried to withdraw *Chance* (but Methuen went ahead with it) on the grounds that it did not give the 'sea' material that the publisher apparently wanted: 'There aren't ten thousand words of what you want of "sea" in the hundred and forty thousand of Chance, nor nearly enough to slake that thirst for salt from which it appears you have been suffering so long'.[9]

In sharp contrast with this bruising exchange with Methuen – over which Conrad must have felt some degree of guilt – was the extremely flattering engagement with his American publisher, Doubleday, and especially with the new young member of the firm, Knopf, who was responsible (later) for the successful sales of *Chance*. Conrad saw that Doubleday had the right attitude to him – they recognized his greatness and were resolved to sell his work and bring him to a wider public. Conrad played to this, showing a surprising degree of acumen about the way in which his reputation could be puffed. Alfred Knopf encouraged him to think in terms of a uniform edition of his novels in fourteen volumes. Conrad responded enthusiastically to this and saw (accurately) that it was desirable to have two preliminary works to bring his name before the American public, a full length critical study by Richard Curle[10] and a new cheap edition of *A Personal Record*: an adulatory study by a young disciple together with his own (oblique) account of his apprenticeship to letters.

We have seen that on 13 May 1912 Conrad wrote a letter to Pinker about 'Dollars' [*Victory*] and added a note about *Suspense*, of which he said: 'I am still in doubt about the form. Whether a narrative in the first person or a tale in the third'.[11] The odd thing about that note is that it has little bearing on *Suspense* but is directly relevant to *Victory*. The strangeness of *Victory* is bound up with the strangeness of its narrative convention. *Chance*'s narrative convention is difficult to follow but it is at least internally consistent. *Victory*'s narrative convention is oddly 'split', designed, it would seem, to mystify and mislead the reader. *Victory* has three dominant narrators who seem to be unrelated to each other. There is an omniscient narrator, the habitué of Schomberg's bar whose perspective dominates Part One of the novel and who repeats nicknames given to Heyst by other Europeans whom he has encountered in the Malay archipelago: 'Enchanted' Heyst (from the Manager of the branch of the Oriental Banking Corporation in Malacca), 'Hard Facts' Heyst (from Mr Tesman of Tesman Brothers, the Sourabaya traders), Heyst the 'perfect gentleman' (from alcoholic McNab) (chapter 1, pp. 7–9), and quotes, impartially, the cruel names given to Heyst by his enemy Schomberg, Heyst 'the spider' (chapter 2, p. 20), Heyst 'the Enemy' and 'that Swede' (chapter 3, pp. 25–6). Heyst, then, to this fairly rough and pragmatic group of men of whom this unnamed narrator is a representative, is an outsider and a potential victim. The second narrator is Davidson, who is much more friendly to Heyst. The contrast between Davidson's sympathy with Heyst and the outer

narrator's callousness towards him is marked by the following comic exchange, where Davidson reflects that Heyst has landed himself with a
difficulty by taking Lena to Samburan: ' "What's he going to do with her
in the end? It's madness." "You say that he's mad. Schomberg tells us that
he must be starving on his island; so he may end yet by eating her," I
suggested' (I, chapter 5, p. 45). Heyst is not a cannibal, but he has met
cannibals, and he knows that Mrs Zangiacomo is 'infinitely more dis-
agreeable than any cannibal I have ever had to do with'. Lena asks 'How
did you come to have anything to do with cannibals?' (II, chapter 1, p.
75). This is neither answered nor explained, and a lost episode – Heyst
among the Cannibals – lingers in the hinterland of the reader's mind so
that when we encounter Pedro and Ricardo, the opposition 'Heyst versus
cannibal-like Caliban' is one with which we feel familiar without being
able to place it. Notice that the dialogue about cannibals comes in a scene
where the narrator has weirdly full access to Heyst's interior consciousness
and to his emerging erotic feeling. Lena 'captured Heyst's awakened faculty
of observation' and he had 'the sensation of a new experience' and 'looked
at her anxiously, as no man ever looks at another man' (II, chapter 1,
p. 71). He falls in love with her voice (II, chapter 2, p. 88) in a manner
which anticipates their later emotional impasse (he cannot love a whole
person). The narrative convention wobbles uneasily here: this delicate
omniscience in part II, chapters 1 and 2 is ostensibly within the same
narrative consciousness as that which is so obviously 'limited' in part I.
Indeed it is this consciousness which introduces these chapters: part II,
chapter 2 starts with another gesture of limitation ('That was how it began. How it was that it ended as we know it did end, is not so easy to state
precisely' (p. 77)), but with chapter 3 this narrator seems to abandon the
pretence of limitation and offers instead observations which are clearly
fully omniscient, as he fills in the story of Heyst's father and of Heyst's
relationship with him. The implication is that it is Heyst senior who has
made Heyst as he is, courteous, unapproachable and a 'queer chap' (II,
chapter 3, p. 91). This narrating voice has full access to the history of
Heyst and his family and is in a position to tell the stories – fully delineated from within – of Schomberg's hatred and jealousy and Heyst's despairing unease in his relationship with Lena.

The 'split' in the narration indicates a generic problem. The form of
Victory is vertiginously unsettling: we find it very hard to say to what genre
it belongs. David Lodge calls it 'not a tragicomedy, but a tragedy of the
absurd'[12] which might seem to suggest that we should think of Conrad as
adumbrating Pinter or Beckett. But in those writers' 'absurd' works the
shapeliness of the work itself is not in question. *Victory* by contrast shows
an agonising refusal to conform to a form: the split narrative displays a
split drama in which the fully registered Heyst coexists with puppets. It
resists our sense of generic neatness.

Jeffrey Meyers makes much of the notion that Heyst may be homosexual: he suggests that Jones is a shadow or double of Heyst and that

Heyst's sexual insufficency is partly a matter of unacknowledged homosexuality within himself.[13] This is too schematic. Sexual disgust and anguish are certainly part of Heyst's consciousness but there is nothing in the novel to support the notion that he is homosexual: it is his *hetero*sexuality that is 'latent'. For much of the novel his own impulses towards Lena fill him with disgust. Only after her death does he see that heterosexual love, if he had learned about it early enough, could have saved him: 'Ah, Davidson, woe to the man whose heart has not learned while young to hope, to love – and to put its trust in life!' (IV, chapter 14, p. 410). Presumably, although he goes to bed with Lena, he does so without sexual desire. He appears to have no sexual fantasies: 'I've never killed a man or loved a woman – not even in my thoughts, not even in my dreams' (III, chapter 3, p. 212). He says this to Lena in the context of a denial: he is not responsible (though the received wisdom, promulgated by Schomberg, says that he is) for the murder of Morrison. He can talk like this to Lena because she is a cliché of the kind that an Edwardian gentleman can understand, the tart with a heart of gold: as she herself says, she is 'not what they call a good girl' (III, chapter 3, p. 198). And the fact that she is a kind of prostitute means that he can talk to her as one outsider to another and sleep with her with indifference: hence his astonishment when she cries 'You should try to love me!' (III, chapter 5, p. 221).

Fathers offer false teaching to their sons in Conrad. Jim's father's stale Christianity is useless to Jim, Gould senior tries to instil defeatism over the mine into Charles Gould, Carleon Anthony has contributed to the low self-esteem suffered by Roderick Anthony and Heyst is unmanned by his father, the philosopher, whose teaching and writing warn him to avoid love: 'Of the stratagems of life the most cruel is the consolation of love – the most subtle, too; for the desire is the bed of dreams' (III, chapter 5, p. 219).

The pattern of topographical contrasts that I referred to at the end of the last chapter (London/Singapore in *Lord Jim*, Geneva/St Petersburg in *Under Western Eyes*, London/the sea in *Chance*) recurs, briefly, in the contrast between his father's dull London house and the very exotic setting – Samburan – in which he now lives (his father dies in the London house with the advice to 'Look on – make no sound' (III, chapter 1, p. 175)). Dull London is the foil for the brilliant strangeness of the setting established in the opening pages of the novel, Heyst's island, formerly the site of the ill-fated Tropical Belt Coal Company set up by the affectionate and inept Morrison, and now the setting for Heyst's solitude. Conrad is very good at openings (think of the first paragraph of *Nostromo*, judged by A. D. Nuttall to be one of the best openings of any novel ever written[14]). Heyst's isolation on Samburan is like that of a man 'perched on the highest peak of the Himalayas' accompanied only by a volcano which at night produces a dull red glow like the glow on the end of Heyst's cigar. The volcano is both his companion and his undoing: his undoing since it is, as Schomberg points out, an excellent landmark for Jones, Ricardo and Pedro to sail by when they make their way to Samburan to destroy Heyst. The contrast between the land people and the sea people in *Chance* has been replaced in *Victory* by a more extreme contrast, that between the denizens of the world and those who, like Heyst and Lena, have renounced the world. The first two parts of *Victory* describe the activity of denizens of the world, people who are to a great or lesser extent busy and self-seeking: the anonymous frame narrator; Davidson, who functions as a secondary or inner narrator; Ricardo, who is effectively a third narrator (telling the stories of Jones, Pedro, and Pedro's brother 'the honourable Antonio' whom Jones put to death); and Schomberg, who with his 'officer of the Reserve' manner is manipulated by Jones and his companions until he hits on the notion of planting in their minds the lure of Heyst's supposed wealth. The activities in parts I and II of the novel take place in time, while Heyst and Lena on Samburan seem to be living out of time, drenched in the peace and stillness of the islands, which to Heyst is perfect and to Lena can seem intolerable. The 'empty space was to her the abomination of desolation,' and she says of it: 'It makes my head swim . . . all that water and all that light' (III, chapter 3, pp. 190–1). In a way, the paragraph in which Lena and Heyst climb to a high point and look out over the sea is the high-point of the arc of the novel, it is a point of stillness and peace which is about to be cruelly invaded and interrupted. It has been preceded by violent purposiveness and it will be followed by violent purposiveness, but in itself it is pure, austere and 'out of time'. This is the paragraph in its entirety:

> Heyst and Lena entered the shade of the forest path which crossed the island, and which, near its highest point, had been blocked by felled trees. But their intention was not to go so far. After keeping to the path for some distance, they left it at a point where the forest was bare of undergrowth, and the trees, festooned with creepers, stood clear of one another in the gloom of their own making. Here and there great splashes of light lay on the ground. They moved, silent in the great stillness, breathing the calmness, the infinite isolation, the repose of a slumber without dreams. They emerged at the upper limit of vegetation, among some rocks; and in a depression of the sharp slope, like a small platform, they turned about and looked from on high over the sea, lonely, its colour effaced by sunshine, its horizon a heat mist, a mere unsubstantial shimmer in the pale and blinding infinity overhung by the darker blaze of the sky (III, chapter 3, pp. 189–90).

In this narrative space which is both out of time and out of the world, Heyst and Lena mythologize each other, he calling her 'princess of Samburan'; a title which is partly mockery, as was 'Lord Jim' in the earlier novel, and partly reality.

The mythical dimension of the people in *Victory* was far more evident in the novel's manuscript. The manuscript, begun (as we have seen) in April 1912, is substantially longer than the published text. Frederick Karl inclines to the view that the length of the manuscript testifies to Conrad's confidence while writing the novel.[15] I take the opposite view: much of the writing shows signs of desperation, as though Conrad were winding a handle to churn out pages of manuscript in order to placate Pinker, and the drastic cuts made for publication indicate – precisely – a lack of confidence, a dismayed recognition that much of what he had written lacked dramatic interest, tended to be repetitive and fell well below his self-imposed standard of excellence. But it is certainly true, as Karl says, that one effect of the changes is that Heyst becomes more fleshly – more male, indeed – in the text than in the manuscript. In the manuscript a great deal of space is given to the Lena-Berg relationship. Lena's names are given as Margaret, then Magdalen, contracted to Lena: the manuscript thus identifies her clearly – much more clearly than does the published text – as a fallen woman associated with a Christlike man. There is also a political dimension to the naming of Lena. In the manuscript she asks why she has been given this name and Berg replies that it is a pet name given to 'many girls in Germany'; presumably Conrad dropped this phrase after Britain went to war with Germany in 1914.[16] The difficulty that Heyst and Lena have in communicating with each other is explored over some hundred sheets of manuscript, as though Conrad is dissatisfied with this theme and hopes by working and reworking it to find the appropriate balance between the two figures. In the published text it is boiled down to fifteen pages of part III, chapter 3. The manuscript version shows them as still strangers even as they approach a sexual relationship. The writing becomes helplessly confused:

> He saw her weak and insincere even in her evasions and all at once without transition he detested her. But only for a moment. He seemed to remember that she was pretty – and more – that she was seductive – that she had a special grace in the intimacy of life. Yes she had that. Such as she was, she was somebody having her own quality. . . . He thought that now they were further from each other than ever. Each of her docilities now would only increase the distance; and as he remembered them in the past, their short common past he seemed to discover in her words, acts, movements, tones in all her impulses and in he [sic] shynesses, in her shrinkings and in her caresses the obscure mental reserves of a sensitive being which thinks itself to be of an inferior essence (MS 594–5).

In the manuscript, then, 'Berg' seems far more sexually incompetent and reluctant than does Heyst in the printed book. And this sexually insubstantial being is also – consistently – wraithlike (as Karl says) in juxtaposition with his adversary 'Smith' [Jones]. The following passage in the manuscript relates to part III, chapter 1, where in the book Heyst is obeying his father's injunction to 'cultivate that form of contempt which is called pity' and to 'Look on – make no sound' (pp. 174–5):

> At first in the presence of the apparent wealth of nature – which is really much poorer than it looks – he thought of taking up some subject for study:

insects, plants, minerals. But he soon perceived the desperate futility of any such occupation – and also its dangers – not to speak of its unworthiness. . . . He looked at the world as one looks into a kaleidoscope. There are infinite combinations of figures. At each turn you saw a different design; but the pieces of glass were always the same. . . . Berg's faintly playful politeness puzzled and amused all sorts and conditions of men in Brazil, in Tripoli, in all the other stations of his erratic progress towards the Islands, where he had remained, enchanted, going round and round like a bit of straw in the eddy of a mill race. But it did not offend either simple or gentle, because they did not know that below the surface he had for gentle and simple, for men and women and achievements labour and expectations, for all the opportunities and dangers of the world and for his own fate in it the same equable impervious indifference – a form of contempt as pronounced and even more hopeless than pity, which his pitiless father had advised him almost with his last breath to practice, either as a concession to some weakness detected in his offspring, or from some secret weakness of his own, or perhaps by a movement of malice to which the wisdom of age will give way sometimes when provoked by the innocence of youth sitting at its feet – or yet perhaps from sheer mistrust of itself.

And it is also possible that Mr Berg the father would have explained and commented and qualified his laconic advice later on if the later on had not slipped away from him [in other words, if death had not come unexpectedly] in the shade of the night, gently like a receding tide that will have no flood. Like the veriest fools and indeed like everyone of us Mr. Berg the elder had been taken unawares by the finality of that ebb leaving some worlds unexplained and taking with him some words unspoken – for no one yet has ever said his last word on earth (MS 456–60).

Berg's passive acquiescence, his willingness to be propelled by random forces, his ostensible mild detachment from human affairs which masks a kind of self-destructive disdain are all present, of course, in Heyst in the published novel, but in the manuscript they are presented much more extensively as though the text itself were enacting, as well as dramatizing, the protagonist's depressed, inert and disengaged state of mind. Although Smith is malignantly active and Berg is helplessly passive, both are 'decadent' in that both echo the styles and prevalent literary conventions of the 1890s. Berg in his inertia resembles Des Esseintes, the protagonist of Huysmans's *A Rebours*, while Smith is like another totemic figure of the 1890s, the eponymous ghoul of Bram Stoker's *Dracula*:

This slow lifeless voice dropping words without passion without insistance [sic] was too much for his fortitude simply because the man who used it affected his imagination with thoughts of death and graveyards and powers from another world. It was livid complexion this faint voice, the spectral slow way of turning his eyes on one and the spidery thinness of his limbs which suggested his having been resurrected and now going about not exactly alive but animated my [by] some unholy spell. There were moments when he gave that impression strongly enough to make you shudder. Schomberg raising his eyes from the floor at last met the two dark caverns hollowed under Mr Smith's thick eyebrows directed upon him impenetrably. (MS 292–3).

Conrad was to reinforce his protagonist's decadent associations by renaming him Axel Heyst, thus recalling the hero of Villiers de L'Isle-Adam's *Axel* (1890), a drama of aesthetic inertia and sexual *impasse* which came to be identified as a quintessentially 'Nineties work. De L'Isle-Adam's Axel is an aristocrat who detaches himself from action and chooses to experience life vicariously, through his servants; in due course he and his mistress commit suicide, preferring death to love.

'Berg' and 'Smith' are fleshless: in the published text Heyst and Jones still mirror each other in that each seems sexually inadequate, but they are both more robust than in the manuscript. Jones, as we have seen, can be read as specifically homosexual (whereas in the manuscript his hatred of women seems supernatural, beyond all recognizable human drives). And Heyst, of course, overcomes his paralysis in order to take the sexual initiative with Lena. If one seeks to locate Heyst and Jones on the spectrum of male sexuality, Ricardo provides a useful fixed point. Ricardo is an aggressive, 'normal' heterosexual male. He instinctively hates Heyst because Heyst 'isn't hearty-like'. Jones remarks in reply that Heyst 'seems to be a very self-possessed man' (III, chapter 10, p. 263). In other words, Jones can relate to sexual repression while Ricardo finds it mystifying and threatening. Ricardo is equally baffled by his master's sexuality, and worried that the disclosure of Lena's presence on the island will prompt unpredictable behaviour in Jones: 'He did not pretend to understand it. . . . All he knew was that he himself was differently inclined . . . the other sort of disposition simplified matters in general; it wasn't to be gainsaid. But it was clear that it could also complicate them. . . . The worst of it was that one could not tell exactly in what precise manner it would act. It was unnatural, he thought somewhat peevishly. How was one to reckon up the unnatural?' (III, chapter 10, p. 266).

Heyst is associated with a number of myths, two of them from the Christian tradition: he is like Christ in his altruism and asceticism, but he is also like Adam. Alone on his island he rules his world and names his animals (one of which is Lena). The myths work against each other, of course, in that Adam as the father of mankind can be assumed to be a figure of sexual energy. Heyst's own father, the philosopher, is associated not with a myth but with nineteenth century philosophers, especially Schopenhauer.[17] In part II, chapter 3 of the novel Adam and Schopenhauer are brought into close and contrasting relation. Of the teaching Heyst has had from his father the omniscient narrator observes:

> The young man learned to reflect, which is a destructive process, a reckoning of the cost. It is not the clear-sighted who lead the world. Great achievements are accomplished in a blessed, warm mental fog, which the pitiless cold blasts of the father's analysis had blown away from the son. 'I'll drift,' Heyst had said to himself deliberately (II, chapter 3, pp. 91–2).

The contrast between the average man's 'warm mental fog' and Heyst senior's 'cold blasts' closely resembles Schopenhauer's distinction between the man who is entangled in phenomena, trapped in his own 'will' (by which Schopenhauer refers to all the desires including sexual desire), and the man of vision who can see the futility and horror of his own impulses and who takes the path of asceticism, of the 'denial of the will to life'. Schopenhauer's *Die Welt als Wille und Vorstellung* was available in a recent translation: *The World as Will and Idea*, tr. Haldane and J. Kemp, 1883. Conrad would certainly have been aware of this translation and may have read it. He knew some German, but it is unlikely that he read Schopenhauer in the original.[18] A curious feature of the novel is that there are also a number of unmistakable verbal echoes (in English translation) of Nietzsche's *Also Sprach Zarathustra*.[19] At one level these references operate as an ironic commentary on the novel's dramatic content, since such themes in Nietzsche's work as self-assertion, will to power and hero-worship, are systematically negated by Heyst and his father. Beyond the irony, though, there is common ground: Heyst, Schopenhauer and Nietzsche agree that man is self-determining and that the universe is an echoing void.

Schopenhauerian asceticism has determined the shape of Heyst's life 'up to that disturbing night', the night on which he is attracted by 'Alma' (Lena): 'It was a shock to him, on coming out of his brown study, to find the girl so near him, as if one waking suddenly should see the figure of his dream turned into flesh and blood' (II, chapter 3, p. 92). Adam here supplants Schopenhauer. The association is with Milton's Adam as well as the Adam of Genesis. In *Paradise Lost* , VIII, 452–90, while God is creating Eve out of one of Adam's ribs, Adam, asleep, dreams of her and wakes to find her 'such as I saw her in my dream'.[20] Part III, chapter 1 gives the most extended comparison with Adam, and explicitly notes the failure of Heyst's father to extinguish the Adam in him:

> 'There must be a lot of the original Adam in me, after all.'
>
> He reflected, too, with the sense of making a discovery, that this primeval ancestor is not easily suppressed. The oldest voice in the world is just the one that never ceases to speak. If anybody could have silenced its imperative echoes, it should have been Heyst's father, with his contemptuous, inflexible negation of all effort; but apparently he could not. There was in the son a lot of that first ancestor who, as soon as he could uplift his muddy frame from the celestial mould, started inspecting and naming the animals of that paradise which he was so soon to lose (III, chapter 1, pp. 173–4).

The old Adam side of himself, combined with the altruistic Christ-like side of himself, impels Heyst to rescue Lena from her hideous destiny with Zangiacomo, and in part III of chapter 4 the two sides wrestle with each other as he tries to overcome his uninitiated state. Immediately before kissing Lena he says: 'I've never killed a man or loved a woman – not even in my thoughts, not even in my dreams' (III, chapter 4, p. 212). In this scene of *éclaircissement* Lena reveals that she had believed Schomberg's story to the effect that Heyst had killed Morrison. Heyst explains the true history of his relationship with Morrison, Lena declares that she could in any case believe nothing bad of Heyst, and the chapter closes with their sexual consummation, obliquely introduced and then decorously elided from the text: 'The girl glanced round, moved suddenly away, and averted her face. With her hand she signed imperiously to him to leave her alone – a command which Heyst did not obey' (III, chapter 4, p. 215). Adam triumphs; but Lena will later relocate their relationship in the Christian myth, seeing the persecution by Jones, Ricardo and Pedro as punishment, 'a sort of retribution from an angry Heaven', visited on the lovers for their sexual relationship. More sexually experienced than Heyst, Lena is a puritan, possessed by sexual guilt: 'It was the way they lived together – that wasn't right, was it? It was a guilty life. For she had not been forced into it, driven, scared into it. No, no – she had come to him of her own free will, with her whole soul yearning unlawfully.' She aligns herself with Eve: 'Woman is the tempter'. Untroubled by Christian belief, Heyst hears in this only a touching expression of her love for him: 'Are you conscious of sin? . . . For I am not . . . before Heaven, I am not!' (IV, chapter 8, p. 354).

Another text contributing to the novel's mythic dimension is *The Tempest*. It has often been remarked that Heyst is like Prospero and Lena is like Miranda. The network of associations with *The Tempest* is extensive, though from a distance comparisons between the texts may not seem close. *The Tempest* a masterpiece of concision, observing the unities of place and time so stringently that only its title seems at odds with its economy. Hallett Smith observes that it could more appropriately be called *The Island*[21] (Dryden, incidentally, used 'The Enchanted Island' as the subtitle for his 1670 and adaptation of the play) though one may remark that to use that title would be to intensify unity of place, while the most striking feature of the play's organization, in the Shakespeare canon, is its unity of time. *Victory* also has an odd title, since its subject is defeat: Lena, the victor, dies in order to save Heyst's life. The working title was 'Dollars' and Conrad's variant working titles were 'Berg' and 'The Man in the Moon'[22] and he occasionally referred to it in his letters as 'the *Island Story*'.[23] He chose *Victory* as the title and finished the manuscript in June 1914.[24]

Like *The Tempest*, *Victory* deals with allegorical figures and with the constraints of an island, and it forces us to acknowledge the coexistence of magical and naturalistic experience, and of types and real people, within the same drama. Heyst is an antitype or adversarial double of Prospero on many fronts. In Milan Prospero is a ruler, on his island he is a ruler and a teacher. He teaches both Miranda and Caliban, and in due course the whole of the intruding court is exposed to his moral education. Heyst's situation is the obverse of this. He counsels his Miranda figure, but cannot save her, he reads deeply in books bequeathed to him by his father but is passive in relation to this legacy, allowing it to make him 'drift altogether and literally, body and soul, like a detached leaf drifting in the wind-currents under the immovable trees of a forest glade' (p. 92). When the monstrous visitors, Jones, Ricardo and Pedro, impact upon Heyst's island the text of *The Tempest* seems to be in Conrad's mind:

> 'Do you see them?' Heyst whispered into the girl's ear. 'Here they are, the envoys of the outer world. Here they are before you – evil intelligence, instinctive savagery, arm in arm . . . fantasms from the sea – apparitions, chimaeras' (IV, chapter 5, p. 329).

The phrase 'the man in the moon' was considered as a title for *Victory* and occurs several times in the text, and it may be a quotation from *The Tempest* where it occurs most significantly in II, ii:

> CALIBAN: Hast thou not dropp'd from heaven?
> STEPHANO: Out o' the moon, I do assure thee: I was the man i'th'moon
> when time was.
>
> (II, ii, 137–9)

In *Victory* the phrase is used jokingly of Heyst, to stress the difference between him and normal human beings. The most interesting use of it occurs when Jones is horrified by the discovery that there is a woman on the island and uses the phrase as a term of abuse, stressing the difference between himself and Heyst. For us, of course, it is Jones, misogynist, skeletal and angular, who is the alien, the creature from outer space, so that when he says 'I have a good mind to shoot you, you woman-ridden hermit, you man in the moon, that can't exist without [a woman]' (IV, chapter 11, p. 387) we feel that two mind-sets, two perceptions of reality are at work. It is important that this line comes at a late stage in the scene and expresses Jones's anger at finding that Heyst resists him: earlier he has sought to establish solidarity with Heyst. As Gentleman Brown did with Jim in *Lord Jim* Jones claims social equality ('It's obvious that we belong to the same – social sphere' (IV, chapter 11, p. 378) and – nauseatingly – clubbable male solidarity. But in the lines in which he does this he exposes the gulf betwen them:

> 'Come! You can't expect to have it always your own way. You are a man of the world.'
> 'And you?'. . . .
> 'I am the world itself, come to pay you a visit'
>
> (IV, chapter 11, p. 379).

In *The Tempest* Alonso, Sebastian and Gonzalo, Ariel's 'three men of sin' are part of Destiny's 'instrument', the 'lower world' come to pay Prospero a visit (III, iii, 53–4). Jones's claim to social equality is important here: in *Victory* we come to recognize that Prospero's real enemies are his social equals; Caliban is not an enemy of any substance.

Lena sees the intruders as figures bringing retribution, punishment 'from an angry Heaven' because of the way she and Heyst live together (IV, chapter 8, p. 354). Heyst reacts with incredulity to this. Lena has about her the relics of naive lower-middle class Christianity while Heyst's scepticism is underpinned, at this stage of the narrative, by Darwin. He regrets, ironically, that he has no religion, 'no Heaven to which he could recommend this fair, palpitating handful of ashes and dust' (IV, chapter 8, pp, 354–55). His perception of his own relationship with mankind is that he as at the end of the evolutionary process while figures like Pedro are at the beginning of it. This is made explicit in IV, chapter 9, where Heyst speaks of Pedro as 'a creature with an antediluvian lower jaw, hairy like a mastodon, and formed like a prehistoric ape' (p. 358) and of himself as 'a man of the last hour' (p. 359). He sounds here the authentic note of *fin de siècle* despair, sounded earlier by Hardy in *Jude the Obscure* (1895). The modern thinking man is an evolutionary disaster, unfitted to live.

Heyst in his purity is doomed to extinction. Lena, who is lower on the evolutionary scale, becomes possessed by purpose at the same juncture of the plot that reduces Heyst to utter impotence. In terms of motivation and philosophical outlook the two characters pass each other, Heyst moving towards emptiness, Lena towards an objective. The desire to save Heyst's life has given her a reason for living: her mind has for long being 'in doubt as to the reason of her own existence' but with this new objective 'she no longer wondered at that bitter riddle, since her heart found its solution in a blinding, hot glow of passionate purpose' (IV, chapter 9, p. 367).

The Conrad who writes *Victory* is also a modern man. The novel is his farewell to the Edwardian period, with its relative certainties, at the onset of the Great War. *Victory* is another example of a Conrad novel which resists our sense of generic neatness. It is powerful but messy, and no consolation is offered. *The Tempest* uses form to exert control; *Victory* does the opposite. Its lack of order indicates that life in 1914 is now beyond hope of control. Conrad is saying, in effect, 'the tidiness of Shakespeare's valedictory romance needs to be countered by something which is both untidy and hopeless. The values by which a creature as noble as Heyst seeks to live have no place in the modern world. The modern world itself is, after all, irredeemably horrible. The coming conflict proves it. Absurdity on this scale cannot be put right by art.'

There is also a Polish source for *Victory*. Andrzej Busza has shown conclusively that parts of the novel are, in effect, quotations from Stefan Żeromski's *Dzieje gzrechu* (*The History of a Sin*) which was published in serial form between 1906 and 1908 and became one of Żeromski's best-known works.[25] *The History of a Sin* is a novel of bold and sensational subject-matter, 'the story of the moral downfall of a virtuous bourgeois girl, who, in turn, eloped with a married man, killed her illegitimate child, became the mistress of a cosmopolitan bandit, murdered another lover at his instigation, entered and left an institution for reformed prostitutes, and finally, at the end of her career, sacrificed her life for the man she loved all along'.[26]

The most striking of Conrad's borrowings from *The History of a Sin* comes at the climax of *Victory*, the death of Lena. The passage from Żeromski is as follows:

> She raised herself from the ground on her elbows, to see his face. Now she would tell him! She saw him. He stood behind wooden bars. He fixed his large eyes on the darkness of the cave, searching it. Their eyes met. A smile of angelic rapture floated down on to Ewa's lips. But together with the smile blood began to flow again from her mouth.
>
> Once again, the neck slightly, very slightly lifted the heavy head. Ewa felt, that two hands had slipped under her hair and lifted the powerless skull off the floor – and that now she was resting in those kindly hands. She could no longer see him. She knew that she was lying on her back, and that he was kneeling and holding her head in his motionless hands.
>
> Her whole being lit with her earliest girlish smile of happiness and with that smile of divine bliss on her lips she died, seeking his glance in the shades of death.[27]

The parallel passage in *Victory* is as follows:

> She tried to raise herself, but all she could do was to lift her head a little from the pillow. With a terrified and gentle movement, Heyst hastened to slip his arm under her neck. She felt relieved at once of an intolerable weight, and was content to surrender to him the infinite weariness of her tremendous achievement. Exulting, she saw herself extended on the bed, in a black dress, and profoundly at peace; while, stooping over her with a kindly, playful smile, he was ready to lift her up in his firm arms and take her into the sanctuary of his innermost heart – for ever! The flush of rapture flooding her whole being broke out in a smile of innocent, girlish happiness; and with that divine radiance on her lips she breathed her last, triumphant, seeking for his glance in the shades of death (Part 4, chapter 13, pp. 406–7).[28]

It must be the case, as Andrzej Busza says, that the Żeromski passage had lodged in Conrad's memory and that he reproduced it in *Victory* by accident. He was particularly pleased with this passage and chose it for a public reading during his American tour of 1923. He would scarcely have selected it for special attention in this way if he had been aware that it was not original.[29]

The end of *Victory* was written against the background of a developing national crisis. The year 1914 divided for Conrad into two parts, the first centring on the publication of *Chance* and the completion of *Victory*, and the second upon his return to Poland for his first visit since 1893.[30] On 19 March 1914 he wrote to Galsworthy about the critical success of *Chance*, as we have seen, to say that although the break-through was welcome it had come too late to compensate for the earlier frustrations of his literary career.[31]

By midsummer Conrad had decided to visit Poland. He and his family had been invited by the Retinger family to visit their estate near Cracow. *Victory* was more or less completed by the end of June 1914, but was subject to further tinkering in July, part of it at the Wedgwoods' country house in Yorkshire.[32] The work was interrupted to visit Sheffield university, where Borys Conrad sat the entrance examinations but did not pass (he was to pass in 1915). Conrad was invited to dine with the Vice-Chancellor of the university – an appropriate mark of Conrad's new-found eminence, but creating a certain awkwardness in retrospect when his son failed to get in. At the final stage of tinkering with *Victory* he alighted upon his title; on 25 July 1914, Conrad wrote to Galsworthy a letter which brings together the two major events of his year, the completion of *Victory* and the visit to Poland. Of the novel he wrote with his characteristic irony and defensiveness:

> The title is *Victory*; there seems to be a fashion just now for short titles and apparently I have been unconsciously influenced: for I could not think of anything else. *Victory: An Island Tale.* I took this *Victory* by the scruff of the neck and 'wrastled' with it till the eighteenth, on which date I managed to fling it out of the house (into Pinker's arms) and then I collapsed.[33]

The trip to Poland arose partly from a meeting in 1912 with J. H. Retinger, son of a successful Cracow lawyer who was visiting England to awaken sympathy for Polish independence. He and his wife Otolia became very friendly with the Conrads and stayed with them in 1913. The friendship did a great deal to renew Conrad's interest in Poland.[34] Clearly to plan to visit in the summer of 1914 was not ideal timing, but he badly wanted to go (although he playfully projects the desire onto Jessie and the boys): 'The mother of Mrs Retinger has invited all the tribe of us to her house in the country, some 16 miles from Cracow but over the Russian border. This caused such an excitement in the household that, if I had not accepted instantly, I would have been torn to pieces by my own wife and children.'

As well as being a famous novelist he was now a commercially successful one, and he could go back to Poland with assured money and status, able to fulfil a natural and understandable desire, on the part on an ambitious emigrant, to show that emigration was the right decision and that he had made a success of his life. He keeps up the fiction that his own role in the expedition is passive: Retinger is making the arrangements, Jessie and the boys have provided the motivation, 'And indeed I am too limp to argue or do anything at all. I shall travel like a bale or a millionaire, Retinger having taken upon himself the duties of courier.' (*Like a millionaire*: and why not, given his distinction and achievements?) Like Jim, he has left his native country to make good. He quotes Stein's famous aphorisms from chapter 20 of *Lord Jim* as he consciously rounds off his earlier decision to emigrate by making this pilgrimage back to his point of departure: 'In

1874 I got into a train in Cracow (Vienna Express) on my way to the sea, as a man might get into a dream. And here is the dream going on still. Only now it is peopled mostly by ghosts and the moment of awakening draws near.'[35] So the visit to Poland was an inner, private matter. It can of course be seen as a somewhat reckless and dangerous expedition. Conrad's attitude towards it seems to have been that even at a time of international crisis nothing could go seriously amiss for himself and his family. He turned out to be right.

Retinger and the Conrads arrived in Cracow on 28 July 1914, the day on which Austria-Hungary declared war on Serbia, and Germany declared war on Russia. Cracow was part of Austria-Hungary, as was Zakopane, a village in the Tatra mountains. The Conrads spent five days in Cracow and then, abandoning the plan to visit the Retinger estate over the Russian border, went to Zakopane (on 2 August) for two months. On 4 August Britain declared war on Germany, and within another week Britain was formally at war with Austria. The Conrads were thus aliens, taking a holiday on enemy territory, and liable at any moment to be interned.

Jessie Conrad remembered that the months in Poland helped her to understand Conrad: 'So many characteristics that had been strange and unfathomable to me before, took, as it were, their right proportions. I understood that his temperament was that of his countrymen'.[36] She was right: his attitude to the war was that of a Pole, and from the Polish viewpoint conflict in Europe meant hope. Najder remarks that 'the mood in Cracow was almost universally buoyant: for Poland, a major conflict between the powers which had partitioned it presented its only chance of regaining national unity, even if it were a unity under an Austrian pro-tectorate'.[37] Many Poles who met Conrad during his visit recorded his views and remarks, among them Kazimierz Górski who recalled Conrad saying that 'the Polish question could be positively solved only if Russia were beaten by Germany and Germany by England and France.[38] As Najder points out that, in the end, is exactly what happened.[39]

At Zakopane the Conrads stayed at first at a pension and then for some two months with Aniela Zagórska and her daughters at Konstantynówka. It seems to me that Conrad at this time is like Heyst on his island, suspended in a timeless place despite hostile forces swirling all around him. He enjoyed talking to the Poles about the future, enjoyed the adulation that he re-ceived from the Zagórska family (especially from the elder daughter, also called Aniela) and immersed himself in Polishness, reading a great deal of Polish literature. The effect of the crisis on him was to lift his depression. On 8 August 1914 he wrote from Zagórska's house to Pinker – without irony – saying 'My health is good. I am getting a mental stimulus out of this affair – I can tell you! And if it were not for the unavoidable anxiety I would derive much benefit from the experience'.[40] Aniela Zagórska, elder of the two Zagórska sisters, recalled that Conrad was in a 'particularly equable and serene frame of mind throughout his visit. His wife commented on it with amazement more than once.'[41] Presumably his mood was sustained partly by freedom from work: since the arrangement in Zakopane was temporary and makeshift he could hardly be expected to fulfil his obligations to Pinker by writing during this period. But there was serious anxiety about getting money into Poland for the Conrads. Conrad's letters to both Pinker and John Galsworthy include specific requests for money and instructions as to how it should be sent out to him – and, of course, about how he and his family were to get home. In August he hoped to get out through France, in September that plan had been replaced by a plan to get out through Italy. On 15 September he wrote to Pinker to say that he was penniless and that money should be sent to him either via the American embassy in Vienna or to an agent in Milan. The letter ends with a paragraph of exoneration, mitigation and protestation. This paragraph is so characteristic of Conrad's relationship with Pinker that I quote it in full:

> I don't apologize for giving you all this bother. I've no option. I have not found myself in this position through any fault of mine. No one believed in the war till the last moment when the mobilization order caught us in Cracow. I had no choice but to rush my people up to this place [he had a choice: Retinger had immediately returned to England]. If you want to know where it is, look due south from Cracow where there is a knot of mountains [the Tatra mountains, now on the Polish-Czech border] marked on the map. I have now exhausted my credit in this place and have no notion what will become of us all unless we get some money from you soon.[42]

He is not responsible for his own life, it is up to Pinker to rescue him, he cannot be blamed for the scrapes into which he gets himself. . . . And so on. As so often, this approach worked: money from Pinker reached him via the American ambassador in Vienna. In early October the Conrads left Zakopane and were driven to Cracow where they arrived on 9 October. They then travelled to Vienna, capital of an enemy country, where Conrad was laid up with gout and they stayed for four days while Jessie Conrad recovered two of their trunks which had been lost on the way from Berlin to Cracow on their outward journey. Najder remarks of Jessie's success with the trunks: 'thus a citizen of a hostile country was given back her luggage, lost several weeks before and a good few hundred miles away.'[43] It is indeed astonishing that the amenities to be expected by grand tourists travelling in style were still available to the Conrads on enemy soil in the third month of the Great War. Conrad's fame helped: the American ambassador to Vienna was courteous and hospitable, and on 18 October the Conrads left for Milan – Italy was a neutral country – and in early November they arrived back in London by boat from Genoa.[44]

What had begun as a private visit had ended as a kind of diplomatic mission in which Conrad sought to arouse sympathy in England for Poland's struggle for independence. In Poland the Poles' optimism had been infectious: back in England he became depressed and pessimistic about the future of Poland because British foreign policy seemed obstinately indifferent to Poland. Russia was Britain's ally and the British did not intend to 'offend the Eastern ally' and regarded Poland's future and her possible self-government as 'Russia's internal affair'.[45] It is against the background of English indifference to Poland that Conrad wrote his fatalistic account of the Polish visit in 'Poland Revisited'.

I call the account 'fatalistic' because its tone suggests that everything Conrad is writing about belongs to a heroic and lost past. He says that the Poles regarded the onset of war with despair: 'A whole people seeing the culmination of its misfortunes in a final catastrophe, unable to trust any one, to appeal to any one, to look for help from any quarter; deprived of all hope and even of its last illusions, and unable . . . to take refuge in stoical acceptance'.[46] We have seen that this was not true – in reality his Polish friends and contacts were optimistic about the outcome of the war – but the myth suits Conrad's mood in 1915, and his valedictory tone tells us that Poland is to be thought of as romantic and doomed: he describes how on his first night in Cracow he took Borys into the market square where 'to our right the unequal massive towers of St Mary's Church soared aloft into the ethereal radiance of the air' (p. 166) and how this brought him back to the day, when he was eleven, on which he led his father's funeral procession through the Florian Gate and out to the cemetery, where his fellow mourners 'were victims alike of an unrelenting destiny which cut them off from every path of merit and glory' (p. 169). Tragedy is to be the tone. The piece is in part an apology: from the perspective of 1915 the trip to Poland in 1914 looked Quixotic and foolish – hence his joky references to overcoming his fear of going there, and his remark that they took the long voyage across the North Sea at the insistence of Jessie (referred to as 'that one of my companions whose wishes are law'[47]), plus his emphasis on the most intelligible reason for going in 1914 – that his two sons should see Poland when they were still at an impressionable age. What his essay does bring out, though, is the inconsequential view of preparations for war that he and his family took:

> The first days of the third week in July, while the telegraph wires hummed with the words of enormous import which were to fill blue books, yellow books, white books, and to arouse the wonder of mankind, passed for us in light-hearted preparations for the journey. What was it but just a rush through Germany, to get across as quickly as possible?[48]

The dramatic point of the essay is demonstrated by its evocation of the English coast in its final paragraph. The Polish child who could not mourn the death of his father and was described by the housekeeper as 'the most callous little wretch on earth' (p. 169) has become the patriotic Englishman; the agony of the funeral in the 'old town of glorious tombs and tragic memories' with at centre stage 'the small boy of that day following a hearse' (p. 169) gives way to his view of the Downs, reminding him of his career as an English sailor: 'The Downs! There they were, thick with the memories of my sea-life' (p. 173). And this is followed by a question about the Great War which is rooted in his new English as against his old Polish identity: 'What were to me now the futilities of an individual past?' Jessie – eternally loyal and uncomprehending Jessie Conrad – will help him to cope with the uncertain future of an Englishman at war. As the ship turns into the mouth of the Thames he hears 'a deep, yet faint, concussion': the distant explosion of a shell in Flanders. This makes an excellent point of closure for the essay on Poland: the emigrant from one troubled country finds that his adopted country is in trouble and needs his loyalty, that fund of fidelity of which, as he tells us in the familiar preface to *A Personal Record*, he has always had his share. From now on he will be more dependent on Jessie, less on his friends:

> Turning instinctively to look at my boys, I happened to meet my wife's eyes. She also had felt profoundly, coming from far away across the grey distances of the sea, the faint boom of the big guns at work on the coast of Flanders – shaping the future (p. 173).

Englishness, not Polishness, will fortify him for the ordeal to come.

10

The Shadow-Line, 1915–1917

'Why! Hang it! You *are the right man for that job'*

The Shadow-Line, p. 31

There can be no possible objection to your recognizing the autobiographical character of that piece of writing – let us call it. It is so much so that I shrink from calling it a Tale. If you will notice I call it A Confession *on the title page. For, from a certain point of view, it is that – and essentially as sincere as any confession can be. The more perfectly so, perhaps, because its object is not the usual one of self-revelation. My object was to show all the others and the situation through the medium of my own emotions. The most heavily tried (because the most self-conscious), the least 'worthy' perhaps, there was no other way in which I could render justice to all these souls 'worthy of my undying regard'.*

Perhaps you won't find it presumption if, after 22 years of work, I may say that I have not been very well understood. I have been called a writer of the sea, of the tropics, a descriptive writer, a romantic writer – and also a realist. But as a matter of fact all my concern has been with the 'ideal' value of things, events and people. That and nothing else.

Letter to Sir Sidney Colvin, 18 March 1917[1]

The first half of 1915 was a restricted and depressed time for Conrad, his mood not greatly lifted by the publication of *Victory* by Doubleday in America on 27 March and the subsequent spectacular sales: 11,000 copies sold in the first three days (as he wrote to Colvin on 28 September of that year).[2] Depression is the dominant mood, as he wrote to Galsworthy: 'I am wretched and coughing dismally. Gouty bronchitis I suppose. Still I am trying to write – I don't know what and I don't know what for – really. The very sunlight seems sinister'.[3] The subject of *The Shadow-Line*, under the title 'First Command', had been with him for many years and was now to occupy him for much of 1915, though progress on this new project was slow because of depression and the competing demands of *The Rescue*, that perennially lingering and blighting project. The estrangement from Ford underwent some softening: Ford sent a presentation copy of his master-piece, *The Good Soldier*, on 18 March, and on 12 August Conrad agreed to act as literary executor for Ford when he enlisted in the army. Perhaps his feelings for his former friend were stirred somewhat by his immediate anxiety over Borys: Borys retook the entrance examination for Sheffield University in June 1915 and passed, but on 3 August chose to enlist. Within two months he was a Lieutenant. On 23 September 1915 Conrad wrote a touching letter to Galsworthy describing how he said goodbye to the newly fledged young officer (not yet eighteen) and then went home and tidied up Borys's room, putting away some of the treasures (including post-cards from Ada, Galsworthy's wife) which reminded him of Borys's childhood:

> 23. ix. 15. Capel House
>
> Borys got his commission last week. He had but a couple of days to complete his list, then a quiet Sunday with his parents and his devoted brother and left home last Monday to join the Mech: Transport Depot of the A.S.C. at Grove Park. I went with him in our extremely old, shabby, disreputable Ford as far as Bromley, within two miles of the camp, whence I caught a 'local' to London and so home. I wanted to be with him as long as possible on the day he had to put his boyhood definitely behind him. He dropped me opposite Bromley Rd. Station, I saw him wriggle between a bus and a van and then I hobbled across the road feeling more old than I have ever felt before. But I have never seen the boy look so happy his $17\frac{1}{2}$ years of life. . . . This is a long screed about Mons' B [Borys] but you are I believe his oldest friend. Putting away the things he left at home I have discovered, preserved most carefully among 'his papers', all the p-crds dear Ada wrote to him when he had scarlet-fever in London just about 10 years ago. I am always a little gouty, wrist or foot. Jessie's only fairly well. John goes about wretched and perfectly insupportable ever since his brother left. The dog either makes dashes upstairs to B's room or else mopes in a corner of the housekeeper's room. This naturally irritates John who want's [sic] him to come out and hunt the last butterflies (They never catch them).
>
> Our dear love to you both,
> Yours ever, J. Conrad.[4]

Fear for Borys's safety was to form a dark background to the Conrads' lives for the duration of the war, and it contributed to the shaping of *The Shadow-Line*, which is dedicated to Borys and was finished in December 1915 shortly before Borys came home for his first leave. In 1916 Borys was given dangerous duties, running munitions convoys under cover of darkness, and displayed considerable courage: Conrad wrote to Galsworthy on 19 March 1916 about Borys's 'cheerful boyish letters in the same tone as his 'Worcester' [training ship] correspondence. We send him a tuck-box now and again. It's as if he were still at school. . . .'[5]

We have seen that Conrad's ambitions in the theatre had been somewhat dashed by his disappointment with the three performances of *One Day More* in 1905. They were revived early in January 1916 by an approach from Basil Macdonald Hastings, who sought to dramatize *Victory*. At first Conrad was not enthusiastic, but when Hastings produced a draft of a proposed adaptation he felt that it had financial possibilities and as the year unfolds we can see him becoming personally interested in the project. The process of getting *Victory* onto the stage took a long time (it was eventually taken on by the great actor-director Henry Irving, and performed at the Globe Theatre in 1919, where it ran from 26 March to 14 June). Involvement with the theatre offered welcome distraction from the isolated business of writing fiction – an isolation exacerbated by the war. Conrad and Macdonald Hastings met Henry Irving at the Garrick Club in August 1916 and he was giving Hastings his help and advice on the adaptation for the rest of the year. It was finished in December. Early in 1917 Conrad involved himself in the casting of the play, and signed a contract with Irving on 3 May 1917. There is no doubt that this venture stimulated Conrad to think about writing other plays. In August 1916 he wrote to Pinker saying that Hastings

> asks for assistance. Very well. One can talk to him anyhow and I may learn a few things on this occasion. . . . I intend to make my profit in the way of knowledge this time and get into close contact with the stage. Who knows?. . . . You will admit I have some faculty of dialogue . . . the bulk [of my work] *is* dramatic. And if I can only learn to adapt my faculty for dialogue and drama to the conditions of the stage, then . . . I am not ossified yet. I am still impressionable and can adapt my mind to various forms of thought – and, perhaps, of art.[6]

Other theatrical schemes were considered: early in 1917 Conrad was thinking of dramatizing *Under Western Eyes* and of collaborating with Hastings on an original play. These plans came to nothing, but after the war he was to dramatize *The Secret Agent* and 'Because of the Dollars' (as *Laughing Anne*[7]). In 1916 Conrad needed distractions: illness, depression, misery over his writing and anxiety about the war dogged him and he was upset, too, by the terminal illness of Arthur Marwood, who died on 13 May (Conrad was not well enough to go the funeral). Henry James had died earlier in the year (28 February) but that did not affect Conrad at the emotional level: his and James's mutual admiration had been sincere but the personal relationship was never close, and the professional warmth had been damaged by James's adverse remarks about *Chance*.

Shaping the future is the subject of *The Shadow-Line*, and a preoccupation of Conrad's throughout the war years. It is normal for literary people to take an interest in the morally questionable.[8] In his greatest fictions Conrad consistently displays such interest: the guilt of such figures as Kurtz, Jim, Nostromo, Verloc, Leggatt and Razumov is the subject of extended meditation. Many changes overtake his later fiction. One of these changes involves a change in dramatic focus: in *Chance* and *Victory* the morally questionable figure is no longer centre stage. Anthony, Flora and Heyst are all complex and divided figures, but their problems are emotional rather than moral: they may feel guilty, but they do not need to – they cannot be convicted of wrong-doing in the way that Jim or Razumov can. The corollary – of course – is that in these books the wicked (the governess, de Barral, Schomberg, Jones) look a bit flat when compared with the guilty heroes of the earlier works. Part of the interest of *The Shadow-Line* is that guilt – though in this case guilt by association, the young skipper's sense of association with the dead skipper who sold the ship's quinine – returns in the protagonist.

The Shadow-Line is based on Conrad's first and only command – of the *Otago* in 1888 – and because of this is sometimes seen as closely autobiographical. Andrzej Wajda's film of *The Shadow-Line* casts the skipper as the young Conrad (admirably played by an extremely well-cast Polish actor who memorized his English phonetically for the film) and has him equipped with Korzeniowski and Bobrowski family photographs. The young Pole in the film encounters the xenophobia that Conrad himself certainly encountered, in reality, in the British merchant marine. But to see the novella thus is to misread it. The bones of the plot are taken from Conrad's experiences in early 1888 when he sailed from Bangkok – the source is used also, as we have seen, for 'The Secret Sharer'[9] and for 'Falk' – but the skipper in *The Shadow-Line* is English. He is given a consciously upperclass English manner in his early dialogue with the hostile Mr Burns, where he asks 'in a *dégagé* cheerful tone: "I suppose she can travel – what?"' (chapter 3, p. 55). His problem (like that of the skipper in 'The Secret Sharer') is not foreignness but inexperience.

The first two chapters of *The Shadow-Line* are a comic red herring – the business with Hamilton, Captain Giles, the Chief Steward of the Officer's Sailors' Home and Captain Ellis, the Master Attendant, has no bearing at all on the story of the young skipper's struggle with the calm, the malaria and cholera, his predecessor's villainy, the sceptical first mate and the heroic cook with the weak heart – but they heighten the reader's expectation. The story really gets going in chapter 3 where the young skipper, intoxicated and awed by his first command, sits in his cabin and listens to the imagined voices of the skippers who have preceded him 'as if a sort of composite soul, the soul of command, had whispered suddenly to mine'. The composite soul says 'you, too, shall taste of that peace and that unrest in a searching intimacy with your own self' (p. 53). The phrasing takes us back to the first of Conrad's great sea novels because it recalls the famous opening of chapter 4 of *The Nigger of the 'Narcissus'* ('On men reprieved by its disdainful mercy, the immortal sea confers in its justice the full privilege of desired unrest'). Here in *The Shadow-Line* Conrad writes of the effect of the sea not on the whole crew but on this single young man, experiencing himself as king as he looks in the mirror of the Captain's cabin: 'I stared back at myself with the perfect detachment of distance, rather with curiosity than with any other feeling, except of some sympathy for this latest representative of what for all intents and purposes was a dynasty' (p. 53).

In a letter to Richard Curle, 14 July 1923, Conrad complained that Curle's account of him restated a cliché: 'I was in hopes that on a general survey it could . . . be made an opportunity for me to get freed from that infernal tail of ships. . . . I may have been a seaman, but I am a writer of prose. . . . The nature of my writing runs the risk of being obscured by the nature of my material.'[10] In this somewhat peevish letter Conrad continues: 'Of course, there are seamen in a good many of my books. That doesn't make them sea stories, any more than the existence of de Barral in *Chance* (and he occupies as much space as Captain Anthony) makes that novel a story about the financial world. I do wish that all those ships of mine were given a rest'.[11] And yet *The Shadow-Line* ensures that they will not be 'given a rest' since it seems to close an outer ring of narratives, starting with 'Youth' and *The Nigger of the 'Narcissus'* and continuing with a number of minor stories and major ones such as 'Falk' and 'The Secret Sharer'. It restates many of the central preoccupations of the earliest fictions of liminality. Conrad writes to Henry S. Canby, Literary Editor of the New York *Evening Post*, 7 April 1924, in similar terms (Canby had written an article on the publication in the USA of the 'Limited Edition' of Conrad's work):

> Surely those stories of mine where the sea enters can be looked at from another angle. In the *Nigger* I give the psychology of a group of men and render certain aspects of nature. But the problem that faces them is not a problem of the sea, it is merely a problem that has arisen on board a ship where the conditions of complete isolation from all land entanglements make it stand out with a particular force and colouring.[12]

This aspect of his reputation was preoccupying and annoying Conrad in his last years. Which does not mean that those who saw him as supreme master of the sea-story were wrong. *The Shadow-Line*, like much of Conrad's best writing, is about work. The skipper, Burns, Ransome, Captain Giles, the Steward, Ellis the Harbour Master and the others are men whose energies are channelled and defined by the nature of their employment and whose personalities are being carved by the fact of work, which is experienced both as constraint and as liberation. In Part One of the narrative the young skipper is experiencing the odd imprisoning lassitude of freedom; he has given up his previous ship and is idling in the sailor's home. He has done so partly because of a fit of existential despair which we are free in retrospect to link to Conrad's own experience of depression: 'The whole [conversation] strengthened in me that obscure feeling of life being but a waste of days, which, half-unconsciously, had driven me out of a comfortable berth, away from men I liked, to flee from the menace of emptiness . . . and to find inanity at the first turn' (pp. 22–23).

'Freedom' – in the sense of leisure, that idleness and pursuit of pleasure which filled many of the young Korzeniowski's days and nights – has brought him not self-determination and a sense of purpose but further despair. Once Captain Giles's oblique remarks have been decoded as the heralding of the offer of a command (a slight weakness of the narrative is that the reader decodes this long before the protagonist does) the young man's despair vanished. He is supremely – naively – happy in the new identity conferred on him by his command and by the sensation of being a 'king' who is set apart from his crew, 'as remote from the people and as inscrutable almost to them as the Grace of God' (chapter 3, p. 62). It is employment which gives him both this reinforced sense of identity and the vexation he experiences when calm and illness block the ship's progress. The skipper reacts to this in commercial, business terms: 'A mankind which has invented the proverb, "Time is money," will understand my vexation. The word "Delay" entered the secret chamber of my brain' (chapter 3, pp. 65–6). Stress on this word helps to account for the novella's odd shape: the fact that two out of its six chapters elapse before we get onto the ship. Delay for the reader – a kind of agonizingly protracted reading foreplay – enacts the postponement of action which is a central feature of the story's plot.

In all work situations a new person in a position of authority needs to learn management skills, and there will be a period of 'storming', of attempts to buck the new man's authority, before the group settles down and starts to function properly. The captain of a merchant ship in the nineteenth century had a great deal of power, and displays of insubordination and hostility, even from his officers, did not need to be experienced as major threats. Part of Conrad's frustration in his own experience as sailor was that of having to obey skippers who were far less intelligent and cultivated than himself, and who had absolute power: hence the pathos of 'Command is a strong magic' in *The Shadow-Line* (chapter 1, p. 29). It was a magic which Conrad himself, as we have seen, had tasted only once. Still, at the start of chapter 3 of *The Shadow-Line*, where the readerly 'delay' is rewarded and the story proper at last gets going, the young skipper's first experience of the need to exercise management skills – his dialogue with Burns – is daunting. The narcissistic relishing of status – the moment of silent communing with his own image in the captain's stateroom – is ruptured and challenged by the intrusion of Mr Burns. The scene that follows is a beautifully understated power-struggle, a competitive stand-off of two fragile male egos. The chief mate has been looking at and 'appraising' (itself a term loaded with competitiveness and aggression) the young skipper. The feeling is reminiscent of that most primitive of male competitive situations, the boys' public school, in which the new boy is scrutinized to see whether he can be upset and bullied. The discomfort that the young skipper attributes at first to his own 'inexperience' and the disadvantage of 'youth' (which is 'a fine thing, a mighty power – as long as one does not think of it', chapter 3, p. 55) is in fact the product of a real threat: Burns' bitter resentment, rooted in the fact that he himself expected to gain command of the ship. Like Iago, Burns is an ambitious older man who has been passed over for promotion by a young man but unlike Iago he is too stupid and innocent to be dangerous. It is a mark of his stupidity that after the death of the old skipper he had sailed into Bangkok rather than Singapore in the belief that no suitable skipper would be found in Bangkok and that he himself would get the appointment, but this clumsy guile fails to pay off: he has overlooked the fact that Singapore can easily be contacted by telegraph. The young skipper finally wins this battle because Mr Burns lacks 'discretion' – the quality constantly praised in *Lord Jim* – and cannot protect himself from bursting out with the fact that he would leave the ship rather than serve under the young skipper if it weren't for his family. This gives the skipper the opportunity to administer a direct rebuke ('I shall expect you to attend to your duty', chapter 3, p. 64) and establish his authority. This formal closure of the scene is preceded by Burns' important narrative presenting the old skipper. The old skipper looks a bit like a parody of *The Ancient Mariner*, which is present here as in 'The Secret Sharer'.[13] Burns shows the skipper a photograph of the former skipper and his mistress. The old man, aged sixty-five, is 'bald, squat, grey, bristly, recalling a wild boar somehow' and his mistress, 'a professional sorceress from the slums' has a musical instrument, 'guitar or mandoline' in her hand (chapter 3, p. 59). Here I feel that Coleridge's other great supernatural poem *Kubla Khan* is being parodied: the damsel with a dulcimer who brings inspiration to the blocked poet becomes this mature, rapacious woman with a mandoline who brings solace to the mad old man whose only other companion is his violin. *The Ancient Mariner* and *Kubla Khan* converge later in the narrative. Specific features from *The Ancient Mariner* include 'inconceivable terror' and 'inexpressible mystery', absolute immobility, a sense that the sea has become 'solid', the terror of an 'unearthly substance' replacing the air (chapter 5, p. 108), the 'eerie, disturbing' moment at which wind disturbs the topmasts while failing to move the ship (chapter 5, p. 116) and this: 'I moved forward too, outside the circle of light, into the darkness that stood in front of me like a wall. In one stride I penetrated it. Such must have been the darkness before creation' (chapter 6, pp. 112–13). The 'one stride' and the supernatural darkness seem to be echoes of these two lines from *The Ancient Mariner*:

> The sun's rim dips: the stars rush out:
> At one stride comes the dark.

General alignment with features of *The Ancient Mariner* is found, of course, in the whole of the novella's plot: especially in the sense that the ship suffers a supernatural curse, that it is crewed by dead men (and is thus a ship of life in death) and that the curse is lifted more or less arbitrarily. A binary system suggests itself. It is possible to read Coleridge's poem as a nightmare or as a Christian allegory. The same is true of Conrad's novella. As nightmare it is dominated by Burns and his interpretation of the ship's plight: the old skipper's malevolent ghost is cursing the ship and needs to exorcised before the ship can reach harbour. The young skipper at times goes along with this reading, and adds to it a strong hint of Coleridge's light and dark spirits accompanying the ship: 'By the exorcising virtue of Mr Burns' awful laugh, the malicious spectre had been laid, the evil spell broken, the curse removed. We were now in the hands of a kind and energetic Providence' (chapter 6, p. 125).

As Christian allegory *The Shadow-Line* becomes a story in which the immature man, the skipper, is rescued by a Christ-like figure whose name indicates that he is a type. Ransome, the consummate seaman with the weak heart, is the true hero of the novella, the only man (other than the Captain himself) not affected by the illness which decimates the crew. Ransome is clearly perceived as a romantic hero (the stereotype is that of the strong man in pain): 'He sat upright on the locker in front of the stove, with his head leaning back against the bulkhead. His eyes were closed; his capable hands held open the front of his thin cotton shirt baring tragically his powerful chest, which heaved in painful and laboured gasps' (chapter 6, p. 122).

It has been pointed out by Allan Ingram that *Hamlet* as well as *The Ancient Mariner* underlies *The Shadow-Line*.[14] The hero suffers from despair, guilt, worthlessness and desire to do away with himself, and the play ponders the mysteries of destiny, honour and stoicism. There are many echoes of *Hamlet* in Conrad's text. 'Well, it was an impulse of some sort; an effect of that force somewhere within our lives which shapes them this way or that' (chapter 1, p. 25) echoes *Hamlet*, V. ii, 'There's a divinity that shapes our ends,/ Rough-hew them how we will' and 'This stale, unprofitable world of my discontent' echoes *Hamlet*, I, ii, 'How weary, stale, flat, and unprofitable/ Seem to me all the uses of this world!'.[15] Where the skipper speaks of having thrown off the 'mortal coil of shore affairs' (chapter 4, p. 73) he refers to the 'To be, or not to be' speech: 'For in that sleep of death what dreams may come,/ When we have shuffled off this mortal coil,/ Must give us pause' (III, i). We have seen that *Hamlet*'s meditation on suicide is a central text for Conrad: it gives Stein his key quotation in chapter 20 of *Lord Jim*, the pivotal chapter of that work.[16]

Much of the readerly experience is that the story delays, but after this meditative passage in which the young skipper contemplates his own destiny in Shakespearian terms the story introduces, in chapter 4, its counter- or sub-plot. With his crew sick the young skipper depends wholly on quinine to cure them; he goes confidently to the medicine cupboard for fresh supplies and makes the appalling discovery that the former captain has sold most of the ship's supply of quinine and put sugar and salt in the bottles. The reverse of 'delay' takes place here. This discovery is thrown at the reader with disconcerting speed, as though the disaster is too distressing for its communication to call on the resources of art: 'Why record all the swift steps of the appalling discovery. You have guessed the truth already. There was the wrapper, the bottle, and the white powder inside, some sort of powder! But it wasn't quinine' (chapter 4, pp. 88–9). This is,

of course, 'art'. The protracted narrative is balanced here by preternaturally swift narrative, abrupt foreshortening and closure of expectation.

The former skipper was insane and wicked, and the first mate is jealous
and difficult. Norman Sherry's work has shown that *The Shadow-Line* departs from its sources in crucial respects: Captain John Snadden, who had
commanded the *Otago* before Conrad, was a good Captain and a loving
husband and father and was on good terms with Born, his first mate. He
had a weak heart and died stoically at sea, having dictated a last letter
to his family (which survives in Born's handwriting[17]). In some superficial
respects he resembled the former skipper in *The Shadow-Line*: a photograph of him reproduced in Sherry's book show that he did indeed look
as though he were in his sixties, though he was in fact fifty when he died
(he was born in 1837) and the description in *The Shadow-Line* of him as
bald, squat, grey, bristly and recalling a wild boar could have been based
on this photograph: Snadden was bald and had somewhat wild eyes and
ferocious-looking beard. He also played the violin (though he didn't throw
it overboard: it was returned with his belongings after his death) and he
was buried at sea.[18] The photograph found by Burns in the skipper's cabin
in *The Shadow-Line* resembles the photograph found in the skipper's violin
case in 'Falk', where the predecessor looks slightly different: less bald but
still boarlike and accompanied by a woman who is not respectable.[19] There
seems no doubt that Conrad did in fact see such a photograph of Snadden
in 1888, a photograph of roughly the same date as the photograph found
by Sherry.

In the light of Sherry's discoveries about Snadden it seems to me that
Conrad had done what he often did, that is to say he has split his source
figure into opposing parts. He invents a mad, wicked side to his predecessor to accompany the illness and delay that dogged the *Otago* and he draws
on the same man's stoicism, seamanship and weak heart for the personality of Ransome. And, human nature being what it is, he has altered the
facts so that they reflect better on his own role than the reality did. John
Snadden was a good skipper, and to follow him invited comparisons: in
The Shadow-Line the dead skipper was mad and wicked, so that comparisons are bound to be favourable. Charles Born, first mate of the *Otago*, was
a warm-hearted, not very educated man, judging from the surviving part
of his letter of condolence to John Snadden's widow.[20] The portrait of Mr
Burns in *The Shadow-Line* plays up the lack of education and sophistication to make him naively superstitious and riddled with anxieties about
status, and nasty to boot.

In his letters Conrad described *The Shadow-Line* as exact autobiography,
and its subtitle is 'A Confession'. The effect of work by Sherry and others
is to push *The Shadow-Line* into the world of fiction. But I want now to
redress the balance and to note that *The Shadow-Line* is closer to lived
experience than Conrad's other works, and that Conrad himself wrote
and spoke about it as though it were autobiography: in other words, we
need to regard it as a work set somewhat apart from the other narratives

based on the *Otago* command ('Falk', 'The Secret Sharer' and 'The End of the Tether') and to think of it instead as another of those semi-fictional works in which Conrad radically recreates the past in the act of recalling it: it thus joins a group which includes *The Mirror of the Sea* and *A Personal Record*. Najder has said that *Victory* is somewhat apart, artistically, from Conrad's other works.[21] I think a change has come over his writing which is not confined to *Victory* or to any other one work. It seems to me that what we have in Conrad's career – and we can see it clearly from the vantage point of *The Shadow-Line* – is a series of concentric arcs, like concentric rainbows. The outer and largest of these arcs runs from the earliest work, *Almayer's Folly, An Outcast of the Islands, The Nigger of the 'Narcissus'* and 'Youth' to *Victory* and *The Shadow-Line*. These are works, to put it crudely, in which we know who is the good guy. An inner arc has more moral relativity (*Heart of Darkness, Lord Jim, Chance*) and the inmost arc consists of the great political works and a major novella (*Nostromo, The Secret Agent, Under Western Eyes*, 'The Secret Sharer'). As a work of fiction *The Shadow-Line* belongs with my outer arc, but it also, as I have said, belongs with the autobiographies. Conrad himself thought of it as autobiography, as is clearly indicated in the letter of 18 March 1917 (to Sir Sidney Colvin) that I have quoted as epigraph to this chapter, where he calls the book a sincere confession; in his earlier letter of 27 February 1917 to Colvin; and in his letter to Pinker of early 1917, where he says that *The Shadow-Line* is 'not a story really but exact autobiography'.[22] The 27 February letter to Colvin indicates that *The Shadow-Line* came directly out of the declaration of war in 1914. The Conrads had returned from their Polish visit. Conrad felt impelled to write something but felt that it was wrong to write fiction in wartime. So he writes this record, with 'experience . . . transposed into spiritual terms – in art a perfectly legitimate thing to do, as long as one preserves the exact truth enshrined therein'.[23] This brings us back to the preoccupation of the *Preface* to *The Nigger of the 'Narcissus'*, the requirement that the artist shall communicate 'truth' to his reader. 'Truth', as the *Preface* to *The Nigger of the 'Narcissus'* understands it, is the beginning and the end of this arc.

The 'lived experience' of *The Shadow-Line* has its own arc, which is shaped by Captain Ellis. Ellis is the only figure in *The Shadow-Line* whose name is not altered at all. Burns, Snadden and others have been 'spiritualized' but Captain Henry Ellis appears with his name and identity exactly as he was in life. He was the Master-Attendant at Singapore who gave Conrad his command of the *Otago* in 1888. As Captain Whalley's friend in 'The End of the Tether' and in *Lord Jim* he had appeared as 'Captain Ellot', but since he had died in 1908 Conrad probably felt free to use him without any kind of disguise. His reputation was that of a dominant personality, normally goodnatured and generous but conscious of his own power and capable of ferocious bad temper. As a young seaman Conrad was obviously forced to feel Ellis's power and this is felt in the satirical description of him as a 'Deputy-Neptune'. Power is the real subject of *The Shadow-Line*.

The young skipper is possessed of power by the time the story closes, and it is sealed, in a way, by the fact that once he has got his crippled ship into port he wants to report to Ellis, as though to a father figure, but learns that the old man has retired and gone home 'about three weeks after I left the port. So I suppose that my appointment was the last act, outside the daily routine, of his official life' (chapter 6, p. 130).

I have quoted as the epigraph to this chapter the letter to Colvin in which Conrad said that *The Shadow-Line* is a confession, as 'sincere as any confession can be. The more perfectly so, perhaps, because its object is not the usual one of self-revelation. My object was to show all the others and the situation through the medium of my own emotions'. I dwell on this because I think that Jacques Berthoud is right to say of this: 'His aim was not self-disclosure, but committed perception. Such autobiography cannot be called "subjective", for it does not project a preestablished self; nor can it be called "objective", for it does not seek to reproduce a ready-made world. The exactness is fidelity to an existential apprehension of the world.'[24]

Berthoud is right to suggest, I think, that the whole of *The Shadow-Line* is an oblique commentary on the Great War. It displays many of the same preoccupations as his declared works of art – what Berthoud calls 'a conception of life as . . . that which resists our illusions'[25] – but it is different in its point of origin, as we are told by the Author's Note: 'Before the supreme trial of a whole generation I had an acute consciousness of the minute and insignificant character of my own obscure experience' (p. xxxviii). His reaction to his son Borys going off to be a soldier was to do something which begins as egoistic self-assertion but becomes generosity: he competes with his son by writing about a test of action in his own young life, and then makes this into a testimony to his son's courage by saying that this experience is universal. Being part of his humanity it is part also of Borys's and of that of all the other young men.

The Shadow-Line is both competitive and self-deprecating: competitive in that Conrad matches his courage against his son's, self-deprecating in that its comedy and callowness register Conrad's consciousness of the 'enormous difference' that his 'single drop' of courage is 'measured against the bitter and stormy immensity of an ocean [of the war]' (pp. xxxviii–xxxix). This is where the supernatural business associated with Mr Burns comes into play. Conrad was vexed by the obtuseness of readers who focused on the supernatural comedy at the expense of the rest of the tale, but the supernatural is there – Conrad put it there – and there is more of it in the manuscript of the story. There is, for example, the young skipper's dream about the Bull of Bashan – a dream associated with fear of Burns – which is present in the Beinecke manuscript and was cut from the final state. This is a crude and striking piece of writing. I quote part of it:

> I dreamt of the Bull of Bashan. He was roaring beyond all reason on his side of a very high fence striking it with his forehoof and also rattling his [??horn]

horns against it from time to time. On my side of the fence my purpose was (in my dream) to lead a contemplative existence. I despised the brute, but gradually a fear woke up in me – that he would end by breaking through – not through the fence – through my purpose. A horrible fear.[26]

Presumably Conrad cut this and other passages because he was struck by precisely the feature of his story that I am referring to here: there is too much supernatural comedy. As he says in the Author's Note 'The Shadow-Line' as title has a ghost-story feel to it, and if he had called it 'First Command' readers would not have thought it a supernatural tale. The supernatural element is, I have said, *comic* and is part of the characterization of the superstitious and naive Burns. As Conrad said in a letter to his friend Helen Sanderson, 1917,

> I never either meant or 'felt' the supernatural aspect of the story while writing it. It came out somehow and my readers pointed it out to me. I must tell you that it is a piece of as strict autobiography as the form allowed, – I mean, the need of slight dramatization to make the thing actual. Very slight. For the rest, not a fact or sensation is 'invented.' What did worry me in reality was not the 'supernatural' character, but the *fact* of Mr Burns's craziness.[27]

Insofar as the young skipper feels terror of the supernatural he is displaying his immaturity: when he gets his ship safely into port the immaturity is overcome. The journey from immaturity to maturity is stressed in the Author's Note: 'Primarily the aim of this piece of writing was the presentation of certain facts which certainly were associated with the change from youth, care-free and fervent, to the more self-conscious and more poignant period of maturer life' (p. xxxviii). He releases the younger self from immaturity. But he also celebrates immaturity and envies the immaturity of his son: he is very conscious of the ageing process, he knows that he is of little use in this war. He did some reconaissance work at the invitation of the admiralty late in 1916 and his most exciting experiences were a flight in a hydroplane in September and a twelve day trip aboard the H.M.S. *Ready* in November.[28] The most poignant, in his word, moment of *The Shadow-Line* is that in which he laments the loss of his own youth, 'a fine thing, a mighty power' (chapter 3, p. 55). The artistic heart of *The Shadow-Line* is here, where Conrad, ageing and ill, narcissistically contemplates his own youthful self-image, notes its innocence and mourns its loss.

The Shadow-Line is a major work, and it enhanced Conrad's reputation. Sales of *Chance* and *Victory* had been excellent, and the tendency among reviewers now was to see Conrad as the outstanding senior novelist of his generation. Historical simplification tends to see 1917 as a hey-day of modernism, but in terms of the novel the benchmarks were still provided by James, Meredith and Hardy; the great modernist novelists, Joyce, Lawrence and Woolf, had all published but they had yet to make any impact. A review by Clement Shorter in *The Sphere* is representative:

A new book by Mr Joseph Conrad is a literary event to many of us, and so it has been for nearly a quarter of a century. Since Mr George Meredith died and Mr Thomas Hardy ceased to write novels no novelist other than Mr Conrad has appeared who has been able to give me that particular thrill – the thrill which came to an earlier generation as each of the novels of Dickens and Thackeray came from their publishers. And it was gratifying to find that with his eighteenth book, *Victory,* Mr Conrad became not only one of the favourite novelists of the elect but one of the favourite novelists of the many.[29]

After the writing of *The Shadow-Line* this favourite novelist of the many found himself increasingly preoccupied with, and depressed by, the war. In March 1917 the revolution in Russia gave a new perspective to the war. Temperamentally Conrad was opposed to revolution. Russia was one of England's allies against the Germans, and Conrad felt that the revolution would weaken the chance of victory. Also he worried about the prospect of a blood-bath in Russia, especially with regard to its possible impact on his birth-place, the Ukraine, his 'foster-brother' (the son of the wet-nurse who suckled him when he was a baby) and his fellow-gentry. On 18 May 1917, he wrote to Hugh Walpole:

> I feel startled when I remember that my foster-brother is an Ukranian [sic] peasant. He is probably alive yet. What does he think? I am afraid that what he thinks bodes no good to the boys and girls with whom I used to play and to their children. Are those gracious Shades of my memory to turn into blood-stained Spectres? *C'est possible, vous savez.* And those houses where, under a soul-crushing oppression, so much noble idealism, chivalrous traditions, the sanity and the amenities of Western civilization were so valiantly pre-served, – are they to vanish into smoke? *Cela aussi est très possible.*[30]

The English press was enthusiastic about the Russian revolution. Conrad felt that this was naïve: he found himself asked 'to join in public ecstasies of joy' but 'begged to be excused'.[31] In fact, though, the revolution had given cause for moderate rejoicing among Poles in that on 30 March 1917 the Russian Provisional Government which succeeded acknowledged Poland's right to independence. In an earlier letter (to Christopher Sandeman) Conrad had noted this but had taken a sceptical view of it: 'The Russian proclamation is very fine but – 2/3 of the Polish territory (on the basis of the 1772 frontier) are in German hands. And peace will have to come soon' (3 April 1917).[32]

Conrad's feelings about the progress of the war and the fate of Poland were bound up with his feelings about himself and his writing. The letters of this sixty-year old world-famous novelist often seem to combine the attention getting antics of a child with the lamentations of hypochondriac. To Garnett, in May 1917, he writes: 'I am like you, my dear fellow; broken up – and broken in two – disconnected. Impossible to start myself going, impossible to concentrate to any good purpose. It is the war – perhaps?

Or the end of Conrad, simply? I suppose one must end someday, some-how. Mere decency requires it.'[33]

Conrad felt secure with disciples: younger men whose hero-worship was assured, and with whom he felt free to express his – often violent – emotions in ways that would have embarrassed him with his contemporaries. Hugh Walpole, recipient of the letter about Conrad's Ukrainian foster-brother, wrote an adulatory study of Conrad (published 1918) and was an adored favourite of the older man. In May, 1918, while Conrad was writing *Chance*, Walpole found him: 'A child, nervous, excitable, affectionate, confidential, doesn't give you the idea anywhere of a strong man, but *real* genius that is absolutely *sui generis*' and again 'like a child about his various diseases, groaning and even crying aloud'.[34] The portraits of Conrad made in his last years – especially Epstein's sculpture, showing a cadaverously intellectual head, and the painting by Walter Tittle in the National Portrait Gallery, which shows an old sea-dog who has become an exhausted sage – are balanced by Hugh Walpole's warm and friendly account which is of a charming, volatile and emotional personality, displaying the insecurity, vulnerability and dependence of a child.

11

The Arrow of Gold, The Rescue, The Rover and *Suspense,* 1917–1924

She never even raised her eyes, giving me the opportunity to contemplate mutely that adolescent, delicately masculine head, so mysteriously feminine in the power of instant seduction, so infinitely suave in its firm design, almost childlike in the freshness of detail: altogether ravishing in the inspired strength of the modelling.

The Arrow of Gold, p. 288.

It may seem unkind to quote this puzzlingly protean account of Rita's head (adolescent, masculine, feminine and childlike – and, of course, 'suave') from *The Arrow of Gold*: presumably Conrad was tired and in-attentive when he dictated it. Much of *The Arrow of Gold* was taken from dictation, and I take it that some of the novel's worst features – boring dialogue, magniloquent but empty description and flagging action – can be blamed on that procedure. Conrad himself knew in the process of writing that *The Arrow of Gold* was meagre stuff: to the Sandersons, 31 December 1917, he wrote that it had 'no colour, no relief, no tonality; the thinnest possible squeaky bubble',[1] and to Galsworthy – in a letter of 8 August 1919, folded inside a presentation copy of the novel – he acknow-ledged that he was less happy about this than about any of his previous works: 'Never before was the act of publication so distasteful to me as on this occasion. Not that I shrink from what may be said. I can form a pretty good guess as to what will be said'.[2] (An odd feature of that last remark is that some of what 'may be said' had already been said: Conrad had read several somewhat adverse notices of *The Arrow of Gold* in the newspapers on the previous day[3]). So why did Conrad write it? Artistically disastrous though it is, Edward Said is probably right to say that *The Arrow of Gold* was written from the same kind of motivation as that very different work, *The Shadow-Line*. These were his 'plain narratives of fact' and his job in them was: 'To discipline himself to writing according to a fixed and acceptable sense of his own distant past. By analogy, it was the kind of sense that modern sailors might develop if they could undergo training aboard a sailing vessel.'[4]

Conrad's experiences of late 1916 had served to show him how physically frail he was. *The Shadow-Line* allowed him to compensate for this frailty imaginatively by revisiting the first major professional responsibility of his young manhood, and *The Arrow of Gold* enabled him to go even further back in his life, to the late adolescent Polish *flâneur* encountering his first sexual adventures in Marseille in the 1870s. The difference between the two works, though, is that the former is based on real memory, the latter on willed fiction. Like many of his novels it was initially conceived as a short story (called 'The Laugh'), and – again, like many of his works – it was conceived as a conscious formal experiment. It was to be an epistolary novel, 'selected passages from letters' between Rita and M. George. The notion of an epistolary novel survives in a rudimentary form in the first two pages of *The Arrow of Gold* which quotes from letters between Rita and M. George. He wrote the first ninety-four pages out in long-hand. The rest he dictated:[5] a procedure that he had not used before for a novel (though he had for *The Mirror of the Sea* and *A Personal Record*). He wrote fast. A letter to S. A. Everitt, Doubleday's publicity agent, in February 1918 indicates that it was conceived somewhat in the spirit of *Romance* – that's to say, a commercial historical novel about the adventures of Don Carlos's mistress – and that Conrad did not yet envisage it as having autobiographical interest. The novel still had no title:

Lots of titles pass through my head (in my idle moments – which are few) but not one of them gives me the exact feeling of rightness. If it had been a book in French I believe I would have called it *L'Amie du Roi*, but as in English (The Friend of the King) the gender is not indicated by the termination, I can't very well do that. People would think perhaps of a friend with a great beard and that would be a great mistake. The title of *The Goatherd*, which would have been possible too, is open to the same objection. They would be both a little misleading, because the connection of the story both with goats and kings is very slender. *Two Sisters* would be a title much more closely related to the facts, but I don't like it. It's too precise and also too commonplace. On the other hand, *Mme de Lastaola* is foreign in appearance, besides looking pretentious. *The Heiress*, which is closest to the facts, would be the most misleading of all; and it is also very unimaginative and stupid. We must wait for the title to come by itself.

As you see, the above are all connected with a woman. And indeed the novel may best described as the Study of a Woman who might have been a very brilliant phenomenon but has remained obscure, playing her little part in the Carlist war of '75–6 and then going as completely out of the very special world which knew her as though she had returned in despair to the goats of her childhood in some lonely valley on the south slope of the Pyrenees. The book, however, is but slightly concerned with her public (so to speak) activity, which was really of a secret nature. What it deals with is her private life: her sense of her own position, her sentiments and her fears. It is really an episode, related dramatically and in the detailed manner of a

study, in that particular life. That it is also an episode in the general experience of the young narrator (the book is written in the first person) serves
only to round it off and give it completeness as a novel.[6]

A woman centred novel: thus, of course, a *seller* as *Chance* had been; also,
risqué in the manner of Flaubert and Maupassant, so that a sophisticated
French-sounding title might be appropriate (but for the beard); a historical romance about a Basque peasant girl who makes good, and thus a
Cinderella-shaped romance with a strong flavour of *La Bohéme* or *Trilby*,
inviting a popular audience; a novel which could compete for the market
of Arnold Bennett's novels, such as *Anna of the Five Towns* and *The Old Wives'
Tale*, but which needs to avoid prosaic Arnold Bennett-type titles (such as
Two Sisters or *The Heiress*); a novel where the emphasis is on the erotically
charged female protagonist, not on the narrator.[7]

Conrad does not seem, then, to have envisaged *The Arrow of Gold* as an
autobiographical work from the beginning: the notion that he was recreating his younger self in the 1870s grew as the novel grew. But as he
rejected *The Heiress* and *Two Sisters* as titles he must have remembered his
early abandoned work (to be published posthumously as *The Sisters*) which
dealt partly with the same subject, the charms of two Basque sisters acting
on the sensibilities of a rootless young European painter. That work is
clearly autobiographical and it must have become obvious to Conrad quite
soon in the writing that this novel could be a vehicle for an account of his
own emotional awakening, however elaborately disguised. Once the book
was published Conrad referred to is as though it was as close to autobiography as *The Shadow-Line*. In the Author's Note to *The Arrow of Gold*,
for example, he wrote that the story was one that he had been 'carrying
about' with him 'for many years', and that it is a private memory about
which he feels shy, a 'product of my private garden'. He says that the story
of M. George and Dominic Cervoni gun-running for the Carlists is true,
as the story of Cervoni and the *Tremolino* in *The Mirror of the Sea* were true
(it seems certain that they are fictions). The most truthful – in absolute
terms – remark in the author's note is this: 'What the story of the *Tremolino*
in its anecdotic character has in common with the story of "The Arrow of
Gold" is the quality of initiation (through an ordeal which required some
resolution to face) into the life of passion.' In *The Arrow of Gold* Conrad
is indeed telling a story about his own emotional initiation, but as far as
the facts are concerned he is not recreating that story but inventing it.

In *The Mirror of the Sea* and *The Arrow of Gold* Conrad sets out a version
of the events of 1877 to 1878 in Marseille which goes roughly as follows:
as one of a syndicate of four and in the company of Dominic Cervoni
(whom he had met on board the *Saint-Antoine* in 1876) and his 'nephew'
César Cervoni he was engaged to smuggle guns from Marseille to Spain
in support of the Carlist pretender to the Spanish throne. This venture
was organized by Rita de Lastaola, with whom Conrad fell in love. He
fought a duel over her and was wounded through the chest in March

1878. It seems clear that Conrad was using *The Mirror of the Sea* and *The Arrow of Gold* to lie to himself about a period of immature silliness and failure which culminated in the dishonourable act of shooting himself through the chest in Marseille in 1878. The 'duel' version of this story was put about by Conrad and endorsed by Uncle Bobrowski. Obviously, as we have seen, it was felt to be more honourable for a Polish gentleman to have been involved in a duel than to have attempted suicide.

In *The Arrow of Gold* 'M. George' (one of the names by which Conrad had been known in Marseille – and an acknowledgement in fiction, incidentally, of Conrad's non-English identity) fights his duel with Captain John Blunt. John Young Mason Key Blunt was a real historical figure, an American from the South (and thus recently defeated in the Civil War) who fought in the Carlist war; his mother, Mrs Ellen Key Blunt, who also appears in the novel, was also a real historical figure. It is not clear that Conrad had any first-hand knowledge of the Blunts, though he could well have heard of them in Marseille in 1878.[8] Rita de Lastaola, a former goat-girl and subsequently an artist's model who had been a mistress of the Carlist pretender to the Spanish throne, seems to be wholly a fiction, although the existence of the fragment called *The Sisters* may indicate that Conrad knew a pair of Basque sisters and was attracted to one of them in Marseille in the 1870s.

The Sisters, written in 1895, consists of seven chapters, four describing a Ukrainian artist, called Stephen, travelling in Europe, and then three presenting the Basque sisters, Rita and Teresa (not Thérèse, as in *The Arrow of Gold*) and the Ortegas. In the fragment there is no meeting between Stephen and the sisters (though some such encounter would presumably take place) and nothing at all – as Najder points out – to support Ford Madox Ford's guess (in his introduction to the 1924 edition) that the plot turned on an incestuous relationship. Najder makes the intriguing point that *The Sisters* translates successfully into Polish, and that this is partly because it contains many Polish literary tricks and mannerisms which contribute, paradoxically, to its failure in English.[9] Conrad often abandoned novels to take them up again and finish them later (*The Rescue* and *Chance* are cases in point). Unless one regards *The Arrow of Gold* as a rewriting of it – and the texts are so remote from each other that that seems untenable – then *The Sisters* is the only instance of a work being abandoned entirely.

The early pages of *The Arrow of Gold* recover some of the attraction of Conrad's earliest narratives, especially the opening paragraphs of 'Youth'. M. George, the narrator, represents himself as one who has lived 'a rough, a very rough life' and is going back to an almost irrecoverable state of mind, that of virginal – indeed, possibly literally virgin – late adolescence, 'that part of my life in which I did not know a woman. These are like the last hours of a previous existence' (p. 13). Greek myth is invoked to suggest the primal flavour of this experience: M. George (being a sailor) is christened 'Young Ulysses' by his boisterous friends (just as a sculptor in the group is dubbed 'Prax', short for Praxiteles). Good looking Captain

Blunt, a dark, elegant hero who 'lives by his sword', with mobile black eyes, reduces M. George to breathless hero-worship, and many of the earlier scenes with Mills and Blunt are saved from tedium by the freshness of M. George's responses to these experienced men as they talk about Rita: 'A woman is always an interesting subject and I was thoroughly awake to that interest' (p. 24), says M. George, and he swallows attentively the paternal advice that he gets from Mills: 'Young man, beware of women with small mouths. Beware of the others, too, of course; but a small mouth is a fatal sign' (p. 25). Sadly, *The Arrow of Gold* rapidly becomes tedious: the gun-smuggling with Dominic Cervoni is given far too little space, and the betrayal of the smuggling is given obliquely and confusingly. Indeed the whole novel is structured on a tiresome principle which Conrad has probably got from Ford's less interesting novels: action is to be given in very spare outline while reflection is given at tedious length. The Conrad who could play out the scene in which Nostromo and Decoud get the lighter of silver across the Golfo Placido over several chapters of *Nostromo*, has M. George and Dominic ambushed, betrayed and abandoning the Carlist cause in a couple of pages, and the culminating betrayal is indicated in retrospect:

> At last came the day when everything slipped out of my grasp. The little vessel, broken and gone like the only toy of a lonely child, the sea itself, which had swallowed it, throwing me on shore after a shipwreck that instead of a fair fight left in me the memory of a suicide. It took away all that there was in me of independent life, but just failed to take me out of the world, which looked then indeed like Another World fit for no one else but unrepentant sinners. Even Dominic failed me, his moral entity destroyed by what to him was a most tragic ending of our common enterprise (p. 256).

The comparison with *Nostromo* can be taken further, since Dominique [sic] Cervoni was a source for Nostromo and Conrad himself was, as we have seen, probably a source for Martin Decoud, the Costaguanero of the Boulevards and *flâneur*, who thus comes to resemble that other French-speaking self-portrait, M. George. In *Nostromo* Conrad displays carefully and at length the moral disintegration of Nostromo, while this novel abandons showing for telling: Dominic's 'moral entity' is 'destroyed' and he 'failed'.

M. George's sexual feeling for Rita is displayed in terms which suggest that the novelist actually hates and resents what he is dramatizing: 'Her image presided at every council, at every conflict of my mind, and dominated every faculty of my senses . . . She enveloped me with passing whiffs of warmth and perfume, with filmy touches of the hair on my face' (p. 274). As though the sexual reality of this woman is too horrible to contemplate, the young narrator seems desperately to fetishize her:

> Man is a strange animal. I didn't care what I said. All I wanted was to keep her in her pose, excited and still, sitting up with her hair loose, softly

glowing, the dark brown fur making a wonderful contrast with the white lace on her breast. All I was thinking of was that she was adorable and too lovely for words! I cared for nothing but that sublimely aesthetic impression. It summed up all life, all joy, all poetry! (p. 304).

Jeffrey Meyers believes that an American journalist called Jane Anderson became Conrad's mistress in 1916–17 and that the portrait of Rita in *The Arrow of Gold* celebrates Conrad's sexual fulfilment with Jane.[10] There are several objections to this simple view of the matter. Jane Anderson was a pushy adventuress who forced herself on the Conrads and to whom Conrad and Jessie were kind and hospitable, but it seems unlikely that Conrad would have wanted a sexual relationship with such a person – he was fastidious and socially discriminating, and by this stage of his life very loyal to Jessie – and, further, it seems very likely indeed that his sex drive was low; he was nearly sixty, and he had been suffering from depression for many years. Also, Conrad had little opportunity for illicit sex: Jessie was vigilant. Jane Anderson certainly set her cap at Conrad: enough to upset Jessie and cause her to regard Jane as spiteful and deceitful.[11] It is possible that Jane Anderson was also attracted to *Borys* Conrad, and the opportunity existed for a brief affair (in Paris) with Borys. If this did happen then Conrad can be seen to have facilitated it, in that he wrote to Borys preparing him for a visit from Jane Anderson, who went to Paris in the summer of 1917 and spent about a week there.[12] One can, therefore, go along with Meyers to the extent of saying that Conrad may have been putting into *The Arrow of Gold* some of the feelings stirred in him by the sexual impact of Jane Anderson on the Conrad household.[13] The descriptions of Rita would seem to be inadvertently hostile accounts of a woman who smothers, neuters, immobilizes and dominates the young male whom she attracts. This portrait doesn't ring true as the product of an ageing man's delighted fulfilment with a young mistress, but it could well reflect a father's mixed feelings about the effect that an experienced woman is having on his son.

I suggested earlier that Conrad's career can be seen as three concentric arcs, the outer arc linking the later works to the earliest works. *The Arrow of Gold, The Rescue, The Rover* and *Suspense* go back to Conrad's early life, resurrect his early writings (*The Arrow of Gold* returns to the two women of *The Sisters*, 1895, and *The Rescue* began as 'The Rescuer', 1896–8) and make use of the interest in the Napoleonic period which had been with Conrad since his honeymoon but which he had not hitherto used extensively in works of fiction.

Conrad felt guilty about the relationship between his later and his earlier work. The anxiety, the sense of underachievement, the need – even at this stage of his life – to counter Pinker's charge of laziness and desultoriness, are felt in the defensive author's note to *The Rescue*:

Those of my readers who take an interest in artistic perplexities will understand me best when I point out that I dropped *The Rescue* not to give myself up to idleness, regrets, or dreaming, but to begin *The Nigger of the 'Narcissus'* and to go on with it without hesitation and without a pause. A comparison of any page of *The Rescue* with any page of *The Nigger* will furnish an ocular demonstration of the nature and the inward meaning of this first crisis of my writing life. For it was a crisis undoubtedly. The laying aside of a work so far advanced was a very awful decision to take. It was wrung from me by a sudden conviction that *there* only was the road of salvation, the clear way out for an uneasy conscience. The finishing of *The Nigger* brought to my troubled mind the comforting sense of an accomplished task, and the first consciousness of a certain sort of mastery which could accomplish something with the aid of propitious stars (p. ix).

He goes on to say that when *The Nigger of the 'Narcissus'* was finished he did not return immediately to *The Rescue* because 'Youth', which was 'on the tip of my pen', could not wait, nor could *Heart of Darkness*. What he does *not* refer to is the glaring fact that *The Rescue* lacks conviction, motivation and narrative energy: in short that he put it on one side for the excellent reason that it is not very good.

The reviewers tended to be generous: Conrad was after all by this time very grand. But Virginia Woolf in the *Times Literary Supplement*, 1 July 1920, saw that *The Rescue* was a played-out and repetitious work, an unconvincing exercise in an earlier manner. She delicately displays the limitations of Conrad's writing about love: to Mrs Travers 'Lingard appeared . . . as a revelation not only of manhood, but of life itself,' but the reader is not interested: 'Mr Conrad has attempted a romantic theme and in the middle his belief in romance has failed him.' Edward Garnett, in a much kinder review in the *Nation*, 17 July 1920, says, accurately, that 'It is perhaps chiefly as an interlude in the life of men that Mr Conrad is interested in women. He does not love them as he loves his heroes'.[14] In general, reviewers of all Conrad's late works tended to play safe. Conrad had become world famous since 1914 and was universally regarded as the leading active living novelist in England (Hardy having 'retired'). But P. C. Kennedy in the *New Statesman*, 26 September 1925, writes that Conrad's later work read as though 'by a student and admirer of the Conrad manner [rather] than by the great man himself. He never wrote without distinction, without a certain loftiness and exactness; but it must be admitted that he was sometimes dull.' And Leonard Woolf, always an independent and judicious reader, says of *Suspense* that it is as empty as a hollow walnut[15] (he is reversing, perhaps consciously, the narrator's remark about the nature of seamen's stories at the beginning of *Heart of Darkness*).

So what are the merits of *The Rescue*? A characteristic that it has in common with many of Conrad's novels (including *The Arrow of Gold*) is that it begins extremely well. Conrad has not lost the gift for setting scenes which was at its best with the opening paragraph of *Nostromo* and is still very much in evidence at the beginning of *The Rescue*: both of the introduction, where we are told that 'The shallow sea that foams and murmurs on the shores of the thousand islands, big and little, which make up the

Malay Archipelago has been for centuries the scene of adventurous under-takings' (p. 3), and of the first chapter where we are shown a seascape comparable with *Nostromo*'s account of the Golfo Placido:

> Out of the level blue of a shallow sea Carimata raises a lofty barrenness of grey and yellow tints, the drab eminence of its arid heights. Separated by a narrow strip of water, Suroeton, to the west, shows a curved and ridged outline resembling the backbone of a stooping giant. And to the eastward a troop of insignificant islets stand effaced, indistinct, with vague features that seem to melt into the gathering shadows (p. 5).

The splendour, the strangeness and the conscious exoticism are all familiar to us from the earliest Conrad. *The Rescue* is the third item in a reverse trilogy, giving us the story of a younger Lingard than the figure who appears in *Almayer's Folly* and *An Outcast of the Islands*. Daphna Erdinast-Vulcan sees the three novels as charting in reversed sequence a myth of decline: in *Almayer's Folly* Lingard is 'a memory of past greatness and for-feited hopes', while *An Outcast of the Islands* gives us the beginning of his decline and the collapse of his trading empire, and *The Rescue* 'an attempt to go back to the glorious beginning' of Lingard's career, so that the writing is 'a project of recovery, an attempt to redeem the present by the power of the past'.[16] This reinforces my sense of Conrad's late works completing an outer arc and going back to his literary and personal beginnings in search of renewal as he faces old age.

In *The Rescue* Lingard is caught up in a plot which involves tension between two cultures: that of his native England, where he is 'working class by contrast with the Travers', stranded on their yacht, and that of his adopted Malay Archipelago, where he is on equal footing with a prince and princess, Hassim and Immada, whom he is trying to help in a struggle to recover their lands. The novel proceeds confidently as long as it is estab-lishing Lingard's personality and his relationship with the Malays and the ruined Norwegian, Jorgensen. The title of the first part, 'The Man and his Brig', tells us that Conrad is on sure footing. As the chapter titles become more mannered ('The Point of Honour and the Point of Passion', 'The Claim of Life and the Toll of Death') so the dramatization becomes less secure. Conrad does not believe in the personality of Mrs Travers, nor in her passion for Lingard, and once this erotic connection has been set up as a feature of the action the plot begins to creak, and creaks more and more woodenly to the end. As a heroine Mrs Travers is a hopeless confec-tion, but as a symptomatic figure of the decadence she occasionally rings true: the bored wealthy woman on her yacht displaying an epicure's pleasure in the sound of men quarrelling is quite well observed: 'Don't stop them. Oh! This is truth – this is anger – something real at last' (part 3, chapter 3, p. 132).

The latter part of *The Rescue* becomes angular and unreal because Conrad is forcing Lingard to act against the grain. Ostensibly he is in love with

Edith Travers, the woman to whom he confides his innermost soul. But the first chapters make it clear, most movingly and eloquently, that Lingard has no loves beyond his little ship the *Lightning*:

> To him she was as full of life as the great world. He felt her live in every motion, in every roll, in every sway of her tapering masts, of those masts whose painted trucks move forever, to a seaman's eye, against the clouds or against the stars. To him she was always precious – like old love; always desirable – like a strange woman; always tender – like a mother; always faithful – like the favourite daughter of a man's heart (part 1, chapter 1, p. 10).

The ship is his mistress and his kingdom. The other two Lingard novels make it clear that his temperament is one of genial self-possession and innocent love of power and patronage: sexual love is not hinted at as he binds Almayer and Willems to himself, and what he badly needs in *The Rescue* is another delinquent young man to patronize. What he gets instead is a woman who is notionally 'irresistible' but comes across as a frigid and demanding hysteric. Jeffrey Meyers remarks that the title is ironic because the plot reverses itself: the rescuer of a victim (Hassim, the young Malay prince whom Lingard has promised to restore as ruler of his country) himself becomes the victim of the woman he rescues.[17] The mutual attraction of Lingard and Mrs Travers is displayed in writing which collapses into leaden absurdity. Conrad has no faith at all in what he is doing: Lingard declares to Mrs Travers that he is 'Providence'. We are then given Mrs Travers as seen by Lingard, 'this vision, so amazing that it seemed to have strayed into his existence from beyond the limits of the inconceivable' (p. 214) followed on the next page by Lingard as seen by Mrs Travers: 'The glamour of a lawless life stretched over him like the sky over the sea down on all sides to an unbroken horizon. Within, he moved very lonely, dangerous and romantic. There was in him crime, sacrifice, tenderness, devotion, and the madness of a fixed idea' (p. 215). The most interesting of these features ('the madness of a fixed idea') is a near-quotation from the characterization of Charles Gould in *Nostromo*, of whom his wife says: 'A man haunted by a fixed idea is insane' (III, chapter 4, p. 379).

Biographically, an important point about the finishing of *The Rescue* was that it returned to, and in a sense 'completed', one of his earliest friendships, that with Edward Garnett.[18] Edward Garnett had of course been a major prop for Conrad's confidence at the beginning of his career, and had acted as literary midwife for *Almayer's Folly, An Outcast of the Islands* and *The Nigger of the 'Narcissus'*. Conrad had not sent his manuscripts to Garnett on a regular basis since *Lord Jim* and it seems likely that he was hurt by Garnett's adverse criticism of the latter part of that novel. Conrad had formed closer and more flattering literary friendships with younger men, and he and Garnett differed sharply over their attitudes to Russia at the time of the publication of *Under Western Eyes*. But Conrad had continued to send Garnett his books and with *The Arrow of Gold* resumed his earlier practice of asking Garnett to read his novels in manuscript. As he resumed work on *The Rescue,* and submitted it to Garnett to read, so the friendship with Garnett strengthened again. Maybe both parties felt some remorse over having allowed the friendship to lapse. There is certainly remorse on Conrad's side: in a letter of 27 October 1917 he remarks that it is so long since the Conrads saw David Garnett that the boy will have forgotten them, and in another letter written over a year later (22 December 1918) Conrad says: 'I missed you immensely my dear old friend during all these days. The resumption of our intercourse has been very precious to me. It was a great and comforting experience to have your ever trusted and uncompromising soul come forward again from the unforgotten past and look closely at my work with the old, old, wonderful insight, with un-impaired wisdom and in unalterable friendship.'

Throughout the war Conrad had expected that Borys would be killed and had felt that writing was a kind of mechanical and second-rate activity compared with soldiering. And yet he had written fast. It is characteristic of depressives that they find that their condition lifts in wartime and in countries which are perpetually at war, such as Northern Ireland, the depression and suicide rates are low. The end of the great war had brought anticlimax and a sense of unreality which is reflected in Conrad's letter of 22 December. He remarks that although it is the first Christmas of peace-time it 'doesn't feel so festive as one expected it to be. A cloud of unreality hangs about men, events, discourses, purposes. The very relief from long-drawn anguish is touched with mistrust as it were if not a delusion then at least a snare'.[19] The war had given him the best and the worst of his late works – *The Shadow-Line* and *The Arrow of Gold* – and with the end of the war he is revisiting an old dramatic theme (Lingard's kindness to displaced persons) and the previous great European conflict. The Great War stirs Conrad's imagination to go back a hundred years to the Napoleonic war, and he writes *The Rover* and *Suspense.*

These two works conform to what we can now see as a pattern. *Lord Jim* was a major work accompanied by a great novella, *Heart of Darkness; Under Western Eyes* was a major work interrupted for the writing of another outstanding short narrative, 'The Secret Sharer', and *Suspense,* the enorm-ously ambitious and incomplete final novel, was interrupted for the writing of *The Rover. The Rover* has freshness, narrative energy and grace, and it dramatizes two early and favourite themes: the contrast between ship-societies and land-societies and the nature of friendship between men. The last of these is treated lyrically in the relationship of Peyrol and Symons, the 'Brothers of the Coast', one French and the other English, who now (1810) find themselves notionally at war. Peyrol has struck the Englishman on the head and then recognizes him as a 'Brother of the Coast' from twenty years earlier, when Peyrol was thirty-eight and Symons was twenty. Peyrol tenderly takes the wounded head of the younger man on his knee and bandages it in a scene which is unworried by its homoeroticism. Peyrol carefully reads Symons's face: 'A face of brown clay, roughly modelled, with a lot of black eyelashes stuck on the closed lids and looking artificially youthful on that physiognomy forty years old or more. And Peyrol thought of his youth' (chapter 9, p. 125). A great virtue of this novel is that it does not shrink from clear – indeed obvious – expression to communicate the emotional lives of its characters. Symons escapes from Peyrol's tartane and the English ship comes back to find him – 'the ship was calling to her man' (chapter 12, p. 191) – and Peyrol's feelings for the younger man are feminine and tender: 'No nurse could have watched with more anxiety the adventure of a little boy than Peyrol the progress of his former prisoner' (chapter 12, p. 199). The plot now moves in symmetrically planned counterpoint: as Peyrol and Symons part, Réal and Arlette come together, united under the light of the moon. This could be inert cliché, but it isn't. Conrad has recovered the virtues of transparent narrative and can often write, in *The Rover*, with the freshness and directness of 'Youth' and *The Nigger of the 'Narcissus'*. The lovers have names which give them an allegorical status, contributing to the feeling that mythical romantic archetypes are being recreated here: Arlette is thus named because her mother was an Arlesienne, Eugene Réal's name translates as 'well-born and royal'.

The politics of *The Rover* are expressed in these names. Conrad has always been conservative in his dramatization of heroism. In earlier works such as *Chance* the conservatism was overlaid by complexity. Here it is un-embarrassed. Scevola Bron, the sans-culotte who supported the revolution which took the lives of the gentry – including Arlette's and Réal's parents – is a straightforward embodiment of spite and evil, and of nationalism in its nastiest forms. Scevola, imprisoned by Peyrol on his little ship, his tartane, believes that Peyrol is selling out to the English:

'I believe you are one of those wretches corrupted by English gold,' he cried like one inspired. His shining eyes, his red cheeks, testified to the fire of patriotism burning in his breast, and he used that conventional phrase of revolutionary time, a time when, intoxicated with oratory, he used to run about dealing death to traitors of both sexes and all ages (chapter 15, p. 243).

In reality, of course, Peyrol is planning a supreme patriotic sacrifice. He saves Réal's life by deception: Real believes that it is his mission to take out false dispatches which will be intercepted by the English fleet and will confound their strategy. Peyrol has determined to take the dispatches himself, leaving Réal ashore (Réal thus finds his true destiny, marriage to Arlette and the life of a farmer on the Escampobar farm). National loyalty is subordinated to brotherhood and solidarity, as it was in the earliest works. The bond that Peyrol feels with the Brotherhood of the Coast is stronger, as we have seen, than his sense of himself as a Frenchman. Much of Conrad's personal history is reflected here. Like Réal, he was the son of betrayed gentry. Like Peyrol, he is fond of the English but never feels fully one of them. And he is refreshing himself by recovering the energies and allegiances of his sea-going years.

As it moves rapidly towards its conclusion *The Rover* gains in dramatic simplicity. As Peyrol takes out the tartane on its final mission the writing becomes energized. The deaths of Peyrol, his companion the fisherman Michel and of Scevola – two from heroism, one from scheming – are well-paced, and Conrad enjoys the touch of gallantry with which the English, the crew of the *Amelia*, fly the French flag on the *Amelia* before sinking her with the three corpses still aboard. As Captain Vincent says, 'After all they never surrendered and, by heavens, gentlemen, we will let them go down with their colours flying' (chapter 16, p. 280). Peyrol, a fine old seaman who has given up his life for his country, is paired dramatically with the British admiral Lord Nelson, who says to Captain Vincent 'I am like that white-headed man [Peyrol] you admire so much . . . I will stick to my task till perhaps some shot from the enemy puts an end to everything' (chapter 16, pp. 275–6). France was Poland's ally (and of course the first of Conrad's adopted countries after his departure from Poland, England being the second). It is appropriate that this, the last of Conrad's completed fictions, should end in mutual admiration between the French and the British. Captain Vincent admires French courage, seamanship and shipbuilding, while detesting 'their political principles and the characters of their public men' (chapter 16, p. 275), an opinion coinciding very closely with Conrad's own. The French – Peyrol and Réal – admire Nelson's cunning, and the friendliness, courage and staying-power of the British. Peyrol says in one of his dialogues with Réal: 'Don't you know what an Englishman is? One day easy and casual, next day ready to pounce on you like a tiger. Hard in the morning, careless in the afternoon, and only reliable in a fight, whether with or against you' (chapter 8, p. 110).

The Rover is in many ways a summing up. It reiterates many dramatic patterns from the earlier works. The ship as a model for political debate is from *The Nigger of the 'Narcissus'*, the older man cherishing the younger from *Almayer's Folly*, *An Outcast of the Islands* and *Lord Jim*, the evil intruder disrupting paradise from *Lord Jim* and *Victory*, the rough man of action undertaking a decisively heroic mission from *Nostromo* (like Nostromo, Peyrol is drawn from Conrad's memories of Dominique Cervoni), an older seaman surrendering his life so that the younger gets the girl from Captain Anthony's behaviour in *Chance*. Another pattern (again from *Chance*) is the older woman impeding the younger – the interaction between Catherine and Arlette is a milder form of that between the governess and Flora. *The Rover*'s use of these patterns is simpler, of course, than in the earlier works. The political model is suffused by the mutual gallantry of the French and the English (Peyrol saves the lives of two younger men, Symons and Réal, one an 'enemy' the other a comrade in arms), the evil intruder – Scevola, who has forced himself on Escampobar and Arlette's saviour – is powerless once the revolution has been succeeded by Napoleon, and the older woman – Catherine, Arlette's aunt – is against marriage because of her own doomed love for a priest, but she repents (she somewhat resembles Dickens's Miss Havisham). Hostile critics of *The Rover* could see it as a tired and oversimplified reworking of older materials. I do not find this. For me Conrad is revisiting, with directness and pace, a central conviction, that action has a redemptive function in men's lives.

Such a belief is peculiarly apt for a depressive. In old age Conrad continued to suffer from depression. He now had a great deal of money but he spent it more quickly than it came in, as though compensating himself for the many years of hardship and claiming by force his status in England as a gentleman. The last and largest of his houses, to which he moved in 1919 – Oswalds, at Bishopsbourne near Canterbury – became the setting for prodigal hospitality. The tradition of lavish hospitality is Polish, and confirmed his sense of himself as a Polish gentleman. It is also characteristic of depressives to reassure themselves of their own worth by experiencing the power of money in spending sprees. While *The Rover* is the work of a man recovering his younger self, *Suspense* is very much the work of a depressive. *Suspense*, the huge fragment of the historical novel that Conrad had been planning for many years, is Conrad's least-read work. It is set in 1815, on the eve of Napoleon's invasion from Elba, and has to do with a group of his sympathisers in Genoa. Like *The Rover* it displays rightwing politics and a simple division between good and evil. The wicked figure in *Suspense*, Count Helion de Montevesso, is quite interestingly developed (and resembles George Eliot's and Henry James's matrimonial sadists, Grandcourt in *Daniel Deronda* and Osmond in *Portrait of a Lady*). He is a parvenu who has made good during the revolution and married Adèle, the daughter of one of France's best families, who accepts him in desperation and with the open declaration that she does not love him. Montevesso devotes himself to bullying and humiliating her into submission. Her childhood friend, the Englishman Cosmo Latham, is greatly attracted to her and as the fragment breaks off it is obvious that in due course Montevesso will get his come-uppance and Cosmo will get the girl. The fragment closes with Cosmo smuggling messages to Elba in a scene reminiscent of Decoud and Nostromo smuggling the silver out of Costaguano (the Nostromo figure in *Suspense* is another Italian, Attilio, the last of Conrad's embodiments of Dominique Cervoni). The novel complements the satellite novella: the title of the *The Rover* tells us that the novel is about action while the title of *Suspense* tells us that this will be a a study of failure to act, of sexual and political frustration, of conspiracy and delay. If he had finished it it would have been Conrad's biggest political novel, and a study of a theme as important to him as that of *Under Western Eyes* had been, since Napoleon was the hero and hope of the Poles, who always believed that France and Poland, the two biggest Catholic countries in Europe, had linked destinies and that Napoleon would liberate Poland from the Russians and reunite it.

Conrad was materially well off after 1914. For the last ten years of

Conrad's life there is a striking contrast between his personal circumstances – living in comfortable seclusion in the Kentish countryside, fussing obsessively about his health and his diet and being pampered by wife and servants – and external events, which included the European war, the Russian revolution and the establishment of the Polish republic under Pilsudski (chief of state 1918–22). From 1914 to 1919 the Conrads lived at Capel House, at Orlestone in Kent, a moated farmhouse surrounded by pleasant countryside where Conrad had for company his wife, servants, and his younger son, John. John Conrad, who became an architect by profession, has recorded these later family homes with great sensitivity and detail in his memoir.[20] From this younger son's account Capel House seems to have been a charming, not overgrand, family house where Conrad was happy with his immediate circle of family and friends: the friends included congenial neighbours like Maisie and Perceval Gibbon and Arthur Marwood, old friends like Galsworthy, Cunninghame Graham and Garnett and new, younger and more flattering friends like Richard Curle, Norman Douglas, Hugh Walpole and André Gide. Apart from Gide the new friends are clearly not Conrad's literary equals. His position was secure. If he had been part of literary London he might have been closer to the new generation of major writers whom we now identify with 'Modernism' – Yeats, Pound, Lawrence, Woolf and Joyce – but his security might have been somewhat shaken. With historical hindsight we can see Conrad as one of the founding fathers of Modernism, but that is not a view that he himself would have welcomed or understood.

John Conrad must have been a rather lonely little boy – his brother Borys was much older and was away at the war for many of these years – and the Conrads made some effort to find him company. For two or three years – partly to provide a friend for John – they gave a home to Robin Douglas, the son of Norman Douglas, traveller and novelist (author of *South Wind*, 1917). Douglas and Conrad had first met on Capri in 1905. Conrad helped Douglas by recommending his writing to British publishers and established contacts for him with the *English Review*, of which Douglas became assistant editor for a time. In 1915 Douglas was arrested for homosexual behaviour and had to leave England; this led to a cooling in the friendship with Conrad. Conrad's attitude to homosexuals is hard to fathom. He had several friends whose homosexuality was more or less common knowledge (Walpole, Gide and Sir Roger Casement as well as Douglas) but he does not seem to have been any more liberal than the average Edwardian gentleman would be expected to be – he dropped Douglas when his behaviour caused scandal and distanced himself when Casement was arrested for treason in 1916 and his homosexual diaries were used to inflame opinion against him and thus secure the death penalty. Douglas was a fairly shabby character and perhaps didn't deserve much sympathy. Casement, on the other hand, was a heroic figure. Conrad had greatly admired him when he first met him in the Congo in 1890, and was in touch with him again in 1903. One might have expected Conrad to sympathize with Casement's objectives: to an objective observer there are parallels between Casement's attempt to free Ireland from English tyranny and Apollo Korzeniowski's attempt to free Poland from Russian tyranny. But although Conrad described Casement as 'tragic' in a letter to John Quinn (24 May 1916), he refused to add his name to an appeal for clemency.[21]

The friends of his later life included a number of young male disciples. An anecdote from February 1918 is of biographical interest for the portrait that it gives of the mature Conrad seen through the eyes of a young admirer and for Conrad's judgement, quoted here, that *Nostromo* is the greatest of his own works (he is more often recorded awarding the highest honours to *Lord Jim*). The source of the anecdote is the writer and journalist Cecil Roberts, who was twenty-six at the time of this conversation. The scene is a London flat which Conrad had rented for the winter of 1917–18, not far from the nursing home in which Jessie Conrad was having tests and treatment for her damaged knee. The Conrads had invited Roberts to dinner with Edward Garnett. Garnett left early, Jessie went to bed and Conrad and Roberts were alone:

> Our talk had turned to the art of writing, and he questioned me closely upon my own experience regarding the speed of composition, the need of revision, the fluidity of ideas. He confessed he had never known the pleasure of writing, only the ardour that drove him to it, and that his progress was painful, a long wrestling with the spirit within. 'Perhaps that is because I began late, when experience checked the singleness of youthful thought. I have never been fluent. Easy writing – and I do not say it cannot be good writing – is not possible to me. My success seems in proportion to my effort, to my striving. I feel that generalship has brought me whatever victories I may claim – if any.'
>
> I watched his face as he pronounced the last two words, with a sadness, a quiet resignation that surprised me.
>
> 'If any?' I repeated, the surprise in my voice. He had risen and stood, one foot resting upon the fender, one hand adjusting the position of the black marble clock on the mantelpiece, his face looking into the fire.
>
> 'You may think I am childish, perhaps,' he said, very slowly and quietly, so that I seemed to overhear his thoughts, 'but I could be content if I could think something of mine, something however small, might endure a while. One has expressions of immortality – there are my boys – but one's writing is one's own immortality, if it can be achieved.'
>
> I expressed my surprise that he could doubt his own achievement. Could he not feel assured, I asked. Had he not realized that his recognition, no popular one in its beginning, was soundly based, that his work had an enduring quality by virtue not only of its singularity of treatment but also because it appealed neither through sensation nor cleverness?
>
> 'My dear young man – if I could think that . . .' he answered, and then, fixing his eyes steadily upon me as I sat there on the opposite side of the fireplace, 'In what book do you feel I have done this?'
>
> '*Nostromo* undoubtedly', I said, without hesitation.

Conrad takes a long time to reply to this and during his silence Roberts takes note of his appearance. This is an accurate (if somewhat adulatory) account of Conrad's appearance in later life: 'The fine tenuous hand, the long Slavonic head. His hair was straight and dark, with a greying trimmed beard and thin moustache. The droop of the lids over the eyes gave him an imperious expression, and the skin, lightly furrowed with lines that marked the impress of nervous tension and high sensibility, had a yellow tinge which is the legacy of those who have braved the tropic suns.' At length Conrad speaks:

'My poor *Nostromo* – you think that? . . . you shall know a secret, if it interests you, which I could not have told to you except for those words of yours. *Nostromo* is my best book, it is more Conrad than anything I have written, that is, in the sense that it embarks upon my greatest imaginative adventure, and that it involved the severest struggle. I stand by *Nostromo*, out of the frailty of flesh, hoping it may last a while for a memorial. And yet it did not succeed with the public. They will not have my poor *Nostromo*. They prefer *Lord Jim*.'[22]

It is refreshing to be reminded that the rather self-regarding figure of this anecdote was also a greatly loved family man. John Conrad's memoir, while it doesn't disguise his father's capacity for being difficult and auto-cratic, recalls him as affectionate, playful and good with children. He recalls at length his father's deep interest in his Meccano set (initially an avuncular gift from André Gide, much added to by Conrad):

As I became more proficient at building models some form of power was often needed so JC bought me various steam engines which between us we managed to adapt to drive the models. I use the word 'we' because he had a knack of spotting weakness in the design or arrangement of machinery and very often made suggestions for its improvement.[23]

A charming picture – the ageing, hugely distinguished artist and the little boy building Meccano together. Conrad was engagingly childlike: he could also be maddeningly child*ish*. John has good anecdotes about Conrad's unreasonable behaviour. When Conrad had toothache John had to ac-company him to the dentist's surgery in Ashford – Conrad couldn't bear to go to the dentist alone – and Conrad would walk up and down outside until after the time of his appointment and would then say 'we will go home now. It has stopped aching'[24] (neglect of his teeth was to cause him serious problems and would exacerbate his temper). John also recalls that a wasp stung Conrad on his bottom one late summer before the war. This produced 'quarter-deck' yells, swearing, a whole hot morning of querulous demands on Jessie to treat the wasp-sting with such homely remedies as raw onion and 'bluebag' (used in laundry) culminating in Conrad requiring Jessie to pile cushions on his chair at lunchtime. Conrad hobbled to the lunch-table on two sticks, John laughed, and Conrad then laughed with him: 'took the cushions and threw them into the corner of the room, remarking that he did not want all that "damned fuss" just because of a wasp sting. My mother was really put out'.[25] Life was often boring during the Great War. As John Conrad puts it: 'So the weeks and months passed by and my mother became more crippled with her damaged knee, my father writing, with occasional periods in bed with gout, and myself being more or less good and not getting into mischief too often'.[26]

From 1919 until his death Conrad lived at Oswalds, Bishopsbourne, near Canterbury. This was by far the grandest of the Conrad family homes, an opulent mansion nestling in a valley among woods, but the Conrads were never as happy there as they had been at Capel House (which had been reclaimed by its owner). John Conrad remarks that Oswald's was very much a 'residence' in contrast with the homely and friendly farmhouse that they had left.[27] Conrad was upset that it had no outlook and constantly complained about being stuck 'in a hole' and having no view, and at the time of his death in 1924 he was seeking to move house again. Conrad at Oswald's was regal: the day would begin with his manservant, Foote, waiting on him at breakfast, and he would then receive visitors and read the newspapers in his study until ten-thirty, he would then write letters and perhaps work on a book until the ceremony of luncheon (which usually included guests). Shopping outings in the chauffeur-driven car were equally regal: the managers of the shops in Canterbury of Ashford would be informed in advance of Conrad's approach and would be there in person to receive him. The grandeur of this seems somewhat stifling and dull: it is not surprising that Conrad was increasingly obsessional and querulous, and Jessie, according to John, now had so many servants that she had literally nothing to do and was very bored. Both of them were in poor health: although she outlived him for a good many years Jessie was nearly as fragile as Conrad. She was obese, subject to periodical major invasive surgery on her knees and in more or less constant pain.

The completion and serialization of *The Arrow of Gold* and the completion and serialization of *The Rescue* are the major literary events (patiently cherished and promoted by Pinker) in the two years following the war. Conrad attached great importance to *The Rescue*, the work which had been with him for so many years, and fervently hoped that it might win him the Nobel Prize for literature. There were other projects. Plans for the production of Macdonald Hastings' stage adaptation of *Victory* stimulated Conrad to write his own adaptation of *The Secret Agent*; we find him planning this early in 1919 and completing the first draft in 1920, showing it to friends in the professional theatre for their advice (it was performed in 1922[28]). *Victory* was staged at the Globe Theatre on 26 March 1919, and ran for eighty-two performances.[29] A collected edition of Conrad's work was planned by Doubleday, Conrad's American publisher, and plans for this were agreed early in 1919. In addition to his other work Conrad now had the hugely enjoyable task of re-reading his life's work in order to

write the 'Author's Notes' for this edition. For this task he had before him
the daunting example of Henry James's prefaces. It seems to me un-
controversial to say that James's prefaces are steeped in self-veneration:
that they are both indispensable works of literary intelligence and elaborate
displays of immodesty. By comparison with James's performances Conrad's
notes are relatively self-deprecating, guarded and oblique. Many of them
have a valedictory feeling: for example, the note to *Notes on Life and Letters*
(1921) where Conrad writes that he is consciously 'tidying up' in this
collection of miscellaneous papers, but that even now, when he has an
opportunity to be personal, he has no intention of giving himself away. In
neither of his memoirs, *The Mirror of the Sea* and *A Personal Record*, nor in
this late collection, is he going to relax what he calls in *Lord Jim* 'discretion'. The *Preface* to *The Nigger of the 'Narcissus'* had given a distant view of
the novelist as a peasant labouring in a field; this author's note gives
another vignette of the writer at work, this time as an elderly curator
putting things straight before he goes into retirement:

> This volume (including these embarrassed introductory remarks) is as near
> as I shall ever come to *déshabille* in public; and perhaps it will do something
> to help towards a better vision of the man, if it gives no more than a partial
> view of a piece of his back, a little dusty (after the process of tidying up), a
> little bowed, and receding from the world not because of weariness or mis-
> anthropy but for other reasons that cannot be helped: because the leaves
> fall, the water flows, the clock ticks with that horrid pitiless solemnity which
> you must have observed in the ticking of the hall clock at home (p. vi).

The valedictory note encouraged reviewers of this volume to take the
opportunity to sum up Conrad's career. One of the most famous of these
reviews was by E. M. Forster, whose sympathetic tone is at odds with the
bleak conclusion that he draws: he says that Conrad does not address
major questions or attempt major answers, that no philosophy can be
found in him, that we need not seek meaning in his work. Forster comes
very close to saying that Conrad's novels are empty and overrated. He
does this partly by making an illogical transition from the elusiveness of
Conrad the man to elusiveness in the work: 'a proud and formidable
character appears rather more clearly here [in *Notes on Life and Letters*] than
in the novels; that is all we can say.' Conrad dreads 'intimacy', he has 'a
rigid conception as to where the rights of the public stop, he has determined we shall not be "all over" him', but 'behind the smoke screen of his
reticence' there is – and here Forster uses his smoke metaphor to facilitate
his unsignalled switch from the personality to the art – a 'central obscurity': 'These essays do suggest that he is misty in the middle as well as at the
edges, that the secret casket of his genius contains a vapour rather than
a jewel; and that we need not try to write him down philosophically because there is, in this particular direction, nothing to write'.[30] The suggestion that Conrad's novels had more rhetoric than content was to be

heard more often after his death and contributed to his loss of popularity in the 1930s.

From time to time the formal and quiet routine of Oswalds was dramatically interrupted. By May 1920 Conrad had started work on *Suspense,* but work on the novel went badly and by the autumn of that year Conrad was suffering from depression, feeling 'gouty, seedy, crusty moody . . . and lame' (letter to Harriet Capes, 17 November 1920[31]). In an attempt to lift his depression and recharge himself for work on *Suspense* he arranged to leave in January, 1921, for a three month stay on Corsica. Borys Conrad drove his parents as far as Rouen and Jean-Aubry accompanied them on the second leg of the journey as far as Lyon. In late January/early February they stayed in Marseille for a few days – Conrad revisited the scenes of his youthful pleasures, excesses and suicide attempt – and they spent February, March and April on Corsica, accompanied by the Pinkers. Jessie liked Corsica, her knee improved there and her spirits rose, but Conrad felt depressed and blocked and was unable to get on with the novel. In February he was full of complaint: 'I am nervous, irritable, bored. . . . We have made no excursions. The afternoons are rather cold. The hotel is abominable. The Corsicans are charming . . . but the mountains with all those paths which wind and wind endlessly along the coast get on my nerves. One feels like howling'.[32]

As far as writing was concerned the visit was a failure: Conrad continued to suffer from 'moral depression which I cannot shake off'. But when they got back from Corsica in May of that year Conrad's verdict was that he was not displeased with the visit: he had read a great deal and 'picked up some good stuff for the novel'.[33] Writing remained blocked and difficult throughout 1921 and 1922. Conrad himself saw depression as the principal cause of his frustration: late in 1921 he wrote to Cunninghame Graham that he was 'seedy and often in pain; which I would not mind much but for the depression (consequent on the inability to work seriously) – which I can not somehow shake off' and in January 1922 he wrote to Aniela Zagórska complaining that his state of mind caused frustrating waste of time: 'I could not work properly the whole of last year – I could not even concentrate my thoughts without a great effort. This makes me worried and fretful'.[34] Later in 1922 Conrad experienced a grave set-back both personally and professionally, when J. B. Pinker died on 8 February 1922. Pinker was younger than Conrad, and despite their quarrel and two year estrangement (1909–11) he had become by the time of his death one of Conrad's most constant companions: they took holidays together, stayed in each other's houses and had even collaborated with each other (on a film-treatment of 'Gaspar Ruiz'; the script was never used). Conrad knew that he had been lucky to find Pinker, whose patience, tact and vision had gone a very long way to shape the ultimate success of Conrad's career as a writer. Pinker had the self-confidence to back his judgement, and had paid out sums of money which were, by the standards of the day, huge, to an author who might easily have remained an impecunious coterie artist to the end of his life. As we know, Pinker's investment paid off, but the relationship with Conrad could easily have ended with Pinker having to write off a very large unpaid debt. The literary agency was taken over by Pinker's sons: one of whom, Eric, looked after Conrad's interests. It is a terrible irony that both Borys Conrad and Eric Pinker, the sons of these brilliantly successful men, were to be sent to prison for financial dishonesty when their fathers were no longer there to rescue them.

An important event in October and November 1922 was the staging of *The Secret Agent* at the Ambassadors Theatre (the play opened on 2 November). Conrad's feelings about the theatre had always been mixed and he decided not to attend the first night and was disappointed by the play's reception, though he may not have been wholly surprised by it: his dramatization is an awkward affair and he must have been aware as he wrote it that most of the novel's interest was getting lost. And yet in the hands of skilled persons it lends itself very well to adaptation: there is an excellent recent version for radio written and directed by Richard Shannon, 1989. Conrad's treatment depends heavily on exposition and repetition: it begins clumsily with a long scene in which Winnie and her mother fill in the character of Verloc and the background of Winnie's marriage to him, and thereafter Winnie is made to remark rather too often that 'things don't stand looking into'. But Conrad's adaptation adds some intriguing details not displayed clearly in the novel. Heat and Verloc look alike: '*There is a certain similarity in their personal appearance, both big men, clothes same sort of cut, dark blue overcoats and round hats on*' (IV, iii),[35] and the Lady Patroness of Michaelis is more precisely placed in the play than in the novel by her oddly non-aristocratic name, 'Lady Mabel'. Her lines have the insolent absolutism of Wilde's Lady Bracknell: 'Have such people any human feelings at all – I wonder' (of Winnie, Act III, p. 143) and 'They may think what they like. My eccentricity is well known' (of the possibility that her other guests may be offended by the way in which she has allowed the Assistant Commissioner to monopolize her, Act III, p. 145). The division into acts reminds us that the novel was dedicated to Wells: the four acts are entitled '*The Private Life*', '*The Under World*', '*The Upper World*' and '*The Issue*'. The title of Act II adds a sense of a preoccupation of the 1890s reflected in titles like George Gissing's *The Nether World*: the notion that the English working class was as unknown as a remote African tribe, and that to investigate it was an act of quasi-imperial exploration.

The major event of 1923 was Conrad's American tour. Doubleday, his American publisher, felt that an American tour would greatly promote Conrad's audience in the United States and in December 1922 invited Conrad to visit the following spring. Jessie's state of health and Conrad's continuing anxieties about his own health made him uncertain about this, but by February 1923 he had decided that he would go, and on 21 April sailed from Glasgow for America in the *Tuscania*, commanded by an old friend, David Bone. Bone's brother, Muirhead Bone, the artist, accompanied Conrad. He spent the month of May staying with the Doubleday family. He attended press interviews and sat for his portrait, met a large number of celebrities, both American and Polish (including the pianist Paderewski who was now prime minister of the newly established Polish republic) and gave a hugely successful public reading from *Victory*. At the end of May he sailed back to England, accompanied by the Doubledays.

A sad feature of Conrad's visit to America was his refusal to meet John Quinn. Quinn, the lawyer and collector, had had warm correspondence with Conrad and had been in many ways a benefactor, buying Conrad's manuscripts for what at the time seemed large sums which represented a very considerable relief to Conrad's straitened circumstances. Conrad had agreed to sell all his manuscripts to Quinn but had in fact broken this promise by selling some of them to T. J. Wise (the bibliophile and collector who was later to be notorious for his forgeries). Quinn was invited to none of the fêting and lionizing of Conrad that took placed in New York. Quinn was reputed to have a violent temper, and Doubleday advised Conrad not to meet him: Quinn telephoned the Doubledays' mansion several times during the month of Conrad's visit but received no reply. He was hurt and outraged. In November 1923 he sold all his books and manuscripts, including the Conrad manuscripts, at auction. The reasons for this were complex: he was unwell and wanted to settle affairs before his death, he was moving to a smaller house and did not have room for the collection. Further, Conrad's fame in America following his visit in May was such that Quinn could expect good prices for the manuscripts. Conrad had sold two hundred and thirty one items to Quinn for a total of ten thousand dollars. At the sale at the Anderson galleries the Conrad items fetched a hundred and eleven thousand dollars. About three quarters of the items were sold to A. S. W. Rosenbach of Philadelphia for seventy-two thousand dollars.

Quinn had initially promised to keep his collection of Conrad's manuscripts together. Still, Conrad had broken his promise to Quinn by selling to Wise, so Quinn's behaviour could not necessarily be seen as dishonourable. Conrad's reaction to the sale of his manuscripts in America was stoical and ironic. He wrote to Garnett, 21 November 1923:

> Yes, Quinn promised to keep the MSS. together – but the mood passes and the promise goes with it. But did you ever hear of anything so idiotic as this sale? But it is my greatest success! People who never heard of me before will now know my name. Others who have never been able to read through a page of mine are convinced that I am a great writer. If I only could let it get about (discreetly) that the whole thing was a put up job between Quinn and me and that I got my share of the plunder I believe I would become 'universally respected'. But that is too much to hope for.[36]

Jessie, meanwhile, had been coping tactfully with a major domestic problem. Borys had secretly married late the previous year and he told his mother about this just before Conrad left for America at the end of April. Jessie decided to keep this to herself, rather than have Conrad agonizing about it throughout his trip to America, and she gave Conrad the news in a hotel room in London on his return. In her account of the episode Conrad exploded: 'Joseph Conrad started up in bed, gripping my arm with cruel force. "Why do you tell me that, why don't you keep such news to yourself?" ' He took refuge in silence and outraged dignity, refusing to discuss the matter beyond asking her whether she was certain that the information was true: ' "I don't want to know anything more about it. It is done, and I have been treated like a blamed fool, dam" '. They went out to lunch with Doubleday and Conrad expressed his outrage to him:

> 'I have told my wife she should have kept such news to herself.' Mr Doubleday replied incredulously: 'But that would hardly be possible. Let us hope they will be happy'.... 'Well, they won't, then. What has he got to keep a wife on? And let me tell you I don't like the way this has been done in secret. I wasn't to know then, why should I now?'[37]

Jessie's account here shows considerable resentment of both Conrad and Borys, Conrad for his tantrums and unreasonable behaviour, Borys for his improvidence and deviousness. Her account is heavily coloured by later events: she is writing in 1933 or 4, and in 1927 Borys had got himself heavily into debt and had been sent to prison for a year for fraud.[38] Jessie could reasonably blame the marriage, and Conrad's own example of reckless prodigality with money, for Borys's disaster. In fact Conrad was quite soon reconciled to Borys's marriage and to his wife. The rest of 1923 was dogged by illness, though Conrad's spirits were lifted by the publication of *The Rover* in December of that year.

He was offered honorary doctorates at Oxford, Cambridge, Edinburgh, Liverpool and Durham in 1923, but declined them all, and in May 1924 he received an official-looking envelope which he thought was an income tax demand. He left it unopened on his desk for a time until a tactful message from the office of the Socialist Prime Minister, Ramsay MacDonald, revealed that the envelope contained the offer of a knighthood. This offer Conrad also declined. It may be that he hoped for something grander, such as the Order of Merit or the Nobel Prize – which he certainly wanted[39] – or it may be that he felt that it was inappropriate for a member of a family which had inherited its nobility to receive the kind of honour that was coveted by middle-class Englishmen. Also, he may have been influenced by the example of his friend John Galsworthy who had declined a knighthood in 1918.[40] (After Conrad's death Galsworthy was both to win the Nobel Prize and to be elected to the Order of Merit.)

In 1924, the last year of his life, it was 'business as usual' while Conrad continued to work on *Suspense*. Although he was in constantly poor health from June 1923 until his death on 3 August 1924, his death, which was sudden, came as a shock. Because it was a holiday, family and friends, including both his sons (and Borys's wife) and Richard Curle, were in the house. Richard Curle had driven over to stay the weekend with the Conrads on Friday, 1 August. Conrad seemed lively and optimistic, and on the

Saturday, 2 August, they set out together to view a house that Conrad was thinking of renting; Conrad had never liked Oswalds and he and Jessie were hoping to leave it at the end of September. During the drive Conrad suffered a pain in the chest and they turned back to Oswalds. A doctor examined Conrad and said that the pain was caused by indigestion but it now seems clear that it was a heart attack. That evening Conrad's sons, daughter in law and grandson came to stay (by prior arrangement to spend the Bank Holiday at home). Richard Curle says that Conrad asked to see Borys's wife and child immediately 'as though he knew that it was his last chance of seeing them.' His breathing was laboured and the doctor ordered oxygen cylinders for him, but said that his pulse was normal and that he was suffering asthmatic side-effects of acute indigestion. Conrad asked Curle and John, the younger son, not to sit with him in order that his laboured breathing shouldn't distress them. Early the following morning Conrad seemed better:

> Conrad got out of bed and insisted on sitting up in his chair, dozing off for a few minutes at a time. At six in the morning he seemed to be in less difficulty and told his eldest son that he must see about getting a male nurse, as Foote, his faithful manservant, was worn out after many hours of constant attendance. He was full of consideration and gratitude and said how finely Foote had behaved. . . .
>
> At the actual moment of death nobody was in the room. Foote had gone out with a message and Conrad was resting. There was no particular anxiety, for only half-an-hour before his pulse had been taken . . . and found to be normal. His wife, lying powerless next door, heard a cry, 'Here . . .' as if a second word had been stifled, and a fall. People ran in: he had slipped, dead, on to the floor from his chair. It was just on eight-thirty.[41]

The death of a great writer triggers a flood of appraisals and summings-up from his contemporaries. In Conrad's case the process had begun before his death, prompted by the valedictory tone of his note to *Notes on Life and Letters*. Forster's treacherously beguiling common reader approach, suggesting that the high rhetoric of the novels coexisted with a lack of meaning, contributed, as I have said, to a slide in Conrad's reputation[42] which reached a low point in the 1930s and didn't start to recover until he was championed in the 1940s by the forceful Cambridge academic critics, M. C. Bradbrook and F. R. Leavis. Conrad's reputation for his last ten years had been that of the greatest living English novelist (once Hardy had become silent); it was natural for a younger generation of writers to take a certain satisfaction in 'placing' him in their obituary notices. Virginia Woolf, Arnold Bennett and Lawrence took their opportunities. The question raised by Forster – do the novels have meaning that one can grasp? – is still asked today.[43] I am certain that the answer to that question is 'yes' but I would be reluctant to attempt to sum up that meaning in a neat – or even in an untidy – generalisation. At the risk of resorting to cliché I would like to restate my conviction – implicit, I hope, in the whole of this book – that the way to grasp Conrad's meaning is to read all his works. At the same time, I would note that Conrad himself has left us some suggestive formulaic expressions of his beliefs, notably, and famously, in the Familiar Preface to *A Personal Record*, where he said: 'Those who read me know my conviction that the world, the temporal world, rests on a few very simple ideas; so simple that they must be as old as the hills. It rests notably, among others, on the idea of Fidelity' (p. xix).

The funeral service took place at St Thomas's Roman Catholic Church, Canterbury. Among other old friends Edward Garnett, Cunninghame Graham and Richard Curle attended the funeral. Cunninghame Graham remarked of it that the mourners: 'all became Catholics for the nonce. When all is said and done, of all the faiths it is the most consolatory, and tears stood in the eyes of many of the heterogeneous congregation. What, after all, is better for the soul than prayer to an unseen God, in an uncomprehended tongue?'[44]

It is a disconcerting thought that Conrad's Catholicism has lasted longer than his scepticism: for most of his sixty-six years he regarded himself as a man of no religion, but for the seventy years (at the time of writing) since his death he has been a Catholic to the extent that he was buried with Catholic rites and lies in a Catholic graveyard. There is some evidence that Conrad did in fact return to the religion of his baptism to some extent in his last years. On 29 July 1914 Conrad visited his own father's grave in the Rakowicki Cemetery at Cracow, where he knelt and prayed – Borys recalled that this was the only time he saw his father pray.[45] On Corsica in 1921 Jessie reports that Conrad was upset when he thought that Pinker was mocking Catholicism, and cried out 'Yes, and I'm a Catholic, aren't I?' Jessie gives little weight to this incident, but Najder believes that Conrad's attitude to religion was at that time undergoing a change.[46] It is certainly true that the priest in *The Rover* is very sympathetically drawn, and *The Rover* is, of course, a product of Conrad's thinking about his big Napoleonic novel and thus, in a way, a product of the trip to Corsica. John Conrad recalled a later incident, at Oswalds (probably in 1919) when his father invited him to accompany him for a walk and they visited a church:

He stopped me with a slight pressure on my arm, bowed respectfully but did not make the Sign of the Cross. After a few moments we moved on, stopping to look at the memorials and stained glass, entered the sanctuary and went up to the altar, paused for a minute or so, bowed and took two paces backward before turning to retrace our steps to the door which we closed, quietly, behind us. Not a word was spoken while we were in the church. I was curious to know why he had not crossed himself, because my aunt, also a Roman Catholic, always did and I expected JC to do the same. As we continued our walk round the church I asked him why he had not done so. 'My boy, when you are aloft taking in canvas in a gale there is no one between you and death but the Good Lord and you cross yourself many times in the course of a voyage – I think He will pardon me – to make the sign now would be pointless – there is no need.'

We carried on, pausing now and then to look at some tombstone and then, as though thinking aloud he said, 'Profanity is the preserve of the devil'. Then as we passed through the lychgate he said, 'Don't assume that because I do not go to church that I do not believe, I do; all true seamen do in their hearts.'[47]

And in 1923 Conrad wrote to Gordon Gardiner declining an invitation to join a club because eligibility was restricted to members of the Church of England. He remarks that 'I was born a R.[oman] C.[atholic], and though dogma sits lightly on me I have never renounced that form of Christian religion.' He had also declined an invitation to join a Catholic society whose objective was the re-establishment of the temporal power of the Pope. As he continues to Gardiner: 'I am afraid I am a lost soul . . . I have got to stand between the two' ('the two' being Catholicism and Protestantism, the religions of his natural and his adopted country) 'a prey to the first inferior devil that may come along. My only hope of escaping the eternal fires is my utter insignificance. I shall lie low on the Judgement Day, and will probably be overlooked'.[48] The most rugged individualists and sceptics tend to become both socially conformist and conventionally pious in later life: Wordsworth is a conspicuous example. And in John Conrad's anecdote Conrad is content to identify himself as a typical member of a group ('All true seamen') while throughout his major phase he had insisted that he was unclassifiable: he was not to be seen as a sailor novelist, he was not to be seen as a Slav, he was not to be compared with Kipling or Stevenson – he was unique. The man who in the *Preface* to *The Nigger of the 'Narcissus'* had proclaimed the isolation of the writer, the agony of his struggle to communicate, and the desperate difficulty of establishing solidarity with his audience, is here relaxing into the forms of solidarity which had shaped his earliest identity: Catholicism, high birth, family, friendship. He had prayed at his father's grave, just as earlier he had mourned his uncle: with his own burial in a Catholic graveyard the tensions between the Korzeniowski and the Bobrowski inheritance are finally resolved.

Notes

1 Zdzisław Najder, ed., *Conrad Under Familial Eyes* (Cambridge: Cambridge University Press, 1983), p. 113.
2 Poland adopted Latin Christianity in 966, became a kingdom in 1025 and fragmented into a series of principalities, 1138–1295. The kingdom was restored in 1295. By 1500 Jagiellonian Poland had occupied a huge land–mass of central Europe. To reconstruct it one has to look at the map of late twentieth-century Europe and imagine a realm which has modern Poland as its core and which includes much of Hungary, Czechoslovakia and the Ukraine and the whole of Byelorussia and Lithuania, as well as a huge bite out of Russia extending almost as far as Moscow itself. The dominant constituents of this realm were the Kingdom of Poland at the centre, the Grand Duchy of Lithuania (by far the largest area) to the east, the Kingdom of Hungary to the south and the Kingdom of Bohemia to the west. This diversity contributed to the inherent vulnerability of Poland, weakened by a struggle for dominance between competing factions, especially the Lithuanian and the Polish magnates. Part of this vulnerability lay in the fact that at no time could Poland's boundaries be regarded as determined by precedent and right. There were natural frontiers consisting of the Baltic to the north and the Carpathian mountains to the south, and two rivers, the Vistula to the east and the Oder to the west, but the fairly small geographical area thus defined has never corresponded to Poland's political frontiers.

The golden age of Poland, the fourteenth, fifteenth and sixteenth centuries, saw the establishing of an empire, the building of Cracow as a royal city (under Casimir the Great, 1333–70) and formal union with Lithuania which was achieved by the Union of Krewo (1385) and by the betrothal of Jadwiga, Queen of Poland, to Władysław II Jagiello, Grand Duke of Lithuania. Queen Jadwiga, who died at the age of twenty–four in 1399, made a bequest to what is still today Poland's richest and most beautiful university, the Jagiellonian university of Cracow (the university was founded in 1364 and revitalized thanks to the endowment of Jadwiga). The Polish renaissance of the sixteenth century was the most brilliant period of its history: three representative figures of this period, all graduates of the Jagiellonian university and of Padua, one of the leading universities in Europe, were Copernicus (1473–1543), the great heliocentrist, Jan Kochanowski (1530–84), the first major Polish poet writing in the vernacular, and Jan Zamoyski (1542–1605), politician, soldier and man of learning, who rebuilt the city of Zamosc as a model city.

In the course of the seventeenth and eighteenth centuries this huge human achievement decayed. From 1717 Poland was dominated, politically, by other powers. In the course of the eighteenth century Prussia, Austria and Russia carved up Poland in a series of treaties (1772, 1793 and 1795). The 1772 partition was designed to curb Russian ambition: Frederick the Great of Prussia and Maria Theresa of Austria sought to block Russia from controlling all Poland by signing a treaty with Catherine the Great which divided about a third of the country between these powers. The 1793 treaty followed a period in which what was left (from the earlier depradations) of independent Poland had tried to modernize herself under her patriotic and reforming King, Stanisław–August Poniatowski (1732–98), and was forced by the Russians and the Prussians to rescind her reforms. The third and final treaty was a response to the National Rising of 1794, led by a figure ever since regarded as one of Poland's national heroes, Tadeusz Kościuszko. Catherine the Great of Russia and Frederick–William of Prussia were able to represent the moderate reforms of the Poles as dangerous Jacobinism comparable with the violence of the recent revolution in France, and in 1794 the Russian army defeated Kościuszko, put down his Insurrectionary Government, deported King Stanisław–August and forced him to abdicate. Having destroyed the Polish government Prussia, Austria and Russia then took the view that there was no one in authority in Poland with whom they were obliged to negotiate, and they erased the Polish state from the political map. The formerly independent Polish territories were shared out between the occupying powers, the Russians taking the largest, eastern area, the Austrians taking the south, including Cracow (an area they called 'new Galicia') and the Prussians taking the west, including Warsaw ('New South Prussia'). (The above summary is based on Norman Davies, *God's Playground* (Oxford: Clarendon Press, 1981)).

3 Andrzej Busza, *Conrad's Polish Literary Background and Some Illustrations of the Influence of Polish Literature on his Work*, Antemurale, X (1966), p. 153. See my discussion of 'Prince Roman', chapter 8, pp. 191–92.

4 N. Davies, *God's Playground*, II (1981), pp. 315–33.

5 Z. Najder, *Joseph Conrad: A Chronicle* (1983), pp. 18–22.

6 N. Davies, *God's Playground*, II (1981), pp. 347–65.

7 Z. Najder ed., *Conrad's Polish Background* (London: Oxford University Press, 1964), p. 2, and Z. Najder, *Joseph Conrad: A Chronicle* (Cambridge: Cambridge University Press, 1983), pp. 9–10.

8 Z. Najder, *Conrad's Polish Background* (1964), p. 2, and Z. Najder, *Joseph Conrad: A Chronicle* (1983), p. 3. The term derives from two German words *schlagen*, to strike a blow, and *Geschlecht*, sex, species, family, race.

9 N. Davies, *God's Playground*, I (1981), pp. 203–10.

10 Z. Najder, *Joseph Conrad: A Chronicle* (1983), pp. 3–9.

11 *Ibid.*, p. 8.

12 *Ibid.*, p. 18.

13 *Ibid.*, p. 40f.

14 Andrzej Busza, *Conrad's Polish Literary Background* (1966), p. 154.

15 *Ibid.*, pp. 11–15.

16 *Ibid.*, p. 16.
17 Z. Najder, ed., *Conrad Under Familial Eyes* (1983), pp. 66–9.
18 Quoted by Najder in *Conrad's Polish Background* (1964), p. 8.
19 Z. Najder, *Joseph Conrad: A Chronicle* (1983), p. 21.
20 See chapter 7, passim.
21 Z. Najder, ed., *Conrad Under Familial Eyes* (1983), p. 122. See also Andrzej Busza, *Conrad's Polish Literary Background* (1966), p. 130.
22 Quoted by Busza, *ibid.*, p. 119.
23 *Ibid.*, pp. 122–5.
24 Quoted by Busza, *ibid.*, p. 131.
25 *Ibid.*, p. 132n.
26 The argument that Conrad's *Preface* to *The Nigger of the 'Narcissus'* owes a great deal to the Preface to *Lyrical Ballads* is found in studies by Ian Watt and David Thorburn. Ian Watt, *Conrad in the Nineteenth Century* (London: Chatto and Windus, 1980) and David Thorburn, *Conrad's Romanticism* (New Haven, Conn: Yale University Press, 1974).
27 Andrzej Busza in *Conrad's Polish Literary Background* (1966), p. 126.
28 Cited by Najder in Z. Najder, *Joseph Conrad: A Chronicle* (1983), pp. 501 and 609.
29 Z. Najder, ed., *Conrad Under Familial Eyes* (1983), p. 77.
30 *Ibid.*, p. 123.
31 The extraordinary fact is that between 1920 and 1939 and again since 1989 the freedoms for which Korzeniowski and his wife gave their lives seemed, and seem, to be becoming attainable by Poles for Poland. But the Republic of 1920 to 1939 was deeply precarious, and the Solidarity dominated government which came into being in 1989 has yet (at the time of writing, 1993) to solve the economic and political disorder created by forty years of communism.
32 See chapter 11, pp. 279–80.
33 Andrzej Busza, *Conrad's Polish Literary Background* (1966), p. 136.
34 Quoted by Z. Najder, *Conrad's Polish Background* (1964), p. 9.
35 Najder writes: 'At the beginning of this powerful drama [*Dziady*], the hero bears the name Gustaw and is a typical young romantic poet, self-centered, lonely, desperately in love, immersed in fantasies. Then, under the impact of the political persecution by Russian authorities to which he and his friends are exposed, his personality and his poetry undergo a radical transformation. He changes his name to Konrad and becomes a romantic patriot, a poet spokesman for his oppressed people.' Z. Najder, *Joseph Conrad: A Chronicle* (1983), p. 11.
36 Julian Krzyżanowski, *Polish Romantic Literature* (London: Allen and Unwin, 1930), pp. 66–7.
37 Z. Najder, *Conrad's Polish Background* (1964), p. 15.
38 Private communication from Andrzej Busza. See also Czesław Miłosz, *The History of Polish Literature* (London: Macmillan, 1969).
39 Andrzej Busza, *Conrad's Polish Literary Background* (1966), p. 141.
40 Z. Najder, *Conrad's Polish Background* (1964), p. 12 and Z. Najder, *Joseph Conrad: A Chronicle* (1983), p. 31.
41 Andrzej Busza, *Conrad's Polish Literary Background* (1966), pp. 244–7. Andrzej Busza points out that Conrad himself told Jean–Aubry, Richard Curle and J. H. Retinger that he went to the school, and that he had no reason to lie about it. *Ibid.*, p. 246.
42 *Ibid.*, pp. 172–6.

43 *Under Western Eyes* reverses that scenario, with Haldin, the heroic mystic, play-
    ing a role like that of Apollo, and Razumov, the pragmatic self-seeker, playing
    a role like that of Tadeusz. The fact that Razumov is a traitor who is crippled
    and deafened for his treachery could well be an encoded punishment both
    of Uncle Tadeusz and also of the Bobrowski streak in Conrad himself.
44 Z. Najder, *Joseph Conrad: A Chronicle* (1983), p. 105.
45 *Ibid.*, p. 6.
46 Z. Najder, ed., *Conrad Under Familial Eyes* (1983), p. 22.
47 *Ibid.*, pp. 16–17.
48 *Ibid.*, p. 17n.
49 'The son of his beloved sister. On him he bestowed his money and advice,
    trying to steady him both physically and morally; to him he preached his
    gospel of perseverance and duty – which Joseph Conrad adopted, while con-
    verting Bobrowski's idea of duty as accepted in passive resignation into his
    own concept of duty as consciously and actively chosen' (*ibid.*, p. xvii).
50 Z. Najder, *Conrad's Polish Background* (1964), p. 114.
51 Najder remarks that: 'Going abroad was a rather obvious thing to do for a
    young exile, a Russian subject eligible for military service in the army of the
    hated oppressor. Dreaming about adventures and a life out of the ordinary
    is, again, quite normal among young men of all nations and times. In Conrad's
    case the dreams must have been reinforced by his feeling of being misunder-
    stood and superior, and out of tune with his environment. It is obvious that
    he wanted to say good-bye to it all – to free himself from restrictions and
    constant surveillance, to be independent in his thoughts and emotions. That
    he decided to go to sea was perhaps a matter of chance rather than a delib-
    erate choice of profession. Had Conrad felt a vocation to become a seaman,
    he would not have mentioned so often in his letters to his uncle various other
    projects and possibilities; indeed, frequently it was Bobrowski himself who
    reminded Conrad [that is, after 1874] that he should spend less time on
    shore and more under sail. Only much later does Conrad seem to have
    acquired a stronger passion for his profession.' Z. Najder, *Conrad's Polish
    Background* (1964), pp. 13–14.
52 *Ibid.*, pp. 9–10.
53 *Ibid.*, p. 9.
54 Z. Najder, *Joseph Conrad: A Chronicle* (1983), p. 32.
55 *Ibid.*, p. 34.
56 *Ibid.*, p. 32.
57 *Ibid.*, p. 35.
58 Najder admirably expresses Conrad's probable state of mind as he made this
    journey: 'Leaving his home country was for Konrad Korzeniowski not tanta-
    mount to shedding all habitual attitudes. Polish szlachta and Polish intelli-
    gentsia were social strata in which reputation, one's evaluation by one's own
    milieu, was felt to be very important, even essential for one's feeling of self-
    worth. Men strove strenuously to find confirmation of their own self-regard
    and image in "the eyes of others" rather than basing them on their own
    consciousness. Such a psychological heritage forms both a spur to ambition
    and a source of constant stress, especially if the idea of man's public duties
    has been inculcated in his mind.' *Ibid.*, p. 38.
59 Cited by Andrzej Busza, *Conrad's Polish Literary Background* (1966), p. 145, texts
    quoted from Z. Najder, *Conrad's Polish Background* (1964), pp. 37, 47 and 66.

Bobrowski usually gives his letters two dates, the first from the Gregorian calendar standard in the West and used in ethnic Poland since the sixteenth century, the second from the Julian calendar which was used officially in Russia. The difference is twelve days (*ibid.*, p. 35n).

60 A Warsaw weekly, *The Wanderer*, founded in 1863 and carrying literary, geographical and historical articles. Z. Najder, *Conrad's Polish Background* (1964), p. 71n.

61 *Ibid.*, pp. 71–2. Busza remarks that 'Conrad in the long letters to his uncle (as far as one can tell from Bobrowski's replies) poured out his soul, translated his thoughts and experiences into writing and, in fact, first gave vent to his literary talent'. Andrzej Busza, *Conrad's Polish Literary Background* (1966), p. 146.

62 Z. Najder, *Conrad's Polish Background* (1964), p. 110.

63 Tadeusz's letters between August 1883 and July 1885 have been lost, otherwise the collection seems complete (*ibid.*, p. 95n).

64 27 September, old style, *ibid.*, p. 38.

65 *Ibid.*, p. 111.

66 *Ibid.*, p. 115.

67 *Ibid.*, p. 99.

68 *Ibid.*, p. 68.

69 *Ibid.*, p. 69.

70 *Ibid.*, p. 98.

71 *Ibid.*, p. 85.

72 *Ibid.*, p. 101.

73 *Ibid.*, p. 74.

74 As was first shown by Jocelyn Baines, in *Joseph Conrad: A Critical Biography* (Harmondsworth: Penguin, 1971) [1960], p. 93. See also Z. Najder, *Conrad's Polish Background* (1964), p. 72n and Z. Najder, *Joseph Conrad: A Chronicle* (1983), pp. 70–1.

75 Z. Najder, *Conrad's Polish Background* (1964), p. 74.

76 For second mate, 1 June 1880.

77 This is a reference to his service on the *Palestine*, which caught fire, 14 March 1883: the episode was the source for 'Youth'.

78 Frederick R. Karl and Laurence Davies, eds., *The Collected Letters of Joseph Conrad*, I (Cambridge: Cambridge University Press, 1983), pp. 7–8.

79 Z. Najder, *Joseph Conrad: A Chronicle* (1983), pp. 119–21.

80 Karl and Davies, ed., *The Collected Letters of Joseph Conrad*, I (1983), p. 130.

81 *Ibid.*, p. 164.

82 Karl and Davies, ed., *The Collected Letters of Joseph Conrad*, III (1988), p. 89.

83 Andrzej Busza, *Conrad's Polish Literary Background* (1966), p. 150.

84 *Ibid.*, pp. 155–6. Busza says of the ending of *Lord Jim* that Jim's death 'combines in a disturbing way the ideas of honour and supreme courage with the notion of self-destruction. It is not being suggested that Conrad consciously borrowed from family history when he wrote the ending of *Lord Jim*, but that he might have easily had Stefan Bobrowski's story at the back of his mind at the time' (p. 156).

85 Karl and Davies, ed., *The Collected Letters of Joseph Conrad*, IV (1990), p. 138.

86 Z. Najder, *Conrad's Polish Background* (1964), p. 155, cited in Andrzej Busza, *Conrad's Polish Literary Background* (1966), p. 160.

NOTES TO CHAPTER 2

1   Z. Najder, *Conrad's Polish Background* (1964), p. 113.
2   R. R. Hodges, *The Dual Heritage of Joseph Conrad* (The Hague, Paris: Mouton, 1967), pp. 10–11.
3   Graham Hough, 'Chance and Joseph Conrad,' *Image and Experience* (London: Duckworth, 1960), p. 215.
4   R. R. Hodges, 'Deep Fellowship: Homosexuality and Male Bonding in the Life and Fiction of Joseph Conrad,' *Journal of Homosexuality*, 4 (1979), p. 380. See also Wayne Koestenbaum, *Double Talk: The Erotics of Male Literary Collaboration* (London: Routledge, 1989), in which it is argued that the Conrad/Ford Madox Ford collaboration was an expression of displaced homosexual desire.
5   Andrzej Busza, *Conrad's Polish Literary Background* (1966), pp. 190–1.
6   Z. Najder, ed., *Conrad Under Familial Eyes* (1983), pp. 214, 213. Zagórska says that Conrad had received a letter from Orzeszkowa, but Najder is convinced that he did not. Clearly her article on its own would have upset Conrad.
7   *Ibid.*, pp. 187–8.
8   Z. Najder, *Conrad's Polish Background* (1964), p. 44.
9   Owen Knowles, *A Conrad Chronology* (Basingstoke: Macmillan, 1989), p. 6.
10 Z. Najder, *Conrad's Polish Background* (1964), pp. 47–8.
11 Owen Knowles, *A Conrad Chronology* (1989), p. 6.
12 Z. Najder, *Joseph Conrad: A Chronicle* (1983), p. 48.
13 As Najder gives the state of knowledge about this matter: 'Hans van Marle, after detailed research in the archives of the Bouches du Rhône department, ascertained that in the period in question not one out of thirty-five hundred ships that docked at Marseilles [sic] bore the name *Tremolino* or was commanded by Dominic Cervoni. And Norman Sherry discovered César Cervoni's son, who confirmed Dominic's proficiency in smuggling but revealed that his father had not been related to Dominic, had not perished in 1878, and had remained on friendly terms with Korzeniowski.' Z. Najder, *Joseph Conrad: A Chronicle* (1983), p. 49. See also Owen Knowles, *A Conrad Chronology* (1989), p. 7.
14 Hanna Segal adapts a concept from Melanie Klein in order to speak of the 'depressive position' as a source of creativity: the artist experiences loss and seeks in his work to achieve reparation for that loss; Hanna Segal, 'Art and the Depressive Position', chapter 7 of her *Dream, Phantasy and Art* (London: Routledge and Tavistock, 1991). She cites *The Shadow-Line* as an example of a 'depressive position' text: 'The deadly calm, the dying men, the feeling of being haunted by a vengeful ghost of a dead parent, the captain's feeling of total and solitary responsibility to bring life to his dying ship and men is a marvellous picture of depression and the captain's heroic struggle against it,' p. 88. It should be noted, though, that as originally used by Melanie Klein the phrase 'depressive position' is unhelpful and indeed confusing. Klein used it to refer to a normal stage in the development of a small child – her 'depressive' does not refer to the kind of condition from which Conrad was suffering.
15 A view of Conrad proposed by Bernard Meyer, *Joseph Conrad: A Psychoanalytic Biography* (Princeton, New Jersey: Princeton University Press, 1967) and reinforced for me by Ken Robinson.

16 Ken Robinson pointed this out to me in a private letter.
17 12/24 March 1879, quoted in Z. Najder, *Conrad's Polish Background* (1964), pp. 176–7.
18 Z. Najder, *Joseph Conrad: A Chronicle* (1983), p. 50.
19 Gerard Jean-Aubry, *The Sea-Dreamer: A Definitive Biography of Joseph Conrad* (London: Allen and Unwin, 1957), p. 74.
20 Z. Najder, *Joseph Conrad: A Chronicle* (1983), pp. 54–5.
21 Z. Najder, *Conrad's Polish Background* (1964), pp. 54–6.
22 Karl and Davies, ed., *The Collected Letters of Joseph Conrad*, II (1986), p. 35.
23 Z. Najder, *Joseph Conrad: A Chronicle* (1983), p. 58.
24 Z. Najder, *Conrad's Polish Background* (1964), p. 58.
25 Z. Najder, *Joseph Conrad: A Chronicle* (1983), p. 59 and Jocelyn Baines, *Joseph Conrad* (1971 [1960]), p. 85.
26 Z. Najder, *Joseph Conrad: A Chronicle* (1983), p. 60.
27 *Ibid.*, pp. 62–3 and 512n.
28 Z. Najder, *Conrad's Polish Background* (1964), p. 59 and Jocelyn Baines, *Joseph Conrad* (1971[1960]), p. 86.
29 Z. Najder, *Joseph Conrad: A Chronicle* (1983), p. 62.
30 Z. Najder, *Conrad's Polish Background* (1964), pp. 62–3, Z. Najder, *Joseph Conrad: A Chronicle* (1983), pp. 64–5 and Jocelyn Baines, *Joseph Conrad* (1971 [1960]), p. 87.
31 Z. Najder, *Joseph Conrad: A Chronicle* (1983), p. 66.
32 Owen Knowles, *A Conrad Chronology* (1989), p. 137.
33 Jocelyn Baines, *Joseph Conrad* (1971 [1960]), p. 90 and Z. Najder, *Joseph Conrad: A Chronicle* (1983), pp. 67–8.
34 *Ibid.*, p. 69.
35 Chapter 1, p. 17.
36 Owen Knowles, *A Conrad Chronology* (1989), p. 9.
37 Five from Cornwall one, from Ireland, one – the Negro – from the Antilles, one from Australia, one from Holland, one from Norway. Z. Najder, *Joseph Conrad: A Chronicle* (1983), pp. 76–7. See also Jacques Berthoud's Introduction to *The Nigger of the 'Narcissus'* in the World's Classics edition (Oxford: Oxford University Press, 1984).
38 Molly Mahood proposed that this was the way to see Marlow in *Heart of Darkness*: M. M. Mahood, *The Colonial Encounter: A Reading of Six Novels* (London: Rex Collings, 1977), p. 23.
39 I discuss 'Youth' more fully in chapter 4, pp. 76–9.
40 Z. Najder, *Conrad's Polish Background* (1964), p. 79.
41 Z. Najder, *Joseph Conrad: A Chronicle* (1983), p. 78.
42 *Ibid.*, p. 81.
43 Owen Knowles, *A Conrad Chronology* (1989), p. 10.
44 Z. Najder, *Joseph Conrad: A Chronicle* (1983), p. 81.
45 *Ibid.*, p. 82.
46 Z. Najder, *Joseph Conrad: A Chronicle* (1983), p. 86.
47 Karl and Davies, ed., *The Collected Letters of Joseph Conrad*, I (1983), p. 12.
48 G. Jean-Aubry, *Joseph Conrad: Life and Letters* vol. II (London: William Heinemann, 1927), p. 264.
49 The dispute is set out in detail in Jocelyn Baines, *Joseph Conrad* (1971 [1960]), pp. 110–11.
50 Z. Najder, *Joseph Conrad: A Chronicle* (1983), pp. 95–6.

51 The collective significance of these sixteen fictions is discussed in Marialuisa Bignami, 'Joseph Conrad, the Malay Archipelago, and the Decadent Hero,' the *Review of English Studies*, xxxvIII, 150 (May 1987), p. 199.

52 Norman Sherry, *Conrad's Eastern World* (Cambridge: Cambridge University Press, 1976), p. 132, and 90–1n.

53 Z. Najder, *Joseph Conrad: A Chronicle* (1983), pp. 100–1, reviews quoted p. 101.

54 *Ibid.*, p. 103.

55 Norman Sherry, *Conrad's Eastern World* (1976), p. 132.

56 Jeremy Hawthorn, ed., Joseph Conrad, *The Shadow-Line*, World's Classics Edition (Oxford: Oxford University Press, 1985), p. viii.

57 Najder remarks that 'Even the chances of improving his English were slight: one of his officers on the *Otago* was a German and the other a Finn.' Z. Najder, *Joseph Conrad: A Chronicle* (1983), p. 112.

58 *Ibid.*, p. 26.

59 Z. Najder, *Joseph Conrad: A Chronicle* (1983), p. 169. Andrzej Busza has pointed out to me that in this respect Conrad is like his own Willems, who in the opening sentence of *An Outcast of the Islands* forgives himself his own truancy by seeing it as part of an oblique route to higher achievement: 'When he stepped off the straight and narrow path of his peculiar honesty, it was with an inward assertion of unflinching resolve to fall back again into the monotonous but safe stride of virtue as soon as his little excursion into the wayside quagmires had produced the desired effect. It was going to be a short episode – a sentence in brackets, so to speak – in the flowing tale of his life.'

60 Najder also says: 'Writing in a foreign language admits a greater temerity in tackling personally sensitive problems, for it leaves uncommitted the most spontaneous, deeper reaches of the psyche, and allows a greater distance in treating matters we would hardly dare approach in the language of our childhood. As a rule it is easier both to swear and to analyze dispassionately in an acquired language', Z. Najder, *Joseph Conrad: A Chronicle* (1983), p. 116.

61 Jocelyn Baines, *Joseph Conrad* (1971 [1960]), p. 211.

62 Owen Knowles, *A Conrad Chronology* (1989), p. 14.

63 Z. Najder, *Joseph Conrad: A Chronicle* (1983), p. 121.

64 *Ibid.*, p. 136.

65 *Ibid.*, p. 144.

66 *Ibid.*, p. 157.

NOTES TO CHAPTER 3

1 Chapter 1, p. 18.

2 Z. Najder, *Joseph Conrad: A Chronicle* (1983), p. 164.

3 A. J. Guerard, *Conrad the Novelist* (Cambridge, Mass.: Harvard University Press, 1958), p. 11. Bernard Meyer takes the same view: he remarks that although Bobrowski's death affected Conrad profoundly, he 'promptly attacked the closing chapters of his novel, displaying far greater energy than at any time since the beginning of the work'. *Joseph Conrad: A Psychoanalytic Biography* (1967), p. 103.

4 Z. Najder, *Joseph Conrad: A Chronicle* (1983), p. 167.

5 Quoted by Najder, *ibid.*, p. 170.

6 See chapter 7, p. 185, and David R. Smith, 'The Hidden Narrative: The K in

Conrad' in David R. Smith, ed., *Joseph Conrad's Under Western Eyes: Beginning, Revisions, Final Forms* (Hamden, Connecticut: Archon, 1991), pp. 39–81.

7 The Malayan 'reversed epic' is discussed by Frederick Karl, *Joseph Conrad: The Three Lives* (London: Faber and Faber, 1979), p. 245 and by Daphna Erdinast-Vulcan, *Joseph Conrad and the Modern Temper* (Oxford: Clarendon Press, 1991), p. 48.

8 Set out in A. J. Guerard, *Conrad the Novelist* (1958) and Thomas Moser, *Joseph Conrad: Achievement and Decline* (Cambridge, Mass.: Harvard University Press, 1980).

9 See chapter 2, pp. 39–40.

10 Norman Sherry, *Conrad's Eastern World* (1966), pp. 89–118. See also Norman Page, *A Conrad Companion* (Basingstoke: Macmillan, 1986), p. 29 and Owen Knowles, *A Conrad Chronology* (1989), p. 12. All Conrad scholars before Sherry had thought that Conrad actually met 'Tom Lingard': see for example Jocelyn Baines, *Joseph Conrad* (1971 [1960]), p. 117.

11 The *gawęda* is an upper-class oral tradition, characteristic of the *slachta*. Stories which were transmitted from one generation of *slachta* to the next strengthened the Polish gentry's sense of identity and continuity. The tall stories in Conrad's *A Personal Record* and the use of a frame narrator in the Marlow narrations can both be traced back to the *gawęda*. (Personal communication from Stanisław Modrzewski, University of Gdańsk.)

12 N. Sherry, *Conrad's Eastern World* (1966) pp. 132–3.

13 Ian Watt remarks of the background to *Almayer's Folly*: 'Even the layout of the fictional setting corresponds very closely to the actual settlements of Gunung Tabur and Tanjong Redeb astride the Berau river. Olmeijer had indeed been settled there for some seventeen years; he was, in fact, the representative of an actual Captain Lingard, though one called not Tom but William; and this William Lingard really was a famous trader and adventurer, widely known as the *Rajah Laut* – Malay for 'King of the Sea' – whose fortunes had in effect begun to decline soon after Olmeijer's arrival'. Ian Watt, *Conrad in the Nineteenth Century* (1980), p. 37.

14 *Ibid.*, p. 39.

15 *Ibid.*, p. 43.

16 Norman Sherry, ed., *Conrad: The Critical Heritage* (London: Routledge and Kegan Paul, 1973), pp. 47 and 61.

17 *Ibid.*, p. 63.

18 *Ibid.*, p. 74.

19 Karl and Davies, ed., *The Collected Letters of Joseph Conrad*, I (1983), p. 281.

20 The dedication is somewhat ironic, of course; this is discussed further in chapter 6.

21 Owen Knowles, *A Conrad Chronology* (1989), p. 17, Norman Page, *A Conrad Companion* (1986), p. 18, and Jessie Conrad, *Joseph Conrad and his Circle* (London: Jarrolds, 1935), p. 11.

22 Karl and Davies, ed., *The Collected Letters of Joseph Conrad*, I (1983), p. 265. Najder remarks: 'It seems most probable that he met Jessie in an office with which he had business dealings and where she worked as a typist, and also that the intimacy between them (we cannot now know if it went to the point of seduction) developed in the course of her typing some of his manuscripts'. Z. Najder, *Joseph Conrad: A Chronicle* (1983), p. 194.

23 Jessie Conrad, *Joseph Conrad and his Circle* (1935), pp. 12–15.

24 Owen Knowles, *A Conrad Chronology* (1989), p. 23.
25 'Daniel Chaucer', *The Simple Life, Ltd.* (London: The Bodley Head, 1911).
26 Quoted in Norman Page, *A Conrad Companion* (1986), p. 18.
27 Jessie Conrad, *Joseph Conrad as I Knew Him* (London: William Heinemann, 1926) and *Joseph Conrad and his Circle* (1935).
28 See chapter 2, pp. 33–4.
29 Karl and Davies, ed., *The Collected Letters of Joseph Conrad*, I (1983), p. 265.
30 See p. 48.
31 See p. 47.
32 Edward Garnett, ed., *Letters from Conrad: 1895–1924* (London: The Nonesuch Press, [1928]), pp. vii–viii.
33 Karl and Davies, ed., *The Collected Letters of Joseph Conrad*, I (1983), p. 245.
34 *Ibid.*, pp. 246–7.
35 *Ibid.*, p. 272.
36 This work was finally published in 1920, after nearly twenty–five years of obstetric anguish, as *The Rescue: A Romance of the Shallows.*
37 'You' and 'Your' are usually capitalized in Conrad's letters.
38 Karl and Davies, ed., *The Collected Letters of Joseph Conrad*, I (1983), p. 273.
39 See p. 60.
40 Karl and Davies, ed., *The Collected Letters of Joseph Conrad*, I (1983), p. 284.
41 *Ibid.*, p. 285.
42 *Ibid.*, pp. 288–9.
43 *Ibid.*, pp. 295–6.
44 *Ibid.*, p. 251
45 Karl and Davies, ed., *The Collected Letters of Joseph Conrad*, I (1983), pp. 252–3.
46 Chinua Achebe, 'An Image of Africa: Racism in Conrad's *Heart of Darkness*', *Massachusetts Review*, 18 (1977), pp. 782–94. A modified version of this lecture appears in R. Kimbrough, ed., *Heart of Darkness* (New York: Norton, 1988), pp. 251–62.
47 Jessie Conrad, *Joseph Conrad as I knew Him* (1926), p. 108. See p. 58.
48 Discussed with *Heart of Darkness*, chapter 4, p. 85.
49 Karl and Davies, ed., *The Collected Letters of Joseph Conrad*, I (1983), p. 301.
50 See p. 32.
51 Conrad clearly makes an artistic gain by changing the destination to London.
52 These models are discussed in chapter 2, p. 36.
53 Ian Watt, *Conrad in the Nineteenth Century* (1980), p. 91. As Ian Watt says: 'Conrad knew that for him there really was a paradox in the metaphysics of creation, that he worked best not by inventing situations and characters, but by so intensely and questioningly remembering the past that it finally disclosed much more than had actually happened' (p. 93).
54 In her famous essay 'Modern Fiction' (1919) reprinted in Virginia Woolf, *The Common Reader: First Series* (London: Hogarth Press, 1925).
55 'What I Believe' [1939], reprinted in *Two Cheers for Democracy* (New York: Harcourt, Brace, 1951), p. 68.
56 Ian Watt discusses the title, Ian Watt, *Conrad in the Nineteenth Century* (1980), p. 100.
57 I use the word 'solidarity' fully conscious of the central significance that it will come to have in the *Preface* to *The Nigger of the 'Narcissus'* and *Lord Jim.*
58 See the Norton Critical edition of *The Nigger of the 'Narcissus'*, ed. Robert Kimbrough (New York: W. W. Norton, 1979), p. 3n.

59 Conrad to Cunninghame Graham, 14 December 1897, Karl and Davies, ed., *The Collected Letters of Joseph Conrad*, I (1983), p. 53.

60 Norman Sherry, ed., *Conrad: The Critical Heritage* (1973), p. 83.

61 Ian Watt, *Conrad in the Nineteenth Century* (1980), p. 99.

62 As in Byron's *Childe Harold's Pilgrimage*, Canto IV, as Jacques Berthoud has pointed out. Jacques Berthoud, ed., *The Nigger of the 'Narcissus'* (Oxford: Oxford University Press, 1984), p. xx.

63 Quoted in Kimbrough, ed., *The Nigger of the 'Narcissus'* (Norton Critical Edition, 1979), p. 168.

64 Ian Watt, *Conrad in the Nineteenth Century* (1980), p. 88.

65 See Jacques Berthoud's excellent account of the *Preface*: Berthoud, ed. *The Nigger of the 'Narcissus'* (1984), pp. 175–82.

66 'The scientist appeals to what could be called the "driving" emotions, the artist to the "objective" emotions – that is, emotions directed towards an object from which they receive definition as they provide it with illumination.' Berthoud, ed. *The Nigger of the 'Narcissus'* (1984), p. 178.

67 William James, *Principles of Psychology* (Cambridge, Mass.: Harvard University Press, 1983), pp. 984–5. I am indebted to A. D. Nuttall for this suggestion.

68 Ian Watt, *Conrad in the Nineteenth Century* (1980), pp. 78–80.

69 I have discussed this in my book on *Lord Jim*. John Batchelor, *Lord Jim* (Unwin: Unwin Critical Library, 1988), p. 43.

70 To quote Berthoud's elegant essay again: 'A heightening of perception . . . requires a heightening of the medium of perception.' Berthoud, ed., *The Nigger of the 'Narcissus'*, (1984), p. 180.

71 Walter Pater, *The Renaissance* [1873] (London: Collins, 1964), p. 129.

72 Berthoud discusses this with admirable clarity, Berthoud ed., *The Nigger of the 'Narcissus'* (1984), p. 181.

73 Walter Pater, *The Renaissance* [1873] (1964), p. 222.

74 It is printed on p. xxx in Berthoud, ed., *The Nigger of the 'Narcissus'* (1984) and p. 150 in Kimbrough, ed., *The Nigger of the 'Narcissus'* (1979).

75 Karl and Davies, ed., *The Collected Letters of Joseph Conrad*, I (1983), p. 370.

76 Karl and Davies, ed., *The Collected Letters of Joseph Conrad*, I (1983), pp. 424–425.

77 By the editors of the *Collected Letters*, Karl and Davies, ed., *The Collected Letters of Joseph Conrad*, II (1986), p. 16n.

78 Karl and Davies, ed., *The Collected Letters of Joseph Conrad*, II (1986), pp. 16–17.

79 *Ibid.*, pp. 159–60.

80 C. T. Watts, ed., *Joseph Conrad's Letters to R. B. Cuninghame Graham* (Cambridge: Cambridge University Press, 1969), p. 4.

81 Cedric Watts and Laurence Davies, *Cunninghame Graham: A Critical Biography* (Cambridge: Cambridge University Press), 1979, pp. xi–xii.

82 See chapter 5, pp. 129–31.

83 Preface to Thomas Beer, *Stephen Crane: A Study in American Letters* (London: Heinemann, 1924), pp. 9 and 3.

84 Karl and Davies, ed., *The Collected Letters of Joseph Conrad*, I (1983), p. 416.

85 Ford Madox Ford, *Joseph Conrad: A Personal Remembrance* (1924), p. 5.

86 Ian Watt, *Conrad in the Nineteenth Century* (1980), pp. 171–12.

87 Edward Garnett, ed., *Letters from Conrad: 1895–1924* [1928], pp. xv–xvi.

88 Owen Knowles, *A Conrad Chronology* (1989), pp. 29–40.

89 See Nina Galen, 'Stephen Crane as a source for Conrad's Jim', *Nineteenth Century Fiction*, 38, I (1983), pp. 78–96.

NOTES TO CHAPTER 4

1   On 14 July 1900.
2   Karl and Davies, ed., *The Collected Letters of Joseph Conrad*, II (1986), p. 284.
3   Edward Said, *Joseph Conrad and the Fiction of Autobiography* (Cambridge, Mass: Harvard University Press, 1966), p. 4.
4   Quoted by Alan Judd, *Ford Madox Ford* (London: Collins, 1990), p. 62.
5   Ford Madox Ford, *Return to Yesterday* (London: Victor Gollancz, 1931), pp. 52–3.
6   In *The Wings of the Dove* (though a slip in Ford's reference to this suggests that he may not have been very familiar with James's text).
7   Ford Madox Ford, *Return to Yesterday* (1931), pp. 52–3.
8   Alan Judd, *Ford Madox Ford* (1990), p. 81.
9   Z. Najder, *Joseph Conrad: A Chronicle* (1983), pp. 234–6.
10 Jocelyn Baines, *Joseph Conrad* (1971[1960]), p. 262.
11 Z. Najder, *Joseph Conrad: A Chronicle* (1983), p. 273.
12 Bernard Meyer, *Joseph Conrad: A Psychoanalytic Biography* (1967), pp. 134–42. Meyer, a professional psychiatrist, gives a striking list of personality traits that Conrad and Ford had in common: quest for parent-child relationships in marriage to compensate for unstable childhood attachments, nervousness, hypochondriasis, gastrointestinal disturbances, depression, suicidal feelings and sensations of being no longer in this world (p. 137).
13 Najder remarks that 'Ford was fascinated by Conrad to the point of worship'. Z. Najder, *Joseph Conrad: A Chronicle* (1983), p. 271.
14 See Conrad's letter to Ford about the disaster, 24 June 1902, *The Collected Letters of Joseph Conrad*, II (1986), p. 428.
15 Z. Najder, *Joseph Conrad: A Chronicle* (1983), p. 283.
16 Ford Madox Ford, *Joseph Conrad: A Personal Remembrance* (London: Duckworth, 1924), pp. 242–4.
17 It is published in its original state in Sondra J. Stang, ed., *The Ford Madox Ford Reader* (Manchester: Carcanet, 1986), pp. 437–47.
18 Owen Knowles, *A Conrad Chronology* (1989), pp. 52–3.
19 Ford Madox Ford, *Joseph Conrad; A Personal Remembrance* (1924), pp. 212–13.
20 Karl and Davies, ed., *The Collected Letters of Joseph Conrad*, II (1986), p. 107.
21 Owen Knowles, *A Conrad Chronology* (1989), pp. 34–8.
22 Ford Madox Ford, *Joseph Conrad: A Personal Remembrance* (1924), pp. 36–7.
23 Quoted by Alan Judd, *Ford Madox Ford* (1990), pp. 70–1; see also Z. Najder, *Joseph Conrad: A Chronicle* (1983), p. 239.
24 Karl and Davies, ed., *The Collected Letters of Joseph Conrad*, II (1986), p. 365.
25 Ford Madox Ford, *Return to Yesterday* (1931), pp. 200–1.
26 Karl and Davies, ed., *The Collected Letters of Joseph Conrad*, II (1986), p. 408.
27 Karl and Davies, ed., *The Collected Letters of Joseph Conrad*, III (1988), p. 287.
28 Joseph Dobrinsky, *The Artist in Conrad's Fiction: A Psychocritical Study* (Ann Arbor: U.M.I. Research Press, 1989), pp. 8–13. The suggestion that Kurtz is like Conrad's romantic father also appears in Frederick Crews, *Out of my System; Psychology, Ideology and Critical Method* (New York: Oxford University Press, 1967), p. 59.
29 Karl and Davies, ed., *The Collected Letters of Joseph Conrad*, I (1983), p. 294.

30 Karl and Davies, ed., *The Collected Letters of Joseph Conrad*, II (1986), pp. 139–40.

31 John Lester, 'Captain Rom: Another Source for Kurtz?', *Conradiana*, XIV (1982), p. 112. There is no way of knowing whether Conrad was aware of this story, but the coincidence with Kurtz's grotesque behaviour is astonishing.

32 Karl and Davies, ed., *The Collected Letters of Joseph Conrad*, II (1986), pp. 176–7.

33 The relationship between manuscript, serial publication and book publication has been examined by Robert Kimbrough for his edition of *Heart of Darkness* which, although very useful, contains some odd errors. In particular, some of its transcriptions from the pencil manuscript are incorrect. For example, it quotes the last words of the ms. as 'the tranquil waterway that leads . . . to the uttermost ends of the earth flowing sombre under an overcast sky seemed to lead into the heart of an immense blackness'; Robert Kimbrough, ed., *Heart of Darkness* (New York: Norton, 1988), p. 76. If the final word of the manuscript were *blackness* it would be very interesting as it would show that the immensely resonant phrase 'heart of darkness' which gives the novel its title was not firmly established in Conrad's mind. But in fact the last word of the manuscript is quite clearly 'darkness'.

34 Cedric Watts, *Conrad's Heart of Darkness: A Critical and Contextual Discussion* (Milan: Mursia, 1977), p. 7.

35 Passages cut from both the manuscript and the serial form are quoted in helpful footnotes in Kimbrough's Norton critical edition (with the caveat that some of the transcriptions from the manuscript are inaccurate as I have indicated). As Kimbrough says, the effect of most of these deleted passages was to make for greater explicitness.

36 Kimbrough, ed., *Heart of Darkness* (1988), p. 72.

37 *Ibid.*, p. 18.

38 Norman Sherry, *Conrad's Western World* (Cambridge: Cambridge University Press, 1971), pp. 48–52.

39 Z. Najder, *Joseph Conrad: A Chronicle* (1983), p. 134.

40 Najder remarks that the very word 'successful' would be ironic in such a context (private communication to the author, December 1992).

41 Sigmund Freud, *Civilization and its Discontents* (London: The Hogarth Press, 1963), p. 17n.

42 Cedric Watts disagrees with this, quoting Dr Johnson: 'Imitations produce pain or pleasure, not because they are mistaken for realities, but because they bring realities to mind.' Letter to the author, 26 May 1992.

43 *Paradise Lost*, IV, 110.

44 This is discussed by R. G. Hampson, 'The Genie out of the Bottle: Conrad, Wells and Joyce', in Peter L. Caracciolo, ed., *The Arabian Nights in English Literature* (London: Macmillan, 1988), p. 220f.

45 See John Batchelor, *The Edwardian Novelists* (London: Duckworth, 1982), John Batchelor, *H. G. Wells* (Cambridge: Cambridge University Press, 1985), and Bernard Bergonzi, *The Early H. G. Wells* (Manchester: Manchester University Press, 1961).

46 Terence Cave, *Recognitions: A Study in Poetics* (Oxford: Clarendon Press, 1988), p. 465.

47 See John Rewald, *The History of Impressionism* (New York: The Museum of Modern Art, 1980), p. 564.

48 This is discussed in detail in an important article by Michael Levenson, 'The Value of Facts in the *Heart of Darkness*', in Kimbrough, ed., *Heart of Darkness* (1988), pp. 391–405.

49 J. Hillis Miller, '*Heart of Darkness* Revisited', in Ross C. Murfin, ed., *Conrad Revisited: Essays for the Eighties* (University, Alabama: University of Alabama Press, 1985), p. 45.

50 I agree that the surface level is important: we should never forget that it is an exposure of colonial exploitation. See M. M. Mahood, *The Colonial Encounter: A Reading of Six Novels* (1977), p. 23.

51 F. C. Crews, *Out of my System; Psychology, Ideology and Critical Method* (1967), p. 66.

52 Karl and Davies, ed., *The Collected Letters of Joseph Conrad*, II (1986), p. 282.

53 *Ibid.*, p., 223.

54 Jan Verleun, *Patna and Patusan Perspectives: A Study of the function of the minor characters in Joseph Conrad's Lord Jim* (Groningen: Bouma's Boekhuis, 1979).

55 Ian Watt, *Conrad in the Nineteenth Century* (1980), p. 260.

56 Karl and Davies, ed., *The Collected Letters of Joseph Conrad*, II (1986), p. 230.

57 *Ibid.*, p. 231.

58 Optical or otherwise: I discuss their thematic and 'moral' similarities on pp. 99–103.

59 Karl and Davies, ed., *The Collected Letters of Joseph Conrad*, II (1986), p. 237.

60 *Ibid.*, p. 234.

61 *Ibid.*, p. 243.

62 Noted by Karl and Davies., *ibid.* p. 243n.

63 *Ibid.*, p. 244.

64 *Ibid.*, p. 257.

65 *Ibid.*, p. 271.

66 John Batchelor, *Lord Jim* (1988), p. 52.

67 *Collected Letters of Joseph Conrad*, II (1986), pp. 49–50.

68 *Ibid.*, p. 191.

69 *Ibid.*, p. 65.

70 'Tuan Jim: A Sketch' is quoted in full in Thomas Moser's Norton Critical Edition of *Lord Jim* (New York: Norton, 1968), pp. 276–91.

71 Moser, ed. *Lord Jim* (1968), p. 283.

72 Ian Watt, *Conrad in the Nineteenth Century* (1980), p. 269.

73 Gail Fraser, *Interweaving Patterns in the Works of Joseph Conrad* (Ann Arbor: U.M.I. Research Press, 1988), p. 77.

74 *Ibid.*, pp. 27–47.

75 *Ibid.*, p. 47.

76 *Pace* the late Allon White, *The Uses of Obscurity* (London: Routledge, 1981). White says that Conrad 'indulges in indiscriminate, sham universalism' using 'enigma' as a method of 'artificially generating value' (p. 122) and that the name of the 'The Nellie' is a deceptively innocuous name, a piece of random particularity designed to perpetuate the supposed 'aura' (in Walter Benjamin's usage) of the fiction (p. 113). White may have been unaware that there was a real yacht called *The Nellie*.

77 Batchelor, *Lord Jim* (1988), p. 209.

78 This form of pleasure is brilliantly discussed by A. D. Nuttall in *Openings: Narrative Beginnings from the Epic to the Novel* (Oxford: Clarendon Press, 1992).

79 These dramatic dates are proposed by J. E. Tanner, cited in Batchelor, *Lord Jim* (1988), p. 79, note 48.

80   A. J. Guerard, *Conrad the Novelist* (Cambridge, Mass: Harvard University Press, 1958), p. 127.
81   Ford Madox Ford, *Joseph Conrad: A Personal Remembrance* (London: Duckworth, 1924), pp. 24–5.
82   *Ibid.*, p. 11.
83   *Ibid.*, p. 6.
84   Arthur Mizener, *The Saddest Story: A Biography of Ford Madox Ford* (London: Bodley Head, 1971), p. 46.
85   See chapter 7, pp. 169–70.
86   I have discussed this at greater length in John Batchelor, *Lord Jim* (1988), p. 121.
87   Edward Garnett, ed., *Letters from Conrad: 1895–1924 [1928]*, p. 172.
88   See the admirably methodical analysis by Jan Verleun in *Patna and Patusan Perspectives* (1979).
89   Norman Sherry, ed., *Conrad: The Critical Heritage* (1973), p. 123.
90   Tony Tanner, *Lord Jim* (London: Edward Arnold, 1963).
91   I have discussed these patterns more fully in John Batchelor, *Lord Jim* (1988), p. 173.
92   *Ibid.*, pp. 118–20.
93   *Ibid.*, pp. 175–9.
94   Quoted by Andrzej Busza, *Conrad's Polish Literary Background* (1966), p. 131. See chapter 1, pp. 5–6.
95   I have written about the relationship that I see between *Lord Jim* and *Hamlet* in John Batchelor, *Lord Jim* (1988), chapter 8, esp. pp. 160–86.
96   'To be or not to be', etc., *Hamlet* III, i, 56–60.
97   Bernard Meyer, *Joseph Conrad: A Psychoanalytic Biography* (1967), p. 274, gives a list of Conrad's suicides which includes Kayerts ('An Outpost of Progress'), Jim, Decoud, Captain Whalley, Renouard, Heyst, Peyrol, Susan ('The Idiots'), Brierly, Winnie Verloc, Erminia ('Gaspar Ruiz'), Sevrin ('The Informer'), de Barral.
98   I take that date from, especially, E. A. J. Honigmann, 'The Date of Hamlet' (*Shakespeare Survey*, 9, 1956), pp. 24–34.
99   J. E. Tanner shows that Jim is born in about 1859 or 1860, the *Patna* incident takes place in 1882–3, Jim arrives in Patusan in 1886–7, Marlow visits Patusan in 1888–9 and his long oral narrative and Jim's death take place in 1889–90. J. E. Tanner, 'The Chronology and Enigmatic End of *Lord Jim*', *Nineteenth Century Fiction*, XXI (March, 1967), pp. 369–80.
100 In a private communication Andzrej Busza has suggested that in the background there may well be an echo of Mickiewicz's *Pan Tadeusz*. This reinforces Morf's argument, since this work was, as we have seen, the Polish national epic. See chapter 1, p. 8.
101 Gustav Morf, *The Polish Heritage of Joseph Conrad* (London: Sampson, Low, Marston, 1930), pp. 149–66.
102 See chapter 2, p. 22.
103 Quoted in John Batchelor, *Lord Jim* (1988), p. 60.
104 *Ibid.*, p. 65–7.
105 Quoted in *Ibid.*, p. 77.
106 Ian Watt, *Conrad in the Nineteenth Century* (1980), p. 261
107 See pp. 97–8.
108 Karl and Davies, ed., *The Collected Letters of Joseph Conrad*, II (1986), p. 261.
109 Ian Watt, *Conrad in the Nineteenth Century* (1980), p. 359.

NOTES TO CHAPTER 5

1 Karl and Davies, ed., *The Collected Letters of Joseph Conrad*, III (1988), p. 287.
2 Owen Knowles, *A Conrad Chronology* (1989), p. 142.
3 See chapter 4, p. 84.
4 As we have seen in Conrad's account of it to John Galsworthy, 20 July 1900. See chapter 4, p. 76.
5 Owen Knowles, *A Conrad Chronology* (1989), pp. 40–1 and Karl and Davies, ed., *The Collected Letters of Joseph Conrad*, II (1986), p. 295.
6 It was published there in July-December 1902.
7 Karl and Davies, ed., *The Collected Letters of Joseph Conrad*, II (1986), p. 261.
8 Ibid., p. 262.
9 Joseph Conrad and F. M. Hueffer, *The Inheritors: An Extravagant Story* (London: William Heinemann, 1901), p. 297.
10 Morley Roberts, a friend of Hudson and Gissing and a prolific writer: Karl and Davies cite *The Colossus: A Story of Today* (1899) as an example of a political fiction that might have been in Conrad's mind. Karl and Davies, ed., *The Collected Letters of Joseph Conrad*, II (1986), p. 257n.
11 *Ibid.*, pp. 256–7. Ford confirms in his memoir that Conrad had written very little of *The Inheritors*: Ford Madox Ford, *Joseph Conrad: A Personal Remembrance* (1924), pp. 134–42.
12 Arthur Mizener, *The Saddest Story* (1971), pp. 54–5.
13 Karl and Davies, ed., *The Collected Letters of Joseph Conrad*, II (1986), 417–18.
14 Lawrence Graver says ' Whalley, like Kurtz, sees the horror of the life and has his memory perpetuated by an enormous lie.' Lawrence Graver, *Conrad's Short Fiction* (Berkeley and Los Angeles: University of California Press, 1969), p. 118.
15 It is possible that his state of mind reflects Conrad's anxieties about the deceptions of Pinker, Ford and others to which he felt forced to resort in order to provide for his family.
16 Karl and Davies, ed., *The Collected Letters of Joseph Conrad*, III (1988), pp. 93 and (translation by Karl and Davies) 94.
17 'Material which we might expect Conrad to use as the basis of a somebrely sceptical analysis of human nature and civilized society is here firmly contained within a social comedy,' and also 'if the reader's reflexive response to the idea of cannibalism is one of revulsion, Conrad mocks that reflex by attributing it to the mediocre Hermann', Cedric Watts, ed., Joseph Conrad, *Typhoon and Other Tales*, World's Classics edition (Oxford: Oxford University Press, 1986), pp. x–xi. To support this Watts quotes a letter in which Conrad said that the basic idea of the tale was 'Contrast between common sentimentality and the clear viewpoint of a rather primitive man (Falk himself) who considers the preservation of life to be the supreme – and moral – law', *ibid.*, p. xin.
18 Cedric Watts thinks that I am wrong about this. He remarks that 'Falk' challenges our 'Conradian expectations (based on *Heart of Darkness*) that cannibalism by whites is to be regarded with revulsion, and it challenges notions of love by explaining that Falk's love for the women is as natural as cannibalistic appetite had once been. That the narrator says "don't be shocked" implies an expectation of shock as a normal reaction' (letter to the author, 26 May

1992). To my mind an important difference between *Heart of Darkness* and 'Falk' is that *Heart of Darkness* belongs to a radical genre, the anti-imperial tale, which is new, topical and shocking (subverting, obviously, an established genre, the Victorian tale of imperial adventure). The genre of tales of cannibalism among sailors, to which 'Falk' belongs, is much older and more familiar and therefore inherently less shocking. The desensitized narrator can reasonably adopt a fairly light tone because this is basically familiar stuff which on this occasion is getting comic treatment.

19 Quoted in Cedric Watts, ed., Joseph Conrad, *Typhoon and Other Tales* (1986), p. xiii.

20 Fork Madox Ford, *Joseph Conrad: A Personal Remembrance* (1924), pp. 120, 132.

21 Jessie Conrad, *Joseph Conrad as I knew Him* (1926), p. 118.

22 Karl and Davies, ed., *The Collected Letters of Joseph Conrad*, II (1986), p. 372.

23 Jessie Conrad, *Joseph Conrad as I knew Him* (1926), p. 119.

24 Karl and Davies, ed., *The Collected Letters of Joseph Conrad*, II (1986), p. 373.

25 *The Nigger of the 'Narcissus', Typhoon, Falk and Other Stories*, ed. Norman Sherry (London: Dent, 1974), p. 266.

26 Karl and Davies, ed., *The Collected Letters of Joseph Conrad*, III (1988), p. 104.

27 *Ibid.*, pp. 59–60.

28 The collaboraton is examined in detail in Raymond Brebach, *Joseph Conrad, Ford Madox Ford and the Making of Romance* (Ann Arbor, Mich.: UMI Research Press), 1985.

29 A reference to the voyage of the *Saint-Antoine* in August and September 1876, but it is not clear how Conrad got his glimpse; see chapter 2, p. 24.

30 Karl and Davies, ed., *The Collected Letters of Joseph Conrad*, III (1988), p. 45.

31 *Ibid.*, p. 47.

32 *Ibid.*, pp. 51–52 and (translation by Karl and Davies) 53.

33 *Ibid.*, p. 55.

34 Chapter 4, p. 82.

35 Karl and Davies, ed., *The Collected Letters of Joseph Conrad*, III (1988), p. 85.

36 Casement was knighted in 1911, but in 1916 he was arrested for collusion with the Germans – which, from the Irish nationalist viewpoint, was wholly patriotic and honourable behaviour – and hanged. See Owen Knowles, *A Conrad Chronology* (1989), p. 129.

37 Karl and Davies, ed., *The Collected Letters of Joseph Conrad*, III (1988), pp. 101–102.

38 Conrad to Cunninghame Graham, 31 October 1904, *ibid.*, p. 176.

39 See chapter 11, pp. 269–70.

40 Karl and Davies, ed., *The Collected Letters of Joseph Conrad*, III (1988), p. 109.

41 To William Rothenstein, 27 June 1904. *Ibid.*, p. 147. This letter is ostensibly about Jessie's knees but switches quite quickly to Conrad's own misery.

42 See above, chapter 4, p. 184.

43 1 September 1904, *ibid.*, p. 158.

44 The serial ending is reprinted by Keith Carabine in Keith Carabine, ed., *Nostromo*, World's Classics Edition (Oxford: Oxford University Press, 1984), pp. 567–75.

45 Conrad and Pinker hoped for serialization with the Northern Newspaper Syndicate.

46 Karl and Davies, ed., *The Collected Letters of Joseph Conrad*, III (1988), p. 6.

47   See chapter 2, p. 24.
48   Norman Page, *A Conrad Chronology* (1986), pp. 2–3.
49   Norman Sherry has shown the extent to which *Nostromo* is based on Conrad's reading in *Conrad's Western World* (Cambridge: Cambridge University Press, 1971), pp. 147–201.
50   R. B. Cunninghame Graham, *A Vanished Arcadia* (London: William Heinemann, 1901), G. F. Masterman, *Seven Eventful Years in Paraguay* (London: Sampson, Low, 1869), *Garibaldi: An Autobiography* (ed. Alexandre Dumas. London: Routledge, Warne and Routledge, 1860), Edward B. Eastwick, *Venezuela: Or Sketches of Life in a South-American Republic* (London: Chapman and Hall, 1868); Ramon Paez, *Wild Scenes in South America* (New York: C. Scribner, 1862); Frederick Benton Williams [pseud. for Herbert Elliott Hamblen], *On Many Seas: The Life and Exploits of a Yankee Sailor* (New York: G. P. Putnam's Sons, 1897).
51   F. B. Williams, *On Many Seas* (1897), pp. 288–9.
52   *Garibaldi: An Autobiography* (1860), pp. 68–9.
53   Masterman, *Seven Eventful Years in Paraguay* (1869), p. 257.
54   E. B. Eastwick, *Venezuela* (1868), p. 187.
55   See chapter 3, p. 72.
56   Cunninghame Graham spent four-and-a-half weeks in prison for his part in the 'Bloody Sunday' demonstration in Trafalgar Square, 1887.
57   Karl and Davis, ed., *The Collected Letters of Joseph Conrad*, II (1986), p. 16.
58   Karl and Davies, ed., *The Collected Letters of Joseph Conrad*, III (1988), p. 217.
59   Chapter 3, pp. 70–1.
60   Quoted by Watts and Davies, *Cunninghame Graham* (1979), p. 143.
61   *Ibid.*, p. 22.
62   *Ibid.*, pp. 120–121.
63   Quoted in Cedric Watts and Laurence Davies, *Cunninghame Grahame* (1979), p. 145.
64   R. B. Cunninghame Graham, *A Vanished Arcadia* (1901), p. 286.
65   Ford Madox Ford, *Return to Yesterday* (London: Victor Gollancz, 1931), p. 200.
66   Karl and Davies, ed., *The Collected Letters of Joseph Conrad*, II (1986), p. 4.
67   A. J. Guerard, *Conrad the Novelist* (1958), p. 180.
68   Cedric Watts, *Nostromo* (Harmondsworth: Penguin, 1990), pp. 55–6 and letter to the author, 25 May 1992.
69   Jacques Berthoud, *Joseph Conrad: The Major Phase* (Cambridge: Cambridge University Press, 1978), p. 97.
70   See p. 131.
71   See pp. 118–19.
72   Cedric Watts, *Nostromo* (1990), p. 29, and letter to the author, 25 May 1992.
73   A. J. Guerard, *Conrad the Novelist* (1958), p. 199, and Watts, *Nostromo*, 1990, p. 96.
74   A. J. Guerard, *Conrad the Novelist* (1958), p. 176 and Robert Penn Warren, 'Nostromo', *Sewanee Review*, 59, 3 (1951), p. 367.
75   S. T. Coleridge, 'To William Wordsworth, Composed on the Night after his Recitation of a Poem on the Growth of an Individual Mind', January, 1807, line 40.
76   A. J. Guerard, *Conrad the Novelist* (1958), p. 199, Cedric Watts, *Nostromo* (1990), p. 96.
77   A. J. Guerard, *Conrad the Novelist* (1958), p. 215.

78 *Ibid.*, p. 204.
79 Robert Penn Warren, 'Nostromo' (1951), p. 371.
80 Ian Watt, *Joseph Conrad: Nostromo* (Cambridge: Cambridge University Press, 1988).
81 Jan Verleun, *The Stone Horse: A Study of the Function of the Minor Characters in Joseph Conrad's Nostromo* (Groningen: Bouma's Boekhuis, 1978), p. 13.

NOTES TO CHAPTER 6

1   *The Secret Agent*, ed. Bruce Harkness and S. W. Reid (Cambridge: Cambridge University Press, 1990), p. 6. Subsequent references to *The Secret Agent* are to this edition.
2   Karl and Davies, ed., *The Collected Letters of Joseph Conrad*, III (1988), p. 286.
3   *Ibid.*, p. 162.
4   *Ibid.*, p. 160.
5   Keith Carabine's edition gives the original as well as the revised ending.
6   Karl and Davies, ed., *The Collected Letters of Joseph Conrad*, III (1988), p. 178.
7   *Ibid.*, p. 112.
8   *Ibid.*, pp. 127, 129.
9   Karl and Davies, ed., *The Collected Letters of Joseph Conrad*, II (1986), p. 257.
10 Karl and Davies, ed., *The Collected Letters of Joseph Conrad*, III (1988), p. 199.
11 *Ibid.*, p. 208.
12 Conrad to Pinker, 12 April 1905, *ibid.*, p. 228.
13 At Cornell University. The draft was probably written at the beginning of 1904. Z. Najder, *Joseph Conrad: A Chronicle* (1983), p. 314–15.
14 Quoted in Najder, *ibid.*, p. 414.
15 John Galsworthy, introduction to Joseph Conrad, *Laughing Anne* and *One Day More* (London: John Castle, 1924), p. 7.
16 Karl and Davies, ed., *The Collected Letters of Joseph Conrad*, III (1988), p. 272.
17 *Ibid.*, p. 228.
18 *Ibid.*, p. 284, 288.
19 See my discussions of *The Secret Agent* and *Under Western Eyes*, pp. 156–57 and 178–80.
20 Karl and Davies, ed., *The Collected Letters of Joseph Conrad*, III (1988), p. 327.
21 *Ibid.*, p. 349.
22 *Ibid.*, p. 403.
23 *Ibid.*, p. 435.
24 *Ibid.*, p. 434.
25 *Ibid.*, p. 448.
26 *Ibid.*, p. 232–3.
27 G. Jean-Aubry, *Joseph Conrad: Life and Letters* (1927), II, p. 168.
28 See chapter 3, p. 55.
29 Borys Conrad, *My Father: Joseph Conrad* (London: Calder and Boyars, 1970), p. 13, p. 25.
30 Bernard Meyer, *Joseph Conrad: A Psychoanalytic Biography* (1967), p. 188.
31 Ford Madox Ford, *Joseph Conrad: A Personal Remembrance* (London: Duckworth, 1924), p. 231.

32 The background to the novel has been explored by Norman Sherry in *Conrad's Western World* (1971).
33 Sherry, *Conrad's Western World* (1971), chapters 20, 21 and 22.
34 *Ibid.*, p. 243.
35 *Ibid.*, pp. 259, 261, 265, 283, 295, 313.
36 Harkness and Reid, eds., *The Secret Agent* (1990), p. xxviii.
37 *Ibid.*, p. xxix.
38 *Ibid.*, p. xxxi.
39 *Ibid.*, p. xxx.
40 See Anthony Winner, *Culture and Irony: Studies in Joseph Conrad's Major Novels* (Charlottesville, Virginia: University Press of Virginia, 1988), p. 84.
41 Sherry, *Conrad's Western World* (1971), p. 314.
42 Barbara A. Melchiori, *Terrorism in the Late Victorian Novel* (London: Croom Helm, 1985), p. 76.
43 Sherry, *Conrad's Western World* (1971), pp. 325–34. See chapter 1, p. 16.
44 *Collected Letters of Joseph Conrad*, I (1983), pp. 416–17.
45 Sherry, *Conrad's Western World* (1971), p. 329.
46 *Ibid.*, p. 329.
47 *Ibid.*, p. 328.
48 William Blackburn, quoted by Sherry, *Conrad's Western World* (1971), p. 332.
49 Suresh Raval, *The Art of Failure: Conrad's Fiction* (London: Allen and Unwin, 1986), p. 115.
50 Who in turn takes his from Nietzsche, Fredric Jameson, *The Political Unconscious* (London: Methuen, 1983), p. 201.
51 Raval, *The Art of Failure: Conrad's Fiction* (1986), p. 114.
52 Karl and Davies, ed., *The Collected Letters of Joseph Conrad*, III (1988), p. 439.
53 *Ibid.*, p. 460.
54 Ian Watt, ed., *The Secret Agent: A Casebook* (London: Macmillan, 1973), pp. 77, 78–9.
55 Karl and Davies, ed., *The Collected Letters of Joseph Conrad*, III (1988), pp. 370–1.
56 Norman Sherry, ed., *Conrad: The Critical Heritage* (London: Routledge and Kegan Paul, 1973), pp. 186–9.
57 Karl and Davies, ed., *The Collected Letters of Joseph Conrad*, III (1988), p. 355.
58 Norman Sherry, ed., *Conrad: The Critical Heritage* (1973), pp. 191–3.
59 Karl and Davies, ed., *The Collected Letters of Joseph Conrad*, IV (1990), p. 111.
60 John Galsworthy, 'Joseph Conrad: A Disquisition', *Fortnightly Review*, 496 (1 April 1908), pp. 627–33.
61 Thomas Mann, 'Joseph Conrad's *The Secret Agent*' (from *Past Masters and Other Papers*, 1933, originally preface to a German translation of *The Secret Agent*, 1926), reprinted in Ian Watt, ed., *The Secret Agent: A Casebook* (London: Macmillan, 1973), p. 102.

NOTES TO CHAPTER 7

1 Conrad to Pinker, 30 July 1907, Karl and Davies, ed., *The Collected Letters of Joseph Conrad*, III (1988), p. 460.
2 *Ibid.*, p. 477.

3   *Ibid.*, p. 475.
4   Karl and Davies, ed., *The Collected Letters of Joseph Conrad*, IV (1990), pp. 7, 15.
5   *Ibid.*, p. 21.
6   See chapter 2, p. 37.
7   Karl and Davies, ed., *The Collected Letters of Joseph Conrad*, IV (1990), p. 9.
8   *Ibid.*, pp. 14–15.
9   *Ibid.*, p. 55.
10 Karl and Davies, ed., *The Collected Letters of Joseph Conrad*, II (1986), p. 455.
11 Karl and Davies, ed., *The Collected Letters of Joseph Conrad*, IV (1990), p. 62.
12 *Ibid.*, pp. 112–13.
13 *Ibid.*, pp. 318–19.
14 Z. Najder, *Joseph Conrad: A Chronicle* (1983), p. 343.
15 Jessie Conrad, *Joseph Conrad as I knew Him* (1926), p. 57.
16 Frederick Karl, *Joseph Conrad* (1979), chapter 28, (especially p. 663) gives a good account of this tangled episode.
17 Quoted in Jocelyn Baines, *Joseph Conrad* (1971[1960]), pp. 419–20.
18 Karl and Davies, ed., *The Collected Letters of Joseph Conrad*, IV (1990), p. 266.
19 *Ibid.*, p. 299.
20 *Ibid.*, p. 302.
21 *Ibid.*, p. 302.
22 *Ibid.*, pp. 304, 305–6.
23 *Ibid.*, pp. 320–1 and n.
24 *Ibid.*, p. 334.
25 They are in the Berg Collection, New York Public Library.
26 Quoted By Zdzisław Najder, *Joseph Conrad: A Chronicle* (1983), p. 357.
27 Letter to David Meldrum, 6 February 1910, quoted by Norman Sherry in *Conrad: The Critical Heritage* (1973), pp. 26–7.
28 *Conrad: The Critical Heritage* (1973), pp. 238–9.
29 Karl and Davies, ed., *The Collected Letters of Joseph Conrad*, IV (1990), pp. 488–9.
30 A. J. Guerard, *Conrad the Novelist* (1958), pp. 291, 221.
31 Zdzisław Najder sees it as a realistically treated melodrama: 'Joseph Conrad's *The Secret Agent* as the melodrama of reality'. *Melodrama* (ed. Daniel Gerould), *New York Literary Forum* (1980), pp. 159–65.
32 Razumov calls it 'a comedy of errors', see p. 181.
33 See my discussion of *Victory* in chapter 9.
34 Tony Tanner calls this ambition 'bourgeois' ('Nightmare and Complacency: Razumov and the Western Eye', *Critical Quarterly* IV, no. 3 (Autumn, 1962), pp. 197–214). Zdzisław Najder remarks that 'bourgeois' here is a misnomer: bourgeoisie hardly existed in Russia. 'A university professor would (even from the legal point of view) become a member of the nobility' (private communication to the author, January 1993).
35 John Batchelor, *Lord Jim* (1988), pp. 107–8.
36 Cedric Watts, ed., Joseph Conrad, *Typhoon: and Other Tales* (Oxford: Oxford University Press, 1986), 'Introduction', p. xviii.
37 John Batchelor, *Lord Jim* (1988), Chapter 8 passim.
38 In a letter to Curle of 30 March 1914 Conrad thanks Curle for Bradley's book, saying that he admires it and wants to keep it a bit longer. Curle had written an intelligent review of *Under Western Eyes* in the *Manchester Guardian* as a result of which he and Conrad met and became friends in the winter of 1912;

Richard Curle, ed., *Conrad to a Friend: 150 Selected Letters from Joseph Conrad to Richard Curle* (London: Sampson Low, Marston and Co., 1928), p. 18.

39 For example, *Nation*, 22 June 1905: 'no book more cheering than this has appeared for many years', and *Times Literary Supplement*, 10 February 1905, 'a great achievement.'

40 Conrad would have been familiar with Aristotle's *Poetics* since his schooldays and may have referred to it again in English in Bywater's translation (published in 1909 and thus also available to Conrad during the latter part of his work on *Under Western Eyes*). Bywater gives the passage about pity and fear thus: 'A tragedy, then, is the imitation of an action that is serious and also, as having magnitude, complete in itself: in language with pleasurable accessories, each kind brought in separately in the parts of the work; in a dramatic, not in a narrative form; with incidents arousing pity and fear, wherewith to accomplish its catharsis of such emotions.' Ingram Bywater, trans. and ed., *Aristotle on the Art of Poetry* (Oxford: Clarendon Press, 1909), p. 17.

41 M. A. Gillies, 'Conrad's *The Secret Agent* and *Under Western Eyes* as Bergsonian Comedies,' *Conradiana* XX, 1988, pp. 195–213.

42 All these revisions are discussed, and the restaurant scene is printed, by David Leon Higdon and Robert F. Sheard in 'Conrad's "Unkindest Cut", The Cancelled Scenes in *Under Western Eyes*', *Conradiana* XIX, Autumn 1987, pp. 167–181.

43 Private communication from Zdzisław Najder, January 1993.

44 John Batchelor, *The Edwardian Novelists* (1982), p. 74.

45 Cedric Watts, 'Stepniak and *Under Western Eyes*', *Notes and Queries* XIII (1966), 410–11 and Thomas C. Moser, 'An English Context for Conrad's Russian characters: Sergey Stepniak and the Diary of Olive Garnett', *Journal of Modern Literature* Vol. 11, no. 1 (March, 1984), pp. 3–44. Richard Garnett's biography, *Constance Garnett : A Heroic Life* (London: Sinclair-Stevenson, 1991), gives more detail on the Stepniak-Olive-Constance relationship.

46 Moser, 'An English Context for Conrad's Russian characters' (1984), pp. 3–4, 20.

47 *Ibid.*, pp. 4–5.

48 *Ibid.*, p. 16.

49 *Ibid.*, p. 23.

50 Private communication to the author, January 1993.

51 *The Secret Agent* (Cambridge edition, 1990), p. 228.

52 *Ibid.*, p. 55.

53 Moser, 'An English Context for Conrad's Russian characters' (1984), p. 34.

54 *Ibid.*, p. 6

55 *Ibid.*, p. 25.

56 See p. 167.

57 Karl Miller, *Doubles: Studies in Literary History* (Oxford: Oxford University Press, 1985), p. 245.

58 *Conrad: The Critical Heritage* (1973), p. 239.

59 Edward Garnett, ed., *Letters from Conrad: 1895–1924* (London: The Nonesuch Press, [1928], p. 260.

60 *Ibid.*, pp. 260–1.

61 See chapter 11, pp. 279–80.

62 Edward Garnett, ed., *Letters from Conrad* [1928], p. 265.

63 *Ibid.*, p. 237.

64 *Conrad: The Critical Heritage* (1973), p. 26.
65 In his editor's introduction to the World's Classics edition of the novel.
66 *Ibid.*, pp. 210–11.
67 *Ibid.*, p. 252.
68 *Ibid.*, p. 254.
69 'Gaspar Ruiz' was completed November 1905 and published in *Pall Mall Magazine*, July–October 1906; 'The Brute' was completed in December 1905 and published in the *Daily Chronicle*; 5 December 1906; 'An Anarchist' was completed in November–December 1905 and published in *Harper's Magazine*, August 1906; and 'The Informer: was finished in December–January 1905–1906, and published in *Harper's Magazine* in December 1906. Lawrence Graver, *Conrad's Short Fiction* (1969), Appendix, 'A Chronology of Conrad's Short Stories'.
70 *Extracts from a Journal Written on the Coasts of Chili, Peru, and Mexico in the Years 1820, 21, 22* (1824), quoted by Paul Kirschner, 'Conrad's Strong Man', *Modern Fiction Studies* (Spring, 1964), p. 32.
71 Kirschner's argument leans too heavily on the similarity that he sees between Gaspar (whose strength is manipulated by Erminia) and the autobiographical M. George of *The Arrow of Gold* (whose youth is manipulated by Rita): Paul Kirschner, 'Conrad's Strong Man' (1964), pp. 35–6.
72 Quoted in Lawrence Graver, *Conrad's Short Fiction* (1969), p. 149.
73 Edward Garnett, ed., *Letters from Conrad: 1895–1924* [1928], pp. 247–8.
74 *Ibid.*, pp. 262–3.
75 These points are noted by Cedric Watts, in *Typhoon: And Other Tales*, World's Classics Edition (Oxford: Oxford University Press, 1986), p. 309. References to 'The Secret Sharer' are to this edition.
76 *Ibid.*, p. 308.
77 *Ibid.*, p. 308.
78 William Wordsworth, *The Prelude*, Book First, 1805 (New York: Norton, Norton Critical Edition, 1979), p. 50, 11.405–12.
79 Alastair Fowler, ed., *Paradise Lost* (London: Longman, 1971), p. 130, Book II, 11.882–3 and n. *OED* gives 'Erebus' as a 'place of darkness between Earth and Hades'.
80 *Paradise Lost*, II, 11.882–3.

NOTES TO CHAPTER 8

1 Quoted in Norman Sherry, ed., *Conrad: The Critical Heritage* (1973), p. 259.
2 This was Robert Lynd, writing in the *Daily News*, 15th January, 1914. Quoted in Sherry, *ibid.*, p. 271.
3 Karl and Davies, ed., *The Collected Letters of Joseph Conrad*, IV (1990), p. 345.
4 Lawrence Graver, *Conrad's Short Fiction* (1969), p. 162.
5 See chapter 1, pp. 1–2.
6 Joseph Conrad, *Tales of Hearsay*, with a Preface by R. B. Cunninghame Graham (London: Fisher Unwin, 1925), p. 19. All my page references to the stories in *Tales of Hearsay* are to this edition.
7 This actually happened. See chapter 1, p. 2.
8 Karl and Davies, ed., *The Collected Letters of Joseph Conrad*, IV (1990), p. 407.
9 *Ibid.*, p. 440.

10　*Ibid.*, p. 522.
11　Owen Knowles, *A Conrad Chronology* (1989), p. 82.
12　Frederick Karl, *Joseph Conrad* (1979), pp. 708–9.
13　Owen Knowles, *A Conrad Chronology* (1989), p. 82.
14　Karl and Davies, ed., *The Collected Letters of Joseph Conrad*, IV (1990), pp. 472–3.
15　*Ibid.*, pp. 484–5.
16　*Ibid.*, p. 462.
17　Frederick Karl, *Joseph Conrad* (1979), p. 701.
18　*Ibid.*, p. 700.
19　Karl and Davies, ed., *The Collected Letters of Joseph Conrad*, IV (1990), pp. 479–80.
20　These cuts are discussed by by David Leon Higdon and Robert F. Sheard in 'Conrad's "Unkindest Cut"' (1987), pp. 167–81.
21　Karl and Davies, ed., *The Collected Letters of Joseph Conrad*, IV (1990), p. 486.
22　Norman Sherry, ed., *Conrad: The Critical Heritage* (1973), pp. 227–8.
23　*Ibid.*, p. 232, 239.
24　See chapter 7, p. 173.
25　Karl and Davies, ed., *The Collected Letters of Joseph Conrad*, IV (1990), p. 523.
26　Quoted by Frederick Karl, *Joseph Conrad* (1979), p. 713.
27　Quoted by Z. Najder, *Joseph Conrad: A Chronicle* (1983), pp. 387–8.
28　See chapter 3, p. 56.
29　Quoted by Z. Najder, *Joseph Conrad: A Chronicle* (1983), p. 389.
30　Owen Knowles, 'Joseph Conrad and Bertrand Russell: New Light on Their Relationship', *Journal of Modern Literature*, XVII: 1 (Summer, 1990), p. 142.
31　Owen Knowles thinks that it also has the '*frisson* of daring homo-erotic attraction' about it. *Ibid.*, p. 140.
32　Frederick Karl, *Joseph Conrad* (1979), p. 737n and Bertrand Russell, *Portraits from Memory and Other Essays* (1956), quoted in Jocelyn Baines, *Joseph Conrad* (1960), p. 536.
33　Daniel R. Schwarz, *Conrad: The Later Fiction* (London: Macmilllan, 1982), pp. 42 and 45.
34　Ref A. J. Guerard, *Conrad the Novelist* (1958).
35　Norman Sherry, ed., *Conrad: The Critical Heritage* (1973), p. 271.
36　'Henry James: An Appreciation', 1905, reprinted in *Notes on Life and Letters*.
37　Quoted in Frederick Karl, *Joseph Conrad* (1979), p. 746.
38　See my discussion of James's quarrel with H. G. Wells in my *H. G. Wells* (1985), pp. 113–22.
39　Norman Sherry, ed., *Conrad: The Critical Heritage* (1973), pp. 265–6.
40　*Ibid.*, p. 268.
41　Graham Hough, *Image and Experience: Studies in a Literary Revolution* (London: Duckworth, 1960), p. 220.
42　See manuscript version of this, p. 206.
43　As he is now called: the 'Archie' of the opening sheets has been dropped.
44　E. E. Duncan-Jones, 'Some Sources of *Chance*', *Review of English Studies*, XX (November, 1969), pp. 468–71.
45　Frederick Karl argues, reasonably enough, that Henri Bergson's work was so much part of the intellectual climate in 1910 that Conrad 'must have had some sense of its impact'. Frederick Karl, *Joseph Conrad* (1979), p. 743n.
46　Martin Ray, ed., *Chance* (1988), p. 466n.

47 G. Jean-Aubrey, *Joseph Conrad: Life and Letters,* II (London: Heinemann, 1927), p. 152.
48 By Robert Hampson, in an unpublished paper, and Paul Kirschner.
49 Paul Kirschner, 'Making you *see* Geneva: The Sense of Place in *Under Western Eyes*', *L'Epoque Conradienne* (1988), pp. 101–25.
50 *Ibid.,* p. 115.
51 John Batchelor, *Lord Jim* (1988), chapter 8.
52 'Desdemona's suffering is like that of the most loving of dumb creatures tortured without cause by the being he adores', A. C. Bradley, *Shakespearean Tragedy* [1904] (London: Macmillan, 1932), pp. 178–9. See John Batchelor, 'Conrad and Shakespeare', *L'Epoque Conradienne* (1992), pp. 124–51.
53 *Ibid.,* pp. 181–2.

Notes to Chapter 9

1 The manuscript of *Victory* is now in the Harry Ransome Humanities Research Centre, University of Texas at Austin.
2 All quoted in Norman Sherry, ed., *Conrad: The Critical Heritage* (1973), pp. 281–2. The quotations are from the following reviews: David Meldrum in the *Daily Chronicle,* 15 January 1914; the *Standard* (unsigned), 16 January 1914; the *Spectator,* 17 January 1914; Sir Sidney Colvin in the *Observer,* 18 January 1914; W. L. Courtney in the *Daily Telegraph,* 21 January 1914; *Punch* (unsigned), 28 January 1914.
3 To Warrington Dawson, 15 February 1911, *Collected Letters of Joseph Conrad,* IV (1990), p. 413.
4 Lawrence Graver, *Conrad's Short Fiction* (1969), pp. 92–93.
5 *Ibid.,* p. 173.
6 Both letters quoted by Frederick Karl, *Joseph Conrad* (1979), p. 716.
7 See my discussion of references to *The Tempest,* pp. 233–5.
8 All these letters of 1912–13 relating to *Victory* are quoted in Frederick Karl, *Joseph Conrad* (1979), pp. 717–19.
9 Both letters quoted in Frederick Karl, *Joseph Conrad* (1979), p. 727.
10 Richard Curle, *Joseph Conrad: A Study* (London: Kegan Paul, Trench, Trubner and Co.), 1914.
11 Frederick Karl, *Joseph Conrad* (1979), p. 716, see above p. 00–00.
12 David Lodge, 'Conrad's "Victory" and "The Tempest": an Amplification', *The Modern Language Review,* 59 (1964), p. 198.
13 Jeffrey Meyers, *Homosexuality and Literature* (London: Athlone Press, 1977), chapter 6, pp. 76–86 and *Joseph Conrad: A Biography* (London: John Murray, 1991), pp. 280–91.
14 A. D. Nuttall, *Openings: Narrative Beginnings from the Epic to the Novel* (Oxford: Clarendon Press, 1992), p. 152 and passim.
15 Frederick R. Karl, '*Victory*: Its Origin and Development', *Conradiana,* XV (1983), pp. 23–51.
16 See my note in Joseph Conrad, *Victory,* ed. John Batchelor, World's Classics Edition (Oxford: Oxford University Press, 1986), p. 421.
17 The comparison has been explored in Bruce Johnson, *Conrad's Models of Mind* (Minneapolis, Minn.: University of Minnesota Press, 1971).

18 See *Victory*, ed., John Batchelor (1986), p. 418.
19 See *Victory*, ed., John Batchelor (1986), pp. 420–1.
20 *Ibid.*, p. 418. It is possible that Conrad is also thinking of Keats's letter to Bailey, 22 November 1817, itself based on the same passage from Milton. Keats takes Adam's dream as a figure of the poetic imagination: 'The Imagination may be compared to Adam's dream – he awoke and found it truth.'
21 Hallett Smith, *The Tempest, The Riverside Shakespeare* (Boston: Houghton Mifflin, 1974), p. 1606.
22 Frederick Karl, *Joseph Conrad: The Three Lives* (London: Faber, 1979), p. 715.
23 *Ibid.*, p. 718.
24 *Ibid.*, p. 747.
25 Conrad refers to the novel in a letter of 2 September 1921 he wrote to Garnett saying that he did not like it much because of 'gratuitous' sensational content, and that he did not recommend it for translation. The letter reads – as one would expect – as though Conrad is referring to a text which he has known for some years, not one that he has just read. Andrzej Busza, *Conrad's Polish Literary Background and some Illustrations of the Influence of Polish Literature on his work* (1966), p. 217n.
26 *Ibid.*, p. 216.
27 Translated and quoted by Busza, *ibid.*, p. 216.
28 Busza shows a number of other parallels between Ewa and Lena, notably the sense of guilt under which they both labour, and he also notes that Żeromski's villains, Pochroń and Płaza-Spławski, resemble Conrad's villains Ricardo and Jones in that they are (respectively) feral and homosexual. *Ibid.*, pp. 218–23.
29 Busza comments on this in detail, *ibid.*, pp. 217–18.
30 Owen Knowles, *A Conrad Chronology* (1989), p. 90.
31 G. Jean-Aubry, *Joseph Conrad: Life and Letters*, II (1927), p. 152.
32 See p. 214.
33 G. Jean-Aubry, *Joseph Conrad: Life and Letters* (1927), p. 157.
34 Z. Najder, *Joseph Conrad: A Chronicle* (1983), pp. 182–3, 397–9.
35 G. Jean–Aubry, *Joseph Conrad: Life and Letters* (London: William Heinemann, 1927), p. 157.
36 Quoted by Z. Najder, *Joseph Conrad: A Chronicle* (1983), p. 402.
37 Z. Najder, *Joseph Conrad: A Chronicle* (1983), p. 399.
38 Quoted by Z. Najder, *Joseph Conrad: A Chronicle* (1983), p. 401.
39 *Ibid.*, p. 401.
40 G. Jean-Aubry, *Joseph Conrad: Life and Letters*, II (1927), p. 160.
41 Z. Najder, ed., *Conrad Under Familial Eyes*, 1983, p. 211.
42 G. Jean-Aubry, *Joseph Conrad: Life and Letters*, II (1927), p. 161.
43 Z. Najder, *Joseph Conrad: A Chronicle* (1983), p. 403.
44 *Ibid.*, p. 404.
45 *Ibid.*, p. 406.
46 Joseph Conrad, 'Poland Revisited', *Notes on Life and Letters* (London: Methuen, 1921), p. 171.
47 In the first of her memoirs Jessie Conrad says that it was in fact his idea that they should cross the North Sea. Jessie Conrad, *Joseph Conrad as I knew Him* (1926), p. 62.
48 'Poland Revisited', *Notes on Life and Letters*, p. 146.

NOTES TO CHAPTER 10

1   G. Jean-Aubry, *Joseph Conrad; Life and Letters*, II (1927), pp. 184–5.
2   Quoted by Owen Knowles, *A Conrad Chronology* (1989), p. 95.
3   Quoted by Z. Najder, *Joseph Conrad; A Chronicle* (1983), p. 407.
4   The letter is transcribed in D. C. Cross, *One Hundred and Thirty Unpublished Letters from Joseph Conrad to John Galsworthy*. Unpublished M.A. thesis, Birmingham University, 1966, pp. 134–5.
5   *Ibid.*, p. 135.
6   Quoted by Najder, *ibid.*, p. 414.
7   See chapter 11, p. 275.
8   Peter Ure expresses it slightly differently: 'Conrad's heroes, partly fashioned in his own image, are sometimes highly imaginative men, and yet at the same time men who can be punished by what may be described as a degeneration of the imaginative faculty.' Peter Ure, 'Character and Imagination in Conrad', *Yeats and Anglo-Irish Literature* (ed. C. J. Rawson, Liverpool: Liverpool University Press, 1974), p. 229.
9   See chapter 7, pp. 187–88.
10 Quoted by Allan Ingram, ed., Joseph Conrad, *Selected Literary Criticism and The Shadow-Line* (London: Methuen, 1986), p. 106.
11 *Ibid.*, p. 106.
12 *Ibid.*, p. 108.
13 See p. 46 above.
14 Allan Ingram, ed., Joseph Conrad, *Selected literary Criticism and The Shadow-Line* (1986), pp. 228–30.
15 *Ibid.*, p. 261 and Jeremy Hawthorn, ed., *The Shadow-Line* (1985), p. 137.
16 *Ibid.*, p. 264. It is obviously important for Conrad, throughout his writing life, to 'match up' his own work to that of Shakespeare.
17 *Conrad's Eastern World* (1966), pp. 218–27 and plates 10–11.
18 *Ibid.*, pp. 220–3 and plate 10.
19 Quoted by Sherry, *ibid.*, p. 219.
20 *Ibid.*, p. 319.
21 Z. Najder, *Joseph Conrad: A Chronicle* (1983), p. 409.
22 G. Jean-Aubry, *Joseph Conrad: Life and Letters*, II (1927), p. 181.
23 *Ibid.*, pp. 182–3.
24 Jacques Berthoud, ed., introduction to *The Shadow-Line* (Harmondsworth: Penguin, 1986), p. 10.
25 *Ibid.*, p. 12.
26 It is quoted in full in Jeremy Hawthorn, ed., *The Shadow-Line* (Oxford: Oxford University Press, 1985), p. 75.
27 G. Jean-Aubry, *Joseph Conrad: Life and Letters*, II (1927), p. 195.
28 Z. Najder, *Joseph Conrad: A Chronicle* (1983), pp. 417–18. The Captain of the *Ready*, J. G. Sutherland, later wrote a book about the trip called *At Sea with Joseph Conrad* (Boston, 1922).
29 Quoted by Z. Najder, *Joseph Conrad: A Chronicle* (1983), p. 423.
30 G. Jean-Aubry, *Joseph Conrad: Life and Letters*, II (1927), p. 194.
31 *Ibid.*, p. 194.
32 *Ibid.*, p. 188.

33 *Ibid.*, p. 193.
34 quoted by Z. Najder, *Joseph Conrad: A Chronicle* (1983), p. 432.

NOTES TO CHAPTER 11

1 G. Jean-Aubry, *Joseph Conrad: Life and Letters*, II (1927), p. 198.
2 *Ibid.*, p. 226.
3 In the *Morning Post*, the *Daily Mail* and the *Daily News*, as he says in a letter to Sir Sidney Colvin, 7 August 1919, *ibid.*, p. 224.
4 Edward W. Said, *Joseph Conrad and the Fiction of Autobiography* (1966), p. 73.
5 Z. Najder, *Joseph Conrad: A Chronicle* (1983), p. 426.
6 G. Jean-Aubry, *Joseph Conrad: Life and Letters*, II (1927), p. 201.
7 Bennett's *The Old Wives' Tale* (1907) is set partly in Paris and deals with the contrasting lives of two sisters, Constance and Sophia, whose prudence and prodigality respectively may have contributed something to the development of Conrad's characterizations of Therèse and Rita; but Conrad's earlier version of his tale, *The Sisters*, was of course in existence some twelve years before the publication of Bennett's novel.
8 Frederick Karl, *Joseph Conrad: The Three Lives* (1979), p. 170 n. and Z. Najder, *Joseph Conrad: A Chronicle* (1983), pp. 48–9.
9 Zdzisław Najder, ed., *Congo Diary: And Other Uncollected Pieces* (New York: Doubleday, 1978), pp. 40–2.
10 Jeffrey Meyers, *Joseph Conrad: A Biography* (1991), chapter 16.
11 *Ibid.*, p. 304.
12 *Ibid.*, pp. 305–6.
13 Z. Najder, *Joseph Conrad: A Chronicle* (1983), pp. 411–13.
14 Norman Sherry, ed., *Conrad: The Critical Heritage* (1973), pp. 334, 335, 339.
15 *Ibid.*, pp. 365, 368.
16 Daphna Erdinast-Vulcan, *Joseph Conrad and the Modern Temper* (1991), pp. 47–8.
17 Jeffrey Meyers, *Joseph Conrad* (1991), p. 336.
18 See Daniel Schwarz, *Conrad: The Later Fiction* (1982), p. 106.
19 Edward Garnett, ed., *Letters from Conrad: 1895–1924* [1928], pp. 274, 283–5.
20 John Conrad, *Joseph Conrad: Times Remembered* (Cambridge: Cambridge University Press, 1981).
21 Owen Knowles, *A Conrad Chronology* (1989), pp. 129, 132.
22 Martin Ray, ed., *Joseph Conrad: Interviews and Recollections* (London: Macmillan, 1990), pp. 128–30.
23 John Conrad, *Joseph Conrad: Times Remembered* (1981), p. 37.
24 *Ibid.*, p. 82.
25 *Ibid.*, p. 34.
26 *Ibid.*, p. 101.
27 *Ibid.*, p. 127.
28 See p. 275.
29 Owen Knowles, *A Conrad Chronology* (1989), p. 108.
30 Norman Sherry, ed., *Conrad: The Critical Heritage* (1973), pp. 345–6.
31 Quoted by Owen Knowles, *A Conrad Chronology* (1989), p. 113.
32 Z. Najder, *Joseph Conrad: A Chronicle* (1983), p. 459.
33 *Ibid.*, p. 460.

34 Quoted by Najder, *ibid.*, p. 465; Najder remarks that 'Inability to concentrate on any kind of work that is not routine and automatic is another characteristic symptom of depression', p. 465.
35 Joseph Conrad, *Three Plays* (London: Methuen, 1934), p. 159. All my page references to the dramatization of *The Secret Agent* are to this edition.
36 Edward Garnett, ed., *Letters from Conrad* [1928], p. 328.
37 Jessie Conrad, *Joseph Conrad and his Circle* (1935), 255–6.
38 Jeffrey Meyers, *Joseph Conrad* (1991), p. 354.
39 He wrote to Jean-Aubry: 'Yeats has had the Nobel Prize. My opinion about that is that it is a literary recognition of the new Irish Free State (that's what it seems to me), but that does not destroy my chances of getting it in one or two years'. Quoted by Meyers, *ibid.*, p. 355.
40 Conrad wrote prematurely congratulating Galsworthy on his knighthood on 12 January 1918. The letter is transcribed in D. C. Cross, *One Hundred and Thirty Unpublished Letters from Joseph Conrad to John Galsworthy* (1966), p. 140.
41 Martin Ray, ed., *Joseph Conrad: Interviews and Recollections* (1990), pp. 227–8.
42 See pp. 273–74.
43 Najder remarks that: 'Conrad is convinced that human life may have a meaning – but it is for us to confer it.' Z. Najder, *Joseph Conrad: A Chronicle* (1983), p. 495.
44 Quoted by Ray, *ibid.*, p. 231.
45 Z. Najder, *Joseph Conrad: A Chronicle* (1983), p. 399.
46 *Ibid.*, p. 459.
47 John Conrad, *Joseph Conrad: Times Remembered*, (1981), p. 152.
48 Z. Najder, 'Joseph Conrad: A Selection of Unknown Letters', *Polish Perspectives: Monthly Review*, XIII, 2 (February 1970), pp. 44–5.

Bibliography

1 WORKS BY JOSEPH CONRAD

Novels, tales, essays and dramatizations are listed below in chronological order of publication in book form (magazine publication indicated in square brackets). With the exception of the *Congo Diary, The Nature of a Crime, The Sisters* and the dramatizations all the works below are in the Collected Edition of the Works of Joseph Conrad (Dent, 1946–55). The World's Classics edition (Oxford University Press) has been used for reference where it is available (where the pagination differs from Dent this is indicated in the notes). The World's Classics, Norton Critical and Cambridge University Press editions are indicated where appropriate.

1895: *Almayer's Folly: A Story of an Eastern River* (World's Classics).
1896: *An Outcast of the Islands* (World's Classics).
1897: *The Nigger of the 'Narcissus': A Tale of the Sea*, Published in America as *The Children of the Sea: A Tale of the Forecastle* [*New Review*, 1897] (Norton Critical and World's Classics).
1898: *Tales of Unrest* ('Karain: A Memory' [*Blackwood's*, 1897], 'The Idiots' [*The Savoy*, 1896], 'An Outpost of Progress' [*Cosmopolis*, 1897], 'The Return' [never serialized], 'The Lagoon' [*The Cornhill*, 1897]).
1900: *Lord Jim: A Tale* [*Blackwood's Magazine*, 1899–1900] (Norton Critical and World's Classics).
1901: *The Inheritors: An Extravagant Story* by Joseph Conrad and F. M. Hueffer (in *Congo Diary*, 1978).
1902: *Youth: A Narrative; and Two Other Stories* ('Youth' [*Blackwood's*, 1898], 'Heart of Darkness'] [*Blackwood's*, 1899] and 'The End of the Tether,' [*Blackwood's*, 1902]). (World's Classics; also *Heart of Darkness and Other Tales*, World's Classics and *Heart of Darkness*, alone, Norton Critical Edition.)
1903: *Typhoon and Other Stories* ('Typhoon' [*Pall Mall Magazine*, 1902], 'Amy Foster' [*Illustrated London News*, 1901], 'Falk' [never serialized], 'To-morrow' [*Pall Mall Magazine*, 1902].) ('Typhoon', 'Amy Foster', 'Falk' and 'The Secret Sharer' are collected as *Typhoon and Other Tales*, World's Classics.)

1903: *Romance: A Novel*, by Joseph Conrad and F. M. Hueffer.

1904: *Nostromo: A Tale of the Seaboard.* [*T. P.'s Weekly*, 1904] (World's Classics).

1906: *The Mirror of the Sea: Memories and Impressions.* [Essays had appeared in a number of periodicals, notably *Pall Mall Magazine, Harper's Weekly* and *Daily Mail*, 1904–1906] (World's Classics with *A Personal Record*).

1907: *The Secret Agent: A Simple Tale.* [*Ridgway's: A Militant Weekly for God and Country*, 1906–1907] (World's Classics and Cambridge).

1908: *A Set of Six.* ('Gaspar Ruiz' [*Pall Mall Magazine*, 1906], 'The Informer' [*Harper's Magazine*, 1906], 'The Brute' [*Daily Chronicle*, 1906], 'An Anarchist' [*Harper's Magazine*, 1906], 'The Duel' [*Pall Mall Magazine*, 1908], 'Il Conde' [*Cassell's Magazine*, 1908]).

1911: *Under Western Eyes.* [*English Review* and *North American Review*, 1910–1911] (World's Classics and Cambridge).

1912: *A Personal Record* (New York title: London title until 1916 was *Some Reminiscences*) [*English Review*, 1908–1909]. '*Twixt Land and Sea: Tales* ('A Smile of Fortune' [*London Magazine*, 1911], 'The Secret Sharer' [*Harper's Magazine*, 1910], 'Freya of the Seven Isles' [*Metropolitan Magazine*, 1912, and *London Magazine*, 1912]).

1914: *Chance: A Tale in Two Parts.* [*New York Herald*, 1912] (World's Classics).

1915: *Within the Tides* ('The Planter of Malata' [*Metropolitan Magazine*, 1914], 'The Partner' [*Harper's Magazine* 1911], 'The Inn of the Two Witches' [*Pall Mall Magazine* and *Metropolitan Magazine*, 1913], 'Because of the Dollars' [as 'Laughing Anne' in *Metropolitan Magazine*, 1914]).

Victory: An Island Tale [*Munsey's Magazine*, New York, and *Star*, 1915] (World's Classics).

1917: *The Shadow-Line* [*English Review*, Sept. 1916–Mar. 1917] (World's Classics).

1919: *The Arrow of Gold: A Story between Two Notes* [*Lloyd's Magazine*, 1918–20].

One Day More (dramatization of 'To-morrow', limited edition, see *Three Plays*, 1934).

1920: *The Rescue: A Romance of the Shallows.* [*Land and Water*, 1919].

1921: *Notes on Life and Letters.*

The Secret Agent (copyright edition of dramatization, see *Three Plays*, 1934).

1923: *The Rover* [*Pictorial Review*, 1923] (World's Classics). *Laughing Anne* (limited edition)

1924: *The Nature of a Crime* (collaboration with Ford Madox Ford, *Congo Diary*, 1978) [*English Review* 1909], *The Secret Agent* (American Publication of dramatization, see *Three Plays*, 1934), *Laughing Anne* and *One Day More* with an introduction by John Galsworthy (London: John Castle, 1924, see *Three Plays*, 1934).

1925: *Suspense: A Napoleonic Novel.* [*Saturday Review of Literature*, 1935]

1925: *Tales of Hearsay* ('The Warrior's Soul' [*Land and Water*, 29 March 1917], 'Prince Roman' [*Oxford and Cambridge Review*, Oct. 1911, also *Metropolitan Magazine*, Jan. 1912, entitled 'The Aristocrat'], 'The Tale' [*Strand Magazine*, Oct. 1917], 'The Black Mate' [*London Magazine*, April, 1908]).

1926: *Last Essays.*

1928: *The Sisters* (in *Congo Diary*).

1934: *Three Plays: Laughing Anne, One day More and The Secret Agent* (London: Methuen, 1934).

1978: *Congo Diary and other Uncollected Pieces,* edited and with comments by Zdzisław Najder (New York: Doubleday 1978).

Collected Editions of Conrad's works were published by Heinemann (U.K.) and Doubleday (U.S.A.) from 1921.

2 CONRAD'S LETTERS AND PREFACES

Blackburn, William (ed.). *Joseph Conrad: Letters to William Blackwood and David S. Meldrum.* Durham, NC: Duke University Press, 1958.

Conrad, Jessie (ed.). *Joseph Conrad's Letters to his Wife.* Privately printed, 1927.

Cross, D. C., ed. *One hundred and thirty unpublished letters from Joseph Conrad to John Galsworthy.* Unpublished M.A. thesis, University of Birmingham, 1966.

Curle, Richard (ed.). *Conrad to a Friend: 150 Letters to Richard Curle.* London: Sampson Low, Marston and Co., 1928.

Garnett, Edward. *Letters from Conrad.* London: Nonesuch Press, n.d. [1928].

Garnett, Edward. *Conrad's Prefaces to his Works* (with an introduction by Edward Garnett). London: J. M. Dent, 1937.

Garnett, Richard. *Constance Garnett: A Heroic Life.* London: Sinclair-Stevenson, 1991.

Gee, John A. and Sturm J. (ed. and trans.). *Letters of Joseph Conrad to Marguerite Poradowska: 1890–1920.* New Haven, Conn.: Yale University Press, 1940.

Karl, Frederick R. and Davies, Laurence. *The Collected Letters of Joseph Conrad* (8 vols). Cambridge: Cambridge University Press, 1983–.

Najder, Zdzisław (ed.). *Conrad's Polish Background: Letters to and from Polish Friends* (trans. Halina Carroll). London: Oxford University Press, 1964.

Watts, C. T. [Cedric] (ed.). *Joseph Conrad's Letters to Cunninghame Graham.* Cambridge: Cambridge University Press, 1969.

3 SECONDARY WORKS

[Date in square brackets indicates date of first publication]

Achebe, Chinua. 'An Image of Africa: Racism in Conrad's *Heart of Darkness*'. *Massachusetts Review*, 18 (1977), pp. 782–94. Revised in R. Kimbrough, ed., *Heart of Darkness* (New York: Norton, 1988), pp. 251–62.

Allen, Jerry. *The Sea Years of Joseph Conrad.* London: Methuen, 1967.

Anderson, Linda R. *Bennett Wells and Conrad: Narrative in Transition.* London: Macmillan, 1988.

Andreach, Robert J. *The Slain and Resurrected God: Conrad, Ford and the Christian Myth.* New York: New York University Press, 1970.

Andreas, Osborn. *Joseph Conrad: A Study in Non-Conformity* [1959]. London: Vision Press, 1962.

Aristotle on the Art of Poetry. Edited and translated by Ingram Bywater. Oxford: Clarendon Press, 1909.

Auerbach, Erich. *Mimesis: The Representation of Reality in Western Literature* [1946]. Princeton NJ: Princeton University Press, 1974.

Baines, Jocelyn. *Joseph Conrad: A Critical Biography.* London: Weidenfeld and Nicolson, 1960.

Batchelor, John. 'Conrad and Shakespeare.' *L'Epoque Conradienne* (1992), pp. 124–51.

Batchelor, John. *The Edwardian Novelists.* London: Duckworth, 1982.

Batchelor, John. '*Heart of Darkness*, Source of Light.' *Review of English Studies*, NS, XLIII, 170 (May 1992), pp. 227–42.

Batchelor, John. *Lord Jim* (Unwin Critical Library). London: Unwin Hyman, 1988.

Batchelor, John. *H. G. Wells.* Cambridge: Cambridge University Press, 1985.

Beach, Joseph Warren. *The Twentieth Century Novel: Studies in Technique.* New York: Century, 1932.

Beer, Thomas. *Stephen Crane: A Study in American Letters* (with an introduction by Conrad). London: Heinemann, 1924.

Belcher, Edward. *Narrative of the Voyage of the H.M.S. Samarang.* 2 vols. London: Reeve, Benham and Reeve, 1848.

Bergonzi, Bernard. *The Early H. G. Wells.* Manchester: Manchester University Press, 1961.

Berman, Jeffrey. 'Introduction to Conrad and the Russians'. *Conradiana*, XII, 1 (1980), pp. 3–12.

Berthoud, Jacques. *Joseph Conrad: The Major Phase.* Cambridge: Cambridge University Press, 1978.

Bignami, Marialuisa. 'Joseph Conrad, the Malay Archipelago, and the Decadent Hero'. *Review of English Studies*, XXXVIII, 150 (May, 1987), pp. 199–210.

Bohlmann, Otto. *Conrad's Existentialism.* New York: St Martin's Press, 1991.

Bonney, W. W. *Thorns and Arabesques: Context for Conrad's Fiction.* Baltimore: Johns Hopkins University Press, 1980.

Bradbrook, M. C. *Joseph Conrad: Poland's English Genius.* Cambridge: Cambridge University Press, 1941.

Bradley, A. C. *Shakespearean Tragedy* [1904]. London: Macmillan, 1932.

Brebach, Raymond. *Joseph Conrad, Ford Madox Ford and the Making of Romance.* Ann Arbor, Mich.: UMI Research Press, 1985.

Brown, E. K. 'James and Conrad'. *Yale Review*, 1945 (pp. 165–85).

Burden, Robert. *Heart of Darkness* (The Critics Debate Series). Basingstoke: Macmillan, 1991.

Burgess, C. F. *The Fellowship of the Craft.* Port Washington, NY: Kennikat Press, 1976.

Burgess, C. F. 'Conrad's Catholicism'. *Conradiana*, XV, 2 (1983), pp. 111–26.

Busza, Andrzej. *Conrad's Polish Literary Background and some Illustrations of the Influence of Polish Literature on his Work, Antemurale*, X (1966), pp. 109–255.

Busza, Andrzej. 'Reading Conrad's *Poland Revisited*,' *Cross Currents*, 6 (1987), pp. 159–71.

Busza, Andrzej. 'The Rhetoric of Conrad's Non-Fictional Political Discourse,' *Annales de la Faculté des Lettres et Sciences humaines de Nice*, 34, 1978, pp. 159–70.

Cave, Terence. *Recognitions: A Study in Poetics.* Oxford: Clarendon Press, 1988.

Conrad, Borys. *My Father: Joseph Conrad.* London: Calder and Boyars, 1970.

Conrad, Jessie. *Joseph Conrad as I Knew Him.* London: Heinemann, 1926.

Conrad, Jessie. 'Conrad's Share in *The Nature of a Crime* and his "Congo Diary" ', *Bookman's Journal*, XII, 46 (July, 1925), pp. 135–6.

Conrad, Jessie. 'The Romance of *The Rescue*', *Bookman's Journal*, XII, 43 (April 1925), pp. 19–20.

Conrad, Jessie. *Joseph Conrad and his Circle.* London: Jarrolds, 1935.

Conrad, John. *Joseph Conrad: Times Remembered.* Cambridge: Cambridge University Press, 1981.

Cooper, Christopher. *Conrad and the Human Dilemma.* London: Chatto and Windus, 1970.

Cox, C. B. *Joseph Conrad: The Modern Imagination.* London: Dent, 1974.

Crankshaw, Edward. *Joseph Conrad: Some Aspects of the Art of the Novel* [1936]. London: Macmillan, 1976.

Crews, F. C. *After My System: Psychoanalysis, Ideology, and Critical Method.* New York: Oxford University Press, 1975.

Cross, Nigel. *The Common Writer: Life in Nineteenth Century Grub Street.* Cambridge: Cambridge University Press, 1985.

Cunninghame Graham, R. B. *A Vanished Arcadia.* London: William Heinemann, 1901.

Curle, Richard. *Joseph Conrad: A Study.* London: Kegan Paul, Trench, Trubner and Co., 1914.

Curreli, Mario, ed. *The Ugo Mursia Memorial Lectures: Papers from the International Conrad Conference University of Pisa, September 7th–11th, 1983.* Milan: Mursia International, 1988.

Daleski, H. M. *Joseph Conrad: The Way of Dispossession.* London: Faber, 1977.

Darras, Jacques. *Joseph Conrad and the West.* London: Macmillan, 1982.

Davidson, Arnold E. *Conrad's Endings: A Study of the Five Major Novels.* Ann Arbor, Mich.: UMI Research Press, 1984.

Davies, H. S. and Watson, G. (eds.). *The English Mind.* Cambridge: Cambridge University Press, 1964.

Delbanco, Nicholas. *Group Portrait.* London: Faber, 1982.

Dobrinsky, Joseph. *The Artist in Conrad's Fiction: A Psychocritical Study.* Ann Arbor, Mich.: UMI Research Press, 1989.

Dodds, E. R. *The Greeks and the Irrational.* Berkeley and Los Angeles, Calif.: University of California Press, 1951.

Dodsworth, Martin. *Hamlet Closely Observed.* London: Athlone Press, 1985.

Duncan-Jones, E. E. 'Some Sources of *Chance.*' *Review of English Studies,* XX (November, 1969), pp. 468–71.

Eagleton, Terry. *Exiles and Emigrés.* London: Chatto and Windus, 1970.

Eastwick, Edward B. *Venezuela: Or Sketches of Life in a South-American Republic.* London: Chapman and Hall, 1868.

Ehrsam, T. G. *A Bibliography of Joseph Conrad.* Metuchen, NJ: The Scarecrow Press, 1969.

Erdinast-Vulcan, Daphna. *Joseph Conrad and the Modern Temper.* Oxford: Clarendon Press, 1991.

Fiedler, Leslie, A. *Love and Death in the American Novel.* New York: Criterion Books, 1960.

Fisch, Harold. *A Remembered Future: A Study in Literary Mythology.* Bloomington, Ind.: Indiana University Press, 1985.

Fleishman, Avrom. *Conrad's Politics.* Baltimore, Md: Johns Hopkins University Press, 1967.

Fogel, Aaron. *Coercion to Speak: Conrad's Poetics of Dialogue.* Cambridge Mass.: Harvard University Press, 1985.

Ford, Ford Madox. *The English Novel: From the Earliest Days to the Death of Joseph Conrad.* London: Constable, 1930.

Ford, Ford Madox. *Joseph Conrad: A Personal Remembrance.* London: Duckworth, 1924.

Ford, Ford Madox. *Mightier than the Sword.* London: Allen and Unwin, 1938.

Ford, Ford Madox. *Return to Yesterday: Reminiscences 1894–1914.* London: Gollancz, 1931.

Ford, Ford Madox ['Daniel Chaucer']. *The Simple Life, Limited.* London: Bodley Head, 1911.

Ford, Ford Madox (ed. Sondra J. Stang). *The Ford Madox Ford Reader.* Manchester: Carcanet, 1986.

Forster, E. M. *Two Cheers for Democracy.* New York: Harcourt, Brace, 1951.

Fraser, Gail. *Interweaving Patterns in the Works of Joseph Conrad.* Ann Arbor, Mich.: UMI Research Press, 1988.

Friedman, Alan. *The Turn of the Novel.* New York: Oxford University Press, 1966.

Galen, Nina. 'Stephen Crane as a source for Conrad's Jim'. *Nineteenth Century Fiction,* 38, I (1983), pp. 78–96.

Galsworthy, John. 'Joseph Conrad: A Disquisition', *Fortnightly Review,* 496 (1st April 1908), pp. 627–33.

Garibaldi: An Autobiography ed. Alexandre Dumas. London: Routledge, Warne and Routledge, 1860.

Gekoski, R. A. *Conrad: The Moral World of the Novelist.* London: Elek, 1978.

Gibbon, Perceval. 'Joseph Conrad: An Appreciation', *Bookman,* XXXIX, no. 233 (Jan., 1911), pp. 177–179.

Gillon, Adam. *Conrad and Shakespeare.* New York: Astra Books, 1976.

Gillon, Adam. *The Eternal Solitary: A Study of Joseph Conrad.* New York: Bookman Associates, 1960.

Gilmour, Robin. *The Idea of the Gentleman in the Victorian Novel.* London: Allen and Unwin, 1981.

Glassman, Peter J. *Language and Being: Joseph Conrad and the Literature of Personality.* New York: Columbia University Press, 1976.

Goonetilleke, D. C. R. A. *Joseph Conrad: Beyond Culture and Background.* New York: St Martin's Press, 1990.

Gordan, J. D. *Joseph Conrad: The Making of a Novelist* [1940]. New York: Russell and Russell, 1963.

Graham, Kenneth. *Indirections of the Novel: James, Conrad and Forster.* Cambridge: Cambridge University Press, 1988.

Graver, Lawrence. *Conrad's Short Fiction.* Berkeley and Los Angeles: University of California Press, 1969.

Green, Robert. *Ford Madox Ford: Prose and Politics.* Cambridge: Cambridge University Press, 1981.*

Greene, Graham. *The Lost Childhood and Other Essays.* London: Eyre and Spottiswoode, 1951.

Guerard, A. J. *Conrad the Novelist.* Cambridge, Mass.: Harvard University Press, 1958.

Guerard, A. J. *Joseph Conrad.* New York: New Direction, 1947.

Guetti, James. *The Limits of Metaphor.* Ithaca, NY: Cornell University Press, 1967.

Guetti, James. *The Rhetoric of Joseph Conrad.* Amherst College Honours Thesis, no. 2. Amherst, Mass.: Amherst College Press, 1960.

Gurko, Leo. *Joseph Conrad: Giant in Exile.* London: Macmillan, 1962.

Halverson, John and Watt, Ian. 'Notes on Jane Anderson: 1955–1990.' *Conradiana,* XXV, 1 (1991), pp. 59–87.

Hampson, Robert G. 'The Genie Out of the Bottle: Conrad, Wells and Joyce'. In Peter L. Caracciolo, ed., *The Arabian Nights in English Literature.* London: Macmillan, 1988.

Hampson, Robert G. *Joseph Conrad: Betrayal and Identity.* London: Macmillan, 1992.

Harkness, Bruce. 'The Young Roman Trader in *Heart of Darkness*', *Conradiana,* XII, 3 (1980), pp. 227–9.

Hawkins, Hunt. 'The Issue of Racism in *Heart of Darkness*', *Conradiana,* XIV, 3 (1982), pp. 163–71

Hawthorn, Jeremy. *Joseph Conrad: Language and Fictional Self-Consciousness.* London: Edward Arnold, 1979.

Hawthorn, Jeremy. *Joseph Conrad: Narrative Technique and Idealogical Commitment.* London: Edward Arnold, 1990.

Hay, Eloise Knapp. *The Political Novels of Joseph Conrad.* Chicago: University of Chicago Press, 1963.

Hepburn, James. *The Author's Empty Purse and the Rise of the Literary Agent.* Oxford: Oxford University Press, 1968.

Hervouet, Yves. *The French Face of Joseph Conrad.* Cambridge: Cambridge University Press, 1990.

Hervouet, Yves. 'Conrad's Relationship with Anatole France'. *Conradiana,* XII, 3 (1980), pp. 195–225.

Hervouet, Yves. 'Conrad and Maupassant: An investigation in Conrad's Creative Process.' *Conradiana,* XIV, 2 (1982), pp. 83–111.

Hewitt, Douglas. *Conrad: A Reassessment* [1952]. London: Bowes and Bowes, 1975.

Hewitt, Douglas. *English Fiction of the Early Modern Period, 1940–1980.* London: Longman, 1988.

Hilton, C. M. *The Nature and Status of the Human Mind in the Writings of Joseph Conrad Considered with Reference to Contemporary Thought.* Unpublished Oxford D.Phil. thesis, 1988.

Hodges, R. R. 'Deep Fellowship: Homosexuality and Male Bonding in the Life and Fiction of Joseph Conrad.' *Journal of Homosexuality,* 4 (1979), pp. 379–93.

Hodges, R. R. *The Dual Heritage of Joseph Conrad.* Paris: Menton, 1967.

Homberger, Eric. 'Ford's *English Review:* Englishness and its Discontents', *Agenda,* 27, No. 4 and 28, No. 1 (Winter, 1989 and Spring 1990), pp. 61–66.

Hough, Graham. '*Chance* and Joseph Conrad', in *Image and Experience.* London: Duckworth, 1960.

Howe, Irving. *Politics and the Novel.* New York: New Left Books, 1961.

Hunter, Allan. *Joseph Conrad and the Ethics of Darwinism.* London: Croom Helm, 1983.

Hunter, Allan. 'Some Unpublished Letters by Conrad to Arthur Symons', *Conradiana* XVII, 3 (1985), pp. 183–98.

Hunter, Jefferson. *Edwardian Fiction.* Harvard: Harvard University Press, 1982.

Ingram, Allan (ed.). *Joseph Conrad: Selected Literary Criticism and The Shadow Line.* London: Methuen, 1986.

Inglis, Brian. *Roger Casement.* London: Hodder & Stoughton, 1973.

James, William. *Principles of Psychology* [1890]. Cambridge, Mass: Harvard University Press, 1983.

Jameson, Fredric. *The Political Unconscious: Narrative as a Socially Symbolic Act.* London: Methuen, 1981.

Jean-Aubry, G. *Joseph Conrad: Life and Letters* (2 vols). London: William Heinemann, 1927.

Jean-Aubry, G. *The Sea Dreamer: A Definitive Biography of Joseph Conrad* [trans. Hellen Sebba]. London: Allen and Unwin, 1957.

Jean-Aubry, G. *Twenty letters to Joseph Conrad.* London: Curwen Press, First Edition Club, 1926.

Johnson, Bruce. *Conrad's Models of Mind.* Minneapolis, Minn.: University of Minnesota Press, 1971.

Jones, M. P. *Conrad's Heroism.* Ann Arbor, Mich.: U.M.I. Research Press, 1985.

Judd, Alan. *Ford Madox Ford.* London: Collins, 1990.

Karl, Frederick R. *Joseph Conrad: The Three Lives.* London: Faber, 1979.

Karl, Frederick R. *A Reader's Guide to Joseph Conrad.* London: Thames and Hudson, 1960.

Karl, Frederick R. 'Conrad-Galsworthy: A Record of their Friendship in Letters', *Midway,* 9, 2 (Autumn, 1968), pp. 87–106.

Keating, George T. (comp.) *A Conrad Memorial Library: The Collection of George T. Keating.* New York: Doubleday, Doran, 1929.

Kermode, Frank. *Essays on Fiction, 1971–1982.* London: Routledge, 1983.

Kiely, Robert J. *Robert Louis Stevenson and the Fiction of Adventure.* Cambridge, Mass.: Harvard University Press, 1964.

Kirschner, Paul. *Conrad: The Psychologist as Artist.* Edinburgh: Oliver and Boyd, 1968.

Kirschner, Paul. 'Conrad's Missing Link with Kipling', *Notes and Queries,* CCXIX (Sept., 1972), p. 331.

Kirschner, Paul. 'Conrad's Strong Man', *Modern Fiction Studies,* X (Spring, 1964), pp. 31–6.

Kirschner, Paul. 'Making you *see* Geneva: The Sense of Place in *Under Western Eyes.'* *L'Epoque Conradienne* (1988), pp. 101–25.

Knowles, Owen. *A Conrad Chronology.* London: Macmillan, 1989.

Knowles, Owen. *An Annotated Critical Bibliography of Joseph Conrad.* Hemel Hempstead: Harvester Wheatsheaf, 1992.

Knowles, Owen. 'Joseph Conrad and Bertrand Russell: New Light on their Relationship.' *Journal of Modern Literature,* XVII. I (Summer, 1990), pp. 139–152.

Koestenbaum, Wayne. *Double Talk: The Erotics of Male Literary Collaboration.* London: Routledge, 1989.

Krenn, Heliena. *Conrad's Lingard Trilogy: Empire, Race, and Women in the Malay Novels.* New York: Garland, 1990.

Krieger, Murray. *The Tragic Vision.* New York: Holt, Rinehart and Winston, 1960.

Krzyżanowski, L. (ed.). *Joseph Conrad: Centennial Essays.* New York: Polish Institute of Arts and Sciences in America, 1960.

Krzyżanowski, Julian. *Polish Romantic Literature.* London: Allen and Unwin, 1930.

Kuhn, Robert E. *Twentieth Century Interpretations of Lord Jim.* Englewood Cliffs, NJ: Prentice-Hall, 1969.

Land, Stephen. *Conrad and the Paradox of Plot.* London: Macmillan, 1984.

Leavis, F. R. *The Great Tradition* [1948]. London: Peregrine, 1962.

Lee, Robert F. *Conrad's Colonialism.* The Hague: Mouton, 1969.

Lerner, Lawrence. 'Conrad the Historian'. *The Listener* (15 April 1965), pp. 554–6.

Lester, John. *Conrad and Religion.* London: Macmillan, 1988.

Lester, John. 'Captain Rom: Another Source for Kurtz?', *Conradiana,* XIV, 2 (1982), p. 112.

Lester, John A. *Journey Through Despair: 1880–1914: Transformations in British Literary Culture.* Princeton: Princeton University Press, 1968.

Levenson, Michael H. *A Genealogy of Modernism: A Study of English Literary Doctrine 1908–1922.* Cambridge: Cambridge University Press, 1984.

Levenson, Michael. *Modernism and the fate of individuality: Character and novelistic form from Conrad to Woolf.* Cambridge: Cambridge University Press, 1991.

Levenson, Michael. 'The Value of Facts in the *Heart of Darkness'.* Reprinted in Robert Kimbrough, ed., *Heart of Darkness* (New York: Norton, 1988), pp. 391–405.

Lodge, David. 'Conrad's *Victory* and *The Tempest:* an Amplification', *Modern Language Review,* LIX (1964), pp. 195–9.

Lohf, Kennth A. and Sheehy, Eugene P. *Joseph Conrad at Mid-Century: Editions and Studies, 1895–1955.* Minneapolis: University of Minnesota Press, 1957.

Lucking, David. *Conrad's Mysteries: Variations on an Archetypal Theme.* Lecce, Italy: Milella, n.d. [1987].

Mahood, M. M. *The Colonial Encounter: A Reading of Six Novels.* London: Rex Collings, 1977.

Mann, Thomas. 'Joseph Conrad's *The Secret Agent*' [1926]. Reprinted in Ian Watt, ed., *The Secret Agent*, A Casebook (London: Macmillan, 1973), pp. 99–112.

Masterman, G. F. *Seven Eventful Years in Paraguay*. London: Sampson, Low, 1869.

McClure, John A. *Kipling and Conrad: The Colonial Fiction*. Cambridge, Mass: Harvard University Press, 1981.

McLauchlan, Juliet. 'Conrad's Heart of Emptiness: "The Planter of Malata"', *Conradiana*, XVIII, 3 (1986), pp. 180–92.

Melchiori, Barbara A. *Terrorism in the Late Victorian Novel*. London: Croom Helm, 1985.

Meyer, Bernard C. *Joseph Conrad: A Psychoanalytic Biography*. Princeton: Princeton University Press, 1967.

Meyers, Jeffrey. *Homosexuality and Literature*. London: Athlone Press, 1977.

Meyers, Jeffrey. *Joseph Conrad: A Biography*. London: John Murray, 1991.

Michael, Marion and Berry, Wilkes. 'The Typescript of "The Heart of Darkness"', *Conradiana*, XII, 2 (1980), pp. 147–55.

Miller, J. Hillis. *Fiction and Repetition: Seven English Novels*. Oxford: Basil Blackwell, 1982.

Miller, J. Hillis. *Poets of Reality: Six Twentieth Century Writers*. Cambridge, Mass.: Harvard University Press, 1966.

Miller, Karl. *Doubles: Studies in Literary History*. Oxford: Oxford University Press, 1985.

Miłosz, Czesław. *The History of Polish Literature*. London: Macmillan, 1969.

Mitchell, Giles. 'Lord Jim's Death Fear, Narcissism and Suicide', *Conradiana*, XVIII, 3 (1986), pp. 163–79.

Mizener, Arthur. *The Saddest Story: A Biography of Ford Madox Ford*. London: Bodley Head, 1971.

Moore, Gene M., ed. *Conrad's Cities: Essays for Hans van Marle*. Amsterdam: Rodopi, 1992.

Morf, Gustav. *The Polish Heritage of Joseph Conrad*. London: Sampson, Low, Marston, 1930.

Moser, Thomas. *The Life in the Fiction of Ford Madox Ford*. Princeton, N J: Princeton University Press, 1980.

Moser, Thomas. *Joseph Conrad: Achievement and Decline*. Cambridge Mass.: Harvard University Press, 1980.

Moser, Thomas (ed.). *Lord Jim*. Norton Critical Edition. New York: W. W. Norton, 1968.

Moser, Thomas. 'An English Context for Conrad's Russian Characters: Sergey Stepniak and the Diary of Olive Garnett', *Journal of Modern Literature*, XI, 1 (August, 1984), pp. 3–44.

Murfin, Ross C. (ed.). *Conrad Revisited: Essays for the Eighties*. Alabama: University of Alabama Press, 1985.

Najder, Zdzisław (ed.). *Conrad's Polish Background*. London: Oxford University Press, 1964.

Najder, Zdzisław (ed.). *Conrad Under Familial Eyes*. Cambridge: Cambridge University Press, 1983.

Najder, Zdzisław. 'Joseph Conrad's *The Secret Agent* as the Melodrama of Reality.' *Melodrama* (ed. Daniel Gerould) *New York Literary Forum*, 1980, pp. 159–165.

Najder, Zdzisław. *Joseph Conrad: A Chronicle*. Cambridge: Cambridge University Press, 1983.

Najder, Zdzisław. 'Joseph Conrad: A Selection of Unknown Letters', *Polish Perspectives: Monthly Review*, XIII, 2 (February, 1970), pp. 31–45.

Najder, Zdzisław. 'Conrad and the Idea of Honor', in Zyla, W. T. and Aycock, W. M., *Joseph Conrad: Theory and World Fiction* (q.v.).

Nazareth, Peter. 'Out of Darkness: Conrad and Other Third World Writers', *Conradiana*, XIV, 3 (1982), pp. 173–87.

Nettels, Elsa. *James and Conrad.* Athens, Ga: University of Georgia Press, 1977.

Nettels, Elsa. 'Conrad and Stephen Crane', *Conradiana*, X (1978), pp. 267–83.

Newbrook, Carl. *The Workman of Art: An Historical Account of the Career of Joseph Conrad.* Oxford, Unpublished D.Phil. thesis, 1991.

Newell, Kenneth B. 'The Destructive Element and Related "Dream" Passages in the *Lord Jim* Manuscript', *Journal of Modern Literature*, I, 1 (1970), pp. 30–44.

Nuttall, A. D. *Crime and Punishment: Murder as a Philosophical Experiment.* Brighton: Sussex University Press, 1978.

Nuttall, A. D. *A New Mimesis: Shakespeare and the Representation of Reality.* London: Methuen, 1983.

Nuttall, A. D. *Openings: Narrative Beginnings from the Epic to the Novel.* Oxford: Clarendon Press, 1992.

O'Hanlon, Redmond. *Joseph Conrad and Charles Darwin.* Edinburgh: Salamander, 1984.

Paez, Ramon. *Wild Scenes in South America.* New York: C. Scribner, 1862.

Page, Norman. *A Conrad Companion.* London: Macmillan, 1985.

Palmer, John A. *Joseph Conrad's Fiction.* Ithaca, NY: Cornell University Press, 1968.

Parins, J. W., Dilligan, R. J. and Bender, T. K. *A Concordance to Conrad's Lord Jim.* New York: Garland, 1976.

Parry, Benita. *Conrad and Imperialism.* London: Macmillan, 1983.

Pater, Walter. *The Renaissance* [1873]. London: Collins, 1964.

Pettersson, Torsten. *Consciousness and Time: A Study in the Philosophy and Narrative Techniques of Joseph Conrad.* Abo, Finland: Abo Akademi, 1982.

Pick, Daniel. *Faces of Degeneration: A European Disorder, c.1848–1918.* Cambridge: Cambridge University Press, 1989.

Polish Academy. *Joseph Conrad Colloquy in Poland 1972.* Wrocklaw: Polish Academy, 1975.

Price, Martin. *Forms of Life: Character and Moral Imagination in the Novel.* New Haven and London: Yale University Press, 1983.

Purdy, Dwight H. *Joseph Conrad's Bible.* Norman, Okla: University of Oklahoma Press, 1984.

Raval, Suresh. *The Art of Failure: Conrad's Fiction.* London: Allen and Unwin, 1986.

Rawson, Claude. 'Gulliver, Marlow and the Flat-Nosed People.' *Order From Confusion Sprung.* London: Allen and Unwin, 1985.

Ray, Martin, ed. *Joseph Conrad: Interviews and Recollections.* London: Macmillan, 1990.

Retinger, J. H. *Joseph Conrad and His Contemporaries.* London: Minerva Press, 1941.

Rewald, John. *The History of Impressionism.* New York: The Museum of Modern Art, 1980.

Rose, Jonathan. *The Edwardian Temperament.* Athens, Ohio: Ohio University Press, 1986.

Rosenfield, Claire. *Paradise of Snakes.* Chicago: University of Chicago Press, 1967.

Roussel, Royal. *The Metaphysics of Darkness.* Baltimore, Md: Johns Hopkins University Press, 1971.

Rude, D. W. 'The Richard Gimbel Collection of Conrad's Manuscripts and Typescripts at the Philadelphia Free Library'. *Conradiana*, XV, 3 (1983), pp. 231–6.

Ruthven, K. K. 'The Savage God: Conrad and Lawrence', *Critical Quarterly*, X (SpringSummer 1968), pp. 39–54.

Sadoff, Ira. 'Sartre and Conrad: Lord Jim as Existential Hero,' *Dalhousie Review*, 49 (1969), pp. 518–25.

Said, Edward W. *Joseph Conrad and the Fiction of Autobiography*. Cambridge, Mass.: Harvard University Press, 1966.

Said, Edward W. *Beginnings*. New York: Basic Books, 1975.

Sale, Roger. *Modern Heroism*. London: University of California Press, 1973.

Sandison, Alan. *The Wheel of Empire*. London: Macmillan, 1967.

Sandstrom, Glenn. 'The Roots of Anguish in Dostoevsky and Conrad', *The Polish Review*, XX, 2/3 (1975), pp. 71–7.

Saveson, John E. *Joseph Conrad: The Making of a Moralist*. Amsterdam: Rodopi, 1972.

Saveson, John E. *Conrad: The Later Moralist*. Amsterdam: Rodopi, 1974.

Schultheiss, Thomas. 'Lord Hamlet and *Lord Jim*', *The Polish Review*, XI, 4 (Autumn 1966), pp. 101–33.

Schwarz, Daniel R. *Conrad: Almayer's Folly to Under Western Eyes*. London: Macmillan, 1980.

Schwarz, Daniel R. *Conrad: The Later Fiction*. London: Macmillan, 1982.

Segal, Hanna. 'Art and the Depressive Position', *Dream, Phantasy and Art*. London: Tavistock/Routledge, 1991, pp. 85–100.

Sherry, Norman (ed.). *Conrad: The Critical Heritage*. London: Routledge, 1973.

Sherry, Norman. *Conrad and his World*. London: Thames and Hudson, 1972.

Sherry, Norman. *Conrad's Eastern World*. Cambridge: Cambridge University Press, 1966.

Sherry, Norman. *Conrad's Western World*. Cambridge: Cambridge University Press, 1971.

Sherry, Norman (ed.). *Joseph Conrad: A Commemoration*. London: Macmillan, 1976.

Simons, Kenneth. *The Ludic Imagination: A Reading of Joseph Conrad*. Ann Arbor, Mich.: UMI Research Press, 1985.

Smith, David R. *Conrad's Manifesto: Preface to a Career*. Philadelphia: The Rosenbach Museum and Library, 1966.

Smith, David R. ed. *Joseph Conrad's Under Western Eyes: Beginnings, Revisions, Final Forms*. Hamden, Connecticut: Archon, 1991.

Smith, Rosalind Wallis. 'Date of Composition of Conrad's Work,' *Conradiana*, XI, 1 (1979), pp. 63–90.

Smith, Walter E. *Joseph Conrad: A Bibliographical Catalogue of His Major First Editions with Facsimiles of Several Title Pages*. Long Beach, California: Privately Printed, 1979.

Stallman, R. W. (ed.). *The Art of Joseph Conrad: A Critical Symposium*. Michigan: Michigan State University Press, 1960.

Stape, J. H. 'Conrad and Mr "Colesworthy": Two Unpublished Letters and a Reply', *Conradiana*, XIV, 3 (1982), pp. 230–2.

Stape, J. H. 'Conrad's *Notes on Life and Letters*: Some Revised Dates of Completion', *Conradiana*, XV, 3 (1983), pp. 153–5.

Stauffer, R. M. *Joseph Conrad: His Romantic Realism*. Boston: Four Seas, 1922.

Stein, William Bysshe. 'The Lotus Posture and "The Heart of Darkness"', *Modern Fiction Studies*, II, 4 (1956–7), pp. 235–7.

Stevenson, Richard C. 'Stein's prescription for "How to Be" and the Problems of Assessing Lord Jim's Career', *Conradiana*, VII, 3 (1976), pp. 233–43.

Stewart, J. I. M. *Joseph Conrad*. London: Longman, 1968.

Street, Brian V. *The Savage in Literature: Representations of 'Primitive' Society in English Fiction, 1858–1920*. London: Routledge and Kegan Paul, 1975.

Sullivan, Ernest W. *The Several Endings of Joseph Conrad's Lord Jim*. The Joseph Conrad Society, UK, nd [1981].

Sullivan, Ernest W. 'The Genesis and Evolution of Joseph Conrad's "Youth": A Revised and Copy-Edited Typescript page', *Review of English Studies*, N.S., XXXVI, 44 (Nov. 1985), pp. 522–34.

Symonds, A. W. *Notes on Joseph Conrad*. London: Myers and Co., 1925.

Tanner, J. E. 'The Chronology and Enigmatic End of *Lord Jim*,' *Nineteenth Century Fiction*, XXI (1967), pp. 369–80.

Tanner, Tony. *Lord Jim*. Studies in English Literature, No. 12. London: Edward Arnold, 1963.

Tanner, Tony. 'Nightmare and Complacency: Razumov and the Western Eye', *Critical Quarterly*, IV, 3 (Autumn, 1962), pp. 197–214.

Tarnawski, Wit. *Conrad the Man, the Writer, the Pole*. trans. Rosamond Batchelor. London: Polish Cultural Foundation, 1984.

Teets, Bruce E. and Gerber, Helmut (eds). *Joseph Conrad: An Annotated Bibliography of Writings About Him*. De Kalb, Ill.: Northern Illinois University Press, 1971.

Teets, Bruce E. *Joseph Conrad: An Annotated Bibliography*. New York: Garland, 1990.

Teets, Bruce E. 'Realism and Romance in Conrad Criticism', *Polish Review*, XX (1975), p. 133–9.

Tennant, Roger. *Joseph Conrad: A Biography*. London: Sheldon, 1981.

Thorburn, David. *Conrad's Romanticism*. New Haven, Conn.: Yale University Press, 1974.

Tillyard E. M. W. *The Epic Strain in the English Novel*. London: Chatto and Windus, 1958.

Tymms, Ralph. *Doubles in Literary Psychology*. Cambridge: Bowes and Bowes, 1949.

Unwin, (Sir) Stanley. *The Truth about Publishing*. London: Allen and Unwin, 1926.

Unwin, (Sir) Stanley. *The Truth about a Publisher: An Autobiographical Record*. London: Allen and Unwin, 1960.

Ure, Peter. 'Character and Imagination in Conrad'. In Rawson, C. J. (ed.), *Yeats and Anglo-Irish Literature*. Liverpool: Liverpool University Press, 1974. pp. 227–42.

Van Ghent, Dorothy. *The English Novel: Form and Function* [1953]. New York: Harper Torchbooks, 1961.

Van Marle, Hans. 'The Location of Lord Jim's Patusan', *Notes and Queries*, NS, XV (August, 1968), pp. 289–91.

Van Marle, Hans. 'Plucked and Passed on Tower Hill: Conrad's Examination Ordeals', *Conradiana*, VIII, 2 (1976), pp. 99–109.

Van Marle, Hans. 'Conrad's English Lodgings, 1880–1896', *Conradiana*, VIII, 3 (1976), pp. 257–8.

Van Marle, Hans. 'Jumble of Facts and Fiction: The First Singapore Reaction to *Almayer's Folly*', *Conradiana*, X, 2 (1978), pp. 161–6.

Verleun, Jan. *Patna and Patusan Perspectives*. Groningen: Bouma's Boekhuis, 1979.

Verleun, Jan. *The Stone Horse*. Groningen: Bouma's Boekhuis, 1982.

Verleun, Jan. 'Marlow and the Harlequin', *Conradiana*, XIII, 3 (1981), pp. 195–220.

Walpole, Hugh. *Joseph Conrad*. London: Nisbet, n.d. (1916).

Warren, Robert Penn. 'Nostromo,' *Sewanee Review*, 59, 3 (1951), pp. 363–91.

Watt, Ian. *Conrad, in the Nineteenth Century*. London: Chatto and Windus, 1980.

Watt, Ian. 'Joseph Conrad: Alienation and Commitment', in H. S. Davies and G. Watson, eds., *The English Mind: Studies in the English Moralists Presented to Basil Willey*. Cambridge: Cambridge University Press, 1964, pp. 257–78.

Watt, Ian. *Nostromo*. Cambridge: Cambridge University Press (Landmarks of World Literature series), 1988.

Watt, Ian, ed. *The Secret Agent: A Casebook*. London: Macmillan, 1973.

Watts, Cedric. *Conrad's Heart of Darkness: A Critical and Contextual Discussion*. Milan: Mursia Internation, 1977.

Watts, Cedric. *The Deceptive Text*. Brighton: Harvester Press, 1984.

Watts, Cedric. *Joseph Conrad: A Literary Life*. London: Macmillan, 1989.

Watts, Cedric. *A Preface to Conrad*. London: Longman, 1982.

Watts, Cedric. *Nostromo*. Harmondsworth: Penguin, 1990.

Watts, Cedric. 'Stepniak and *Under Western Eyes*'. *Notes and Queries*, XIII (1966), pp. 410–11.

Watts, Cedric, and Davies, Laurence. *Cunninghame Graham: A Critical Biography*. Cambridge: Cambridge University Press, 1979.

White, Allon. *The Uses of Obscurity*. London: Routledge, 1981.

Wilding, Michael. 'The Politics of *Nostromo*', *Essays in Criticism*, XVI (1966), pp. 441–56.

Wiley, Paul L. *Conrad's Measure of Man*. Madison, Wis.: University of Wisconsin Press, 1954.

Williams, Frederick Benton [pseud. for Herbert Elliott Hamblen]. *On Many Seas: The Life and Exploits of a Yankee Sailor*. New York: G. P. Putnam's Sons, 1897.

Willy, Todd G. 'Measures of the Heart and of the Darkness: Conrad and the Suicides of "New Imperialism"', *Conradiana*, XIV (1982), pp. 189–98.

Wise, Thomas J. *A Bibliography of the Writings of Joseph Conrad (1895–1921)*. (Privately Printed, 1921). London: Dawsons, 1964.

Wise, Thomas J. *A Conrad Library: A Catalogue of Printed Books, Manuscripts and Autograph Letters by Joseph Conrad Collected by Thomas James Wise*. London: Privately Printed, 1928.

Woolf, Virginia. *The Common Reader: First Series*. London: Hogarth Press, 1925.

Wright, Andrew. *Fictional Discourse and Historical Space*. London: Macmillan, 1987.

Wright, Walter F. *Romance and Tragedy in Joseph Conrad* [1949]. Lincoln, Nebraska: Nebraska State University Press, 1966.

Yelton, Donald C. *Mimesis and Metaphor: An Inquiry into the Genesis and Scope of Conrad's Symbolic Imagery*. The Hague: Mouton, 1967.

Young, Gavin. *In Search of Conrad*. London: Hutchinson, 1991.

Zabel, M. D. *Craft and Character in Modern Fiction*. London: Gollancz, 1957.

Zabel, M. D. 'Joseph Conrad: Chance and Recognition', *Sewanee Review*, LIII, 1 (1945), pp. 1–22.

Zyla, W. and Aycock, W. M. *Joseph Conrad: Theory and World Fiction*. Proceedings of the Comparative Literature Symposium, vol. VII. Lubbock, Texas: Interdepartmental Committee on Comparative Literature, Texas Technical University, 1974.

Index

[See Conrad, Joseph, for Conrad's publications, names of persons referred to in his writings, names of ships in which he served and houses in which he lived, and (under 'topics') recurrent themes in his life and work. Works by authors other than Conrad appear either by title or after the author's name.]

3. *Topics in Conrad's life and works; see also* general index.